Woke Cinderella

Remakes, Reboots, and Adaptations

Series Editors: Carlen Lavigne, Red Deer College, and Paul Booth, DePaul University

Broad-ranging and multidisciplinary, this series invites analysis of remakes, reboots, and adaptations in contemporary media from videogames to television to the internet. How are we re-using and remixing our stories? What does that tell us about ourselves, our cultures, and our times? Scholars use multidisciplinary approaches from areas such as gender studies, race, sexuality, disability, cultural studies, fan studies, sociology, or aesthetic and technical research. Titles in the series set out to say something about who we are, where we've come from, and where we're going, as read in our popular culture and the stories we tell ourselves over and over again.

Recent titles in the series:

Woke Cinderella

Twenty-First-Century Adaptations

Edited by Suzy Woltmann

LEXINGTON BOOKS
Lanham • Boulder • New York • London

Published by Lexington Books
An imprint of The Rowman & Littlefield Publishing Group, Inc.
4501 Forbes Boulevard, Suite 200, Lanham, Maryland 20706
www.rowman.com

6 Tinworth Street, London SE11 5AL, United Kingdom

British Library Cataloguing in Publication Information Available

Library of Congress Cataloging-in-Publication Data Available

ISBN 9781793625946 (cloth)
ISBN 9781793625960 (pbk)
ISBN 9781793625953 (electronic)

Contents

Introduction

Cinderella and Wokeness

Suzy Woltmann

Conventional representations of the "Cinderella" fairy tale are far from what is currently considered to be woke—that is, culturally competent, sensitive, and aware. In a *New York Post* article ranking Disney princesses from "retro to woke,"[1] Cinderella is placed next to last—furthest from woke, out-retroed only by Snow White. The traditional Cinderella is renowned for her passivity, silence, and uncomplaining indentured servitude to a cruel stepfamily who names her after the cinders that cover her face. However, contemporary "Cinderella" revisionism opens up the princess and her rags-to-riches story to new and wonderful potentialities. A woke "Cinderella" story, what I call elsewhere a "transformative adaptation,"[2] reframes the narrative in a way that empowers not only the titular heroine but also the retelling's audience. While this collection focuses primarily on twenty-first-century adaptations in the Americas, woke "Cinderella" variations have a rich and textured history going back to earlier reimaginings and transnational versions that destabilize traditional hierarchies to allow for new forms of voice and empowerment.

EARLY CINDERELLA

The most published, researched, and highly-rated fairy tale worldwide, "Cinderella" has enjoyed more popularity than warrants the story of a humble girl known for sitting in the ashes: "by all accounts, 'Cinderella' is the best-known fairy tale, and probably also the best-liked."[3] The original rags-to-riches or recovered riches story, the tale has been fleshed out through innumerable revisualizations. But how do we recognize a "Cinderella" story? As Heidi Anne Heiner notes:

1

The tale has its own Aarne Thompson classification which is 510A. The tale always centers around a kind, but persecuted heroine who suffers at the hands of her step-family after the death of her mother. Her father is either absent or neglectful, depending on the version. The heroine has a magical guardian who helps her triumph over her persecutors and receive her fondest wish by the end of the tale. The guardian is sometimes a representative of the heroine's dead mother. Most of the tales include an epiphany sparked by an article of clothing (usually a shoe) that causes the heroine to be recognized for her true worth.[4]

The Aarne-Thompson-Uther system catalogs numerous basic story lines from folktale types and separates the various tales based on prevalent thematic elements. The "Cinderella" story has its own classification (510A), which shares strong similarities with the typical "Furrypelts" classification (510B).

Arguably the first popularized rendition of the "Cinderella" tale, first-century BC Egypt introduces the beleaguered Rhodopis, made by her peers to stay back and perform menial labor while they attend the Pharaoh Amasis's gathering. An eagle steals her shoe and leaves it with the Pharaoh, who then requires all nearby women to try on the sandal. It fits Rhodopis, and so the Pharaoh marries her. The Chinese "Ye Xian" depicts a naturally hard-working and attractive girl who becomes close to the reincarnation of her dead mother in the body of a fish. The bones from the fish prove to be magical and help her meet and fall in love with the prince. Several other variations circulated through Asia and Africa, and the tale eventually made its way to the European canon. Giambattista Basile's "The Hearth Cat" tells the story of a young girl who is abused by her father's mistress but aided by a magical cow and fairies so that she eventually marries into royalty. Basile's tale focuses largely on nature and maternity, two themes that become prevalent in the Perrault and Grimm brothers versions. Thousands of other "Cinderella"-like stories have been discovered worldwide; for the purpose of this collection, I focus mainly on versions from the Americas.

Brazil's "Gata Borralheira" examines race and class structure.[5] Cinderella is Indian and African, and her Portuguese stepfamily treats her as a servant, projecting on her the incapability of having feelings or experiencing sadness. "Gata Borralheira" challenges this racist, classist dynamic and ultimately places the heroine in a place of power as the prince's wife. Gata is described as living with her stepmother and stepsisters, and when her lineage is discussed it is in terms of her mother's ethnicity, reemphasizing the matrilineal and feminine context of the story.

In a similar Brazilian version, "The Maiden and the Fish," Hearth-Cat is mocked by her (biological) sisters for taking care of the household and helping the servants in the kitchen.[6] Racial and class bias are still present but are diluted from the "Gata Borralheira" tale. The fairy godmother role is filled by a golden fish, which Hearth-Cat saves from being eaten—thus demonstrating her inherent kindness—and which gifts the girl a fancy gown and golden slippers for the ball.

A Chilean "Cinderella" story called "Maria Cinderella" dictates the plight of a young girl who begs her father to remarry in order to gain security and happiness.[7] A magical cow gives Maria Cinderella a golden star on her forehead, while her half-sister Maria's failure to competently complete a series of impossible tasks leaves her with burro dung adorning her brow. The prince falls for Maria Cinderella's beauty while at church and eventually takes her away. This version of the "Cinderella" tale emphasizes an ironic mirror-image version of Cinderella; Maria's name mirrors that of Maria Cinderella, but her actions dictate otherwise. The dichotomy of the two Marias is clarified and finalized in the mark each girl carries on her forehead and the Prince's eventual choice. "Domatila," a Mexican "Cinderella," focuses on ethnic relations and the importance of tradition. It portrays a strong bond between the maternal and Cinderella's ability to win over the "prince" of the tale, the governor's oldest son.[8] A Puerto Rican version of the "Cinderella" story became popularized in the late nineteenth century.[9] "Flor Blanca" presents a typically passive Cinderella. Flor Blanca is so beautiful that she is imprisoned by a jealous father and provoked by townspeople who must bother her because "she was so pretty."[10] Her beauty is something to be protected and used by others, not something she truly possesses herself. Instead of providing the Cinderella character with a ball gown or the ability to escape a cruel stepfamily, in this tale the fairy godmother instead leaves Flor Blanca to realize she must dress herself in rags in order to be left alone.

A Native American version of "Cinderella" called "The Toad Prince" opens with a description of traditional wedding practices and introduces the positions and significance of different members of the tribe. Unlike other "Cinderella" tales, this prince does not fall for a girl's beauty and then seek her out in hopes he will find the girl whose foot will fit the slipper. Instead, he fetishizes the material goods that represent his marriage to a wife who can save him from being trapped in the body of a toad. "Goldenstar," a variation on the Spanish American "Maria Cinderella" tale, introduces a Cinderella who encourages her reluctant father to marry a widow neighbor. The most significant difference in this "Cinderella" tale is the attention paid to religion. The fairy godmother character in this version is held by the Virgin Mary, and Goldenstar's one desire is to attend Mass—which allows her to catch the attention of the Prince and thus rise in status. Each time Goldenstar ventures into the public sphere, she causes a striking change to occur: first through encouraging her father to marry the widow, then by acting with goodness and receiving a golden star, and finally by attending Mass and winning the prince's affections.

The next "Cinderella" story popularized in the Americas bears similarities to the Grimm brothers' "Furrypelts." "Furrypelts" is a darker version of the typical rags-to-riches "Cinderella," as the princess literally dresses herself in rags in order to escape the attentions of her lascivious father.[11] Furrypelts's mother's obsessive concern with the perpetuation of her physical beauty resembles the wicked stepfamily of a typical Cinderella; ironically, she is saved from being represented as villainous only through her death, which pushes that role onto the ultimately incestuous king. Furrypelts's patience and kindness is revealed through her unwavering work ethic. Though she is born a princess and could feasibly live in luxury if she claims her title, she prefers to save her integrity and lead a "wretched life."[12] Early eighteenth-century England popularized a story called "Catskin," a more lighthearted version of the German "Furrypelts" tale. In the English version, Catskin resembles a typical Cinderella: she is passive, requests merely to see the ball or serve food rather than chase the Prince, and immediately upon marriage bears children.

The American "Catskin" places the storytellers as part of the narrative; they entice "fathers and mothers, and children also" to come listen to their unusual tale.[13] This Cinderella is intelligent, self-assured, and assertive. She recognizes that her situation is unfair and decides to act to change it by disguising herself in order to learn. Significantly, the man of interest and potential husband in this tale is not a prince, as in the original English version, but merely a squire. This demonstrates the beginning of a move away from class hierarchies and sovereign rule toward a more egalitarian, liberated ideal. The stepmother figure in this tale is embodied in the lady of the house, the squire's mother. However, she does not become the villain of the tale. Despite her abusive ways and attempts to prevent Catskin from attending the ball, she also takes the girl in and becomes a mentor of sorts by offering her a position in the household. Ultimately, the squire's mother's efforts are of little consequence and even made humorous when Catskin tells the squire where she lives. In this tale, Cinderella is defined by her presence rather than her absence, thus moving toward a woke conscious ideal.

Charles Perrault's and the Brothers Grimm's adaptations, as well as the immensely popular Disney film version, further act as foundational texts against which later adaptations can be assessed. Perrault "fixed the ground rules and sexual regulations for the debate" about women in fairy tales.[14] As seen in the title, Perrault's "Cinderella: Or, the Little Glass Slipper" is about desire for social mobility through the lens of artifice. The little glass slipper here is implied to be just as important as the titular character. Perrault's "Cinderella" would ultimately become the most widely used source text, as he gives supplemental features to the story that would become foundational symbols such as the fairy godmother, glass slippers, and metamorphic crea-tures. His tale emphasizes Cinderella's vulnerability and fetishistic material-ism. Even the chosen moral for the tale reflects an appreciation for physical beauty—of course, of "lesser value" than graciousness,[15] which Cinderella's godmother gives to her when she teaches her to behave like a queen. This emphasizes her positionality as patriarchal construct of Woman. As Cristina Bacchilega says, "by showcasing 'women' and making them disappear at the same time, the fairy tale thus transforms us/them into man-made constructs of 'Woman.'"[16] Cinderella only desires that which will in turn make her desirable to men, and this very factor erases her as subject. Perrault's adaptation emphasizes an idealization of beauty, passivity, and heteronormativity.

The Brothers Grimm believed in retaining the "purity" of each fairy tale they gathered but altered the story's form and content "to stress fundamental bourgeois values of behavior and moral principles of Christianity that served the hegemonic aspirations of the rising middle classes in Germany."[17] The stories maintained and promoted Christian ideals and supported the preexisting social structures of the time; however, they were also meant to give hope for what the brothers considered to be true moral ground, extolling the virtues of hard work, wit, and a strong moral compass. The Grimm brothers' "Cinderella" variation emphasizes the original mother-daughter relationship and thus the matrilineal structure of the tale. This version of the "Cinderella" story focuses mostly on retribution and ancestry. Cinderella initially shows she is different from her beauty-seeking stepsisters when her father asks the girls what they would like him to bring home from his journey to the fair. Cinderella's stepsisters seek happiness in the material world of artifice and superficiality while she appreciates the beauty of the natural world, which signifies her beloved mother. Her inner goodness is recognized by external social and political realms when her outer beauty is exposed. However, the stepsisters who actively seek to enhance their physical beauty are found to be inherently ugly.

These variations on the "Cinderella" story set the backdrop for many reimaginations of the tale in contemporary literature and film. The Walt Disney industry revolutionized the tales in filmic culminations of "male fantasizing about women and power."[18] The Disney version makes Cinderella's main characteristic her "lovableness," which takes away her "birthright of shrewdness, inventiveness, and grace under pressure."[19] While Disney's version introduces a vivid visual depiction of the heroine, Cinderella is pushed even further into a position of absence and passivity in the film than her previous incarnations. Her stepfamily is portrayed as hating her because of her beauty; jealous and spiteful, they force her into domestic servitude, which she passively accepts. The film insinuates a gendered dichotomy in which men are valued for their wit, courage, and other active personality characteristics and feminine value is assessed through passive virtue and piety, as externally reflected through physical beauty. Cinderella does not fight back against oppressive forces and domination, making her the perfect malleable victim. This Disneyfied Cinderella is a sympathetic character, but not one with agency. Her every chance for mobility is given to her by magical animals or a fairy godmother rather than earned through subversion or empowerment.

WOKE CINDERELLA

Contemporary adaptations often try to challenge and destabilize oppressive hierarchies in traditional fairy-tale variations. This collection uses the rhetorical lens of *wokeness* to theorize the work that contemporary "Cinderella" adaptations engage with. The term "woke" rose in the American ideological imagination when Erykah Badu released the song "Master Teacher" in 2008.[20] Woke was then further used as a signifier for noticing racial injustice by activists, particularly as part of the Black Lives Matter movement.[21] The term was added to Merriam-Webster and the Oxford English Dictionary in 2017 following widespread appropriation of the term to mean anyone who notices and points out systemic forms of oppression and subjugation. The OED says that by midway through the twentieth century, woke "had been extended figuratively to refer to being 'aware' or 'well informed' in a political or cultural sense."[22] Without denying its significance as founded in African-American activist practices, this collection uses the term to signify an adaptation that destabilizes traditional forms of authoritative voice and extends the legacy of the "Cinderella" fairy tale for a contemporary audience. This may be because the adaptation reframes the tale to point out gender and sexual identity-based oppression and allow for feminist viewpoints; creates space for divergent and diverse forms of representation; reproduces the tale in a manner that creates new avenues for analysis; or encourages post-human and post-truth narratives.

This collection uses woke as a term that indicates societal awareness of traditionally oppressive practices and the ways in which contemporary literature tries to subvert or otherwise destabilize them. Instead of using the term monolithically, then, the collection draws on it as representative of a sea change. An adaptation is not inherently woke or unwoke, but the practices that go into expanding forms of representation as "complex, intersectional, and multifaceted" indicate a move toward a conscionable ideal.[23] Adaptations that rely on these practices "are descriptive and self-reflexive, do not seek to simply subvert stereotypes—replace the old with the new; rather, they rattle the foundational cages of the tale where the power structures reside."[24] By rattling the foundational cages of the tale, they release it for interpretation by an empowered readership.

The majority of fairy-tale scholarship has looked at commonalities in recurring symbolism and archetypes prevalent in these stories in order to argue for a folkloric, psychoanalytic theory of universality. While this collection supports this investigation, it is more interested in seeing how subjects are actively produced in and through these tales. Jack Zipes reads fairy tales as representing the dichotomous shift from idyllic childhood to young adulthood with all its implications of normative behavior, shifting gender expectations, and social becoming.[25] Fairy-tale adaptations, then, trace a rich history of contemporaneous ideology and cultural zeitgeist. Retellings that reflect these ideas through the lens of wokeness, or what Bacchilega calls "activist responses,"[26] are inspired by activist motivations. These adaptations are destabilizing, often postmodern works that allow a transformative reading experience. They are used in multiple communities through a citational practice that undermines the idea of authoritative voice while simultaneously reaffirming the tale's longevity.

"Cinderella" adaptations that extend the representation of previous versions are not limited to the twenty-first century. Past reimaginings create voice for the traditionally silenced heroine or expose ideological flaws. For example, Sylvia Plath's "Cinderella" (1955) depicts the ball, and therefore Cinderella's future with the prince, as both transitory and trapping. Cinderella's passivity and inability to stop the ticking clock or the hectic music represents her lack of self-actualization and reliance on the prince or others to save her; it is a social critique of women's oppression. Similarly, Anne Sexton's "Cinderella" (1971) satirizes the entire system that promises a happy ending to the American rags-to-riches ideal and the supposed domestic happiness brought by marriage. The poem reflects the ways women become jaded through systematic interpellation into happily ever after. In Gail Carson Levine's *Ella Enchanted* (1997), Ella is cursed with obedience; rather than following societal mandates into a passive, docile position as in typical "Cinderella" stories, she is literally forced into an obedient lifestyle by spell. However, she vehemently hates her necessary obedience. Emma Donoghue's *Kissing the Witch: Old Tales in New Skins* (1997) writes a "Cinderella" who upends the normative tale by falling for her fairy godmother. And the 20th Century Fox film *Ever After* (1998) places the "Cinderella" tale into a historical perspective. Its protagonist is an empowered and sympathetic character who revolutionizes Cinderella with agency and autonomy. Unlike the typical Cinderella, who seeks only to dance at the ball, Danielle wishes for love and social change with the prince.

The twenty-first century brought with it a wealth of "Cinderella" adaptations that transform the original tale, including many not discussed in this collection. Brandy became the first Black woman to portray Cinderella onscreen in Rodgers and Hammerstein's racially diverse *Cinderella* (1997); Keke Palmer was then the first to play Cinderella in subsequent Broadway performances (2012). Francesca Lia Block's *The Rose and the Beast* (2000) frames the glass slippers as "made from your words, the stories you have told like a blower with her torch forming the thinnest, most translucent sheets of light out of what was once sand."[27] This implies the power of active readership in fairy-tale (re)creation. Donna Jo Napoli's *Bound* (2004) refashions the "Cinderella" story to reflect issues happening in Ming Dynasty China, including foot-binding and the complexities of female relationships. Malinda Lo's *Ash* (2009) rewrites Cinderella as someone with queer desires who must choose between the world of the living and the fairy realm; the prince hardly factors in. In *Cinder Ella* (2016), S. T. Lynn writes a Black, transgender Cinderella figure. Jennifer Donnelly's *Stepsister* (2019) tells the story of the ugly stepsister who self-mutilates her foot to fit Cinderella's glass slipper. These and other contemporary adaptations extend the legacy of the "Cinderella" story by reconfiguring its core themes to represent more inclusive beliefs.

This collection looks at contemporary "Cinderella" adaptations to examine the epistemological and ideological shifts that take place between hypo- and hypertext. It is filled with fascinating, divergent approaches to the contemporary "Cinderella" story as it intersects with wokeness. In *Girl Power: Feminist and Queer Readings*, Sarah Maier and Jessica Raven's "Gen Z Cinder(f)ellas: Girl Powered Gender Adaptations in the *A Cinderella Story* Films" argues that the *A Cinderella Story* film franchise reflects Gen Z's feminist ideology. Aoileann Ni Eigeartaigh's "'With this Shoe I Thee Wed': Cinderella as Agent of the Backlash in *The Devil Wears Prada* and *Sex and the City*" assesses the "Cinderella" myth as responds to patriarchal oppression and consumerism. Svea Hundertmark's "'Have Courage and be Kind': The Emancipatory Potential of 21st-Century Fairy-Tale Adaptations of 'Cinderella'" analyzes empowered feminist depictions of the Cinderella-type. Christine Case's "Two Centuries of Queer Horizon: Rodgers and Hammerstein's *Cinderella*" argues that the production history of a theatrical "Cinderella" queer-codifies the tale for a modern audience.

In *(Re)Production: A Classic Tale Told Anew*, Loraine Haywood's "Queen of the Ashes: Daenerys Targaryen, Cinderella of the Apocalypse, and Her Mirror Prince, in *Game of Thrones*," argues for two intertwined "Cinderella" motifs in HBO's *Game of Thrones*. Brittany Eldridge's "Forgive me Mother for I have Sinned" investigates the relationship between the wicked stepmother and princess through the lens of forgiveness. Camille Alexander's "Tiana Can't Stay Woke: Reassessing the 'Cinderella' Narrative in Disney's *The Princess and the Frog*" contends that rewriting a Cinderella character as African American without giving her agency detracts from a woke depiction. Christian Jiminez's "Predestination or the Rediscovery of Agency" argues that many contemporary "Cinderella" retellings only allow success under the conceit of white masculinity. Carolina Alves Magaldi's and Lucas Alves Mendes's "Deaf Cinderella: The Construction of a Woke Cultural Identity" assesses the significance of a "Cinderella" adaptation written in SignWriting.

In *Post-human and Post-truth Cinderellas*, Rachel L. Carazo's "Dragons, Magical Objects, and Social Criticism: Reimagining the 'Cinderella' Trope in Tui T. Sutherland's *The Lost Heir*" looks to materialism and multiculturalism as they intersect with a dragon Cinderella. Alexandra Lykissas's "Cyborg-erella: Marissa Meyer's *Cinder* as a New Type of Other" traces the "Cinderella" story through cyborg and post-humanist depictions. Ryan Habermeyer's "Once Upon a Time in Nazi-Occupied France: *Inglourious Basterds*, Cinderellas, and Post-truth Politics" argues that "Cinderella" themes are deliberately employed in Tarantino's filmic corpus to delightful, and often bloody, ends. Finally, my epilogue, "A Postmodern Princess: Rhetorical Strategies of Contemporary 'Cinderella' Adaptations," identifies different literary tools used by adaptations working toward wokeness.

Literary fairy tales take oral tradition and transcribe it as part of a conscriptive process that, among other goals, seeks to interpellate subjects in a normative matrix. Looking within these texts at motifs, themes, and representation shows how later adaptations challenge norms established in source texts. Contemporary adaptations often change the framing of power and empowerment, particularly through agency and desire. However, there are still constraints that limit the possibilities of adaptation. The idea that a fairy-tale adaptation is always pushing back or writing back to a singular authoritative original is inherently problematic. Similarly, the demythologizing process of fairy-tale adaptations and particularly postmodern adaptations can be seen as ruining the magic of these tales. However, by shifting narration from an authoritative space (the "once upon a time" tale that has always been around in some incarnation or another) to a personal one, contemporary adaptations engender an interactive readership.

Through this process, the hierarchy of authoritative myth becomes destabilized. Adaptations transform the narrative itself to expose certain beliefs that permeate previous versions and respond in some way to the shared understanding of a text's cultural legacy. Many adaptations studies scholars focus on adaptations of literary works (as Bacchilega says, "authored and canonical Literature with a capital L"),[28] but fairy-tale adaptations respond to oral/cultural traditions as much as literary inscriptions. Instead of looking at fidelity or variations, the theoretical significance of investigating fairy tales and their adaptations relies instead on the tensions and anxieties that call for new adaptations. By looking at these texts as dialogic and heteroglossic, rather than as simple subversion, readers gain a more comprehensive understanding of how cultural expectations have evolved throughout these retellings. We empathize with Cinderella by placing ourselves in her shoes—or rather, her glass slippers—in these new adaptations.

NOTES

1. Sara Stewart, "Ranking the Disney Princesses from Retro to Woke," *New York Post*, 19 Oct. 2018, nypost.com/2018/10/18/ranking-the-disney-princesses-from-retro-to-woke/.

2. Suzy Woltmann, "'I Can't Pass Away from Her': Adaptation and the Diaristic Impulse of *The Wind Done Gone*," in *Diary as Literature: Through the Lens of Multiculturalism in America*, ed. Angela Hooks (Wilmington: Vernon Press, 2019), 59.

3. Bruno Bettelheim, *The Uses of Enchantment: The Meaning and Importance of Fairy Tales* (New York: Random House, 1976), 236.

4. Heidi Anne Heiner, "The Quest for the Earliest Fairy Tale," *Sur La Lune Fairy Tales*, 28 June 2014, http://www.surlalunefairytales.com/introduction/timeline.html

5. Heiner, "Tales Similar to 'Cinderella,'" *Sur La Lune Fairy Tales*, 02 December 2012, http://www.surlalunefairytales.com/cinderella/other.html.

6. Heiner, "Tales."

7. Ibid.

8. Ibid.

9. William McCarthy, *Cinderella in America* (Mississippi: University Press, 2007), 86.

10. Ibid.

11. Jacob and Wilhelm Grimm, *The Complete Fairy Tales of the Brothers Grimm* (Toronto: Bantam, 1988), 292.

12. Ibid., 296.

13. McCarthy, *Cinderella in America*, 34.

14. Jack Zipes, *The Brothers Grimm* (New York: Palgrave Macmillan, 2002), 7.

15. Zipes, *Brothers*, 7.

16. Cristina Bacchilega, *Fairy Tales Transformed* (Wayne State University Press: Detroit, 2013), 9.

17. Ibid., 90.

18. Jack Zipes, *Why Fairy Tales Stick* (New York: Routledge, 2006), 59.

19. Jane Yolen, "America's Cinderella," *Children's Literature in Education* 8 (1977): 28.

20. Merriam Webster, "What Does 'Woke' Mean?" *Merriam-Webster*, 30 December 3018, www.merriamwebster.com/words-at-play/woke-meaning-origin.

21. Ibid.

22. Oxford English Dictionary, "New Words Note June 2017." *Oxford English Dictionary*, 11 June 2018, public.oed.com/blog/june-2017-update-new-words-notes/.

23. Karlyn Crowley and John Pennington, "Feminist Fraud on the Fairies? Didacticism and Liberation in Recent Retellings of 'Cinderella,'" *Marvels & Tales* 24.2 (2010): 302.

24. Ibid., 304.

25. Zipes, *Why Fairy Tales Stick*, 11.

26. Bacchilega, *Fairy Tales Transformed*, 31.

27. Francesca Lia Block, *The Rose and the Beast* (Harper Collins: New York, 2000), 61.

28. Bacchilega, *Fairy Tales Transformed*, 33.

BIBLIOGRAPHY

Bacchilega, Cristina. *Fairy Tales Transformed*. Wayne State University Press: Detroit, 2013.

Bettelheim, Bruno. *The Uses of Enchantment: The Meaning and Importance of Fairy Tales*. New York: Random House, 1976.

Block, Francesca Lia. *The Rose and the Beast*. Harper Collins: New York, 2000.

Cinderella. Dir. Clyde Geronimi, Wilfred Jackson, and Hamilton Luske. Perf. Ilene Woods. Disney, 1950.

Crowley, Karlyn, and John Pennington. "Feminist Fraud on the Fairies? Didacticism and Liberation in Recent Retellings of 'Cinderella.'" *Marvels & Tales* 24.2 (2010): 297–311.

Grimm, Jacob, Wilhelm Grimm, Jack Zipes, and Johnny Gruelle. *The Complete Fairy Tales of the Brothers Grimm*. Toronto: Bantam, 1988.

Heiner, Heidi Anne. "The Quest for the Earliest Fairy Tale." *Sur La Lune Fairy Tales*, 28 June 2014, http://www.surlalunefairytales.com/introduction/timeline.html.

Heiner, Heidi Anne. "Tales Similar to Cinderella." *Sur La Lune Fairy Tales*, 02 December 2012, http://www.surlalunefairytales.com/cinderella/other.html.

McCarthy, William. *Cinderella in America*. Mississippi: University Press, 2007.

"New Words Notes June 2017." *Oxford English Dictionary*, 11 June 2018, public.oed.com/blog/june-2017-update-new-words-notes/.

Perrault, Charles, Martin Hallett, and Barbara Karasek. *Folk and Fairy Tales*. Toronto: Broadview Press, 2002.

Stewart, Sara. "Ranking the Disney Princesses from Retro to Woke." *New York Post*, 19 October 2018, nypost.com/2018/10/18/ranking-the-disney-princesses-from-retro-to-woke/.

"What Does 'Woke' Mean?" *Merriam-Webster*, 30 December 3018, www.merriamwebster.com/words-at-play/woke-meaning-origin.

Woltmann, Suzy. "'I Can't Pass Away from Her': Adaptation and the Diaristic Impulse of *The Wind Done Gone*," *Diary as Literature: Through the Lens of Multiculturalism in America*, ed. Angela Hooks. Wilmington: Vernon Press, 2019.

Yolen, Jane. "America's Cinderella." *Children's Literature in Education* 8 (1977): 21–29.

Zipes, Jack. *The Brothers Grimm*. New York: Palgrave Macmillan, 2002.

———. *Why Fairy Tales Stick*. New York: Routledge, 2006.

I

Girl Power: Feminist and Queer Readings

Chapter One

Gen Z Cinder(f)ellas

Girl Powered Gender Adaptations in the
A Cinderella Story *Films*

Sarah E. Maier and Jessica Raven

Cinderella was not born but made. She is a metaphoric young woman who repeatedly metamorphoses in meaning to keep pace with the transformations in social conventions and mores which dominate in any given century or culture. Western European archetypal versions[1] begin within aristocratic circles; Giambattista Basile created the first written version of the tale, "Cenerentola," in his *Pentamerone* (1634) followed by Charles Perrault who wrote his own literary *kunstmärchen* "Cendrillon ou la petite pantoufle de verre" within *Histoires du temps passé* (1697) for either society children or his peers,[2] Madame Marie-Catherine Le Jumel de Barneville—the Baroness d'Aulnoy—sought to entertain with "Finette Cendron" in her *Les Contes des Fées* (1697), while just over a century later, the Brothers (Jacob Ludwig Karl and Wilhelm Carl Grimm) collected "Aschenputtel" for their folkloric *Kinder und Hausmärchen* (1812). In all cases, there are remaining questions of originality and authenticity since the stories derived from oral tales told among people; indeed, at least one theorist has called this image of young womanhood found in multiple times and cultures "a princess of and for the people."[3] Twentieth-century history in the United Kingdom has seen this designation of "People's Princess" most famously given to Princess Diana (née Lady Diana Spencer) for her work with early AIDS patients, landmine activism, and kind responses to the public. Tragically, the death of the Princess was a result of the people's desire to know about her life after the traditional fairy-tale life she expected fell apart. More recently, the Duchess of Sussex (née Meghan Markle) is feeling the wrath of some of the British

Public for stealing away their Prince Harry from "The Firm" of Queen Elizabeth's royal court. In the first case, the Prince Charming failed his Princess; in the second, the ginger-haired Prince Charming has chosen to protect his self-defining, self-aware, girl-powered Princess and their son, Archie.

These many examples prove there is no one Cinderella, either historically or in modern times; rather, "there are distinctive characteristics and plots that alert us to regularities in similar works of art, we can trace a marvelous evolution of the oral wonder tale in the western world and see how it contributed to the formation of the literary fairy tale as a genre in the sixteenth and seventeenth centuries and how the oral and literary traditions conspired or colluded to reach out to other forms of art to propagate their wonder and fairy tales"[4] in both traditional and new media. While many filmmakers, beginning with George Méliès through to Tim Burton, use aspects of the fairy tale in their work, in the last few years, specific "Cinderella" stories have attempted to enter the forum for consideration. Novels like *Cinder* (Meyer 2012) or *Ash* (Lo 2009), adaptations like *Ella Enchanted* (Levine 1997, O'Haver 2004) or *Cinderella* (Branagh 2015), and loosely based films like *Ever After* (Tennant 1998) or *Pretty Woman* (Marshall 1990) continue to appear in a nostalgic return to the past in a seeming contradiction in a supposedly post-feminist, post-third wave world. To retain the Cinderella story, new parameters for an empowered young woman, the women who surround her, the men who challenge her, and the young men who partner her must be recast for a young woman who claims her own agency rather than other people's expectations.

The fairy-tale heroine of *Cinderella* and her rags-to-riches narrative is oft recycled, perhaps as a hotel maid who, when mistaken for a hotel guest, catches the eye of a wealthy gentleman, or in an updated story wherein the traditionally chaste Cinderella is transformed from a sexualized prostitute into a lady through an unexpected romance with a handsome businessman.[5] Transmedial and intertextual references to the young woman's story still seek to entice a target audience of women. Neither *Maid in Manhattan* (Wang 2002) nor *Pretty Woman*, or even *My Big Fat Greek Wedding* (Zwick 2002), promised a feminist plot to an adult audience. Just as bridal salons[6] use Cinderella's happy ending to sell extravagant ballgowns that make even the most regular woman feel like royalty, most films that use such an archetype focus primarily on the Cinderella character's transformative romance with a powerful, rich, and attractive man, but ignore her potential growth as an individual without him.

Problematically, "historical changes in Cinderella's characterizations that preceded filmic presentations chart a devolutionary sequence of losses of autonomy and a stripping away of individuating characteristics"[7] that may lead to the further replication of "old masculinist and antifeminist metanarratives."[8] One could argue that the majority of the films to date continue this falling away or degeneration of female individualized character in order to reinstate universalized, traditional gender roles, a move perhaps best exemplified in the animated film by Walt Disney's *Cinderella* where Cinderella's character has been emptied of individuality to be no longer "the shrewd, resourceful heroine of folktales from earlier centuries has been supplanted by a 'passive princess' waiting for Prince Charming to rescue her."[9] The mice seemingly have more agency than the young woman.

While the lack of female empowerment in these films may be escapist fantasy to a target audience of women who have established careers and relationships, the same cannot be said for younger viewers because for many of them, "romance co-habits uncomfortably with women's liberation [and] barely disguised forms of fairy tales transmit romantic conventions through the medium of popular literature."[10] The formula of Cinderella's story has needed to change from one of an "inchoate, unspecified, generalized, universally and undifferentially female woman who marries up the social scale in an exchange of chaste sexuality for monetary security. Folklore cannot be easily dismissed as mere entertainment because it has always been one of culture's primary mechanisms for inculcating roles and behaviours"[11] and enforcing cultural imperatives of passivity, dependency, and self-sacrifice.

Fairy tales are social documents; as such, recent Cinderella narratives target Generation Z, or the population of people "born between 1991 and 2000."[12] The term itself was coined in the media. In a *USA Today* article, there was a call to name the next generation after Generation X.[13] Alex Williams argues that "Demographers place its beginning anywhere from the early '90s to the mid-2000s. Marketers and trend forecasters, however, who tend to slice generations into bite-size units, often characterize this group as a roughly 15-year bloc starting around 1996, making them 5 to 19 years old now. (By that definition, millennials were born between about 1980 and 1995, and are roughly 20 to 35 now)."[14] In addition, "Girl Power" is exemplified by a "free spirit, self-acceptance and self-fulfillment [which] are crucial characteristics."[15]

Born in the wake of third-wave feminism, technologically literate and social media aware, Generation Z has never known a world without the concept of Girl Power—but feminism, according to the Spice Girls, had become "a dirty word. Girl Power is just a nineties way of saying it . . . of course I am a feminist. But I could never burn my Wonderbra. I'm nothing without it!"[16]—a comment that demonstrates the paradoxical feelings of young women. From the 1990s onward, mainstream media programming sought to make girls/young women feel tough and empowered; cartoons were full of characters like a trio of superpowered sisters who fight crime in the *Powerpuff Girls* (1998–2005, reboot 2016) and a high school girl who uses her cheerleading moves to double as a secret agent in *Kim Possible* (2002–2007). Popular films included *Wendy Wu: Homecoming Warrior*

(2006) which tells the story of a teenage girl who is the reincarnation of a powerful warrior and *Cadet Kelly* (2002), about an outwardly girly girl who attends military school while *Buffy the Vampire Slayer* (1997–2003) dominated the teen television scene as a kickboxing demon killer. Compared to these empowered female characters, a traditional Cinderella story—wherein the female protagonist is kind, demure, and takes her stepfamily's abuse with grace until she marries a handsome prince—would not satisfy a typical Gen Z viewer. The formula required reinvention with a feminist flare and some Girl Power punch.

Into the early 1990s, cultural conventions expressed complex understandings of gender roles; sometimes, little girls might think they could either be a girly-girl or a tomboy with no middle ground, separating young women into battle lines while many more enlightened women looked to find common ground that would allow for a multiplicity of femininities and to pursue an empowering agenda. Girls had not been able to reach outside of the traditional realm of femininity without having to sacrifice their identities, not be further marginalized as tomboys just for a preference of dirt bikes and baseball over tea parties and pink dresses. Even authors and publishers, thirty years apart, continually recognize the need to rewrite such archetypes with picture books like *The Paper Bag Princess* (1980) by Robert Munsch and *Not All Princesses Dress in Pink* (2010) by Jane Yolen. If a girl preferred playing in the dirt to having tea parties, then she was a tomboy and anything that individualized a young girl from the habitual patriarchal view of girlhood meant that, by definition, she was less-than a girl. This method of isolation, combined with a world full of parents and teachers telling young girls that boys pulling their pigtails on the playground meant that he liked her or that "a science career would jeopardize their chances for a rewarding future personal life"[17] left girls and young women in desperate need of new messages; they needed to be taught that individuality was okay, that their self-worth and happiness are important, and that they need not limit their dreams.

This intergenerational discomfort is not new; the New Woman of the 1880s included the New Girls, younger women who were seeking to define themselves both as and in difference to the earlier suffragettes. Sally Mitchell has argued that

> the new girl—no longer a child, not yet a (sexual) adult—occupied a provisional free space. Girls' culture suggested new ways of being, new modes of behavior, and new attitudes that were not yet acceptable for adult women [. . .] a change in outlook and supported inner transformations that had promise for transmuting woman's "nature" but is more sure of her own destiny and that marriage is not her necessary destiny; further, girls were consciously aware of their own culture and recognized its discord with adult expectations.[18]

Indeed, the term "girl" only became "dramatically visible about 1880."[19] A century later, and modelling a new girlhood while feeling they had been left out of adult feminism, it was those lessons that are precisely what the Girl Power movement set out to teach Generation Z's budding youth, and the Spice Girls serve as an early example of Girl Power put into motion.

The Spice Girls may not have invented Girl Power but they can be credited with the global girl community embracing the new brand of youth-oriented feminism, which encouraged young girls and women to embrace their individuality, to be confident and to go after what they want—what they really, *really* want. Jude Davies explains that "girl power helped to sell Spice Girls' product while at the same time consumption of the group put girl power on the lips and in the minds of female youth."[20] Sporty, Scary, Ginger, Posh, and Baby Spice, by possessing vastly different identities demonstrated female individuality; Sporty Spice, perhaps the most revolutionary of the five members, wore tracksuits and enjoyed sports but neither made her any less of a Girl than the other Spices, not a tomboy to be feared for deviant gender or sexuality but in and for herself as an athletic woman.[21] At the time, these "varieties of femininity [were] offered as possible and legitimate modes, each with its own identifying characteristics of behavior, facial expressions, clothing, hairstyle and accessories. Appearances [were] closely related to presumptions about 'essence'" and "offer[ed] a freedom to choose from a series of appearance identities, which together constitute[d] a fragmented definition of womanhood."[22] By embracing individuality, the Spice Girls encouraged their fans to do the same. Self-confidence and the drive to follow one's dreams are the traits that the Spice Girls encouraged female youth to have; as they sing in "The Lady is a Vamp:" "She's got something new / She's a power girl / in a '90s world / and she knows just what to do."[23] Tara Brabazon and Amanda Evans make the point that the Spice Girls "grant[ed] a spirit, power and humor to the performance of difference. The Spice Girls could never be feminism's woman" but could be "colorfully affirmative" as a new way to consider feminist politics.[24] The Spice Girls preached Girl Power, and girls listened to their "fashionable, truly popular [form of] feminism"[25] and, subsequently, this image began to shape the media that targeted the Generation Z audience.

At this cultural moment, in *A Cinderella Story* (2004), writer Leigh Dunlap and director Mark Rosman set out to retell Cinderella's story in a way that would appeal to the Girl Power-obsessed youth of Generation Z. In the manner of "chick lit" these "chick flicks" might be seen as "narratives organizing young women after the so-called death of feminism. These not-so-fairy tales mostly feature savvy and single white females [. . .] whose tribulations and elations lead toward greater self-awareness and self-fulfillment" while it "seems to be a barometer for social, cultural, political, and economic issues that concern young women."[26] While film critics like Stephen Hunter at the *Washington Post* commented that "Stories can last forever if they achieve structural, emotional and moral perfection and therefore can survive any telling of them [. . .] I thought it was true, also, of 'Cinderella,' until *A Cinderella Story* proved me wrong. You can say of this movie, truly, that they took the most famous tale in the world and broke it."[27] Perhaps that is the point—white, male, non-Generation Z is not the intended audience; his expectations of the film are too literal or literary. Instead, stories such as these exemplify a kind of intertextuality, "no longer folktales but rather original creations which have a general [or generic] intertextual relationship with folktale schemata"[28] that evoke potential comparative images, scenarios and outcomes for the viewer. While fairy-tale aspects of the Cinderella archetype are adapted to the *Cinderella* films, these films work because as in many modern narrative adaptations, "passivity is not rewarded, sexuality does not masquerade as death, and the speaking subject can begin to articulate her desires rather than simply appearing as the object of another's" desire. [29] One could further argue that such new adaptations negate universality and instead rely on specificity of place, situation, and so forth. A Girl Power Cinderella must demonstrate the self-confidence and drive to follow her dreams, both of which give her the ability to escape her abusive stepfamily without needing to be rescued by Prince Charming.

In order to create a Girl-Power-embodying Cinderella, the writers, directors, and producers of the *A Cinderella Story* films first strip the heroine of the damsel-in-distress persona outlined for her by Walt Disney's film. Produced in a post-WWII environment in which the general societal consensus was that women needed to be "protected"[30] from America's enemies, Disney's film presents its audience with a domestic goddess who is unfairly abused by her cruel stepfamily because she lacks a man to protect her following the death of her father. Subsequently, the role of her hero falls to Jacques and Gus, proving that male mice have more agency than Cinderella.[31] This Cinderella is an utterly dependent damsel who relies upon men (regardless of their size and species) to take care of her—which, in a post-WWII climate, is exactly the message Disney wanted to send to female viewers: Rosie the Riveter should happily step back into the home and take their "natural" domestic place by the hearth. It was, culturally post-WWII, "the thing to think the men were coming back and the women would revert to the role they had before and make the homes ready for them."[32] In a Girl Power era, messaging that promotes female submissiveness grew unacceptable; even Disney changed its positioning with *The Cheetah Girls* (2003). This novel-to-film adaptation capitalized on the surge in popularity of girl groups like the Spice Girls by telling the story of four talented young women who form a band together and dream of making it big. Featuring songs like "Girl Power" and "Together We Can," the film promotes female independence and sisterhood; the Cheetah Girls even go so far as to reject the archetypal Cinderella narrative with the aptly titled song "Cinderella."

In the *A Cinderella Story* franchise, Cinderella is revisioned as an intelligent and ambitious young woman who is capable of being her own hero, a Cinderella who does not intend to sit around and wait for a rich man to save her. These Cinderellas all have aspirations that will carry them away from their stepfamily, even if Prince Charming never shows up. Sam Montgomery, the reinvented Cinderella, plans to graduate high school early so she can study at Princeton; Mary Santiago, the heroine of the sequel *Another Cinderella Story* (Santostefano 2008), dreams of attending the Academy of Performing Arts and becoming a professional dancer; in *A Cinderella Story: Once Upon a Song* (Santostefano 2011), Katie Gibbs writes songs and intends to go to college far away from her family and to become a musician; Tessa dreams of being a performer in *A Cinderella Story: If the Shoe Fits* (Johnston 2016) and in the most recent film in the franchise, *A Cinderella Story: Christmas Wish* (Johnston 2019), Kat Decker has a part-time job in order to save up enough money to move out of what is now her stepmother's house. In each film, the teenage heroine already has life aspirations that either relate to her education or her career, plus she possesses the intelligence, the talent, and the drive needed to achieve her goals. The key to a happy ending is no longer to wait for your prince to come, but to succeed through hard work and dedication to one's dreams as clearly demonstrated by Mary's song, "Tell Me Something I Don't Know." [33]

Refusing to be passive or silent, the new Cinderella girl must chart a new path to self-fulfillment. The reinvention of a story that previously aligned freedom with marriage to a wealthy man, Cinderella's new life must be clearly linked to her own hard work and dedication to self-betterment. In the first film, Sam's late father teaches her how to play baseball but far more importantly he teaches her the value of getting an education and of being self-sufficient. In the flashback sequence at the beginning of the movie, the audience sees Sam's father reading her a bedtime story from a book of fairy tales with the ending as anticipated: "And the beautiful princess and the handsome prince rode off to his castle, where they lived happily ever after;" Sam then asks her father if fairy tales come true to which he responds, "Well, no—but dreams come true." [34] When Sam then asks her father if he has a dream, he tells her, "My dream is that you'll grow up, go to college, and maybe someday you'll build your own castle." [35] Her father disrupts conventional didacticism of perfection and patience to, instead, tell Sam that if she goes to college and gets an education, she will create her own future. The twenty-first-century lesson is that self-reliance will allow her to provide for herself. This pro-active Cinderella decides that she is going to graduate early. Sam's success story is the rags-to-riches tale that Generation Z, fueled by

Girl Power, wants to hear; they want a Cinderella who succeeds through her own hard work and dedication, not by marrying the richest guy in town.

The four films in the *A Cinderella Story* franchise that follow the original continue to enforce Cinderella's position as a Girl Power role model, but other women in the tale support a variety of readings. The paradigm of the stepmother's lack of understanding of young girls—past stories and present adaptations—might be read as an exaggerated dislocation between generations. Much of this intergenerational conflict is emblematic of the discomfort between the new girls who seek "to place their own lives and priorities in relation to those of the generation that preceded them. The girls who came of age during a decade of Girl Power generally considered feminism to be dated and irrelevant to them," causing debates between the past and the present.[36] The reality is that there is still a necessary place for feminist assertion, and that the contradiction of postfeminism is that while it is associated with what has been achieved by women since the Second Wave, it sometimes problematically pushes aside recognition of what they have gained by early feminist movements.[37]

Mary, for one, faces her fair share of adversity along the way from her abusive stepmother, Dominique. To reinforce Mary's role as submissive and subservient to her stepmother's dominance in the domestic sphere, the Cinderella-girl is told she is in no need of intellectual development:

Fiona: What are you doing just standing there? Get to work!

Sam: Fiona, I can't go to work [at the diner] this morning. I've got a really big test I have to study for.

Fiona: Listen, Sam. People go to school to get smarter so that they can get a job. You already have a job, so it's like skipping a step.[38]

Additionally, the stepmother frequently uses Cinderella's financial dependency to manipulate her further; as the widow of Cinderella's wealthy father, the stepmother has control over all of his assets including the funds that he left behind so that his daughter could go to college.[39] Ironically financially empowered by the death of the patriarch, rather than lift the next generation, she seeks their submission, aggressively promising to "find a way for [the] savings . . . to disappear."[40] The stepmother does so by spending Cinderella's college money on beauty treatments that will help her adhere to current standards of youthful beauty. Like mother like daughter, Fiona spends an obscene amount of Sam's late-father's money on breast implants and imported Norwegian salmon for a crash diet she is doing, while Katie's stepmother in *A Cinderella Story: Once Upon a Song* (2011) warns that she can "access that money [Katie's] fool daddy left [for college], should I need it for a medical reason. You know, like to grow longer legs."[41] These older women attempt to prevent or usurp the Cinderellas' feminist educations; often, such tales "point to the complicity of women within a patriarchal culture" since they are "primary transmitters and models for female attitudes" and often the initial enforcer of young female generational conformity.[42]

Although modern adaptations of the Cinderella archetype, these film narratives rely on the previous models wherein female assertiveness is sabotaged and any "exhibitions of feminine force . . . or disruptive non-conformity will result in annihilation or social ostracism."[43] Modern stepmothers know that, if Cinderellas are allowed to enter the public sphere of post-secondary education, the young women will become less passive and will recognize that the women's behavior is unacceptable abuse.[44] The stepmothers often demand deference or seek to marginalize the girls as other to the ideal young woman. One such example has Gail attempt to force Katie to model deferential behavior in *A Cinderella Story: Once Upon a Song* in order to hide her intellect from men who may find it threatening. Deference behavior is a key component in any patriarchal society and is synonymous with the young female phenomena of "playing dumb;"[45] problematically, "deference behavior towards men may sometimes be intentional . . . just as women intentionally try to attract better mates by spending time and resources in order to look as young, healthy and attractive as possible." It is clear that "deferential behavior (more hesitant or tentative speech) does help women gain influence with males"[46] because it allows for male control over women. The separation of girly girls from tomboys not only damages the supposed tomboy's self-worth but teaches the girly girls to marginalize anyone who is different or possibly "deviant" but definitely unfeminine.

In each of the *A Cinderella Story* films, the girly girl is embodied by her stepsister(s) and by an additional character who, for lack of a better phrase, can only be called a mean girl. Ironically, one of the articles surrounding the first *Cinderella Story* makes a connection with the title, "The Power Duff Girls"; in the interview with Hilary Duff and her sister Haylie Duff, Brenda Rodriguez asks the sisters to describe their fashion sense. Haylie says she is a rocker, but Hilary calls her "girly" while Rodriguez assumes that "make[s] Hilary the tomboy" then asks if they "compete for guys,"[47] a proliferation of female stereotypes that can only be described as completely unenlightened. Just a little over two months before *A Cinderella Story* hit theaters, the "onslaught of girl-ness"[48] continued with *Mean Girls* (2004), a film that preaches acceptance and anti-bullying to teens. A cult classic for its campy, Tina Fey brand of humor, *Mean Girls* features the character of Regina George, the reigning queen of a clique called the Plastics and the pop-culture apex of the high school mean girl. While Regina George is certainly not the world's first mean girl, and not even the first mean girl to appear on film, she is the essence of who the mean girl is, "a master of rumor and character assassination, ready to eliminate any pretender to her throne as most popular (and powerful) girl in the school."⁴⁹

The Cinderellas' stepsisters in these film narratives act as mean girls who view themselves as elite because they are popular adherents to the image of popular success; consequently, they instantly go on the attack when they project that Cinderella—individual, outsider—is potentially encroaching with success on their territory: the targeted Prince Charming. The Prince Charmings' interest in characters like Sam and Mary, who do not adhere to the mainstream concept of attractiveness or ideal young womanhood, threatens to recalibrate the patriarchal balance of the social order to which the stepsisters are accustomed and wherein they are always favored. In the most recent entry, *A Cinderella Story: Christmas Wish* (2019), when Dominic, the Prince Charming character, tells one of his popular friends that the mean girl "Skylar's not really [his] type," his friend responds, baffled, that "Skylar is everybody's type."⁵⁰ One *Boston Globe* reviewer of *A Cinderella Story* calls out that "A modern 'tweener-girl movie [. . .] can't exist without a bitchy cheerleader."⁵¹

The mean girl is unquestionably anti-feminist because rather than encouraging girls like Cinderella who have faced discrimination, such a young woman attempts to tear other young women down to preserve her own comfortable social status. A phrase that the respective mean girls use frequently throughout the series is that "people like her don't belong in our world"⁵² and they do their very best to keep Cinderella ostracized, excommunicated from cool girl culture. In the translation from past archetype to current parlance, any "attempt to analyze a formula for these stories might yield an element of royalty (whether literal or high school variety), a romance with the good guy (and/or father), [and] a notable lack of realism."⁵³ When Natalia, the mean girl in *Another Cinderella Story*, learns that Mary is the masked girl whom Joey Parker, the film's popstar Prince Charming, danced with at the Black and White Ball, Natalia enlists Mary's stepsisters to help with Mary's public embarrassment; at the step-sisters' birthday party, they play a home video of a much younger Mary professing her childlike love for Joey and dancing to one of his songs. Both incidents of humiliation are performed to concretise Cinderella's status as an outsider or, as they would say in *Mean Girls*, a "freak,"⁵⁴ or here, "the Pretend Princess,"⁵⁵ or "the Dork Princess,"⁵⁶ epithets intended to insult but more obviously revealing the ignorance of the mean girls who invoke and represent such ugliness.

The new Cinderella follows the folkloric past in her fight against those persons who would see her shamed. Neither Sam nor Mary, despite the mean girl's best efforts, allow public adversity to humiliate them into giving up on their dreams or changing who they are. In a powerful speech that Sam delivers, she declares that, "I know what it feels like to be afraid to show who you are. I was, but I'm not anymore—and the thing is, I really don't care what people think about me, because I believe in myself and I know that things are going to be okay."[57] In spite of public embarrassment and untruths, Sam perseveres.[58] The films still posit that some men still find submissiveness in a woman attractive; toxic, patriarchal behavior exists in Generation Z while worse still, the "predisposition [to defer] is likely unconscious."[59] Katie, in *A Cinderella Story: Once Upon a Song*, proves that she is a Girl Power Cinderella by challenging the need for female deference to male authority. When in the presence of a man, Katie refuses to blend in; her instinct is to allow herself to shine as an intelligent individual. Katie's cruel stepmother, Gail, embodies the ideal of a woman who defers; when Guy Morgan, a hot-shot record producer, arrives at a meeting about enrolling his son Luke in the school where Gail serves as Dean, the first words she utters are, "You look like a man who knows things."[60] Gail flatters him with the implication that he is smarter than her even though she is Dean of a private school which implies intelligence, ambition, and accomplishment; however, she chooses to play dumb in order to appear more attractive to a powerful man. In the same scene, Katie—unlike her stepmother—is not afraid to show off her own intellect in a direct contrast of generational expectations. When Guy Morgan says my son "just produced an album with the Fruity Dangers?" with an element of uncertainty, Katie quickly chimes in to correct him: "Do you mean Danger Fruit?" but Gail scowls at Katie for having the audacity to speak up and make such a man look foolish and when Katie continues to speak about the album recognizing it is a "cult phenomenon," Gail harshly cuts in and asks, "I'm sorry—why are you talking?"[61] Gail's repressive behavior makes her complicit; she believes that Katie should be silent. Katie is smart and unafraid to own her knowledge. Unlike her stepmother, while the conventional, conservative influences around her tell her that she should be quiet, Katie learns a crucial lesson about finding one's voice in the face of pressure, patriarchally motivated or otherwise.

Not only does the franchise revision Cinderella in a way which allows her to be her own hero, the films use the example of Cinderella's reinvention to showcase that young women can embrace their individuality and Girl Power, like the Spice Girls, without sacrificing their individualism. At the time of the film series' conception, women who posed as role models treated feminism like a curse word with young women saying they did not like "the f-word." Deborah Siegal points out that Jennifer Aniston "who directed a film for a series sponsored by *Glamour* magazine as part of a project to address the paucity of female directors working in Hollywood, anxiously reassured an interviewer that she wasn't, like, 'a bleeding heart feminist,' while twenty-six-year-old singer-songwriter Kelis recently told *Essence* not to call her [a feminist]: 'Whenever you say that word, people think of some crazy, hairy lesbian.'"[62] Not only do such statements clearly demonstrate a misunderstanding of the term and its impact on social history, reform, and future possibilities for women, the uninformed stereotype misrepresents feminism to young women. In no way does feminism deny women their femininity; rather, it promotes for each woman to find what it means for and by herself.

The *A Cinderella Story* films, like the Spice Girls' personae and other popular culture fixtures of Generation Z, seek to show girls that they can be champions for self-defined female empowerment that reflects intellectual and gender fluidity. In *A Cinderella Story: If the Shoe Fits*, Tessa stretches her character in that she is unafraid to enjoy masculine activities or to be better at them than the men whom she knows. Tessa's late father was a race car driver and owned an autobody shop; he taught her everything he knew there and now Tessa works there as a mechanic. Her knowledge gives her an advantage over all of the young men who, in a reversal of stereotypes, know plenty about music and theater but nothing whatsoever about auto-mechanics. When she sees a pair of stagehands wheeling a broken-down motorcycle backstage, she asks, "Hey, is that a 500cc twin? 1950, right?" to which they reply, "Yeah, if you say so . . . We're not really bike people."[63] Even when in the presence of Reed West, the Prince Charming character, Tessa does not hesitate to show off her skills. After being recruited once again to fix the show's motorcycle, Tessa offhandedly asks Reed in the midst of her work, "Can you pass me the 9/16th spanner?" to which he hopelessly looks at her tools and responds with, ". . . no?"[64] Realizing that he is not familiar with mechanical terminology, she resorts to calling it "the small silver thing" and, when he successfully passes it to her, he jokes, "You should've just said that."[65] Here, Tessa dumbs down her intellect but not in a way that diminishes it; she is, instead, forced to dumb her request down because she mistakenly assumed that Reed, as a man, would be familiar with cars. Rather than being repulsed by a girl who knows more, Reed actually finds Tessa's capability attractive, later remarking that his ideal girl would "be smart, of course. Smarter than me, probably."[66] Girls and young women who watch the films gain confirmation that not all boys dislike smart girls and that young women do not have to dumb themselves down just to impress. Tessa is a grease monkey and proud of it even if it is not what the society considers appropriately feminine.

Challenging the ongoing, damaging images of physical culture that deeply affect young women's self-perceptions, in *A Cinderella Story: Christmas Wish*, Katherine "Kat" Decker refuses to be defined by what she sees on Instagram and embraces her own sense of self. The most recent of the five films, it is the most heavily influenced by the rise in popularity of social media. While many Millennials did not have cell phones when they were in high school, Generation Z is entangled in the inescapable web of twenty-four-hour social media updates, trending topics and viral vlogs; as a consequence, the mental health of this young group is greatly affected by it. Instagram, a social media app which predominantly features photos and videos, is one of the worst culprits in influencing teen and young adult mental health for the worse, especially young women's self-image. In a discussion of selfies, critics explain that "likes and comments attributed to . . . young women's selfie[s] serve as quantified measures of social acceptance and validation [and] may influence their offline well-being, particularly their body Image."[67] The cause of young women's negative body image is due, in no small part, to the presence on social media glam influencers and waifish models frequently referred to online as Instagram Girls.[68]

Like many pop culture images of Cinderella's stepsisters who ornament and dress themselves to cover their inner insecurities, many Instagram Girls gain their following by being self-proclaimed beauty gurus who post "carefully crafted images"[69] of their makeup, outfits, and fitness regiments online. Because they are influencers, it is assumed by their young and impressionable audience that they are experts in the field of beauty and, as such, they must be emulated. Trouble, therefore, lies in the fact that the photos published by these beauty gurus "are sometimes just as edited and curated as those seen in fashion magazines."[70] Kat's stepsister, Joy, is an Instagram Girl who runs a daily vlog all about her ideal life and, on the particular day when *A Cinderella Story: Christmas Wish* begins, she catches footage on said vlog of Kat slipping and getting covered in pink drinks from Starbucks. Because of Joy's online influence, Kat goes viral as "Starbucks Girl"[71]—awkward, clumsy, and precisely the opposite of what girly girls on Instagram aspire to be. Additionally, appearance is a significant marker of worth for the film's mean girl, Skylar, who is horrified to discover that Kat "totally ruined [Dominic's] shoes" when she fell and spilled Starbucks Frappuccino everywhere. Dominic insists that it is fine, but Skylar exclaims, "It's not fine! . . . They don't sell couture at Nordstrom Rack, sweetie."[72] Showing no concern for Kat's physical well-being when she fell, Skylar's obsession with materialism is a fixation.

Sadly, for many young women, the fixation upon maintaining a perfect image that reflects a perfect—but fraudulent—appearance can result in harmful "self-objectification [which is] a tendency for women to adopt an externalized or outsider view of their own bodies, often due to consistent exposure to objectification of female bodies in media."[73] Kat has no interest in being a picture-perfect Instagram Girl who is unhealthily obsessed with her body image, preferring to live in the moment to do what makes her happy. Kat brings home Chinese takeout for dinner, despite the fact that her stepmother, Deirdra, objects to it when Joy reaches for some, declaring rudely, "No carbs for you. You'll get fat."[74] Body dysmorphia and eating disorders are of serious concern for young persons but this Cinderella sets a strong example of strong womanhood that is unconcerned with industry beauty standards and unhealthy messaging about body image. To counter this emphasis on culturally delineated standards with a body that is strong, *Another Cinderella*

Story includes Mary, a young woman who highlights another area of the Girl Power movement: skater girl culture. Like Sam and Tessa, Mary exists outside of what the patriarchy would classify as normative behavior: she rides a skateboard. Often viewed as a masculine activity, the skater girl culture was also a popular symbol of Girl Power in the 2000s, "with its emphasis on individual self-expression and nonconformity, afforded skater girls room to develop a critique of, and distance from, *emphasized* femininity."[75] Championed in pop culture by female icons like Canadian punk musician Avril Lavigne, skater girls believe in "the importance of being oneself amidst the pressures to conform" (238). A primary example of the phenomena of skater girls refusing to conform to emphasized feminine standards exists in the lyrics of Lavigne's punk anthem, "Sk8r Boi."[76] The implication of the song is that a skater girl is better than the girly ballerina and gets the boy that both girls want because she believes in authenticity over artifice. This pitting of non-conformists like the reinvented Cinderellas against stereotypical girly or mean girls occurs frequently in Girl Power cinema.[77]

It would be remiss to ignore the stepsisters as mean girls; while the root of the mean girl's toxic behavior is not always explicit, the stepsisters in the *A Cinderella Story* franchise are clearly affected by the unhealthy, anti-feminist influence of their mother—Cinderella's stepmother. Nicole Moulding makes clear that "abuse by mothers was [linked to] mental illness" by many of her study's subjects and, because "mothers are positioned in society as almost entirely responsible for the well-being and care of their children"[78] the abuse from the stepsisters' mother from a young age onward predisposes the stepsisters to abuse others; this abusive cycle fits every Cinderella's stepmother's effect on both herself and her stepsisters with a near-constant, negative presence in their lives during formative years of cognitive molding and habit formation. For example, in *A Cinderella Story: Once Upon a Song*, the stepsister Bev agrees to lip-sync; she believes she must in order to become a famous singer because her mother has spent years denigrating her abilities to make her believe that she will never be good enough:

Bev: Guy Morgan will give me a record deal as soon as he hears me sing.

Gail: I doubt that, Puddin'.

Bev: I've been practicing really hard. My voice teacher says that I have transcended to a whole new level.

Gail: Yeah, I doubt it.[79]

Bev has effectively had her self-confidence stripped over years of emotional abuse by her mother, leading her to believe that she is not good at anything and that, like her mother, she will have to get by in the world on her physical appearance:

Katie: All you have to do is stand there and look pretty.

Bev: Have you ever thought about how that makes me feel? You have talent! You can go on *American Idol* and forget about the rest of us! This is like my only chance. Pretty doesn't last very long. Just look at Mom. [80]

Extensive, ongoing abuse by their mothers ultimately leads the stepsisters in the films to lash out at the Cinderellas, most likely out of jealousy. That said, problematically, Cinderella abandons the other abused girl(s) with whom she grew up. The structuralist formula of Cinderella's narrative dictates that there must be an evil stepmother and at least one wicked stepsister, to serve as the good-natured Cinderella's oppressors. But it begs the question: If Cinderella is allowed to be reinvented in the wake of feminism and Girl Power, why are her stepsister(s), who are also subjected to abuse, not given the same chance at transformation? [81]

Patriarchal standards do not just negatively impact young girls and women who do not embody the traditional standard of what it means to be a girl; the conventions of masculinity found in the foundational images of Prince Charming negatively impact young boys and men, too. The *A Cinderella Story* franchise does address some portion of the audience by having the Prince Charming characters become Cinderfellas with their own modern variations to oppose hegemonic male standards. Relevant to the young people for whom the films are intended is an experiment that Celine Kagen conducts annually with her high school students:

On the first day of class, students write for ten minutes in response to the question, "What is a man?" Inevitably, the discussion that follows begins with a student posing, "A man is someone with a penis." From this point, the conversation moves into a listen of male stereotypes: strong, tough, tall, rich, brave, independent, likes cars, doesn't cry, has lots of sex, watches sports and pornography, etc. [82]

Any deviation from type intended to create the old school, perfect Prince Charming risks social isolation and self-doubt. Viewers can witness isolation in action during the dance competition in *Another Cinderella Story*; when a young man takes to the stage to perform a solo ballet routine, Dominique, Mary's stepmother, shouts derogatorily from the audience, "Ballet is for girls!" [83] Just as young girls and women are shamed for nonnormative activities, young boys and men may be self-conscious if they pursue traditionally feminine dreams. Much of culture will assume effeminacy and since the feminine is seen as weak, young boys and men who reject such categorizations are perceived as weakening the patriarchy's power. Nontraditional young men who wish to avoid replicating stereotypes require new possibilities of Prince Charmings, just like young women need revised Cinderellas so they might advocate for social change.

The newly embodied Cinderfella defies the toxic, patriarchal standards set for him in *A Cinderella Story*; for example, Austin Ames vehemently rejects his father's patriarchal dream for his life when he takes control of his destiny.[84] In a modern imitation of patrilineage, Austin's father wants him to play football at his alma mater, University of Southern California, and then take over their family's car dealership, an emulation of the traditionally masculine pastimes of sports and cars. Austin wants to go to Princeton (Prince/town) like Sam and pursue a writing career. In a radical act of defiance, Austin stands up to presumptive expectations when he skews the crucial football game that would have gained him admission to his father's university:

Mr. Ames: You're throwing away your dream!

Austin: No, Dad. I'm throwing away yours.[85]

Likewise, Luke Morgan in *A Cinderella Story: Once Upon a Song* refuses to be forced into a profession; his father, Guy Morgan, wants him to follow in his footsteps and become a successful record producer, claiming "there are two types of people in the music biz: artists and businessmen. Luke is a businessman."[86] The father intentionally sets business against the arts, oblivious that Luke's passion lies in song writing.[87] Effectively, through such resistance to patriarchal forces in their lives, Austin and Luke all encourage young boys and men to reject the conventionally restrictive roles into which they are cast.

One of the central challenges young men face as social expectations change is found in interactions between fathers and sons, particularly for the sons who prefer to enact a supportive, rather than dominant, role in society. Unlike Joey, Luke, and Reed, who yearn to be in the spotlight, Dominic Wintergarden prefers to work behind the scenes. He admits to Kat that he wants to manage bands but is afraid of disappointing his father because he does not "think it's what [his] dad had in mind for [him]."[88] It is worth noting that Dominic's father is the wealthy CEO of a chain of luxury hotels; therefore, by necessity, he exudes dominance, focus, and power at the forefront of his company, not from the shadows. The key difference between Dominic and the previous incarnations is that, while the adversity they faced was genuine, Dominic's experience leads him to assume that his father will not approve of a nontraditional career path without even consulting him—shockingly, his expectations are contra to his father's actions. Remodelling the archetype, it is not his father's opinion which Dominic must conquer, but his own complicity and patriarchal understanding of how the world works for men. His father's unexpected, active support for his unconventional dream, insisting that Dominic has "an excellent ear for talent" and that he will make "a great manager,"[89] helps to dismantle male fear of the disapproval of society. Patriarchs, too, can embrace change, or even provide change much like a fairy godfather.

While the main focus of the *A Cinderella Story* franchise is the self-growth of the Girl Power Cinderella and the changing Cinderfella Prince Charming, the films do still feature the inevitable relationship between the two characters and, much like their individual story lines, their romance now exists for a feminist purpose: to teach this demographic the importance of equality and support in any healthy relationship. A noteworthy and energizing part of this franchise, apart from other adaptations, is that these Prince Charmings have no real power over the Cinderellas. The male is merely popular, and not literal royalty, with the accompanying dominion. He cannot punish her for speaking her mind. The scenario in *Pretty Woman* is an obvious contrast—Edward, as Vivian's Prince Charming, is not actually a prince—that said, Edward's money and status give him immense monetary and elevated class power over Vivian, a sex worker who is on the margins of social discourse. In the *A Cinderella Story* series, the Prince Charmings exercise no power and refuse to exert conventional gender dynamics in their romances, while all of the Cinderellas are smart, confident, and driven young women who can survive on their own without trading themselves for access to male fortune; these women honor themselves, be it by obtaining a college scholarship or getting a high-paying job in the music industry. Cinderella's independence allows her to advocate for herself when she feels that Prince Charming is not treating her with the respect that she, as a strong young woman with Girl Power, deserves.

The best example of a Cinderella who places her self-worth first is Sam in *A Cinderella Story*. There is a telling moment when Sam stands up for herself after Shelby publicly humiliates her; the traditional male protector, fearing for his reputation, does nothing to stop it:

Austin: I know that you think I'm some—

Sam: Coward? Phony?

Austin: Just listen—

Sam: No, *you* listen . . . I came to tell you that I know what it feels like to be afraid to show who you are. I was, but I'm not anymore. And the thing is, I really don't care what people think about me because I believe in myself . . . I know that the guy who sent me those emails is in there somewhere, but I can't wait for him because waiting for you is like waiting for rain in this drought: useless and disappointing.[90]

In contrast, the concept of mutual support is evident between Mary and Joey in *Another Cinderella Story* and Kat and Dominic in *A Cinderella Story: Christmas Wish*. Joey is, without a doubt, Mary's support system and is emphasized by the lyrics of the song that he writes about her: "You're the new classic; / You're the new P.Y.T. / It stands for 'paid', 'young', and 'taking on the world from the driver's seat.'"[91] Joey admires Mary's ambition, so much so that when he finds out that the Academy of Performing Arts "changed their minds" about letting Mary audition, he insists that he can help "change it back"[92] by having Mary dance in his music video competition. Joey recognizes that his celebrity status does give him some power and, rather than using it to control Mary, he uses it to help her, transforming from a Prince Charming to a potential fairy godfella figure. In reciprocity, Mary supports Joey in his decision to reject a duet with Dominique. The profound impact that Mary's support has on Joey, when he has only faced adversity from his family, is clear when he evokes her when he sings, "You're bringing back the real me; no judgement in your eyes."[93] Kat and Dominic provide each other a similar support system. Kat, after two years of ruthless emotional abuse from her stepmother and stepsisters, has grown full of fear, unable to accept basic acts of kindness or to trust anyone. Dominic offers her an invitation to his family's charity gala with no strings attached; when she tells him that she cannot accept the invitation, Dominic insists, "Yes, you can."[94] Likewise, Kat helps Dominic get over his fear of disappointing his father when she insists, "I think your dad would be proud of you."[95] The equality of emotional support that these Cinderellas and Prince Charmings provide for each other serves as a model for the Generation Z viewers of what a healthy relationship looks like, no longer dictated by restrictive binaries of gender roles that assume women are emotional and helpless while men are intellectual and powerful.

When Dunlap and Rosman set out to create a Cinderella story with Girl Power, they successfully appealed to an increasingly feminist audience of Generation Z viewers and, along the way, they taught girls and boys alike several valuable lessons about their sense of self-worth and healthy romantic relationships. While still fraught with remnants of folkloric conventions, Sam and Austin, Mary and Joey, Katie and Luke, Tessa and Reed, and Kat and Dominic do present the film franchise's attempt to legitimize more modern versions of Cinderellas and Cinderfellas as alternative types to emulate in a world still full of negative messaging in popular culture. Adaptations and other portraits of strong women influence the women watching, young or old.

Following the immense popularity of the science fiction drama *The X-Files* (1993–2002, reboot 2016–2018), critics argued for a link between young women watching the show and pursuing an education and career in STEM because of Dana Scully. At The Geena Davis Institute on Gender in Media, a study was done to evaluate how and if the "medical doctor and FBI agent, played by Gillian Anderson, inspired a generation of women to enroll in careers related to science, technology, engineering or medicine (STEM), a pattern they are calling the Scully Effect"; they asked two thousand women over the age of twenty-five "how frequently they watched *The X-Files* and what influence it had on their career aspirations" and the result was decisive—"half of those [women] familiar with Anderson's character said she increased their interest in STEM careers. Women who watched the show regularly were more likely to have considered a STEM career, studied these subjects at college and entered these professions."[96] Similar examples of aspirational STEM characters include Dr. Ellie Sattler, the paleobotanist portrayed by Laura Dern in the film *Jurassic Park* (1993). Just as the team of the *A Cinderella Story* franchise revised Cinderella's character to make her a stronger role-model for girls, so too did the team of *Jurassic Park* (1993); in Michael Crichton's original novel (1990), Lex is the younger of the two Murphy siblings and serves no purpose to the plot aside from the reader's discomfort with knowing that a helpless little girl is trapped on an island overrun with man-eating dinosaurs. Her older brother, Tim, is the more significant character because he possesses a nearly encyclopedic knowledge of dinosaurs and is skilled with computers; however, in the film adaptation, the screenplay flips the roles of the Murphy siblings to make Lex the elder and, by default, the protector of her younger brother. The STEM skill sets of the children are split equally with Tim, still a dinosaur expert, but Lex as the computer genius which gives her a more significant role in the film's plot. Lex saves the survivors from being devoured by velociraptors when, in the control room, she uses her skills as a self-taught hacker to reboot the Park's computer system to enable the door locks and prevent an imminent raptor attack. By giving Lex a scientific skill set, *Jurassic Park* includes a strong role model for young girls watching the film, just as Dana Scully was an inspiration to female fans of *The X-Files*. Scully encouraged women to become doctors and Lex, in much the same way, encourages girls to become computer scientists.

Just as STEM heroines have been proven to encourage young women to pursue careers in STEM fields, it is safe to assume that intelligent and aspirational Cinder(f)ellas could have a profound impact on the lives of their Generation Z viewers.

NOTES

1. The Aarne-Thompson-Uther system classifies Cinderella as Tale Type 510A, Persecuted Heroine.
2. Jack Zipes believes the tales were specifically crafted not for children but for Perrault's "peers in the literary salons." In *The Oxford Companion to Fairy Tales* (New York: Oxford UP, 2000), 379.
3. Ruth Bottingheimer, "Cinderella: The People's Princess," *Cinderella across Cultures*, ed. Martine Hennard Dutheil de la Rochère, et al. (Detroit: Wayne State University Press, 2016), 27.
4. Jack Zipes, "Grounding the Spell: The Fairy Tale Film and Transformation," *Fairy Tale Films*, ed. Pauline Greenhill and Sidney Eve Matrix (Boulder: University Press of Colorado, 2010), x.
5. The initial screenplay treatment, *3,000* by J. F. Lawton, began as "a dark fable about a financially destroyed America and the perils of showing the good life to people who had never experienced it before" (Kate Erbland, "The True Story of Pretty Woman's Original Dark Ending," *Vanity Fair*, 23 March 2015, www.vanityfair.com/hollywood/2015/03/pretty-woman-original-ending). The original film, according to actress Julia Roberts, "really read like a dark, gritty art movie" and she remembers reading the original ending in the script "where a man tosses her character Vivian Ward out of the car, 'threw the money on top of her, as memory serves, and just drove away leaving her in some dirty alley'" (Bryan Alexander, "Julia Roberts Reveals the Dark, Original *Pretty Woman* Ending," *USA Today*, 14 June 2019, www.usatoday.com/story/life/movies/2019/06/14/julia-roberts-reveals-pretty-womans-origi-nal-dark-ending/1462720001/). Ironically, when CNN airs the clip by Roberts on its website, the preceding DNN documentary clip is Prince Harry speaking about his love for the Duchess of Sussex in their series, *The Windsors* (2020). See www.cnn.com/videos/entertainment/2019/06/16/julia-roberts-pretty-woman-ending-wxp-vpx.hln.
6. Even Disney-inspired wedding dresses have become trendy, the inference being that the happy ever after will follow the dress; for an example, see www.dailymail.co.uk/femail/article-4925968/Disney-inspired-gowns-let-brides-princess-day.html.
7. Bottingheimer, "Cinderella," 29.
8. John Stephens and Robyn McCallum, *Retelling Stories, Framing Culture: Traditional Story and Metanarratives in Children's Literature* (London: Taylor and Francis, 1998), 22.
9. Maria Tatar, "Introduction: Cinderella," *The Classic Fairy Tales* (New York: Norton, 1999), 102.
10. Karen Rowe, "Feminism and Fairy Tales." *Women's Studies* 6 (1989): 237.
11. Ibid., 238-9.
12. Carolina Herrando et al., "Tell Me Your Age and I Tell You What You Trust: The Moderating Effect of Generations." *Internet Research*, 29.4 (2019): 800.
13. Bruce Horovitz, "After Gen X, Millennials, What Should Next Generation Be?" *USA Today*, 4 May 2012, www.usatoday30.usatoday.com/money/advertising/story/2012-05-03/naming-the-next-generation/54737518/1.
14. Alex Williams, "Move Over, Millennials, Here Comes Generation Z," *NY Times*, 18 September 2015. www.nytimes.com/2015/09/20/fashion/move-over-millennials-here-comes-generation-z.html.
15. Dafna Lemish, "Spice World: Constructing Femininity the Popular Way." *Popular Music and Society* 26.1 (2003): 21.
16. Ginger Spice qtd. in Lemish, "Spice World," 26.
17. Jane Stake and Shannon Nickens, "Adolescent Girls' and Boys' Science Peer Relationships and Perceptions of the Possible Self as Scientist," *Sex Roles* 52.1-2 (2005): 3.
18. Sally Mitchell, *The New Girl: Girls' Culture in England, 1880–1915* (New York: Columbia University Press, 1995), 3.
19. Ibid., 6.
20. Jude Davies, "'It's Like Feminism, But You Don't Have to Burn Your Bra': Girl Power and the Spice Girls' Breakthrough 1996–7," *Living through Pop*, ed. Andrew Blake (London: Routledge, 1999), 160.

21. For an excellent discussion of nonconformist images of young girls, see Megan Friddle, "Who Is a 'Girl'? The Tomboy, the Lesbian, and the Transgender Child," *Gender(ed) Identities: Critical Rereadings of Gender in Children's and Young Adult Literature*, eds. Tricia Clasen and Holly Hassel (London: Routledge, 2017), 117–136.

22. Lemish, "Spice World," 20.

23. This song appears on the album *Spiceworld* (1997).

24. Tara Brabazon and Amanda Evans, "I'll Never Be Your Woman: The Spice Girls and New Flavours of Feminism," *Social Alternatives* 17.2 (1998): 39.

25. Ibid., 42.

26. Sarah Rasmussen, "Chick Lit," *Girl Culture: An Encyclopedia*. Edited by Claudia Mitchell and Jacqueline Reid-Walsh (Westport: Greenwood Press, 2008), 228.

27. Stephen Hunter, "Skip This Ball: 'Cinderella' Is a Limp Take on the Tale," *Washington Post* (July 16, 2004): C01.

28. Stephens and McCallum, Retelling, 220.

29. Elisabeth Rose Gruner, "Telling Old Tales Newly: Intertextuality in Young Adult Fiction for Girls," *Telling Children's Stories: Narrative Theory and Children's Literature*, ed. Michael Cadden (Lincoln: University of Nebraska Press, 2011), 5.

30. Krisztina Robert, "Constructions of 'Home,' 'Front,' and Women's Military Employment in First-World-War Britain: A Spatial Interpretation," *History and Theory* 52.3 (2013): 331.

31. The mice actually enact the beginning of her escape; when her stepmother locks her in the attic so that she cannot try on the glass slipper, the mini-men must retrieve the key from the enemy and rush to Cinderella's rescue. The Grand Duke and Prince Charming save Cinderella from her abusive situation by fitting her with the glass slipper since marriage to the Prince is the only way she can escape. Clues provided by the characters' clothing suggest that this version of the tale stylistically appears to take place in the nineteenth century and, as a result, there would have been no other options for an uneducated young woman like Cinderella to get away from her family aside from, potentially, prostitution and a life as a fallen, disgraced woman.

32. Phil Goodman, "'Patriotic Femininity': Women's Morals and Men's Morale during the Second World War," *Gender & History*, 10.2 (1998): 290.

33. *Another Cinderella Story*, directed by Damon Santostefano (Warner Premiere, 2008).

34. Ibid.

35. *A Cinderella Story*, directed by Mark Rosman (Warner Bros. Pictures, 2004).

36. Kathleen Karlyn, *Unruly Girls, Unrepentant Mothers: Redefining Feminism on Screen* (Austin: University of Texas Press, 2011), 2.

37. Kathleen Karlyn makes a similar point in her discussion of James Cameron's film, *Titanic* (1997), wherein she points to the influence of "Girl Power" or "Girl Culture" as well as riot grrrls and Spice Girls on the expectations of the female Edwardian protagonist, Rose, as well as her power to draw young women to the box office.

38. *A Cinderella Story*, Rosman.

39. Verbal abuse is rampant; for example, Dominique threatens, "Don't you sass me, smarty-pants, or I'll revoke your school privileges" and demands Mary's obedience; she is aware that Mary sees school, both secondary and the possibility of post-secondary, as an escape from the home and uses that leverage as a form of manipulation.

40. *Another Cinderella Story*, Santostefano.

41. Ibid.

42. Rowe, *Feminism*, 243.

43. Ibid, 247–248.

44. For example, Dominique links Mary's self-confidence with the feminist values that she is engaging with at school and, as a result, the stepmother attempts to put a stop to it by negating Mary's chances at going to post-secondary school by lying to the director of the Academy of Performing Arts who calls to set up Mary's audition with the claim that Mary "broke both of her legs [and] can't dance."

45. Rosemary Hopcroft, "Gender Inequality in Interaction: An Evolutionary Account," *Social Forces* 87.4 (2009): 1855.

46. Ibid., 185–186.

47. Brenda Rodriguez, "The Power Duff Girls," *People,* 62.5 (2004): 77–78.

48. Lauren Adams, "Chick Lit and Chick Flicks: Secret Power or Flat Formula?" *The Horn Book Magazine* 80.6 (Nov/Dec 2004): 670.

49. David Resnick, "Life in an Unjust Community: A Hollywood View of High School Moral Life." *Journal of Moral Education* 37.1 (2008): 102.

50. *A Cinderella Story: If the Shoe Fits*, directed by Michelle Johnston (Warner Home Video, 2016).

51. Ty Burr, "Updated 'Cinderella' Will Please 'Tweens, It's Perfectly Plain to See." *Boston Globe,* 16 July 2004, www.archive.boston.com/ae/movies/articles/2004/07/16/updated_cinderella_will_please_tweens_its_perfectly_plain_to_see.

52. *A Cinderella Story*, Rosman.

53. Adams, "Chick Lit," 674.

54. *Mean Girls*, directed by Mark Waters (Paramount Pictures, 2004).

55. *A Cinderella Story*, Rosman.

56. *Another Cinderella Story*, Santostefano.

57. *A Cinderella Story*, Rosman.

58. In much the same way Mary, too, refuses to let others define her; to assert herself, she performs in Joey's dance competition and proves to the director of the Academy of Performing Arts that she deserves inclusion in the advanced program. Immediately offered admission into the school based upon her talent, she has earned the escape from her abusive stepfamily and her dream: a young woman empowered is her own heroine.

59. Hopcraft, Gender Inequality, 1848.

60. *Another Cinderella Story*, Santostefano.

61. Ibid.

62. Jennifer Aniston and Kelis, quoted in Deborah Siegal, *Sisterhood, Interrupted: From Radical Women to Grrls Gone Wild* (Basingstoke: Palgrave, 2007), 9.

63. *A Cinderella Story: If the Shoe Fits,* Johnston.

64. Ibid.

65. Ibid.

66. Ibid.

67. Chelsea Butkowski et al., "Body Surveillance on Instagram: Examining the Role of Selfie Feedback Investment in Young Adult Women's Body Image Concerns," *Sex Roles,* 81.5-6 (2019): 385.

68. Social media influencers are "people who have established credibility with large social media audiences because of their knowledge and expertise on particular topics, and thereby exert a significant influence on their followers' and peer consumers' decisions" (Ki and Kim 2019, 905).

69. Chandra Feltman et al., "Instagram Use and Self-Objectification: The Roles of Internalization, Comparison, Appearance Commentary, and Feminism," *Sex Roles,* 78 (2018): 313.

70. Ibid.

71. *A Cinderella Story: If the Shoe Fits*, Johnston.

72. Ibid.

73. Butkowski, "Body Surveillance," 386.

74. *A Cinderella Story: If the Shoe Fits*, Johnston.

75. Dierdre Kelly et al., "Skater Girlhood and Emphasized Femininity: 'You Can't Land an Ollie Properly in Heels.'" *Gender and Education* 17.3 (2005): 238 (emphasis added).

76. Avril Lavigne, "Sk8rboi," *Let Go* (Arista Records, LLC, 2002).

77. Examples of this form of cinema is found in other films, like Disney Channel's *High School Musical* (2006–2008) trilogy (wherein popular, blonde, wealthy, pink-clad Sharpay Evans seeks to destroy bookish Gabriella Montez and steal her boyfriend in every film); *A Walk to Remember* (2002), in which pretty, popular, and blonde Belinda gets revenge on Jamie, the outcast reverend's daughter, for "stealing" her boyfriend by plastering the school with sexual, photoshopped posters of her; and, the most well-known example of them all, *Mean Girls* (2004).

78. Nicole Moulding, "Damned If You Do, Damned If You Don't: Conflicted Femininities in Women's Narratives of Childhood Emotional Abuse," *Affilia* 23.2 (2017): 321.
79. Santostefano (2011, 00.13.15).
80. Ibid (1.07.40).
81. The most discomforting example of Cinderella's individualistic behavior can be seen in *A Cinderella Story: Once Upon a Song*; prior to the school's big talent showcase, Katie and Bev have a heart-to-heart that implies Bev is capable of redemption and was only cruel because her mother conditioned her to act in such a manner. There is an opportunity here for a rekindled sisterhood, for a chance at unity, and for the sisters to stand up to Gail but the narrative's arc takes another path. While Bev is lip-syncing on stage to Katie's live singing, Luke Morgan grabs a camera and exposes their act then Katie's friend pushes her out onto the stage to sing in front of the crowd. Katie then gets her moment in the spotlight and, ultimately, gets to escape Gail's abuse by making an album with Luke and his father but she participates in Bev's suffering. Viewers are left with a lingering feeling of unease. The implication appears to be that because the stepsister was mean, she deserves punishment and humiliation—she deserves to be abused. Such a message is anti-feminist and anti–Girl Power, both of which promote girls supporting girls. Until the *A Cinderella Story* film showcases Cinderella not only being her own hero but as a hero to other abused girls, the franchise cannot be praised for promoting feminist behavior, strong sisterhood, and female empowerment.
82. Celine Kagen, "Reading for Masculinity in the High School English Classroom," *Thymos: Journal of Boyhood Studies* 6.1/2 (2012): 214.
83. *Another Cinderella Story*, Santostefano.
84. There have been versions of male Cinderellas, including a film around the same time by Ron Howard, *Cinderella Man* (2005), based on the true story about a Depression-era, working poor boxer, James J. Braddock Jr. See Halbfinger 2005.
85. *A Cinderella Story*, Rosman.
86. *Another Cinderella Story*, Santostefano.
87. In a similar way, Joey Parker rejects the patriarchal path laid out for him in *Another Cinderella Story* when he refuses to sacrifice his artistic integrity. His parents want him to record a duet with Mary's stepmother, Dominique, because he could buy them "another house" with the song's profits, but Joey refuses to allow his family to force him into a money-making scheme. Convention dictates that as a man, it is his duty to provide for his family but he somewhat rejects those standards by setting moral boundaries for what he will and will not do to make money.
88. *A Cinderella Story: If the Shoe Fits*, Johnston.
89. Ibid.
90. *A Cinderella Story*, Rosman.
91. The revamped acronym starkly contrasts Michael Jackson's version of a "P.Y.T." which relegates the song's subject to an objectified "pretty young thing" (1982).
92. *Another Cinderella Story*, Santostefano.
93. Ibid.
94. *A Cinderella Story: If the Shoe Fits*, Johnston.
95. Ibid.
96. "Feedback," *New Scientist* 238.3176 (May 2018): 56.

BIBLIOGRAPHY

Adams, Lauren. "Chick Lit and Chick Flicks: Secret Power or Flat Formula?" *The Horn Book Magazine.* 80.6 (Nov/Dec 2004): 669–678.
Alexander, Bryan. "Julia Roberts Reveals the Dark, Original 'Pretty Woman' Ending." *USA Today* (June 14, 2019) www.usatoday.com/story/life/movies/2019/06/14/julia-roberts-reveals-pretty-womans-original-dark-ending/1462720001/.
Bottingheimer, Ruth B. "Cinderella: The People's Princess." *Cinderella across Cultures*, ed. Martine Hennard Dutheil de la Rochère, et al. Detroit: Wayne State University Press, 2016. 27–51.

Brabazon, Tara and Amanda Evans. "I'll Never Be Your Woman: The Spice Girls and New Flavours of Feminism." *Social Alternatives.* 17.2 (1998): 39–42.

Burr, Ty. "Updated 'Cinderella' Will Please 'Tweens, It's Perfectly Plain to See." *Boston Globe.* (July 16, 2004). www.archive.boston.com/ae/movies/articles/2004/07/16/updated_cinderella_will_please_tweens_its_perfectly_plain_to_see.

Butkowski, Chelsea P., Travis L. Dixon, and Kristopher Weeks. "Body Surveillance on Instagram: Examining the Role of Selfie Feedback Investment in Young Adult Women's Body Image Concerns." *Sex Roles.* 81.5-6 (2019): 385–397.

Davies, Jude. "'It's Like Feminism, But You Don't Have to Burn Your Bra': Girl Power and the Spice Girls' Breakthrough 1996–7." *Living through Pop.* Edited by Andrew Blake. London: Routledge, 1999. 159–174.

Erbland, Kate. "The True Story of Pretty Woman's Original Dark Ending." *Vanity Fair.* (March 23, 2015). www.vanityfair.com/hollywood/2015/03/pretty-woman-original-ending.

"Feedback." *New Scientist.* 238.3176 (May 2018): 56.

Feltman, Chandra E. and Dawn M. Szymanski. "Instagram Use and Self-Objectification: The Roles of Internalization, Comparison, Appearance Commentary, and Feminism." *Sex Roles.* 78 (2018): 311–324.

Friddle, Megan E. "Who Is a 'Girl'? The Tomboy, the Lesbian, and the Transgender Child." Edited by Tricia Clasen and Holly Hassel. *Gender(ed) Identities: Critical Rereadings of Gender in Children's and Young Adult Literature.* London: Routledge, 2017. 117–136.

Geronimi, Clyde, Hamilton Luske, and Wilfred Jackson (directors). *Cinderella.* Walt Disney Studios, 1950.

Goodman, Phil. "'Patriotic Femininity': Women's Morals and Men's Morale during the Second World War." *Gender & History.* 10.2 (1998): 278–293.

Gruner, Elisabeth Rose. "Telling Old Tales Newly: Intertextuality in Young Adult Fiction for Girls." *Telling Children's Stories: Narrative Theory and Children's Literature,* Edited by Michael Cadden. Lincoln: University of Nebraska Press, 2011. 3–21.

Halbfinger, David M. "Russell Crowe's Cinderella Story." *New York Times.* (May 8, 2005): B3.

Herrando, Carolina, Julio Jimenez-Martinez, and M. J. Martin-De Hoyos. "Tell Me Your Age and I Tell You What You Trust: The Moderating Effect of Generations." *Internet Research.* 29.4 (2019): 799–817.

Hopcroft, Rosemary L. "Gender Inequality in Interaction: An Evolutionary Account." *Social Forces.* 87.4 (2009): 1845–1871.

Horovitz, Bruce. "After Gen X, Millennials, What Should Next Generation Be?" (May 4, 2012). www.usatoday30.usatoday.com/money/advertising/story/2012-05-03/naming-the-next-generation/54737518/1.

Howard, Ron (director). *Cinderella Man.* Miramax, 2005.

Hunter, Stephen. "Skip This Ball: 'Cinderella' Is a Limp Take on the Tale." *Washington Post.* (July 16, 2004): C01.

Jackson, Michael. "P.Y.T." *Thriller.* Epic & CBS Records, 1982.

Johnston, Michelle (director). *A Cinderella Story: Christmas Wish.* Warner Bros. Home Entertainment, 2019.

—— (director). *A Cinderella Story: If the Shoe Fits.* Warner Home Video, 2016.

Kagan, Celine. "Reading for Masculinity in the High School English Classroom." *Thymos: Journal of Boyhood Studies.* 6.1/2 (2012): 213–219.

Karlyn, Kathleen. *Unruly Girls, Unrepentant Mothers: Redefining Feminism on Screen.* Austin: University of Texas Press, 2011.

Kelly, Deirdre M., Shauna Pomerantz, and Dawn Currie. "Skater Girlhood and Emphasized Femininity: 'You Can't Land an Ollie Properly in Heels.'" *Gender and Education.* 17.3 (2005): 229–248.

Ki, Chung-Wha 'Chloe' and Youn-Kyung Kim. "The Mechanism By Which Social Media Influencers Persuade Consumers: The Role of Consumers' Desire to Mimic." *Psychology and Marketing.* 36 (2019): 905–922.

Lavigne, Avril. "Sk8er Boi." *Let Go,* Arista Records, LLC, 2002.

Lemish, Dafna. "Spice World: Constructing Femininity the Popular Way." *Popular Music and Society.* 26.1(2003): 17–29.

Mitchell, Sally. *The New Girl: Girls' Culture in England, 1880–1915.* New York: Columbia University Press, 1995.

Moulding, Nicole. "Damned If You Do, Damned If You Don't: Conflicted Femininities in Women's Narratives of Childhood Emotional Abuse." *Affilia.* 23.2 (2017): 308–326.

Oxford English Dictionary. "girly, adj." *OED Online*, Oxford University Press, 2019, www. oed.com/view/Entry/78490.

———. "tomboy, n. and adj." *OED Online*, Oxford University Press, 2019, www.oed.com/ view/Entry/203097.

Rasmussen, Sarah. "Chick Lit." *Girl Culture: An Encyclopedia.* Edited by Claudia Mitchell and Jacqueline Reid-Walsh. Westport: Greenwood Press, 2008. 227–234.

Resnick, David. "Life in an Unjust Community: A Hollywood View of High School Moral Life." *Journal of Moral Education.* 37.1 (2008): 99–113.

Robert, Krisztina. "Constructions of 'Home,' 'Front,' and Women's Military Employment in First-World-War Britain: A Spatial Interpretation." *History and Theory.* 52.3 (2013): 319–343.

Rodriguez, Brenda. "The Power Duff Girls." *People.* 62.5 (2004): 77–78.

Rosman, Mark (director). *A Cinderella Story.* Warner Bros. Pictures, 2004.

Rowe, Karen E. "Feminism and Fairy Tales." *Women's Studies.* 6 (1989): 237–257.

Santostefano, Damon (director). *A Cinderella Story: Once Upon a Song.* Warner Premiere, 2011.

——— (director). *Another Cinderella Story.* Warner Premiere, 2008.

Siegel, Deborah. *Sisterhood, Interrupted: From Radical Women to Grrls Gone Wild.* Basingstoke: Palgrave, 2007.

Spice Girls. "The Lady Is a Vamp." *Spiceworld.* Virgin Records, 1997.

Stake, Jayne E. and Shannon D. Nickens. "Adolescent Girls' and Boys' Science Peer Relationships and Perceptions of the Possible Self as Scientist." *Sex Roles.* 52.1–2 (2005): 1–11.

Stephens, John and McCallum, Robyn. *Retelling Stories, Framing Culture: Traditional Story and Metanarratives in Children's Literature.* London: Taylor and Francis, 1998.

Tatar, Maria. "Introduction: Cinderella." *The Classic Fairy Tales.* Edited by Maria Tatar. Norton, 1999, pp. 101–108.

Waters, Mark (director). *Mean Girls.* Paramount Pictures, 2004.

Williams, Alex. "Move Over, Millennials, Here Comes Generation Z." (September 18, 2015). www.nytimes.com/2015/09/20/fashion/move-over-millennials-here-comes-generation-z.html.

Zipes, Jack. "Grounding the Spell: The Fairy Tale Film and Transformation." *Fairy Tale Films.* Edited by Pauline Greenhill and Sidney Eve Matrix. Boulder: University Press of Colorado, 2010. ix–xiii.

———. *The Irresistible Fairy Tale: The Cultural and Social History of a Genre.* Princeton: Princeton University Press, 2012.

———. *The Oxford Companion to Fairy Tales.* New York: Oxford UP, 2000.

Chapter Two

"With This Shoe I Thee Wed"

Cinderella as Agent of the Backlash in The Devil Wears Prada *and* Sex and the City

Aoileann Ní Éigeartaigh

This chapter assesses two twenty-first-century iterations of the Cinderella myth, *The Devil Wears Prada* (2006) and *Sex and the City: The Movie* (2008), focusing on the contradiction between the ostensibly empowering message of female fulfillment articulated by the central protagonists and their structural entrapment within a "happy ending" that is predicated upon their submission to normative gender behaviors. Both movies situate themselves in the contemporary postfeminist world of consumerism where the protagonists, raised on an ideological diet of female achievement, nevertheless find themselves struggling with what Betty Friedan defined in 1963 as the "mystique of feminine fulfillment."[1] My argument will draw upon Susan Faludi's persuasive indictment of postfeminism as little other than a thinly disguised attack on feminism by patriarchal institutions like the media, who coined terms such as "man shortage" and "biological clock" in an attempt to push women back into their "acceptable roles."[2] Much of this hostility was directed at career-minded women who were beginning to threaten the hegemonic values and gender composition of the American workplace. A key strategy of the backlash was its claim that feminism itself was the root cause of much of this stress and unhappiness.

Analyses of contemporary adaptations of fairy tales tend to interrogate their potential to destabilize traditional conceptions of gender norms, suggesting that the narrative structure can be opened up to alternative, perhaps even resistant, interpretations. Cristina Bacchilega argues that adaptations serve as vehicles for multivocality, thus activating: "multiple—and not so predictable—intertextual and generic links that both expand and decenter the narrow conception of the genre fixed in Disneyfied pre-1970s popular cultural memory."[3] The "transformation" which she sees as central to the fairy-tale narrative offers at least some potential to challenge traditional hegemonic conceptions of gender roles.[4] The proliferation of movie adaptations of Cinderella at the start of the twenty-first century would appear to support Bacchilega's assertion that the fairy tale can accommodate the multiple voices and perspectives expected by media-literate contemporary audiences. Rosalind Sibielski notes that critiques of contemporary Cinderellas tend to herald her "transformation from paragon of patriarchal feminine virtue to unruly female rebel," in line with the pervasive "girl power discourse" that suffuses many postfeminist media representations of women.[5] Sibielski cautions against an overly optimistic reading of such revisionist Cinderellas, however, arguing that in spite of their ostensibly "smart, sassy, self-reliant" heroines, such texts rarely offer a valid feminist rewriting of the canonical tale, functioning instead to reinscribe women within the patriarchal order they claim to challenge.[6]

Sibielski's observation points to the inherent complication in assessing contemporary texts targeting women, namely that the language of empowerment associated with feminism can very often be co-opted in postfeminist texts, which offer at best revisionist, at worst anti-feminist, messages about women's social roles and identities. This co-option is what Linda Pershing and Lisa Gablehouse define as "faux feminism," namely narratives that trivialize the concerns of feminism and push women back into the traditional conventions of romance while—crucially—"maintaining that they are her choice, not actions instilled by patriarchal teaching and values."[7] In her book *Backlash: The Undeclared War against Women* (1991), Faludi offers copious evidence of a clear and growing hostility to feminism in media discourse in the closing decades of the twentieth century. She identifies this backlash as the most effective of the myths peddled by patriarchy in its fight to roll back on the advances won by second wave feminism and persuade women to reclaim their ostensibly natural roles as wives and mothers. The backlash is particularly effective because it operates as a myth, hiding its ideology beneath an appeal to common sense and its disdain for women beneath a veneer of concern for their well-being. A key strategy of the backlash is its claim that feminism itself is the root cause of much of this stress and unhappiness: "Women are unhappy precisely *because* they are free. Women are enslaved by their own liberation. They have grabbed at the gold ring of independence, only to miss the one ring that really matters."[8] The backlash thus projects all blame for society's ills onto women and suggests that if women can be corralled back into their "natural" roles in the private sphere, society will thrive once again.

A particular target of the backlash is the single career woman, a figure who simultaneously resists her "natural" destiny of marriage and motherhood while threatening male hegemony in the workplace. Diane Negra notes that the neoconservative determination to reinscribe women within the domestic sphere has led to the pathologizing of the single woman as "deviant" and "deficient."[9] Feminism, it would seem, has wronged women by persuading them to abandon the life choices that would make them happiest. Faludi also notes the "divide-and-conquer strategy" pursued by the backlash, a strategy that pits women against each other, effectively encouraging them to self-police each other's choices: "It manipulates a system of rewards and punishments, elevating women who follow its rules, isolating those that don't."[10] Rather than being forced to behave in particular ways, women are invited to recognize themselves in the unhappy women the media portray to them and thus to sign up to the solutions being offered.

Many theorists cite postfeminism as the narrative that most successfully recruits women to an ideology that fundamentally undermines their autonomy and freedom. For Sarah Gamble, postfeminism's triumph lies in its ability to define itself as an ironic, postmodern critique of feminism rather than as an overtly hostile one.[11] In a society which defines itself largely through media images, women are easily persuaded that feminism is *passé* and embarrassing. Angela McRobbie states that postfeminism is more dangerous to women than any other element of the backlash as it is more overtly "antifeminist" in its message, casting feminism as a malign, joyless denial of femininity.[12] Media texts and advertisements encourage women to resist this attack on their essential femininity. Now that the fight for equality has been won, they proclaim, women are free to dress as they wish, use as many cosmetics as they like, and choose their own identities, even those rejected by feminism as repressive. Natasha Walter notes that in spite of the widespread language of empowerment and choice, sexualized images of women are effectively replacing all other representations of women across popular culture, including in fairy-tale texts ostensibly aimed at younger women and children.[13] This pressure on women to be both sexual and feminine is, according to Peggy Orenstein, part of a general move to reclaim the fairy-tale princess as the female role model *par excellence*, a move she describes as inducing a: "paralyzing pressure to be 'perfect': not only to get straight As and be the student body president, editor of the newspaper, and captain of the swim team but also to be 'kind and caring,' 'please everyone, be very thin, and dress right.'"[14] These so-called freedoms limit rather than increase women's autonomy across a broad spectrum of social practices, with the result that what is hailed as empowerment routinely demands acceptance of a diluted role for women.[15]

The movie genre most closely aligned with the narrative of postfeminism is the chick flick, a genre that privileges: "a return to femininity, the primacy of romantic attachments, girlpower, a focus on female pleasure and pleasures, and the value of consumer culture and girlie goods, including designer clothes, expensive and impractical footwear, and trendy accessories."[16] The very term "chick flick" embodies the uneasy contradiction at the heart of postfeminist culture. It suggests both a confident, insouciant embrace of a previously reductive word for women but is not fully able to shake off its patronizing, derogatory implications. Critical responses to chick flicks also encapsulate these differing perspectives on postfeminism, with advocates emphasizing the empowerment protagonists derive from their ability to celebrate their femininity and sexuality; while detractors accuse them of: "promoting a retreat into pre-feminist concerns and the unthinking embrace of consumerism, of endorsing not true freedom but 'the freedom to shop (and cook).'"[17] Certainly chick flicks closely align female empowerment with consumption, which in turn reinforces patriarchal expectations of ideal female behavior. Moreover, the much-lauded choices on offer to women reveal themselves on the whole to be predictable and traditional. A key element of many chick flicks is the "makeover," defined by Karen Hollinger as a paradigmatic structure that hides its ostensible interest in the development of its female protagonist behind a thinly veiled determination to force her to conform to socially acceptable ideals of beauty: "They show a young independent woman who does not meet the criteria of conventional beauty experiencing an external transformation that places her much more in accord with mainstream beauty standards."[18] What is significant is the implication that a woman's innate femininity is insufficient, rather she must be tutored in the performance of femininity as constructed for her by the beauty industry. This leads not to empowerment but rather to homogeneity and ever narrowing conceptions of female beauty.

The Devil Wears Prada centers around Andrea "Andy" Sachs, an ambitious aspiring journalist with a social conscience, who reluctantly takes a temporary job as second assistant to Miranda Priestly, editor of *Runway*, an influential fashion magazine. Although she is assured on a number of occasions that "a million girls would kill for this job,"[19] Andy feels the job is beneath her and is initially disparaging of the superficial world of fashion it represents. Ironically, she performs this distance from the world of *Runway* through her own clothing choices. The opening scene contrasts Andy's casual preparations for her workday, which involve little more than brushing her teeth and pulling a sweater over her unbrushed hair, with the meticulous preparations of other women, who are seen dutifully smearing drawers full of cosmetics onto their faces and squeezing their bodies into tight clothing and stilettos. Although Andy's deliberately unfashionable clothes and sensible shoes are used in the movie to signify her natural, free-spirited persona, it is worth noting that hers is a wardrobe that has long been associated by Hollywood with the intellectual ingénue. Moreover, Anne Hathaway, who plays

Andy, played the Cinderella role in two previous incarnations, *The Princess Diaries* series (2001, 2004) and *Ella Enchanted* (2004).[20] The audience thus knows from the very start that this movie will adhere to a conventional retelling of the Cinderella story and that Andy will blossom and embrace the beautiful clothes associated with the princess before too long.

Miranda, the "devil" of the title, is a demanding boss, whose high standards cause her employees to panic when she arrives early, a panic apparent in the scenes of women swapping their comfortable shoes for stilettos and redoing their lipsticks as she approaches. Miranda is thus allied from the very start of the movie with the prescriptions of the fashion and beauty industries, and she is indeed merciless in the standards she imposes on the subjects of her magazine, including a group of female paratroopers whose brave career choice is clearly insufficient to warrant their inclusion: "They're all so deeply unattractive. Is it impossible to find a lovely, slender female paratrooper?"[21] Emily, newly promoted to "first assistant," is hostile to Andy from the start, directing her distain primarily toward her clothes: "Human Resources clearly has an odd sense of humor. . . . *Runway* is a fashion magazine so an interest in fashion is crucial."[22] She takes every opportunity to mock Andy's clothes, clearly occupying the snide role of Ugly Sister, a role she shares with her colleague who is played, with delicious irony, by supermodel Gisele. Nigel, *Runway*'s camp art director, makes the most effort to be friendly toward Andy, but even he cannot hide his horror at the challenge she poses to the airbrushed perfection demanded of all *Runway* employees: "Who is that sad little person? Are we doing a before and after piece I don't know about?"[23] There is, unsurprisingly for a movie based in the world of fashion, a huge focus on women's bodies, with fat-shaming a theme in many of the interactions between Andy and her new colleagues. Miranda refers to her as the "smart fat girl," while Nigel questions her decision to eat any food for her lunch, sarcastically informing her that "cellulite is one of the ingredients in corn chowder," and ignoring her very valid defense of her slim figure, "I'm a six," by suggesting that six "is the new fourteen."[24] Andy is initially confident about her identity and ignores the barbed comments about her body: "I'm not going to be in fashion forever and I don't really see the point in changing everything about myself just because I have this job."[25] However, it is not too long before she has begun to internalize the disdain with which her appearance is greeted and panics that she has "nothing to wear" to work. Both of the significant male figures in her life offer their help in very different ways. Her boyfriend Nate, who seems resentful from the start of the demands of her new job, dismisses her concern with the sarcastic comment that: "You're going to be answering phones and making coffee—you need a ballgown for that?"[26] Nigel more helpfully presents her with a pair of stilettos, answering her protestation that "Miranda hired me, she knows what I look like" with the pointed "Do you?"[27] These clear references to the Cinde-

rella myth give an early indication that Andy is about to transform from the
ragged girl enslaved in the kitchen to the beautiful swan who will be
launched into the world of fashion with a little help from her fairy godmother
and the magical shoes he offers her.

That this blossoming is predicated on her willingness to embrace the
dictates of conventional fashion is made implicit during the run-through
scene, which not only represents a turning point in Andy's self-transformation but also brings the underlying message of the movie to the fore. The run-
through is when Miranda assesses all of the options designers send to her and
decides which will be included in the magazine. Complaining that designers
are not producing anything truly original, Miranda pauses to weigh up two
similarly colored blue belts. When Andy naively fails to see much difference
between the belts and smirks at the earnest attention her colleagues are paying to them, Miranda mocks her lack of insight into the dominance of the
fashion industry. Andy's mistake, she scathingly states, is that she believes it
is possible to opt out of the prescriptions of the fashion industry simply by
wearing unfashionable clothes: "You think this has nothing to do with you.
You go to your closet and you select . . . that lumpy blue sweater . . . because
you're trying to tell the world that you take yourself too seriously to care
about what you put on your back."[28] Miranda's statement encapsulates the
hegemonic dominance of consumerism, which not only sets the agenda for
what is perceived as fashionable, but can also easily accommodate resistance
to its dictates because it alone produces the means through which this resistance is performed. This is identified by John Fiske as the central dilemma
that theories of popular culture confront: "The people's subordination means
that they cannot produce the resources of popular culture, but they do make
their culture from those resources."[29] Fiske does suggest that the potential is
there for the subordinate to construct alternative meanings that "are not those
preferred by the dominant ideology,"[30] but this potential is dismissed by
Miranda who assures Andy that the "lumpy blue sweater" is not after all a
symbol of resistance but rather of capitulation to the dominance of the fashion industry: "That blue represents millions of dollars and countless jobs and
it's sort of comical how you think you have made a choice that exempts you
from the fashion industry when in fact you're wearing a sweater that was
selected for you by the people in this room."[31] Of course, as argued above,
hegemony derives much of its power from its ability to hide any evidence of
coercion behind a smokescreen of consent. Andy is not forced into changing
her style but rather seeks out a new image, much to the delight of Nigel who
musters the considerable resources of the *Runway* wardrobe to assist her in
her transformation. Although he snidely comments that "I don't know what
you expect me to do, there's nothing in this whole closet that will fit a size
six,"[32] before too long, Andy's glossy hair and radiantly made-up face trium-
phantly parade through a sequence of fashion looks that are filmed as though

she was participating in an advertising campaign, with Madonna's anthemic "Vogue" contributing an appropriate soundtrack. The movie at this point affirms what Ferriss argues is one of the key tropes that link the fairy tale with the chick flick: "the makeover . . . promising self-transformation through shopping."[33]

The function of the makeover and its link to transformation is a key theme in critiques of postfeminist cultural texts, with arguments ranging from those who read the makeover as indicative of the worst excesses of the fashion industry, to those who insist that the makeover functions only as a source of pleasure for its female viewers. Key to the latter position, as Ferriss notes, is that the makeover is ultimately superficial, necessary only to unveil the true beauty of the protagonist to a world that is too blind to see it for itself.[34] Indeed, Andy—in spite of Nigel's concerns—easily fits into a range of sample sizes, and she emerges from her makeover a still recognizable, if slightly glossier, version of herself. The approval she now receives from Emily and Miranda fills Andy with self-confidence, and this alone seems to enable her to do her job with ease. Her makeover can thus be read as providing little other than tangible evidence to Andy of her own self-worth, an indication that consumerism can indeed lead to women's empowerment. However, Ferriss's suggestion that the makeover serves merely to reveal the beauty Andy already possessed is not entirely accurate, for it is clear that she is hailed primarily for her obedience to the prescribed standards of beauty. This is most evident in continuing references to her shrinking body size. Complimenting her on her svelte appearance during Paris fashion week, Nigel remarks admiringly that: "My work here is done . . . you bet your size six ass."[35] Andy's proud qualification that she is now a "four" and the admiring look this wins from Nigel emphasizes the very limited definition of feminine beauty permitted by the fashion industry. Andy's triumph in fitting into a model size recollects what Bettleheim notes is the function of the glass slipper in Cinderella: "the common stereotype contrasted the bigness of the male with the smallness of the female, and Cinderella's small feet would make her especially feminine,"[36] its tiny size assuring the reader of the innate femininity and passivity of its wearer. As noted earlier in the chapter, postfeminism claims to empower women to choose their own individual style, but in fact the term "choice" is misleading and serves only to force women into increasingly narrow ideals of beauty.

Andy's willingness to embrace a conventionally acceptable style is not merely about her own personal transformation but more significantly signifies her inscription within the wider values of the consumerist society. Rook explains that costume has a ritualistic function in society, linking the wearer to their prescribed role within the social order and thus: "contributing to social cohesion."[37] Andy may not *need* fabulous clothes to answer the phone, but wearing them amounts to a public declaration of her allegiance to the values of the magazine. Her new style is thus an act of what Althusseur calls "interpellation,"[38] the way in which we answer the "hail" or call of the ideological forces operating in our society, whose function is to persuade us to act, dress and think in a manner that is considered socially appropriate. Many theorists point out that consumerism is an intrinsically ritualistic practice, and that through our shopping and branding choices, we are ritually connecting ourselves with the values of our culture.[39] The significance of the makeover trope in the movie is thus not limited to its function within the plot. It is equally significant in inviting its audience to subscribe to the values being articulated.

What is interesting about Andy's transformation is how hard the movie works to deny any element of underlying patriarchal coercion. In fact, Nate, Andy's boyfriend, is wholly unenthusiastic about her new style, stating that he "liked the old clothes."[40] Unlike in the traditional fairy tale, Andy's makeover is not directed at attracting the handsome prince. Rather, as Suzanne Ferriss notes, she transforms "only when she senses her job, and hence her future career . . . is at risk."[41] This denial of patriarchal coercion is, in fact, a common theme in postfeminist movies where, as Sibielski explains, the protagonist may have to overcome numerous obstacles on her path to self-determination but discrimination "on the basis of being a woman/female-identified is not one of the oppressions that Cinderella must liberate herself from in order to achieve her happily ever after."[42] This is one of the hallmarks of postfeminist discourse, suggesting that "gender equality is achieved" and, therefore, that feminism is "no longer needed."[43] In fact, under this veneer of an ungendered, postfeminist society, where women are now free to celebrate both their empowerment and their femininity, *The Devil Wears Prada* embodies many of the characteristics of the backlash thesis, in particular when it focuses on the intersections between the careers and personal lives of the female characters.

When we first meet Andy, she is living what in Hollywood passes for a "bohemian" lifestyle, in a small apartment with her boyfriend Nate, eating grilled cheese sandwiches and meeting their friends for impassioned conversations in cozy wine bars. Andy's job at *Runway* is seen as a betrayal of their carefully cultivated self-image, although it is worth noting that her friends work as a chef and a photographer, hardly jobs associated with the working class. Immediately after her makeover, Andy's personal life is hanging by a thread, a development that does not surprise Nigel: "That's what happens when you are good at your job."[44] What angers her friends most is Andy's ostensible betrayal of the certainties that defined them as a group, specifically her relationship with Nate and their smug sense that they are living authentic lives that somehow transcend the cheap lure of consumerism: "The Andy I know is madly in love with Nate. . . . and thinks that Club Monaco is couture."[45] The judgmentalism and distain for Andy's new awareness of fashion suggest that, to her friends, her transformation is not merely superficial but has fundamentally altered her identity. Their absolutist insistence on the incompatibility of her career and personal life is central to the final fight Andy has with Nate before they break up: "You used to say this was just a job. You used to make fun of the *Runway* girls. . . . Now you've become one of them."[46] As Lillian Barger notes: "The message is that high-powered careers for women are incompatible with love. Instead of the freedom to construct diverse lives, women have a false choice between love and work."[47] Because love remains the only path to happiness for the female characters, when they make the misguided decision to prioritize their careers, they are putting themselves on a path that can only lead to unhappiness and regret. The bullying, masquerading as concern, to which Andy is subjected by her friends is reflective of what Caryl Rivers describes as the dominant approach of postfeminist media texts: "the media no longer tells women . . . that we can't achieve. . . . It's simply too obvious that we can achieve. The new message is that the price of achievement is too high. . . . Today, it's more subtle: *Poor dears, the price of your accomplishment will be unhappiness, regret, failed marriages, wretched children.*"[48] The hegemonic media thus hide their determination to reinscribe women in their traditional roles with a faux concern for their well-being

The movie reserves its most bitter condemnation for Miranda, the publicly lauded editor, whose pout is enough to destroy a designer's season. Such influence, according to the backlash theory, can only come at huge cost to a woman's personal life and, indeed, it becomes clear that Miranda is the poster girl for failure on the domestic front. Barger notes that: "The film reeks with fear of female power . . . (Miranda) is held up as an example of the dangers of unrestrained female ambition and the negative consequences of choosing power."[49] Our first introduction to Miranda sees her managing her private life through her assistant Emily: "Call my ex-husband and remind him that the parent-teacher conference is . . . tonight and then call my husband and ask him to please meet me for dinner."[50] Clearly the audience is supposed to condemn her for managing her relationships as though they were business encounters, although it must be noted that Miranda appears in both cases to be taking responsibility for scheduling many of the core activities of family life. Her lowest and most vulnerable point in the movie is when she learns that her second husband is filing for divorce. Andy encounters her sitting alone and symbolically unmade up and disheveled in her Paris hotel room. Miranda appears to be less heartbroken at the end of her marriage than concerned about the negative press her second divorce will engender: "Another divorce splashed across page six. Just imagine what they are going to write about me. The Dragon Lady. Career-obsessed Snow Queen drives away another Mr. Priestley."[51] Miranda's sarcastic recitation of the language used to undermine career-focused women as unnatural, cold-hearted, and monstrous appears to hint that the movie might be moving toward a feminist critique of the unequal treatment of women in the workplace. Moreover, Andy acknowledges that much of the criticism Miranda receives is due to her sex rather than her behavior: "If Miranda was a man, nobody would say anything about her except how good she was at her job."[52] Although both of these comments clearly identify the key themes of the backlash thesis, the movie quickly shies away from overt critique and, in fact, Andy quickly reinscribes herself as a fairy-tale heroine, reacting with horror when Miranda unveils a Machiavellian scheme to ensure her continued stewardship of *Runway*, in the process vanquishing her younger French challenger and betraying her devoted assistant Nigel. When Miranda suggests that Andy harbors the same ruthless ambition, she is forced to confront the age-old dilemma facing women, namely how to be successful in the workplace without losing one's mythical femininity.

Andy's decision to throw away her career at *Runway* to reclaim the values of kindness and fairness is what Collette Dowling defines as the contemporary manifestation of the "Cinderella Complex."[53] No longer confined to "Intimations of Helplessness" and the need for a handsome prince to save her, the contemporary Cinderella is instead so fearful of being successful, that she sabotages herself through: "a network of largely repressed attitudes and fears that keeps women in a kind of half-light, retreating from the full use of their minds and creativity."[54] Andy does not end the movie in the arms of a man, but she does spend much of the closing sequence atoning for the ambition that caused her temporarily to value her professional success above her duties to her friends and family. The almost ritualistic sequence of apologies she offers to Emily and Nate affords them the opportunity to remind her how damaging ambition can be for that most precious feminine attribute, the heart: "You sold your soul the first time you put on a pair of Jimmy Choos"; "You were right about everything . . . I turned my back on my friends and my family and everything I believed for, and for what? . . . For shoes and shirts and jackets and belts."[55] The movie thus conforms to what Sibielski notes is Cinderella's reinforcement of women's subordination within patriarchy, particularly in this context its: "valorization of submissiveness, passivity, and self-abnegation as feminine virtues."[56] Having reclaimed her feminine kindness and sacrificed her individual desire to the feelings of others, Andy successfully achieves her final transformation. Dressed in jeans, a sartorial choice Fiske links to the "mythic dignity of labor,"[57] Andy is now ready to begin her journalistic career at *The New York Mirror*, a publication that values her research into "the janitor's union" and will enable her to pursue her true calling as a compassionate, socially committed writer. Andy's trendy outfit and glossy hair suggest that she will continue to subscribe to conventional notions of feminine beauty, while the glowing reference and benign smile she receives from Miranda in the final scene of the movie assures the audience that this Cinderella has accepted her place within the patriarchal order and will continue to blossom now that she has learned to temper her ambition with kindness.

Sex and the City was a phenomenally successful television show, created by Darren Star, which ran from 1998 to 2004. The series followed the lives of four close friends as they navigated love, sex, and relationships in contemporary New York. Its unapologetic celebration of consumerism and championing of designer labels was a significant source of voyeuristic pleasure for its predominantly female audience. The show's success was also due to its mainly positive, even resistant, representations of women's choices that transcended the narrow roles generally suggested for them in traditional media texts. Negra notes that although the show did not specifically address misogynistic cultural representations of women, it did at least attempt to address "some of the most pernicious mythologizing of contemporary female experience,"[58] particularly those directed at the perceived deviance of thirty-something single career women. Potential anxiety about the women's single status was, according to Camille Kreaplin, "made tolerable" by their nurturing, platonic friendship, which exhibited: "the ethical qualities of respect, affection, support and loyalty."[59] The complex portrayal of its protagonists also enabled the series to resist what Negra describes as "a cultural postfeminism that leaves behind the more challenging, complex, and unresolved questions and issues of earlier feminisms."[60] It was able to do so at least partly because the television series as a genre facilitates open endings and ambiguous resolutions: "frequently closing an episode in a bittersweet mode that would be off limits to the mainstream chick flick whose ideological conservatism demands positive resolution."[61] The limitations a closed ending imposes on a text is in fact apparent in the final episode of the series, in which Carrie, previously an independent woman well able to fight her own battles, is "rescued" from an abusive relationship by Mr. Big, her perennially unfaithful on-off boyfriend, who reenters the series to bring about a somewhat unconvincing "happy ending." The movie, which begins ten years after the series ends, suffers even more, evidently from the limitations imposed by its structural need to work toward the conventional ending that demands that Carrie finally marries Big. In order to do so, it loses much of the potential for resistance celebrated in the series, subsuming its female protagonists within a recognizable narrative structure predicated on their acceptance of their traditional gender roles.

The movie continues to revolve around the lives of the four female characters but gone is the uncritical acceptance of difference that was so important to the empowerment of the series. In its place, the movie offers a significantly more judgmental and divisive narrative, that recruits the women to attack each other's life choices. This, according to Faludi, is typical of the backlash, which, "pursues a divide-and-conquer strategy: single versus married women, working women versus house-wives."[62] The movie can thus be read as an example of the false choice this chapter has argued is central to postfeminism: it ostensibly celebrates the different choices embodied by its four protagonists, but, in fact, ultimately rewards only those women who conform to the narrow categories of ideal female behavior. While browsing for Halloween outfits with Carrie, Miranda ruefully notes that there are only two costume choices available to women: "witch and sexy kitten."[63] The accuracy of Miranda's statement is borne out in the movie which directs its patriarchal backlash primarily toward the women who threaten its hegemony. Charlotte and Samantha, who happily adhere to their roles as "sexy kittens," albeit in very different ways, pose no threat to prescribed categories of femininity and as a consequence suffer little criticism over the course of the movie. Charlotte's contented embrace of her role as homemaker, which she performs in twinsets, pearls, and pretty dresses, is rewarded at the end of the movie with the unexpected news of a pregnancy. Charlotte's happiness confirms one of the promises of the backlash thesis: "morality tales in which 'the good mother' wins."[64] As Carrie's voiceover notes: "I guess in certain houses, fairy tales do come true."[65]

Samantha, the movie's other "sexy kitten," is the sexually aggressive woman identified by Walter as central to postfeminist conceptions of empowerment.[66] Samantha's frequent articulation of her sexual desire and the alignment of her confidence with her sexuality may be celebrated as a sign of her strength within the movie, but it also suggests an adherence to an externally derived form of affirmation which interpellates Samantha as a subject of the male gaze. Her appetite for and adoration of men makes her no threat to their dominance. In pursuit of a traditional happy ending, she has moved to Los Angeles to live with her much younger boyfriend Smith, only to find that a life of domestic bliss is a choice for which she is unsuited. Her attempt to deny her sexuality is mocked in the movie when she attempts to fill the emptiness by adopting a small dog (clearly a substitute baby) which, like its owner, shivers constantly with unsatisfied sexual desire. Even more objectifying is the comfort she begins to take in food: "I eat so I won't cheat."[67] The amount of weight she gains is so miniscule as to be almost unnoticed by the viewer—the camera helpfully lingers on her waist—but it elicits cries of horror from her supposed friends who subject her to concerted and misogynistic body-shaming: "'I didn't realize how big I was until I saw it on your faces' . . . 'How, and I say this with love, *how* could you not realize it?'"[68] The faux concern in Carrie's comment is reminiscent of the tactics used by the backlash to enforce compliance among its subjects. Having been suitably shamed, Samantha realizes the error of her ways and leaves her boyfriend to reclaim her former life in New York, her newly gained svelte figure and the heroic tone of her break-up speech clearly signifying that it is meant to be read as an act of female empowerment: "I love you but I love me more."[69]

Samantha is the ultimate postfeminist in the movie: she does not need a man to define her, is sexually confident and financially independent, but crucially confines her empowerment to terms that are acceptable to the patriarchal hegemony.

Miranda is the most evident target of the backlash in the movie. Combining her pressurized job with a husband and family, Miranda exhibits no signs of the despair and misery the backlash insists is the lot of the over-stretched career woman. Rather than celebrating her, however, the movie is keen to emphasize that all of this comes at a cost. Like her namesake in *The Devil Wears Prada*, Miranda is indicted for deprioritizing her marriage and forsaking her husband Steve for the sake of her career. Her abnegation of her duties as a wife is most clearly linked with her unsatisfactory sex life and, in fact, Rivers notes that career and a satisfying sex life are generally portrayed as being incompatible in backlash texts.[70] The movie clearly supports this thesis, with Miranda's infrequent sex a theme in conversations both with her husband and with her friends. Like Nate, Andy's boyfriend in *The Devil Wears Prada*, Steve is intent on blaming Miranda for their problems. During a conversation, which symbolically takes place in their kitchen as Miranda is putting away the groceries and attempting to share out their considerable family duties: "While I run over to see your mother tomorrow, maybe you could take Brady to the first birthday party alone, and then I can meet you at the twins' party and you can leave and be at the bar by six"; Steve confesses to having had sex with another woman, offering as justification the fact that: "you and I hadn't had sex in a really long time."[71] Miranda is thus to blame for his infidelity.

What is most astonishing is that Miranda's friends concur with his assessment, all of them advising Miranda to think carefully about her decision to leave her marriage. Carrie's first reaction is the distinctly unsupportive: "I don't know if this question is allowed but how is Steve handling this?"; while Samantha dismisses the significance of Steve's cheating, suggesting that Miranda will regret what she clearly views as her overreaction: "Miranda honey are you sure you want to do this? It's just one time. Anyone can have a slip."[72] Miranda is criticized for not having sex with her husband as regularly as her friends, although as she rather defensively points out, she is the only one of them to combine a job with a child and other family responsibilities: "I have a full-time job. . . . you don't also have a five year old and PTA meetings and playdates and a mother-in-law in a care home with advancing Alzheimer's."[73] She is also brutally body-shamed by Samantha, who reacts with horror at the sight of a few stray hairs visible when Miranda is wearing her bathing costume: "Jesus honey, wax much?"[74]—the camera helpfully lingers on Miranda's crotch to ensure the viewer sees the full "horror" for themselves. Miranda feels justifiably bullied by her friends and is under no illusion as to where they place the blame for the breakdown of her marriage:

"So what, it's my fault? I let the sex go out of my marriage and I deserve what I got?"[75] The behavior of the other women in these scenes is akin to what Ariel Levy calls "Female Chauvinist Pigs," women whom Walter explains are complicit in the coercive culture promoted by patriarchy: "women who are happy to work alongside men to promote this waxed and thonged image of female sexuality."[76] It is significant that the male characters in the movie play very marginal roles—it is the women who, in their guise of friends and supporters, impose these judgmental and, in their treatment of Miranda, overtly misogynistic restrictions on the choices they make.

Unlike her namesake in *The Devil Wears Prada*, Miranda is given the opportunity to save her marriage, but only when, like Andy, she has acknowledged her role in its failure and has crucially learned to forgive, a quality the movie seems intent on inscribing as central to femininity. After unrelenting pressure from her friends, Miranda agrees to attend couple's therapy with Steve, where she learns that he holds her equally to blame for the break-up of their marriage: "I mean, yeah, I broke a vow but what about the other vows? Like promising to love someone for better or for worse."[77] By this twisted logic, Miranda's reaction to Steve's cheating is somehow equal to his cheating. Perhaps unsurprisingly, Miranda cedes to the dominant reading of her situation and begins to internalize blame for her role in it. On the day the therapist has appointed for their final decision, Miranda is shown mulling over long lists of reasons to stay or leave her marriage. A woman's use of logic is, of course, never likely to lead her to the correct decision, and instead a memory of happier times fills Miranda's heart with love and she hurries off to reconcile with Steve. Her decision is praised by Carrie's voice-over which intones that: "It suddenly dawned on Miranda that Steve's list might have had more cons than pros"[78]—a conclusion that is not justified by anything the viewer witnesses in the movie but that succinctly embodies the backlash which this chapter argues underlines the plot. Miranda's return to Steve might be portrayed as a choice she is making for herself, but it is clear that her happy ending depends on her willingness to change her behavior and commit to performing the loyal and adoring qualities expected of the ideal wife. She exemplifies in this way the contradiction at the heart of postfeminist representations of women.

Carrie, the free-spirited writer, is the character most clearly connected to the Cinderella narrative, the single woman who after years of tortured juggling of career and relationships is about to grasp the ultimate happy ending through marriage to her handsome prince. The obstacles she must overcome on her path to eternal happiness, most notably being publicly jilted on the day of her wedding and slowly learning to believe in true love again, can be read as the conventional plot devices at the heart of any romance movie, where the happy ending must be earned to be emotionally satisfying for the viewer. However, like Miranda, there are clear links made between Carrie's humiliation and the lessons the backlash demands that women learn. Even though it is Big who loses his nerve on the morning of their wedding, it is Carrie who is forced over the course of the movie to confront her role in precipitating his crisis. Big is unchanged when they reunite at the end of the movie—even his love letters are copied from the love letters of great men, suggesting that he has not undergone any meaningful emotional development during their separation. Carrie, on the other hand, undergoes significant soul-searching, finally concluding that her selfishness and narcissism are what almost robbed her of her happy ending.

Carrie's first mistake, it seems, is to be too complacent about her relationship. When a realtor refers to her as Big's wife, she is unconcerned, but Big is uncomfortably aware that language does not easily accommodate their relationship status, his reaction an indication perhaps that his masculinity is offended by the terminology: "'He's my boyfriend' . . . 'aren't I a little old to be introduced as your boyfriend?'"[79] As well as the unclear social status of their long-term relationship, Carrie is also made aware of the tenuous legal position she occupies when she and Big make the decision to move into a bigger apartment. The decision to purchase the apartment brings previously invisible tensions to the fore, as evident in the tussle over pronouns in an exchange between Carrie and Big: "'Welcome home, Baby'. . . 'Can we afford this?' . . . 'I got it.'"[80] Big is clearly asserting his masculinity here, although it is couched in the language of a prince determined to sweep his princess into the security of their fairy-tale castle. Charlotte, who is living her own fairy tale (ironically in the huge apartment she got as part of the divorce settlement after the end of her first marriage!), is ecstatically happy for Carrie, but the more pragmatic Miranda cautions her to protect herself by retaining control over her financial future. When Carrie shares her concerns with Big, they decide to get married, a decision they make together. It may not be conventionally romantic but it is egalitarian and realistic for a couple who have been living together for ten years.

The movie does not blame Carrie for entering into marriage for security. On the contrary, she is subjected to numerous stories involving divorces and breakups, all of which had a detrimental impact on the lives of the women involved. The threat of divorce is, according to Faludi, a key weapon employed by the backlash to frighten women into prioritizing their romantic relationships, with career women identified as particularly at risk of the inevitable fall in living standards, not to mention social status, that results from: "legal slingshots that 'threw thousands of middle-class women,' as a typical chronicler put it, 'into impoverished states.'"[81] Carrie's excitement that she and Big will move into the beautiful penthouse apartment is tempered slightly when she is told the apartment is on the market due to a nasty divorce. The four women also attend an auction of jewelry that a jilted mistress is selling after the public break-up of her relationship. The trajectory of the woman's life serves as a salutary tale to the crowds of women picking over her belongings: "Blair Elkin was a waitress, turned model, turned actress, turned billionaire's girlfriend, who came home one night to find herself unceremoniously turned out on the street."[82] Her mistake, according to her friend, was to trust in the stability of her relationship, a naïve decision that has now left her penniless: "We all told her to get married but she didn't want to listen. . . . She came home one night and he had locked her out. She didn't even have anywhere to live. Such a shame. After ten years. She was a smart girl until she fell in love."[83] This summation delivers a direct attack on Germaine Greer's exhortation to women to free themselves from the patriarchal repression of the monogamous marriage and embrace what Walter calls a "guilt-free promiscuity, which she was certain would deliver more fulfilment."[84] Somewhat ironically, given its title, *Sex and the City: The Movie* insists that this central tenet of second wave feminism did not serve women well and that they are better off retreating to the security of marriage.

Given the overwhelming threat posed by the single life, it is understandable that news of Carrie's engagement is treated less as a tale of individual happiness than as a public beacon of hope for all women of a certain age. A brief newspaper column on the subject declares excitedly that: "the ultimate single gal Carrie Bradshaw will be married in Manolos to New York financier John James Preston come Fall."[85] It is notable that Carrie is defined by her single status and love for shoes, while Big is introduced through his job. The column goes on to state that this news proves "to single gals everywhere that there can be happiness over forty."[86] The use of the breezy yet patronizing "gals" in conjunction with the reference to their age is an exemplar of the methods employed in postfeminist texts, which assure women that they are empowered to make their own choices while simultaneously warning them that they will be left alone if they do not choose wisely. Carrie is also invited to participate in a feature for the annual Age Issue of *Vogue* magazine—not to write a column, which her career might warrant, but rather to star in one, as befits the fascinating change in the single girl's fortunes that she now represents: "I want you to be featured in the magazine as the forty year old . . . and here's the brilliant twist . . . *bride.*"[87] The editor has no doubt that Carrie will agree to be featured, assuring her that no expense—or technology—will be spared to help her look her best: "It's bridal couture. . . . *Vogue* designers. *Vogue* photographers. *Vogue* airbrushing.*"[88] When Carrie objects to the emphasis on her age, suggesting that it undermines the empowering ethos supposedly at the heart of the Age Issue: "I thought the issue was great style at every age," the editor corrects her and states that there are clear limits on women's right to dress as they wish and that "forty is the last age that a woman can be photographed in a wedding gown."[89] Carrie's tentative objection to this blatant sexism is silenced immediately by her delighted participation in the fashion shoot, a sumptuously filmed sequence of scenes which enables the movie to merge its focus on the wedding as the ultimate prize for the single woman and the fashion industry which offers the best vehicle for the channeling of her inner princess. Observing Carrie posing in the wedding dresses, Samantha succinctly observes that: "She's looking quite at home for someone who didn't think she had the bride gene."[90] Carrie, like many single girls it seems, may have thought she was satisfied with her life, but underneath the surface all she wanted was to be married.

Carrie's impending wedding allows the movie to morph into another dependable subgenre of the chick flick, namely the wedding flick, described by Brook as an effective way for a movie to appear to mock the conventions of fairy tales, while celebrating its key motifs, including its: "ephemerally coy homoerotics, its fetishization of clothes," all of which facilitate the reinforcement of the "highly conservative, even misogynistic, performances of gender on screen."[91] Carrie's initial decision to stay true to her own style by wearing a vintage suit is dismissed by Anthony, her self-appointed wedding planner, as too simple given the public investment in her big day: "the bride wore a dress by no-one."[92] Carrie's wedding, it becomes clear, is not so much about her personal happiness as an opportunity for her to participate in a public ritual designed to confirm the central role of the hegemonic institution of marriage. Moreover, the wedding also enables the movie to include another key trope of the chick flick, the bridezilla. The term "bridezilla," according to Emine Saner, emerged in the mid-1990s and has become a popular stereotype in postfeminist films of over-wrought, over-competitive brides.[93] It is also used in media articles to describe brides in the real world, although the subjects of these critiques often exhibit little other than perfectionism and attention to detail. The term is thus indicative of what Ruggerio describes as a determination to mock assertive women: "our culture is really uncomfortable with the idea of women having power. . . . It speaks to this deep anxiety we seem to have with women who assert themselves, want to take control and have a voice."[94] The demonization of women who assert themselves is evident in the movie when Carrie, who has survived her public humiliation and has worked hard to regain her self-confidence, comes across the *Vogue* bridal shoot, published rather symbolically just in time for Valentine's Day. Leafing through the glossy pages, Carrie is not upset that she was so badly let down by the man she believed loved her. On the contrary, the photographs reflect an image of her own behavior she begins to read as culpable for her heartbreak. Like Miranda, Carrie must identify her internal flaws and atone for them if she is to have a chance at achieving her happy ending: "I deserve what I got, running all over New York, believing that I'm finally getting my happy ending. . . . In that article, I did not say we once. . . . The whole article was 'I think' and 'I want'. . . I let the wedding get bigger than Big. . . . I am the reason that he did not get out of that car."[95]

Carrie realizes that she was guilty of believing that she had the right to celebrate herself and her choices, rather than adopting the modesty that society demands of women. Once she accepts her subservient role, she is rewarded with a second chance at happiness. Arriving at the never inhabited penthouse apartment an hour before it is sold to collect a pair of shoes she had symbolically placed in the huge closet, Carrie encounters Big for the first time since their wedding. Assuring us that "It wasn't logic, it was love," they fall into each other's arms, before apologizing to each other for "what I put you through."[96] Carrie decries that they ruined their perfect relationship by allowing the outside world to pressure them into committing to marriage. For Big, however, it was clearly the nature of their decision that rankled with him: "and the way we decided to get married, it was all business, no romance. That's not the way you propose to someone. This is . . . Carrie Bradshaw, love of my life, will you marry me?"[97] Big's second proposal, delivered as convention demands on bended knee, is certainly intended to be read as the ultimate romantic ending. However, as in their earlier discussion, the pronouns he uses suggest a determination on his part to win back control of the narrative—he is the one doing the proposing, while Carrie is firmly reinscribed within her traditional gender role of passive recipient. Observing that the lack of an engagement ring was another problem with their first attempt to get married: "See this is why there's a diamond, you need something to close the deal,"[98] Big picks up the conveniently diamond-encrusted shoe, signifying his capturing of Carrie by symbolically placing the shoe on her foot. Bruno Bettelheim offers an interesting reading of the function of the glass slipper in Cinderella, noting that the prince slips it on Cinderella's foot to ensure that she is indeed his princess in spite of the rags with which she is clothed: "By handing her the slipper to put her foot into, the prince symbolically expresses that he accepts her the way she is, dirty and degraded. . . . At this moment, what had been a borrowed appearance of beauty while at the ball becomes Cinderella's true self."[99] Accordingly, when Carrie does marry Big it is as her (supposedly) authentic self, dressed in her vintage suit and celebrated at an intimate gathering of her closest friends. The movie makes one final attempt to assure us that its central message is one of women's empowerment, when Carrie rather confusingly—at the end of a movie in which all the female protagonists have their roles within normative gender relationships affirmed—intones that relationships are not after all the most important signifiers of identity: "Maybe when we label someone bride, groom, husband, wife, married, single, we forget to look past the label to the person."[100] The only thing that really matters, we are assured in true princess-speak, is: "Love . . . the one label that never goes out of style."[101]

This chapter has argued that both *The Devil Wears Prada* and *Sex in the City* can most fruitfully be read as postfeminist movies, with their wholesale embrace of the values of the fashion industry and articulation of their message of female empowerment through the consumer goods with which the characters surround themselves, so that "A Woman's Right to Shoes," the title of an episode of the *Sex and the City* television series, becomes a manifesto of female choice. The seemingly ironic and playful use of the conventions of the Cinderella story enable the movies to present themselves as empowering the strong female characters at their heart, while in actuality working hard to ensure their compliance to traditional gender roles. An interesting similarity between the movies is their lack of a male antagonist. Instead, the female protagonists, each representing different life choices, are pitted against each other. To use Faludi's terminology, they internalize the hegemonic representations of femininity and essentially enforce the backlash on themselves.

NOTES

1. Betty Friedan, *The Feminine Mystique* (UK: Penguin Classics, 2010), 5.
2. Susan Faludi, *Backlash: The Undeclared War against Women* (London: Vintage, 1993), 21.
3. Cristina Bacchilega, *Fairy Tales Transformed? Twenty-First-Century Adaptations and the Politics of Wonder* (Detroit: Wayne State University Press, 2013), ix.
4. Ibid., 4.
5. Rosalind Sibielski, "Reviving Cinderella: Contested Feminism and Conflicting Models of Female Empowerment," in *Quarterly Review of Film and Video*, vol. 36, no. 7 (2019), 585.
6. Ibid., 590.
7. Linda Pershing and Lisa Gablehouse, "Disney's *Enchanted*: Patriarchal Backlash and Nostalgia in Fairy Tale Film," in *Fairy Tale Films: Visions of Ambiguity*, eds. Pauline Greenhill and Sidney Eve Matrix (Logan, CO: Utah State University Press, 2010), 145.
8. Faludi, *Backlash*, 2.
9. Diane Negra, "Quality Postfeminism: Sex and the Single Girl on HBO," in *Genders* (April1, 2004). https://www.colorado.edu/gendersarchive1998-2013/2004/04/01/quality-post-feminism-sex-and-single-girl-hbo.
10. Faludi, *Backlash*, 16.
11. Sarah Gamble, "Postfeminism," in *The Routledge Companion to Feminism and Postfeminism*, ed. Sarah Gamble (London: Routledge, 2001), 45.
12. Angela McRobbie, *The Aftermath of Feminism: Gender, Culture and Social Change* (London: SAGE, 2009), 1.
13. Natasha Walter, *Living Dolls: The Return of Sexism* (GB: Virago, 2015), 6.
14. Peggy Orenstein, *Cinderella Ate My Daughter* (New York: Harper, 2012), 17.
15. Yvonne Tasker, "*Enchanted* (2007): Postfeminism: Gender, Irony, and the New Romantic Comedy," in *Feminism at the Movies: Understanding Gender in Contemporary Popular Cinema*, eds. Hilary Radner and Rebecca Stringer (New York: Routledge, 2011), 69.
16. Suzanne Ferriss and Mallory Young, eds., *Chick Flicks: Contemporary Women at the Movies* (New York and London: Routledge, 2008), 4.
17. Ibid., 4–5.
18. Karen Hollinger, "Afterword: Once I Got beyond the Name Chick Flick," in *Chick Flicks: Contemporary Women at the Movies*, eds. Suzanne Ferriss and Mallory Young, 226.
19. *The Devil Wears Prada*, directed by David Frankel, 20th Century Fox, 2006.
20. Suzanne Ferriss, "Fashioning Femininity in the Makeover Flick," in *Chick Flicks: Contemporary Women at the Movies*, eds. Suzanne Ferriss and Mallory Young, 51.
21. *The Devil Wears Prada*, 2006.
22. Ibid.

23. Ibid.
24. Ibid.
25. Ibid.
26. Ibid.
27. Ibid.
28. Ibid.
29. John Fiske, *Understanding Popular Culture* (Boston: Unwin Hyman, 1989), 4.
30. Ibid., 2.
31. *The Devil Wears Prada,* 2006.
32. Ibid.
33. Suzanne Ferriss, "Fashioning Femininity in the Makeover Flick," 42.
34. Ibid, 44.
35. *The Devil Wears Prada*, 2006.
36. Bruno Bettelheim, *The Uses of Enchantment: The Meaning and Importance of Fairy Tales* (GB: Penguin Books, 1991), 268.
37. Denis W. Rook, "The Ritual Dimension of Consumer Behaviour," in *The Journal of Consumer Research*, vol 12 (December 1985), 255.
38. Louis Althusseur, "Ideology and Ideological State Apparatuses," in *A Critical and Cultural Theory Reader*, eds. Antony Easthope and Kate McGowan (Buckingham: Open University Press, 1997), 55.
39. Judith Williamson, *Decoding Advertisements: Ideology and Meaning in Advertising* (GB: Marion Boyars, 2010), 40–42.
40. *The Devil Wears Prada*, 2006.
41. Ferriss, "Fashioning Femininity in the Makeover Flick," 52.
42. Sibielski, "Reviving Cinderella," 594.
43. Ibid., 595.
44. *The Devil Wears Prada,* 2006.
45. Ibid.
46. Ibid.
47. Lilian Calles Barger, "Backlash: From *Nine to Five* to *The Devil Wears Prada*," in *Women's Studies*, 40 (2011), 348.
48. Caryl Rivers, *Selling Anxiety: How the News Media Scare Women* (Hanover and London: University Press of New England, 2007), 13.
49. Barger, "Backlash," 345.
50. *The Devil Wears Prada*, 2006.
51. Ibid.
52. Ibid.
53. Colette Dowling, *The Cinderella Complex: Women's Hidden Fear of Independence* (London: Fontana, 1982), 18.
54. Ibid.
55. *The Devil Wears Prada*, 2006.
56. Sibielski, "Reviving Cinderella," 592.
57. Fiske, *Understanding Popular Culture*, 1–2.
58. Negra, "Quality Postfeminism," n.p.
59. Camille Kreaplin, "*Girlfriends* and *Sex and the City*: An Intersectional Analysis of Race, Gender and Commodity Feminism," in *Media Report to Women*, 40.1 (Winter 2012), 14.
60. Negra, "Quality Postfeminism," np.
61. Ibid.
62. Faludi, *Backlash*, 17.
63. *Sex and the City: The Movie*, directed by Michael Patrick King, HBO, 2008.
64. Faludi, *Backlash*, 141.
65. *Sex and the City: The Movie*, 2008.
66. Walter, *Living Dolls*, 6.
67. *Sex and the City: The Movie*, 2008.
68. Ibid.
69. Ibid.

70. Rivers, *Selling Anxiety*, 24.
71. *Sex and the City: The Movie*, 2008.
72. Ibid.
73. Ibid.
74. Ibid.
75. Ibid.
76. Walter, *Living Dolls*, 33.
77. *Sex and the City: The Movie*, 2008.
78. Ibid.
79. Ibid.
80. Ibid.
81. Faludi, *Backlash*, 37.
82. *Sex and the City: The Movie*, 2008.
83. Ibid.
84. Walter, *Living Dolls*, 84.
85. *Sex and the City: The Movie*, 2008.
86. Ibid.
87. Ibid.
88. Ibid.
89. Ibid.
90. Ibid.
91. Heather Brook, "Die, Bridezilla, Die! *Bride Wars* (2009), Wedding Envy, and Chick Flicks," in *Feminism at the Movies*, eds. Hilary Radner and Rebecca Stringer, 228.
92. *Sex and the City: The Movie*, 2008.
93. Emine Saner, "How 'Bridezilla' Became This Summer's Biggest Sexist Slur," in *The Guardian* (August 15th, 2019). https://www.theguardian.com/lifeandstyle/2019/aug/15/how-bridezilla-became-this-summers-biggest-sexist-slur.
94. Quoted in Saner, n.p.
95. *Sex and the City: The Movie* 2008.
96. Ibid.
97. Ibid.
98. Ibid.
99. Bettelheim, *The Uses of Enchantment*, 270–271.
100. *Sex and the City: The Movie*, 2008.
101. Ibid.

BIBLIOGRAPHY

Althusseur, Louis. "Ideology and Ideological State Apparatuses," in Easthope, Antony and Kate McGowan, eds. *A Critical and Cultural Theory Reader*. Buckingham: Open University Press, 1997.

Bacchilega, Cristina. *Fairy Tales Transformed? Twenty-First-Century Adaptations and the Politics of Wonder*. Detroit: Wayne State University Press, 2013.

Barger, Lilian Calles. "Backlash: From *Nine to Five* to *The Devil Wears Prada*," in *Women's Studies*, 40 (2011): 336–350.

Bettelheim, Bruno. *The Uses of Enchantment: The Meaning and Importance of Fairy Tales*. GB: Penguin Books, 1991.

Brook, Heather. "Die, Bridezilla, Die! *Bride Wars* (2009), Wedding Envy, and Chick Flicks," in Radner, Hilary and Rebecca Stringer, eds. *Feminism at the Movies: Understanding Gender in Contemporary Popular Cinema*. New York: Routledge, 2011.

The Devil Wears Prada, directed by David Frankel, 20th Century Fox, 2006.

Dowling, Colette. *The Cinderella Complex: Women's Hidden Fear of Independence*. London: Fontana, 1982.

Faludi, Susan. *Backlash: The Undeclared War against Women*. London: Vintage, 1993.

Ferriss, Suzanne. "Fashioning Femininity in the Makeover Flick," in Ferriss, Suzanne and Mallory Young, eds. *Chick Flicks: Contemporary Women at the Movies.* New York and London: Routledge, 2008.

Ferriss, Suzanne and Mallory Young, eds. *Chick Flicks: Contemporary Women at the Movies.* New York and London: Routledge, 2008.

Fiske, John. *Understanding Popular Culture.* Boston: Unwin Hyman, 1989.

Friedan, Betty. *The Feminine Mystique.* UK: Penguin Classics, 2010.

Gamble, Sarah. "Postfeminism," in *The Routledge Companion to Feminism and Postfeminism,* ed. Sarah Gamble (London: Routledge, 2001), 45.

Hollinger, Karen. "Afterword: Once I Got beyond the Name Chick Flick," in Ferriss, Suzanne and Mallory Young, eds. *Chick Flicks: Contemporary Women at the Movies.* New York and London: Routledge, 2008.

Kreaplin, Camille. "*Girlfriends* and *Sex and the City*: An Intersectional Analysis of Race, Gender and Commodity Feminism," in *Media Report to Women,* 40.1 (Winter 2012), 12–20.

McRobbie, Angela. *The Aftermath of Feminism: Gender, Culture and Social Change.* London: SAGE, 2009.

Negra, Diane. "Quality Postfeminism: Sex and the Single Girl on HBO," in *Genders* (April 1, 2004). https://www.colorado.edu/gendersarchive1998-2013/2004/04/01/quality-postfeminism-sex-and-single-girl-hbo.

Orenstein, Peggy. *Cinderella Ate My Daughter.* New York: Harper, 2012.

Pershing, Linda and Lisa Gablehouse. "Disney's *Enchanted*: Patriarchal Backlash and Nostalgia in a Fairy Tale Film," in Greenhill, Pauline and Sidney Eve Matrix, eds. *Fairy Tale Films: Visions of Ambiguity.* Logan, CO: Utah State University Press, 2010.

Rivers, Caryl. *Selling Anxiety: How the News Media Scare Women.* Hanover and London: University Press of New England, 2007.

Rook, Denis W. "The Ritual Dimension of Consumer Behaviour," in *The Journal of Consumer Research,* vol. 12 (December 1985): 251–264.

Saner, Emine. "How 'Bridezilla' Became This Summer's Biggest Sexist Slur," in *The Guardian* (August 15, 2019). https://www.theguardian.com/lifeandstyle/2019/aug/15/how-bridezilla-became-this-summers-biggest-sexist-slur.

Sex and the City: The Movie, directed by Michael Patrick King, HBO, 2008.

Sibielski, Rosalind. "Reviving Cinderella: Contested Feminism and Conflicting Models of Female Empowerment," in *Quarterly Review of Film and Video,* vol. 36, no. 7 (2019): 584–610.

Tasker, Yvonne. "*Enchanted* (2007): Postfeminism: Gender, Irony, and the New Romantic Comedy," in Radner, Hilary and Rebecca Stringer, eds. *Feminism at the Movies: Understanding Gender in Contemporary Popular Cinema.* New York: Routledge, 2011.

Walter, Natasha. *Living Dolls: The Return of Sexism.* GB: Virago, 2015.

Williamson, Judith. *Decoding Advertisements: Ideology and Meaning in Advertising.* GB: Marion Boyars, 2010.

Wolf, Naomi. *The Beauty Myth: How Images of Beauty are Used against Women.* London: Vintage, 1990.

Chapter Three

"Have Courage and Be Kind"

The Emancipatory Potential of Twenty-First-Century Fairy-Tale Adaptations of "Cinderella"

Svea Hundertmark

Fairy tales are among the oldest stories told by humanity. Nevertheless, they always seem to be up-to-date. The recent trend to adapt fairy tales in literature, film and television supports this claim since these adaptations often address current sociopolitical issues, for example, gender equality. This article addresses the modernization of what I call the "Cinderella-type" in recent fairy-tale films and TV series. Along with the eponymous Cinderella or *Aschenputtel*, the Cinderella-type also includes other characters that experience a similar "rags to riches" story. To pin down instances of renewal in modern day versions of "Cinderella," I first consider the story before the twenty-first century, referring to the Aarne-Thompson-Uther Index by Hans-Jörg Uther. In combination with an overview of tendencies of modernization in other contemporary fairy-tale adaptations, this provides the basis for my investigation into the depiction of gender roles. I argue that contemporary adaptations of "Cinderella" can only achieve a portion of the reimagination of gender roles that is present in many recent fairy-tale films because they have to perpetuate female gender roles that are inherent in the fairy tale. Nevertheless, they try to evade gender stereotypes and use other means to modernize their title characters, for example, by revising initially minor characters. I therefore examine the portrayal of men and women in films and TV series that are either based on the fairy tale "Cinderella" or include a character of the Cinderella-type, exploring their potential to promote emancipation from gender stereotypes.

CINDERELLA BEFORE THE TWENTY-FIRST CENTURY

"Cinderella" is one of the most popular fairy tales worldwide: A young woman is forced to become a servant to her stepmother and stepsisters in her own house and is mistreated by them. While secretly attending a royal ball that lasts three nights the prince falls in love with her. When she loses one of her unique shoes on the third night the prince vows to marry only the woman whom the shoe fits. Upon marrying the prince, she is rescued from her miserable life. *The Types of International Folktales* by Hans-Jörg Uther, also known as the Aarne-Thompson-Uther Index (ATU), lists the story of Cinderella as tale type 510A.[1] It belongs to the grouping of "Tales of Magic" (ATU 300-749), and, more specifically, to that of "Supernatural Helpers" (ATU 500-559). The focus of this categorization is, therefore, not on the heroine herself but on the entities that help her. Depending on the version of the fairy tale, these may be a fairy godmother, or a variety of birds and the tree on her mother's grave.

Two of the best-known versions of tale type 510A are "Cendrillon" by Charles Perrault from 1697 and "Aschenputtel" by Jacob and Wilhelm Grimm from 1857. Though the plot is very similar in both texts, the central motives differ to a great extent. In "Cendrillon," the orphaned title character receives beautiful dresses and slippers made of glass from her fairy godmother. She is sent to the royal ball in a coach made out of a pumpkin, drawn by mice transformed into horses, a rat as the coachman and six lizard footmen.[2] In the end, she forgives her stepsisters and pairs them up with two noblemen.[3] Cendrillon does not only stand out from her stepsisters in terms of beauty but because of her goodness and sweetness of temper.[4] Despite the cruelty she has to endure from them, she helps them to prepare for the ball voluntarily.[5] Even in her disguise she remains friendly and shares with them fruit, which the prince has given her.[6] Above all, she never complains about the ill-treatment she experiences.[7] At the same time, Cendrillon is very witty: she asks her stepsisters to lend her a dress so that she can go to the ball to see the beautiful princess they met there. Being the beautiful princess herself and anticipating that her sisters will not give her a dress, her request is a strategy to divert her stepsisters' attention.[8]

Aschenputtel of the Brothers Grimm receives her dresses and the golden slippers from a bird that sits in the hazel tree on the grave of her mother. Her father is still alive and well aware of the abuse of his daughter.[9] Aschenputtel makes her way to the festival on foot, where the prince is supposed to choose a bride.[10] In the end, her stepsisters are punished for mistreating her: not only do they cut off their toes and heels respectively in hope of marrying the prince once the shoe fits, but on Aschenputtel's wedding day they also have their eyes picked out by her birds.[11] Following her mother's orders, Aschenputtel is pious and good.[12] In terms of character, she is sometimes rather naïve: Although her stepmother had broken her promise to let her attend the festival after she has finished her chores, Aschenputtel still hopes that she will take her there after all.[13] Yet, she is determined to go and asks the wish-fulfilling bird to provide her with a suitable dress.[14] She also tricks other characters, for example, when she repeatedly escapes from the prince who is trying to accompany her on her way home.[15] In contrast to Cendrillon, Aschenputtel is not friendly to her stepsisters of her own accord. She simply fulfills the tasks that are given to her.[16]

All versions of a fairy tale can influence later adaptations of it. Fabienne Liptay points out that the medial variety of fairy tales explains why fairy-tale films are not always only based on one or several classic fairy tales. They rather refer to other adaptations in literature, illustrations, theater, film, television, opera and ballet.[17] Therefore, an additional account of the story should be mentioned when talking about tale type 510A and the Cinderella-type. In 1950, Walt Disney released the very influential animated film *Cinderella*. The film is based on the version by Perrault with some alterations made to it. The protagonist is described as being gentle and kind.[18] At the same time, Cinderella firmly defends her right to attend the ball.[19] In addition, she reacts defiantly against being teased by her stepfamily.[20] Similarly to Brothers Grimm's Aschenputtel, she completes her chores but obviously does not enjoy it.[21] In contrast to the literary version, the fate of the stepsisters is not mentioned in Disney's *Cinderella*.

Considering these versions of the story of Cinderella, characters of the Cinderella-type can be described as follows: They are generally of a good nature and diligent. Nevertheless, they do not necessarily like the hard work. Additionally, they face a rather tough life and even maltreatment. Magical intervention is needed to help them break free from this situation and their escape is followed by an advantageous marriage. The characters responsible for the Cinderella-type character's misery are either forgiven or punished for their actions.

TENDENCIES IN RECENT FAIRY-TALE FILMS AND TV SERIES

Since the beginning of the twenty-first century, more than thirty feature films based on fairy tales have been theatrically released in the United States. Moreover, at least three TV series referring to fairy tales have been broadcast in the same time. Films produced for television and online streaming services are likely to raise those numbers. Fantasy films and series alluding to fairy-tale plots and structures can be added as well. Similar tendencies in other countries, for example, the high amount of fairy-tale films produced by German television networks, prove that this is not a phenomenon limited to the United States but that adapting films from fairy tales is a global trend.[22]

Recent fairy-tale films and TV series have a tendency to modernize the fairy tales they are based on. Nevertheless, most films retain the essence of those tales: The basic structure of the plot, central motifs and the main characters stay the same. Even in a rather free adaptation like *Snow White and the Huntsman* (Universal Pictures, 2012) the title character, her evil stepmother, a huntsman and the dwarfs remain true to the original. Snow White first flees into the woods and later takes a bite from a poisoned apple, just like her counterpart in the "Snow White" fairy tale. In the end, the evil queen is defeated as well.

In terms of modernization, the plots are updated considering current trends of thought. The result may be a film that seems to have only little left in common with the literary fairy tale. As described above, it nevertheless builds on the tale's tradition. A renewal might entail the representation of marginalized groups without major changes to the fairy tale itself, for example, by employing a cast that is not all white. Other recent films and TV series try to incorporate discourses of gender and sexual identity. One strategy is to set female characters apart from their literary and filmic predecessors: They become proactive, they go into battle if necessary and they liberate themselves from suppression. Disney's *Maleficent* (2014), for instance, negotiates the role of women in society and the ways they can react toward what men do to them. By accentuating the villain and entitling her to her own story, the former image of women in "Sleeping Beauty" is revised. First, the focus is shifted from a passive female character to an active one. She is then equipped with a coherent motivation for her actions. Thus, this version of the fairy tale moves away from the hysterical and vengeful female villain to a more profound portrayal of women.

Another possibility for innovation is to depict characters with nonheteronormative sexual identities. LeFou in Disney's *Beauty and the Beast* (2017) alludes to the existence of LGTBQ+ characters. According to director Bill Condon, "LeFou is somebody who on one day wants to be Gaston and on another day wants to kiss Gaston."[23] In the end, he even dances with another man, albeit the scene only lasting two seconds.[24] This scene has, nevertheless, been met with some critique because of the discrepancy between the announcement of an openly gay character and his depiction.[25] In the TV series *Once Upon a Time* there are two attempts to offer representation of nonheteronormative romances. The first is the love story of Ruby and Dorothy in season 5. Viewers, however, heavily criticized the portrayal of their relationship, which evolved over the course of only one episode. In an article for bustle.com, Jennifer Still writes, "[r]epresentation doesn't mean throwing the audience a bone in the form of a throwaway romance that we saw for a few minutes and then never have to deal with again. In fact, that's actually the definition of tokenism."[26] In the seventh season, the more complex relationship of Alice and Robin is introduced to the series. It seems that the creators took the initial critique very seriously. In return, this love story is met with rather positive reviews.[27]

These examples show that discourses of gender and sexual identity are gradually implemented in modern fairy-tale films. However, they are largely not connected to the main protagonists of the fairy tales, but they are generally associated with minor characters. Those characters can, nevertheless, advance to become the heroes of the film adaptations, as is the case with Maleficent.

CORPUS AND RESEARCH QUESTION

Considering these trends, the question remains as to how far similar tendencies to modernize the narrative of Cinderella can be found. I therefore focus on the revision of gender roles in fairy-tale films and TV series that include characters of the Cinderella-type. The chosen films are *Cinderella* (Disney, 2015) and *Into the Woods* (Disney, 2014), in which Cinderella herself is present. Additionally, *Aladdin* (Disney, 2019) and *The Princess and the Frog* (Disney, 2009) are examined because of their Cinderella-type characters. Furthermore, I take a closer look at two of the aforementioned German productions. Both films portray the story of Cinderella. The ZDF released *Aschenputtel* in 2010 and the ARD followed in 2011 with a film also called *Aschenputtel*. Individual episodes of the series *Once Upon a Time* (ABC, 2011–2018) and *Grimm* (NBC, 2011–2017) serve as additional examples. As this paper is concerned with representations of the Cinderella-type in fairy-tale adaptations, films that are based on the story of Cinderella but do not include magic are not investigated. Consequently, films like *Maid in Manhattan* (Sony Pictures, 2002) and *A Cinderella Story* (Warner Bros., 2004) are not part of the corpus.

It should be noted that both literary versions of the fairy tale (Perrault and Brothers Grimm) are used as the basis for the filmic adaptations of "Cinderella." Earlier films, like Disney's 1950 *Cinderella*, influence recent fairy-tale films as well. Some features of the fairy tale, however, are altered in comparison to previous versions of the story. These are mainly the fate of the stepfamily and the part the prince plays in the narrative. In combination with the representation of the Cinderella-type characters, these aspects offer the greatest potential in terms of examining modernized gender roles in this fairy tale.

CINDERELLA AND OTHER CHARACTERS OF
THE CINDERELLA-TYPE

In terms of the portrayal of character traits, all Cinderella-type characters in recent fairy-tale films are more resolute than their literary counterparts. They contradict their stepmothers more strongly, they argue with their stepsisters, and they exhibit confidence when talking to the prince. This becomes especially apparent in the German version by the ARD. Aschenputtel screams at her stepmother as well as the prince. While her stepmother concludes that this behavior renders Aschenputtel unfit to go to the ball,[28] the prince is of a different opinion. He is rather impressed by her fiery temper.[29] Likewise, the young women are even more reluctant to serve their stepfamilies. However, this intensifies the already existing conflicts. When Cinderella in *Into the Woods* gives way to her anger while dressing her stepsister's hair, she hurts her. In response, Cinderella is slapped in the face so hard that she falls to the ground.[30] Nevertheless, when considering the 1950 animated film, it becomes clear that these tendencies have been inherent in earlier adaptations as well.

The situations in which Cinderella-type characters are depicted do not differ considerably from film to film. They mainly serve to highlight the contrast between housework and ball scene. The protagonist is shown primarily in four situations: doing housework, meeting the prince before the ball, at the ball and when trying on the shoe. While the first meeting of Aschenputtel and the prince is only very short in the ZDF-film, she attends all three balls. Every time her dress is more beautiful than the one before.[31] In between those ball scenes, she is primarily seen doing housework.[32] In the ARD version, Aschenputtel spends most of her time carrying out various tasks. While doing this she meets the prince several times.[33] Fulfilling her tasks, therefore, gives her the opportunity to get to know the prince before reuniting with him at the ball.[34] In *Cinderella*, the title character looks after the house herself after her father dies because the family cannot afford employees anymore. She endures this demotion and the maltreatment from her stepfamily by repeatedly reminding herself of her mother's mantra, "have courage and be kind."[35] Cinderella meets the prince only once before the ball,[36] where her entrance is very lavishly staged.[37] Like Aschenputtel in both German films, she is portrayed as being very modest, especially when trying on the shoe.[38] The prince then waits for her to indicate if she wants to marry him.[39] This is not always the case as sometimes the Cinderella-type character is simply declared to be the true bride, for example, in the ZDF production,[40] and in *Into the Woods*.[41]

Even with characters that are based on the Cinderella-type more loosely, there is a tendency to emphasize the difference between housework and ball gown. Tiana is the protagonist of *The Princess and the Frog*, which is an adaptation of "The Frog Prince" (ATU 440). In spite of the film's title, Tiana is not a princess but a waitress who wants to open her own restaurant.[42] In the course of the events, she meets a prince who was turned into a frog. Upon kissing the prince in an attempt to help him to return to his human self and to obtain the money she needs for the restaurant, she turns into a frog herself.[43] While in her human form, she is almost exclusively shown doing housework and waiting tables.[44] The only exceptions to this are her dream sequences and the wedding with the prince.[45] Her portrayal, however, does have emancipatory potential, as she is a very ambitious woman who works hard to fulfill her dream, particularly so, since she faces explicit prejudices against her as she is a black woman from a working-class background.[46] Nevertheless, this potential remains unused: Tiana can only fulfill her dream once she has a man by her side she did not know she needed or wanted.[47] Thus, the end of the film even undermines what is left of this emancipatory potential by adhering to traditional gender stereotypes about men and women.

The portrayal of the Cinderella-type in *Into the Woods* differs from the other films. While Cinderella is introduced cleaning the kitchen,[48] she is almost exclusively shown in the woods later on. Most of the time she is running from the prince because she is not sure if she wants him at all.[49] Even though Cinderella usually wears an evening gown, the three festivals are not staged. Shortly after having been declared the true bride and marrying the (unfaithful) prince, she decides against living in the palace. Mentioning that she enjoys cleaning from time to time, she wants to help the baker with his household instead.[50] The possibility to decide against her predestined fairy-tale life does hold emancipatory potential. Nevertheless, since the film lacks a truly happy ending this Cinderella faces a rather sobering future.

The films' level of modernization in terms of the depiction of women can also be determined by the names that are given to the Cinderella-type characters. As the labels "Aschenputtel" and "Cinderella" are intended to mock the young women, the question remains if they should have this name substituted or at least complemented by a real name. In *Cinderella* the protagonist is called Ella. Ridiculing her, her stepsisters add the prefix "Cinder," referring to the ashes on her face.[51] In the ZDF version the young woman's name is actually Marie.[52] The ARD production leaves the protagonist nameless apart from the scornful "Aschenputtel." What is very striking in this case is the fact that many of the other characters do have names: The prince is called Viktor, her stepsister is Annabella and the farm hand goes by the name of Johanna.[53] In contrast, in *Into the Woods*, most of the characters do not have a name, including the Cinderella character and the prince. It seems that most adaptations that refer to the narrative of Cinderella more loosely tend to give names to their characters. Apart from Tiana in *The Princess and the Frog*, *Once Upon a Time* features two Cinderella-type characters, Ashley[54] and Jacinda,[55] whose names retain the association with the ashes but omit the negative connotation. The humanizing potential of a name provides the characters with more dignity. Granting the female protagonist a real name rather than only labeling her with a derogatory term therefore reinforces a more differentiated portrayal of women.

Overall, recent Cinderella-type characters are either shown in a situation of great splendor or performing housework associated with the female sex. This is not a balanced portrayal of female characters but an opposition of two extremes. Sometimes, the Cinderella-type characters do not even receive a name, even if the prince and other characters do. If a film exhibits any emancipatory potential, it is often not explored successfully. Thus, Tiana is convinced that she needs to have a royal husband if she wants to become the owner of a restaurant. Despite the more modern portrayal that makes the female characters appear more determined and independent, it seems that the prince still has to rescue all of them in the end. The one exception is Cinderella in *Into the Woods* who ultimately ends the unhealthy relationship with her unfaithful prince.

CINDERELLA'S STEPSISTERS

The films that directly refer to the fairy-tale version by the Brothers Grimm retain the disfiguring of the stepsisters' feet. The sisters cut off their toes and heels respectively to make the shoe fit and, consequently, marry the prince. In the versions by the ZDF and the ARD, there is only one stepsister. In both films the mother mutilates her daughter's feet in spite of her fearful protests.[56] Cinderella's stepsisters in *Into the Woods* suffer a similar fate. One of them loses her toes; the other one, her heel,[57] and their additional punishment is depicted as well when Cinderella's birds peck out their eyes.[58] There would have been some emancipatory potential in refusing to submit to such a violent act that aims at conforming to an ideal of beauty (small feet) in order to secure an advantageous marriage, but none of the films makes use of that potential. One could cite faithfulness to the original as a possible reason for this. The abundance of situations in which the films divert from this original, however, render this rather unlikely.

Another motivation to keep the mutilation of the stepsisters might be a current trend called "Grimmification":

> This term [. . .] has so far been defined in direct opposition to the belittling, harmonizing, and commercializing effects of "Disneyfication" (Bendix 1993) as "the act of allegedly de-bowdlerizing a story, but going to the other extreme: making it Grimmdark," ("Grimmification" [1]) or else "making a traditional fairy tale even darker and edgier than it may have already been."[59]

Tzvetan Todorov describes the fantastic genre using a spectrum in which the marvelous is on the one end and the uncanny on the other. A narrative can be called fantastic if it is uncertain to which of the two it belongs. The fairy tale is considered to be a prime example of the marvelous.[60] Many recent fairy tale films highlight the violent and eerie aspects of those stories, thereby moving them to the uncanny end of the fantastic spectrum. In doing so they position themselves closer to the horror genre to appeal to adolescent and adult audiences, as can be seen in *Hansel & Gretel: Witch Hunters* (Paramount Pictures/Metro-Goldwyn-Mayer, 2013).

The version by Perrault grants the stepsisters a good ending. However, the films and TV series that refer to this version do not necessarily adhere to this. In Disney's *Cinderella*, a concluding voice-over gives insight into their fate: Although Cinderella forgives them, her stepmother and her stepsisters leave the kingdom and never return.[61] Whether this is their own choice or whether they are banished does not become clear. In the series *Once Upon a Time*, one of the stepsisters finds her true love—one of the prince's footmen—while her mother is punished for her deeds.[62] At the end of the spin-off series *Once Upon a Time in Wonderland* the second stepsister receives a happy ending as well: together with her true love she rules over the Wonderland of Lewis Carroll's *Alice* books.[63] Cinderella and her stepsisters are only marginally considered in the first six seasons of *Once Upon a Time*. In *Once Upon a Time in Wonderland* one of the stepsisters is explored further but she remains one of the villains for most of the series. In the seventh season of *Once Upon a Time*, however, the Cinderella-character is recast and she becomes one of the protagonists. Because of that, her stepfamily takes up a bigger part of the plot as well. For most of the season, they are regarded as evil, although their backstories are explored and therefore the motivation behind their actions becomes clearer. The now more rounded characters change sides once an even more evil villain starts to endanger them as well: in the end, Cinderella's stepmother gives her life to save one of her daughters[64] and the two sisters leave town to make a fresh start together.[65]

The TV series *Grimm* differs from both patterns. The episode dealing with "Cinderella" is only loosely based on the fairy tale. The Cinderella-type character Lucinda is a supernatural being who kills her stepmother and one of her stepsisters with supersonic screams.[66] She attempts to murder her other stepsister as well to become the lone heir to her father's fortune. In the course of the struggle, her equally supernatural godfather kills her.[67] Aside from this, it is not clear if Lucinda has been treated badly by her stepfamily or if she was the one oppressing them.[68] Therefore, the violence is not a question of punishing the stepfamily. The Cinderella-type character, who is portrayed as being at least mildly psychopathic,[69] kills out of hatred and greed. This episode, like the series as a whole, exhibits another trend in fairy-tale adaptations. In a growing number of films and series, the classic fairy tales are not only subject to Grimmification; many fairy tales are turned around completely. This might include the reversal of the plot or the transposition of good and bad characters. Cinderella becoming a "bat out of hell" includes both.[70] Another example would be Little Red Riding Hood turning out to be the wolf herself, as is the case in *Once Upon a Time*[71] and *Red Riding Hood* (Warner Bros., 2011).

In many recent adaptations of the story of Cinderella, the protagonist's stepfamily is punished in some way. While the films that are based on the version by the Brothers Grimm retain the maiming of the stepsisters' feet, most of them leave out the picking out of the eyes and include a punishment for the stepmother instead. Their actions toward Cinderella are nevertheless mostly not explained. Thus, the characters remain one-dimensional. The mutilation of the female body for the sake of a beauty ideal does not contribute to an interrogation of female gender roles either. Films and TV series that are based on the version by Perrault focus on the punishment of the stepmother. Cinderella's stepsisters often find their happiness in the end, be it in form of a love relationship or with one another. Because of its serial format, *Once Upon a Time* is able to devote more time to the development of the stepfamily. As a result, the characters become more rounded and exhibit a deeper motivation for their actions, which leads to a more nuanced portrayal of female characters.

THE PRINCE

In comparison to the literary versions and Disney's animated film, the prince plays a bigger role in all the analyzed adaptations. While the prince is supposed to find a bride at the king's festival in the version by the Brothers Grimm,[72] the prince's ball in Perrault's version does not have such a background.[73] The pressure to find a wife, mainly for political reasons, is nevertheless incorporated in almost all of the films. This leads to a closer examination of this character who is now introduced to the narrative before the ball. Thus, the prince advances from the object of the sisterly contest to a psychologized character. This change is often accompanied by a reinterpretation of the prince. Consequently, he has to be saved from an arranged marriage and the Cinderella-type character is the one to rescue him.

This is, for example, the case in the *Aschenputtel* film by the ZDF. Here, the prince wants to save his country from his legal guardian by becoming king himself. To do so he has to marry before turning twenty-one.[74] Despite being aware of his responsibility he does not want a wife who wants him only because of his royal status.[75] This conflict offers a potential to modernize the male part in the Cinderella narrative. However, this potential is undermined by the shallowness of the prince as he only invites the beautiful women of his kingdom to the ball.[76] Likewise, his declarations of love for Aschenputtel/Marie always refer to her outer appearance and beauty.[77]

In Disney's *Cinderella* and in *Aschenputtel* by the ARD the prince is pressured by the king to marry in the near future.[78] In both films, he meets the Cinderella-type character before the ball but does not reveal his true identity. The young woman makes an impression on him because of her unpretentious behavior and openness.[79] Therefore, the prince is allowed to fall in love and can be loved because of who he is instead of choosing a wife based on her looks. Additionally, he is granted some vulnerability, for example, when he cries over the death of his father in *Cinderella*.[80]

In *Into the Woods*, the king holds a festival to find a bride for the prince who does not object to this.[81] The appeal Cinderella has for the prince, however, lies in the fact that she runs from him. His courting is therefore mainly portrayed in scenes of hunting.[82] His conquest of Cinderella does not make him happy permanently, though. In the end, he cheats on her so they agree to go their separate ways.[83] This prince does by no means stand for a differentiated portrayal of men. Instead, sexist clichés about unfaithful husbands are called upon to parody the ideal fairy-tale prince.

One of the freer adaptations seems to be a special case in terms of the part of the prince. In Disney's most recent version of "Aladdin," that has only little in common with the tale from *One Thousand and One Nights*, this role is taken on by the princess. Aladdin, who lives on the streets but then marries into royalty with the help of magic, is the Cinderella-type character of the story. Since the princess wants to follow her father as sultan and has studied all her life to be able to do that, she declines all proposals for a political marriage.[84] In this film, the emancipatory potential of the Cinderella narrative is realized by casting a female character for the role of the prince. In the end, the princess is actually crowned "sultan" by her father and decrees that she may marry whomever she wants.[85] In the 1992 animated film, it is her father who changes the law, allowing the princess to choose her husband and therefore the future (still inevitably male) sultan.[86]

Compared to the literary versions, the prince takes up a bigger part of the story of Cinderella in many recent adaptations. The portrayal of the character varies widely from film to film, though. The prince might be a modern character, searching for his true love. This does not mean, however, that he is immune to choosing his bride based on superficial criteria, such as beauty. The role of the prince can be occupied by a female character, as well. By doing this, *Aladdin* questions prevailing male and female gender roles. The prince can also be characterized as a macho-type womanizer. In *Into the Woods*, this parodic perspective is used to undermine and question stereotypical portrayals of masculinity.

CONCLUSION

To what extent can we speak of a modernization of gender roles in recent film adaptations of the Cinderella narrative and in connection with characters of the Cinderella-type? As my analysis illustrates, the female protagonist is further developed in terms of character, consequently becoming more independent. Nevertheless, following the source narrative, Cinderella is still shown doing housework and is rescued by a man in the end. Therefore, her portrayal does not question female gender roles to a significant extent. The same is true for the fate of the stepsisters. Although Cinderella's behavior is modernized and her stepsisters, at least in some formats, receive a deeper motivation for their actions, the female characters mostly stay the same. With reference to the version by the Brothers Grimm, the stepsisters' bodies are mutilated to please a man. This man in turn receives considerably more room in the story when he is introduced before the ball. The prince, a minor character in the fairy tale, is elaborated on in recent adaptations to revise male gender roles. Like in other recent fairy-tale films, the revision of gender roles is therefore connected to a minor character who then becomes a more central character. If stereotypes about men are not challenged, they are parodied and, therefore, undermined. The depiction of the Cinderella-type characters does not equally subvert female gender stereotypes. Therefore, recent Cinderella fairy-tale films revise and question male gender roles rather than female ones. Nevertheless, the rewriting of the prince does influence the other characters as well: The prince is not a mere object for the sisters to climb the social ladder anymore. He is a psychologized character who is allowed to fall in love and to be loved. Cinderella only later finds out that the one she loves is royalty and realizes that he may help her to start a new life. The female protagonist, thus, becomes more rounded herself since she does not simply use the prince to escape her horrible life.

NOTES

1. Uther, Hans-Jörg, *Animal Tales, Tales of Magic, Religious Tales, and Realistic Tales, with an Introduction* (Helsinki: Suomalainen Tiedeakatemia, 2004), 293–95.
2. Perrault, Charles, "Cendrillon ou La Petite Pantoufle de Verre / Aschenputtel oder Das Gläserne Pantöffelchen," in *Contes de Fées: Märchen* (Munich: dtv, 2001), 86–91.
3. Ibid., 89–90.
4. Ibid., 80–83.
5. Ibid., 84–87.
6. Ibid., 92–93.
7. Ibid., 82–83.
8. Ibid., 92–95.
9. Grimm, Jacob and Grimm, Wilhelm, "Aschenputtel," in *Kinder- und Hausmärchen: Ausgabe letzter Hand mit den Originalanmerkungen der Brüder Grimm. Mit einem Anhang sämtlicher, nicht in allen Auflagen veröffentlichter Märchen und Herkunftsnachweisen*, ed. Heinz Rölleke (Stuttgart: Reclam, 2014), 132.

10. Ibid., 133–35.
11. Ibid., 139.
12. Ibid., 131.
13. Ibid., 134.
14. Ibid., 134–35.
15. Ibid., 135–37.
16. Ibid., 133.
17. Liptay, Fabienne, *WunderWelten: Märchen im Film* (Remscheid: Gardez-Verlag, 2004), 133.
18. *Cinderella*, directed by Clyde Geronimi, Wilfred Jackson and Hamilton Luske.
19. Ibid.
20. Ibid.
21. Ibid.
22. Zipes, Jack, "The Great Cultural Tsunami of Fairy-Tale Films," in *Fairy-Tale Films beyond Disney: International Perspectives*, ed. Jack Zipes, Pauline Greenhill and Kendra Magnus-Johnston (New York: Routledge, 2016), 1–6.
23. Lee, Ashley, "'Beauty and the Beast': Josh Gad Plays Disney's First-Ever Gay Character," accessed January 7, 2020, https://www.hollywoodreporter.com/news/beauty-beast-disneys-first-ever-gay-character-is-lefou-voiced-by-josh-gad-981928.
24. *Beauty and the Beast*, DVD, directed by Bill Condon (2017; Munich: Walt Disney Studios Home Entertainment, 2017).
25. Lawler, Kelly, "'Beauty and the Beast's 'Gay Moment' May Have Been Much Ado about Nothing," accessed January 7, 2020, https://eu.usatoday.com/story/life/entertainthis/2017/03/20/beauty-and-the-beast-gay-moment-audience-reaction/99407168/.
26. Still, Jennifer, "Why Ruby and Dorothy's Relationship on 'Once Upon a Time' Missed the Mark," accessed January 7, 2020, https://www.bustle.com/articles/155329-why-ruby-dorothys-relationship-on-once-upon-a-time-missed-the-mark.
27. Roker, Sarah, "Once Upon a Time Stars Open Up about Alice and Robin's 'Big Love Story,'" accessed January 7, 2020, https://www.digitalspy.com/tv/ustv/a853105/once-upon-a-time-alice-robin-relationship/.
28. *Aschenputtel*, DVD, directed by Uwe Janson (2011; Eisingen: KNM Home Entertainment, 2011).
29. Ibid.
30. *Into the Woods*, DVD, directed by Rob Marshall (2014; Munich: Walt Disney Studios Home Entertainment, 2015).
31. *Aschenputtel*.
32. Ibid.
33. Ibid.
34. Ibid.
35. *Cinderella*, DVD, directed by Kenneth Branagh (2015; Munich: Walt Disney Studios Home Entertainment, 2016).
36. Ibid.
37. Ibid.
38. Ibid.
39. Ibid.
40. *Aschenputtel*.
41. *Into the Woods*.
42. *The Princess and the Frog*, DVD, directed by Ron Clements and John Musker (2009; Munich: Walt Disney Studios Home Entertainment, 2010).
43. Ibid.
44. Ibid.
45. Ibid.
46. Ibid.
47. Ibid.
48. *Into the Woods*.
49. Ibid.

50. Ibid.
51. *Cinderella.*
52. *Aschenputtel.*
53. *Aschenputtel.*
54. "The Price of Gold," *Once Upon a Time*, 1x04. DVD, directed by David Solomon, ABC: November 13, 2011 (Munich: Walt Disney Studios Home Entertainment, 2013).
55. "Hyperion Heights," *Once Upon a Time*, 7x01. Amazon Prime Video, directed by Ralph Hemecker, ABC: October 6, 2017 (Munich: Amazon Digital Germany GmbH, 2017).
56. *Aschenputtel.*
57. *Into the Woods.*
58. *Into the Woods.*
59. Marzolph, Ulrich, "The Grimmification of Narrative Tradition," in *From the Tana River to Lake Chad: Research in African Oratures and Literatures; in Memoriam Thomas Geider*, ed. Hannelore Vögele et al. (Cologne: Köppe, 2014), 125.
60. Todorov, Tzvetan, *The Fantastic: A Structural Approach to a Literary Genre* (Cleveland: Press of Case Western Reserve University, 1973), 41–57.
61. *Cinderella.*
62. "The Other Shoe," *Once Upon a Time*, 6x03. Amazon Prime Video, directed by Steve Pearlman, ABC: October 9, 2016 (Munich: Amazon Digital Germany GmbH, 2016), 00:36:06–00:36:14.
63. "And They Lived . . . ," *Once Upon a Time in Wonderland*, 1x13. Amazon Prime Video, directed by Kari Skogland, ABC: April 3, 2014 (Munich: Amazon Digital Germany GmbH, 2014).
64. "Secret Garden," *Once Upon a Time*, 7x11. Amazon Prime Video, directed by Mick Garris, ABC: March 2, 2018 (Munich: Amazon Digital Germany GmbH, 2018).
65. "Sisterhood," *Once Upon a Time*, 7x15. Amazon Prime Video, directed by Ellen S. Pressmen, ABC: March 30, 2018 (Munich: Amazon Digital Germany GmbH, 2018).
66. "Happily Ever Aftermath," *Grimm*, 1x20. Netflix Video, directed by Terrence O'Hara, NBC: May 4, 2012 (Amsterdam: Netflix International B.V.).
67. Ibid.
68. Ibid.
69. Ibid.
70. Ibid.
71. "Red-Handed," *Once Upon a Time*, 1x15. DVD, directed by Ron Underwood, ABC: March 3, 2012 (Munich: Walt Disney Studios Home Entertainment, 2013).
72. "Aschenputtel," 133.
73. "Cendrillon," 82–83.
74. *Aschenputtel.*
75. Ibid.
76. Ibid.
77. Ibid.
78. *Cinderella.*
79. Ibid.
80. Ibid.
81. *Into the Woods.*
82. Ibid.
83. Ibid.
84. *Aladdin,* DVD, directed by Guy Ritchie (2019; Munich: Walt Disney Studios Home Entertainment, 2019).
85. Ibid.
86. *Aladdin,* DVD, directed by Ron Clements and John Musker (1992; Munich: Walt Disney Studios Home Entertainment, 2017).

BIBLIOGRAPHY

Aladdin. DVD. Directed by Ron Clements, and John Musker. 1992. Munich: Walt Disney Studios Home Entertainment, 2017.

Aladdin. DVD. Directed by Guy Ritchie. 2019. Munich: Walt Disney Studios Home Entertainment, 2019.

"And They Lived . . ." *Once Upon a Time in Wonderland,* 1x13. Amazon Prime Video. Directed by Kari Skogland. ABC: April 3, 2014. Munich: Amazon Digital Germany GmbH, 2014.

Aschenputtel. DVD. Directed by Susanne Zanke. 2010. Munich: FM Kids, 2011.

Aschenputtel. DVD. Directed by Uwe Janson. 2011. Eisingen: KNM Home Entertainment, 2011.

Beauty and the Beast. DVD. Directed by Bill Condon. 2017. Munich: Walt Disney Studios Home Entertainment, 2017.

Cinderella. DVD. Directed by Clyde Geronimi, Wilfred Jackson, and Hamilton Luske. 1950. Munich: Walt Disney Studios Home Entertainment, 2014.

Cinderella. DVD. Directed by Kenneth Branagh. 2015. Munich: Walt Disney Studios Home Entertainment, 2016.

Grimm, Jacob, and Wilhelm Grimm. "Aschenputtel." In *Kinder- und Hausmärchen: Ausgabe letzter Hand mit den Originalanmerkungen der Brüder Grimm. Mit einem Anhang sämtlicher, nicht in allen Auflagen veröffentlichter Märchen und Herkunftsnachweisen.* Edited by Heinz Rölleke, 131–39. Stuttgart: Reclam, 2014.

"Happily Ever Aftermath." *Grimm,* 1x20. Netflix Video. Directed by Terrence O'Hara. NBC: May 4, 2012. Amsterdam: Netflix International B.V.

"Hyperion Heights." *Once Upon a Time,* 7x01. Amazon Prime Video. Directed by Ralph Hemecker. ABC: October 6, 2017. Munich: Amazon Digital Germany GmbH, 2017.

Into the Woods. DVD. Directed by Rob Marshall. 2014. Munich: Walt Disney Studios Home Entertainment, 2015.

Lawler, Kelly. "'Beauty and the Beast's 'Gay Moment' May Have Been Much Ado about Nothing." Accessed January 7, 2020. https://eu.usatoday.com/story/life/entertainthis/2017/03/20/beauty-and-the-beast-gay-moment-audience-reaction/99407168/.

Lee, Ashley. "'Beauty and the Beast': Josh Gad Plays Disney's First-Ever Gay Character." Accessed January 7, 2020. https://www.hollywoodreporter.com/news/beauty-beast-disneys-first-ever-gay-character-is-lefou-voiced-by-josh-gad-981928.

Liptay, Fabienne. *WunderWelten: Märchen im Film.* Remscheid: Gardez!-Verlag, 2004.

Marzolph, Ulrich. "The Grimmification of Narrative Tradition." In *From the Tana River to Lake Chad: Research in African Oratures and Literatures; in Memoriam Thomas Geider.* Edited by Hannelore Vögele et al., 123–32. Cologne: Köppe, 2014.

"The Other Shoe." *Once Upon a Time,* 6x03. Amazon Prime Video. Directed by Steve Pearlman. ABC: October 9, 2016. Munich: Amazon Digital Germany GmbH, 2016.

Perrault, Charles. "Cendrillon ou La Petite Pantoufle de Verre / Aschenputtel oder Das Gläserne Pantöffelchen." In *Contes de Fées: Märchen,* 80–101. Munich: dtv, 2001.

"The Price of Gold." *Once Upon a Time,* 1x04. DVD. Directed by David Solomon. ABC: November 13, 2011. Munich: Walt Disney Studios Home Entertainment, 2013.

The Princess and the Frog. DVD. Directed by Ron Clements, and John Musker. 2009. Munich: Walt Disney Studios Home Entertainment, 2010.

"Red-Handed." *Once Upon a Time,* 1x15. DVD. Directed by Ron Underwood. ABC: March 3, 2012. Munich: Walt Disney Studios Home Entertainment, 2013.

Roker, Sarah. "Once Upon a Time Stars Open Up about Alice and Robin's 'Big Love Story.'" Accessed January 7, 2020. https://www.digitalspy.com/tv/ustv/a853105/once-upon-a-time-alice-robin-relationship/.

"Secret Garden." *Once Upon a Time,* 7x11. Amazon Prime Video. Directed by Mick Garris. ABC: March 2, 2018. Munich: Amazon Digital Germany GmbH, 2018.

"Sisterhood." *Once Upon a Time,* 7x15. Amazon Prime Video. Directed by Ellen S. Pressmen. ABC: March 30, 2018. Munich: Amazon Digital Germany GmbH, 2018.

Still, Jennifer. "Why Ruby and Dorothy's Relationship on 'Once Upon a Time' Missed the Mark." Accessed January 7, 2020. https://www.bustle.com/articles/155329-why-ruby-dorothys-relationship-on-once-upon-a-time-missed-the-mark.

Todorov, Tzvetan. *The Fantastic: A Structural Approach to a Literary Genre*. Cleveland: Press of Case Western Reserve University, 1973.

Uther, Hans-Jörg. *Animal Tales, Tales of Magic, Religious Tales, and Realistic Tales, with an Introduction*. Helsinki: Suomalainen Tiedeakatemia, 2004.

Zipes, Jack. "The Great Cultural Tsunami of Fairy-Tale Films." In *Fairy-Tale Films beyond Disney: International Perspectives*. Edited by Jack Zipes, Pauline Greenhill and Kendra Magnus-Johnston, 1–17. New York: Routledge, 2016.

Chapter Four

Two Centuries of Queer Horizon

Rodgers and Hammerstein's Cinderella

Christine Case

Fairy tales have a knack for taking root, and carving out *the possible*, in unexpected ways, places, and times. Due to the ubiquity of the fairy story, we can often, erroneously, think we know all there is to know. However, de-historicized, metonymic "knowing" is scarcely knowing at all. Rather, nuanced attendance to the particular histories and diegetic offerings of certain fairy stories may help intervene on their "seemingly exhausted status," including that of "Cinderella today."[1]

Rodgers and Hammerstein's 1957 *Cinderella* is strangely equipped at finding new life.[2] Seventy-two years following its live television debut, *Cinderella*'s lyrics and melodies may be found woven into the sonic landscape of the twenty-first century with Chance the Rapper's album *The Big Day*. In the album's final number, "Zanies and Fools," Chance plucks from the musical's songs of transformation, "Impossible" and "It's Possible," originally sung by Cinderella and her Fairy Godmother. He manipulates the musical's tracks to both advance a critique of the American Dream and endorse the seeming foolishness of love of desire, demonstrating these tracks' political, artistic malleability. Mobilizing *Cinderella*'s rhetoric of "zanies and fools," Chance the Rapper taps into the possibilities of these musical numbers, endorsing their message of the "wonderfully crazy" or nonsensical. In this way, the improbable proffers a sonic and affective linkage between twenty-first-century rap and mid-century Americana. Not only is *Cinderella* present in multiple historical periods, but it is capable of responding to new, contextualized historical questions and ideological debates. At large, this chapter understands the iterative, recurring nature of this production to displace and disperse 1957 as its historical moment, instead reading *Cinderella* as very much of the twenty-first century.

The eve of March 31, 1957, saw the debut of Rodgers and Hammerstein's new musical, *Cinderella*; this live television spectacular (boasting rising star Julie Andrews) premiered on CBS to a historic audience of over 100 million, nation-wide. This *Cinderella*, however, has refused to stay put in this given historical moment, instead, traveling across generations through revivals in the form of television films in 1965 and 1997, and a Broadway show in 2013. The material and circulation histories of this *Cinderella* are testament to its fervid, flexible reappearance across generations. Continually relevant, Rodgers and Hammerstein's *Cinderella* is a cultural artifact with a queer orientation to time.

As Elizabeth Freeman argues, the "stubborn lingering of pastness . . . is a hallmark of queer affect."[3] She continues, "Longing produces modes of both belonging and 'being long,' or persisting over time."[4] The sense and sensibilities of queerness, then, are linked with both the temporally distended, and with longing. In playing with time, longing may both represent and enact a queer defiance and desire. José Esteban Muñoz posits, "queerness exists for us as an ideality that can be distilled from the past and used to imagine a future."[5] Queerness plucks from the past to imagine and engender alternate possibilities; nominally of the past, Rodgers and Hammerstein's *Cinderella* queerly resists becoming passé, spreading its "Impossible" possibilities across generations and mediums.

First marking the disciplinary echoes between fairy-tale studies and gender and sexuality studies, I proceed to employ the feminist, queer lens well-suited to the material at hand. In the myriad reviews of this production, both historical and recent, it is the hetero-romantic duet between the Prince and Cinderella ("Ten Minutes Ago") which has been granted analytic and affective centrality. However, what queer horizons are obscured by this insistent emphasis on the marriage plot? I turn, instead, to the pivotal sequence of transformation, a duet between Cinderella and her Fairy Godmother that blurs between "Impossible" and its seeming inverse, "It's Possible." Such is a moment of willed and willful *wishing*, co-constructed by two women; this focus upon the potentials of *female* duet queerly refocuses the musical's generic coupling away from the hetero-romantic. Through this sequence, in particular, Rodgers and Hammerstein indulge the "zanies and fools" and their own, *non-* "sensible rules."[6] *Cinderella* thereby performs and advocates a queer critical utopianism, which imagines the present and future in a manner beyond and *otherwise to* the known and the now.

CRITICISM AND HISTORICIZATION: THE STAKES

Critical discourses of the fairy tale carve out the terrain of the allowable and imaginable. Fairy-tale scholar Jennifer Schacker understands the historicization of fairy-tale discourse as a pedagogical imperative for students, instructors, and critics alike. Though often overlooked "paratextual and metacommunicative features" of fairy-tale texts, readers and viewers may better understand the fairy tale as a polyvalent genre whose purported traditions are constantly, actively reconstituted.[7] To this end, Schacker critically interrogates Frank L. Baum's introduction to the first of his Oz series (1990), in which Baum advocates for a transition from "the old-time fairy tale" of the Grimm Brothers and Hans Christian Andersen to a "modernized" "wonder tale."[8]

However, in characterizing the Grimm and Andersen stories as fully "historical . . . [and] having served for generations," Baum contorts the truth.[9] In fact, their works predated Baum's by no more than seventy years. In this way, Baum offers a falsely-narrativized, or fictional, genealogy which behooves his project. Plumbing the motivation behind this gap between the historical record of the fairy tale and the discursive construction thereof, Schacker asks: "What is at stake in Baum's framing of those relatively recent chapters in fairytale history as canonical but also old and out of date?"[10] She highlights the potential existence of political stakes in the rhetorical mobilization of categorizes such as the tradition and the modern, or modernized. I follow her lead in questioning the consequences of erasing Rodgers and Hammerstein's *Cinderella*—and the characterizations of female presence and wishing presented therein—as a worthy or fitting manifestation of the fairy-tale genre.

As Jennifer Nash reminds us, criticism is constantly engaged in re-making the boundaries of what is designated as appropriate engagement with a fundamental concept or text.[11] Promotion of, or adherence to, a "language of textual fidelity," in fact, performs a certain originalism, all the while obscuring the role of criticism in policing the applications of foundational conceptions.[12] In the name of "a mode evaluation and a practice of rescuing," this originalism "is also a practice of *forgetting*."[13] This forgetting functions as a practice of foreclosure which shuts down "the very thinking of what is possible" in life.[14] Though centered upon Kimberley Crenshaw's theory of intersectionality, Nash's warning also applies to assertions of the genre boundaries of the fairy tale.

The fairy tale historically functioned as an "authorless genre" which "invited free adaptation and retelling."[15] As with the category "woman," there is not an original incarnation of the fairy tale; rather, each fail to reference a stable "subject who stands 'before'" representation, or discursive formation.[16] As Butler notes, subsequent "performative invocation[s] of a nonhistorical 'before'" may often serve the political aims of the status quo.[17] Among the wide array of social scripts and cultural texts that produced *through* representation, fairy-tale representations function (if you care to glance askance) precisely as re-presentations, as unstable productions of alteration, translation, revision, and interpretation. Because of this, the lauding of only *certain* tales as exemplary, faithful, or traditional must ruffle our feathers and raise our suspicion. We must resist the erasure and over-writing that such originalist "forgetting" entails, instead interrogating the possibilities of the text at hand—especially those shut down by critical disavowal.

GOULD'S CRITIQUE: UPHOLDING A "TIMELESS" TRANSFORMATION

As cultural critics, reviewers possess immense power, "mediat[ing] the encoding and decoding" of meaning.[18] In this way, "Just as every rewriting of a tale is an interpretation, so every interpretation is a rewriting."[19] Embedded in and advancing Nash's politics of reading, the act of reviewing a cultural artifact may threaten to overwrite the artifact itself, and the meanings readily available to the general populace.

Following its debut, *New York Times* critic Jack Gould regarded the 1957 *Cinderella* as indisputably "wanting in some respects," with a striking lack of "that elusive quality of fragile spirit that makes a fairy tale universally loved."[20] In declaring what makes for the fairy tale's universal popularity, Gould both essentializes the genre and audience reception thereof. The fragility he presents as a genre requirement is further linked with a specific, scripted femininity, as seen in Gould's elaboration:

> Cinderella was lovely to look at, but that is not quite the same as sharing her enchanting transition from a drab and dirty kitchen maid to the radiant and mysterious princess of the ball [. . .] a young girl's magical transfer to happiness ever after.[21]

With Andrews's loveliness apparent throughout the film, Gould believes Rodger and Hammerstein to have "discarded the element of contrast," which he understands as "the whole point of make-believe in 'Cinderella.'"[22] "Make-believe," in Gould's conception, functions to wow with visualizable contrast, rather than impress with thought-provoking wonder. Gould cannot seem to image a purpose to the tale beyond a "drab and dirty kitchen maid" *becoming*—as distinct from *being*—an enchanting femme figure.

Gould's emphasis on visual aesthetics is further evidence by his reaction to the 1965 revival. Gould centralizes the material artistry of George Whittaker, particularly the white, fur-lined gown he crafted for Cinderella's ballroom debut.[23] In this "sumptuously mounted production," the sartorial was central in rendering Leslie Anne Warren's Cinderella "an enchanting vision as the peasant girl turned into a dream by her fairy godmother."[24] Gould praises the transmogrification of woman into something more, something *else*: Warren into vision, girl into dream. He limits "dream" to a teleological endpoint, one brought about by an outside force and through outward appearance; it is not the act of dreaming, with all its possibility. Intentional or not, Gould's discursive construction of the respective pitfalls and successes of 1957 and 1965 *Cinderella*s asserts and habituates certain norms which, in turn, discipline the genre and police possibility.

Gould fears for the "ageless durability of the fairy tale," wary of the consequences of widespread technological innovation.[25] His dis-ease betrays an attachment, which also runs at the societal level, to the nostalgic and purportedly essential, or timeless. "The warmth of ageless make-believe sometimes was submerged in the efficiency of the modern touch," he bemoans of the inaugural 1957 production.[26] In doing so, he offers another polemical contrast: that between the "ageless" and the "modern." However, what defines the modern—and what politics are involved in the establishment of such a definition? The politics of empire, for one.

The establishment of "contrastive pairs" such as the traditional and the modern abets understandings of "teleological plots" of progression which marks the moving away from an atavistic past or underdeveloped state and toward an enlightened, Western subjectivity.[27] Strictly linear conceptions of time, notes Bliss Cua Lim, serve "the temporal logic[s] of colonialism" and "contemporary capitalist governance"; such logics limit the terrain of imaginable futurities.[28] Here, Lim echoes Butler's concern for the role of habituated norms that may take in the (often violent) foreclosure of certain modes of living and their projected futures.[29] In this way, the policing of the categories of "tradition" and "modern" by cultural critics, as in the case of Rodgers and Hammerstein's *Cinderella*, functions to establish habituated dismissals of certain proffered socialities—dismissals often bound up in hegemonic temporal logics.[30] The critical dismissal of this *Cinderella* entails the deprioritization of the communal forging of desired futures and imagined horizons advanced by "zanies and fools."

Ironically, while Gould deemed the "modern" sensibility of the 1957 performance an impediment to its fairy-tale spirit, the historicized mid-century nature of this performance was later credited as part and parcel of its magic. As Andrews herself states, "I guess now it is almost a period piece, or . . . a beloved curiosity."[31] Ironically, what was then disparaged as being too "modern" (i.e., contemporary) rather than endearingly antiquated is now, from the standpoint of the twenty-first century, considered historical. This demonstrates the tenuousness of the categories upon which Gould founds his respective criticism and praise of the 1957 and 1965 productions, and disintegrates a particular set of aesthetic conventions from simple alignment with the category "modern." Such is an example of Rodgers and Hammerstein's *Cinderella* demanding a loosening of time and strict temporal affiliations, thereby advancing a queer temporality which destabilizes the known and the now.

Despite their rediscovery in the old office of the Rodgers and Hammerstein Organization in 1981, the "three reels of this 16-millimeter of [1957] *Cinderella*" were not returned to the home screen (PBS) or released on DVD until December 2004.[32] Due to this delay, the 1957 *Cinderella*, though materially extant and located, did not reappear for public consumption until the early twenty-first century. Moreover, in February of 2002, the presumed-discarded rehearsal tape from the Andrews broadcast was unearthed "in the CBS tape archive in Hollywood,"[33] further amplifying the twenty-first-century resurfacings of the 1957 production. Unviewed for forty-five years, this "primitive . . . artifact is a piece of entertainment history that had been given up for lost."[34] Through the lens of later decades, these tapes and their housed performances are read as "primitive" and yet unforeseen, belonging to both the past/passed *and* the very horizon of possibility. This dual temporal location, along with its latent existence and unanticipated rediscovery, queers and complicates the original midcentury timestamp of said production. This iterative reemergence of the 1957 performance also attests to the material defiance of the possible. The tapes survived, however unlikely, implausible, or impossible that may have appeared.

QUEER ACTS, POSSIBLE AND IMPROBABLE

Hope advances its own methodology.[35] Muñoz aligns hope, or critical utopianism, with queerness—which, though "We may never touch . . . we can feel . . . [as] the warm illumination of a horizon imbued with potentiality."[36] In the full, trans-temporal assemblage which is Rodgers and Hammerstein's *Cinderella*, this warm horizon of potentiality is expressed in the form of "the pale pink mists of a foolish dream."[37] With "Impossible"/"It's Possible" serving as a diegetic hinge which imagines, and thereby makes possible, the plot's subsequent actions, these numbers also function as an enactment of queerness, that "structuring and educated mode of desiring that allows us to see and feel beyond the quagmire of the present."[38] Notably, in this understanding, "desiring" moves *through and beyond* the foolish or idealistic to be an "educated" and critical avenue toward change. Muñoz continues: "we must dream and enact new and better pleasures, other ways of being in the world, and ultimately new worlds."[39] This invective, this demand, this urgency of "must" calls upon dreaming (and desiring) as both method and hermeneutic through which to envision and pursue imagined pleasures and socialites. In defending the transformative potential of the possible, the imagined, and the imaginable, *Cinderella* enacts and advocates what Muñoz deems a "queer utopian hermeneutic," in which the utopian is a critical construction birthed from and through the daydreams and "hopes of a collective, an emergent group, or even the solitary oddball who is the one who dreams for many."[40]

Cinderella and her Fairy Godmother constitute such a community of believers, their duo performing queerness in multiple ways. In her feminist genealogy of "Broadway Musical Theatre's Histories,"[41] Stacy Wolf positions "two women singing together in a duet, their voices intertwined and overlapping, their attention toward one another" as an intimate and queer act, a disruption within and of the common hetero-romantic focus of the genre.[42] In this way, Rodgers and Hammerstein's "Impossible"/"It's Possible" sequence both advances the queer potentiality of desiring, or wishing for, the seemingly impossible and does so through a queerly disruptive female duet. The following section takes up the 1957, 1965, 1997, and 2013 productions of *Cinderella* to plumb each incarnation's enactment of collaborative female wish-making, as well as varying degrees of agency on the part of the titular character.

Let us begin with the inaugural production of 1957. Herein, the initial appearance of Edie Adams's Godmother interrupts and interweaves with Cinderella's own harmonies. Cinderella's reprise of "In My Own Little Corner" transitions quickly into the bare beginning of dialogic wishing: "Oh, I wish, I wish . . ."[43] This, in turn, is interrupted by the Godmother's appearance and performance of the first stanza of "Impossible," which posits "all the wishes in all the world [as] poppycock and twaddle."[44] The Godmother then reprises Cinderella's own "In My Own Little Corner," singing, "I just knew I would find you in that same little chair, in the pale pink mist of a foolish dream."[45] Then just as quickly out as in, the Godmother returns to the melody and lyrics of "Impossible."

This dialogic interweaving, as well as the Godmother's taking-up of Cinderella's own melody, blurs the boundaries between their voices (and, arguably, personae) in what Wolf deems a queer relationality. What is more, this duo's first moment on screen together reaches both backward and forward, to previous or forthcoming full numbers. This positions their meeting, their unification, as on a temporal cusp, or horizon of possibility. Such is a site of queer temporality. What is more, the Godmother's singing is situated within and as a response to a conversational moment with Cinderella, presenting the two as engaged in communal forging of a relation, and rhetorical scene. In this way, Cinderella is, at the least, partially responsible for the production of possibility.

Andrews's Cinderella performs a sustained rhetorical unpacking of the power of wishing, and takes up an agentive role in envisioning the logistics of her transportation to the ball. As her stepmother and stepsisters flit off to the ball, the audience sees her gingerly approaching a large pumpkin in the yard, her contemplative glance pregnant with possibility.[46] From here, Andrews's Cinderella proceeds to imaginatively engineer all "the magical substitutions" that would be required for her to attend the ball, and "can almost be credited with turning her godmother, who comes calling in a conventional way, into a *fairy* godmother through the force of her wishing."[47] (This "turning" of her godmother is also applicable in the later 2013 production). In this way, we may understand Cinderella herself as conjuring, through craftiness and a critical utopianism, the trappings of the upcoming transformations.

Andrews's Cinderella beseeches of her Godmother:

> I am wishing. In the name of every young girl who ever wanted to go to a dance but was told that she couldn't, I wish that I may go to that dance tonight. I wish that by some kind of magic or abracadabra or folderol and fiddle-lee-dee that all the kind hearts of the world could put their heads together . . . that all the kind hearts and good souls would wish with me and that you Godmother would help me with every ounce of strength and cleverness that you possess.[48]

Whereas Gould upholds the notion of magical transfer ("*to* happiness ever after" as a teleological endpoint),[49] Cinderella offers magic as linked to the gerundial act of wishing. Magic (and its fellows, "abracadabra" and "folderol and fiddle-lee-dee," the latter of which runs through the upcoming number "Impossible") is thus a modality through which wishing may bring together "the kind hearts of the world" in a compounding, communal wish(ing). In other words, magic and wishing function as a queer critical utopianism. Hearts, heads, and souls merge; they are all and each appealed to in a rhetorical gesture put forward by Cinderella herself.

With tears welling, 1965's Cinderella welcomes the musical chimes and magical appearance of Celeste Holm's Fairy Godmother with a simpering, "Oh, how beautiful you are!"[50] Holm's Godmother replies: "I am made of all your most beautiful dreams and hopes and wishes."[51] In such a way, the story's introduction of literalized magic is linked immediately with feminine beauty, and audiences may be wary that only, seemingly, those desires deemed sufficiently beautiful may comprise this Fairy Godmother and the enchantments she shall enact. Nevertheless, by rendering the Fairy Godmother as "made *of*" (my emphasis) Cinderella's own "dreams and hopes and wishes," this Cinderella still offers us a queer union of its Godmother and Cinderella, through the key of desire.

The revised book for 1965 appears uninterested in proposing, if briefly and sardonically, that wishing may be only impossible "folderol." Instead, Holm's Godmother quickly presents herself as in the business of accomplishing the impossible. Throughout the sequence, the Fairy Godmother of 1965, strikingly more than her Cinderella, enacts the rhetorical unpacking of what is and is not possible; Cinderella merely follows her lead. Less agentive than her 1957 incarnation, Warren's 1965 Cinderella cautions us against the assumption that the passage of time inherently indicates increased "progressive" content. Instead, to uncover the full potential of cultural productions, we must often loop backward and revisit the past.

In 1997, and at the dawn of the twenty-first century, the Wonderful World of Disney, in tandem with executive producer Whitney Houston, brought a third iteration of Rodgers and Hammerstein's *Cinderella* to the television screen. When Houston's Fairy Godmother brandishes her swirls of magic, conjuring fires from ash, Brandy's Cinderella asks, "How'd you do that?" The response? "Practice."[52] In this way, 1997's Godmother renders magic practice, and praxis. This emphasis on the magical *act* continues as this Fairy Godmother bemoans those who "dream about doing something instead of really doing it."[53] Instead, she encourages, "Cinderella, if you want to get out of here, you're going to have to do it yourself. The music's in you, deep down in your soul."[54] The task, then, becomes about finding the "music" within—the magical hinges upon enactment; the sonic is united with self, and becomes a means toward liberation.

Houston's Godmother embodies a brash undeniability of the magical. As she belts out "Impossible," she whirls a skeptical Cinderella into a circling dance. In kinetic frenzy, their bodies are united in a twirling embrace; this dance between two women precedes and, ultimately, enables the later spectacle of Cinderella and the Prince at the ball. Enchantment thereby engenders socialities beyond the hetero-romantic, and the Godmother's remark that "Everything starts with a wish" functions to enfold all actualities ("Everything") into the purview of the magical.

Despite garnering over 60 million viewers on the evening of November 2, 1997, this iteration, like its predecessors, did not escape critical disparagement. Caryn James of the *New York Times* laments that "Some things"—including Rodgers and Hammerstein's *Cinderella*—"never change."[55] He continues: "In fairy tale terms, the musical was always a pumpkin that never turned into a glittering coach, despite large audiences," with the new version "often charming and sometimes ordinary," ultimately failing to "take that final leap into pure magic."[56] Here, we may locate echoes of Gould in James's privileging of the "pure" and fully transformed over that which may hover upon the horizon of possibility, oscillating between the known (ordinary) and the idealized (charming).

In certain ways, Rodgers and Hammerstein's *Cinderella* has embodied Broadway its whole life. Conceived by this singer-songwriter duo and originally headlining Andrews fresh with fame from *My Fair Lady*, *Cinderella* is easily misunderstood to have long been a Broadway production. However, despite global theater productions, *Cinderella* arrived late to the Broadway ball, taking up that esteemed cultural location only in 2013, with a new book by Douglas Carter Beane.

The evening of the ball, a disguised Fairy Godmother joins Cinderella outside her cottage, interrupting her fanciful reprise of "My Own Little Corner" with "folderol and fiddle-lee-dee."[57] As in 1957, the Godmother comes to rearticulate Cinderella's own reprise, taking up Cinderella's previous fantasies and joining her in an exercise of sonic wish-fulfillment.

Her voice takes up Cinderella's previous fantasies, joining her in an exercise of sonic wish-fulfillment. Like in 1957, the characters are tethered in a communal enactment (duet) of desire. The Godmother sings, "I just knew I would find you in that same little chair, in the pale pink mists of a foolish dream."[58] Having fallen into absence in the 1965 and 1997 productions, this quintessential Hammerstein line returns here, fifty-six years later, to both embody and engender queer temporal imaginings.

To Cinderella's contestation to the notion that she, Cinderella, "can change it all, could make it all happen," her Godmother responds, "You're right" and picks back up the refrain: "It's all so . . . Impossible!"[59] Cinderella's dialogic interjection (unique to the 2013 production) of "But you said . . ." is cut off by Marie's singing, by her apparent insistence on the *im*possible.[60] The next stanza has Cinderella come in with another qualification, this time triumphant: "But! The world is full of zanies and fools . . ."[61] The characters of Cinderella and her Fairy Godmother are thereby dialogically, lyrically tethered in this communal, gerundial *building* of a moment of magical affirmation.

When Cinderella admits foolishness, her Godmother's response—"Then let's be foolish together!"—indicates a queer sociality which privileges the communal and the so-called nonsensical, the alternative to normative value-systems ("And now I must make all the dreams *we joked about* come true," my emphasis).[62] "What shall we dream of?" functions as an invitation, an invocation of the enchanted and desired beyond and through notions of foolishness and limitation.[63] "We" pulls in the audience into this wish-making, as does her Godmother's later benediction: "In the name of every girl who ever wanted to change the world she lived in, go! With the promise of . . . possibility!"[64] The promise of possibility hereby functions as the queer horizon when rents open the terrain of the imaginable. Imagining is coupled with action ("Go!") here in a manner similar to the 1997 production, and is presented as a viable mode of effecting change in the world around you.

The resonances in content between the 1957 and 2013 productions carry over to critical discourses thereof. Through Ben Brantley's theater review, the *New York Times* of 2013 conceives of *Cinderella* in terms similar to Gould's nearly seventy years prior. Brantley introduces *Cinderella* as "that ultimate and most enduring of makeover shows," with its 2013 incarnation knotted up by the desire to be "both traditional and up to date . . . reassuringly old-fashioned and refreshingly irreverent . . . all at once."[65] In this way, Brantley, like Gould, centralizes transformation and appeals fervently to the comfortingly "traditional," though articulating no set parameters by which to define or identify that category. He does, however, speak to the driving tensions of desire the show manifests. In my reading, this emphasis on desire is a key component in *Cinderella*'s proffering of a queer critical imaginary, which takes us wishing as valuable action.

Whereas Brantley understands this 2013 *Cinderella* as not quite knowing what it wants to be, Nelson Pressley understands this revived production as, simply, "'Cinderella,' being what it wants to be."[66] Pressley continues on: "You can't say that 'Rodgers + Hammerstein's Cinderella' has finally been perfected; it has been altered so often that by now it's sort of a Frankenstein creation . . . Our dear 'Cinderella' changes and spins and changes again, and this version will do, handsomely. Its spirit is right."[67] Like Gould, Pressley appeals to the notion of the production's "spirit" in his evaluation of its merits; in this way, praise aside, he also fortifies a notion of the fairy tale's purported essence. But whereas Gould's appeal to transformation hinged upon an aesthetically differentiable Cinderella, Pressley regards the centrality of transformation to the production's history. For this 2015 reviewer, *Cinderella* the performance, rather than Cinderella the character, is teeming with transformative potential, changing and spinning and changing seemingly forevermore. It is this kaleidoscopic, Frankenstein nature which helps comprise the fairy spirit of *Cinderella* and contributes to its queer defiance of any singularized historical period.

In each iteration, as Cinderella and her Fairy Godmother's duet begins in earnest, the delineation between what is not possible ("Impossible") and what can *become* possible ("It's Possible") breaks down further. With "It's Possible" functioning as a reprise of "Impossible," the two are linked by melody, and share a stanza.[68] This stanza begins by challenging the preceding articulation that "folderol and fiddle-lee-dee" such as pumpkins turning to coaches and "plain country bumpkin[s]" wedding princes "is Impossible."[69] The linkage through "but" suggests that the existence of "zanies and fools" and their disavowal of so-called sensibility *matters*, in a manner which erodes the perceived truthfulness of those possibilities previously deemed *im*possible.[70] In fact, it is *"because* these daft and dewy-eyed dopes / Keep building up impossible hopes" that the "impossible" may transpire, and "everyday!"[71] These lyrics thereby further the production's commitment to defiant, communal, and gerundial wishing, or hoping.

Rather than transform such "zanies and fools" and "daft and dewy-eyed dopes" into a new model of rationality, with an updated or redefined set of "sensible rules," Rodgers and Hammerstein endorse the potential of nonsense itself.[72] In "failing" to subscribe to, or uphold, a standard model of rationality (and the related standard bifurcation of the im/possible), the duo advances a project of *troubling*. And as Butler has stated, "Perhaps trouble need not carry such a negative valence";[73] perhaps "trouble" is more critically and creatively generative than its sanitized, cohered opposite. Jack Halberstam positions failure as a queer art, with "unmaking, undoing, unbecoming, [and] not knowing" functioning, "under certain circumstances," to actually "offer more creative, more cooperative, more surprising ways of being in the world."[74] In this instance, we may regard even the rhetorical blurring—and musical merging—of the notions of *it's possible* and *impossible* as an intentional failure, or refusal, of the epistemologically discrete. This "undoing" and "not knowing" exist on the cusp of an epistemic horizon, defiantly imagining new methodologies and structures for possible presents and futures; as such, purported failure advances and is advanced by any dedication to a Muñoz-style queer critical hermeneutic. And not to forget the queer interventions of Wolf, we ought to note (and rejoice in) the fact that it is the female team of Cinderella and her Godmother that advocate this dismantling of hegemonic knowledge systems in defiant favor of the queerly wishful, wished, and wishing.

CONCLUSION

Rodgers and Hammerstein's *Cinderella*, a 1950s production, survives defiantly in the present, exceeding any presumed boundaries of the historical "artifact." Per Freeman, it is through critical attendance to "culture's throwaway artifact" (even those which may harbor "outmoded masculinities and femininities")[75] that history may be opened up to its fullest potential,[76] that past articulations of futurities may be revisited, mobilized, and manipulated, for present and future cause. De-historicized and critical disavowal of such artifact-assemblages as Rodgers and Hammerstein's *Cinderella* forecloses the very horizon of the imaginable.

The iterative reappearances of this *Cinderella* production evoke the temporality—replete with its queer lingering and longings—of the fairy tale itself. As Maria Nikolajeva notes, the iterative moves beyond including and encompassing the present to, "in fact, *eliminat[ing]* the actual, chronological sequence of time."[77] In this way, the continued rendering of past *as* present refutes a model of time in which one period cleanly supplants the last. Nikolajeva further argues that in the "idylls," or enchanted places, of children's literature "linear development rounds back into the circular pattern."[78] The queer temporalities that often mark the contained plots of the fairy tale here mark the material histories of *Cinderella* itself, bringing fairy-tale modalities into the quotidian. The queer time of fantasy, as such, is locatable within our lived realities and traceable through our affective and cultural archives. Rodgers and Hammerstein's *Cinderella* leads us in a whirling song and dance which prompts a delighted evaluation of the queer, critical affordances provided by the enchanted, the wished-for, and the "impossible." To continue this seventy-year project of proffering alternative modalities of living and knowing, we must peer beyond the typical hetero-romantic focus of this fairy tale, and swell the ranks of "zanies and fools."

NOTES

1. Cristina Bacchilega, "Forward," *Cinderella across Cultures: New Directions and Interdisciplinary Perspectives* (Wayne State University Press, 2016), xiii.
2. Jack Zipes, for one, cannot seem to fathom why Rodgers and Hammerstein's *Cinderella* is granted such an array of rebirths. He laments the class of Cinderella musicals which "create sweet and hollow entertainment" ("The Triumph of the Underdog: Cinderella's Legacy," *Cinderella across Cultures* [Wayne State University Press, 2016], 372). He posits Rodgers and Hammerstein's 1957 *Cinderella* as "a classic example of live-action trash" (Ibid.). With a plot "so artificial and contrived" and songs "so mushy and saccharine," Zipes questions "why such an adaptation has been reproduced" time and again (Ibid.). As Judith Butler notes, the life of a text may run amuck, defying authorial expectations and even original presentations—in large part as "the result of the changing context of its reception" (*Gender Trouble* [New York: Routledge, 1990], vii). In this way, one possible answer to Zipes's question is that the very criticism which has historically reacted to this *Cinderella* has functioned as the very fodder for its continued cultural relevance and re-genesis.
3. Elizabeth Freeman, *Time Binds: Queer Temporalities, Queer Histories* (Durham: Duke University Press, 2010), 13.
4. Ibid.
5. Jose Esteban Muñoz, *Cruising Utopia: The Then and There and Queer Futurity* (New York: NYU Press, 2009), 1.
6. Chance the Rapper, "Zanies and Fools," Released July 2019. Track 22 on *The Big Day*, self-released, audio recording.
7. Jennifer Schacker, "Long Ago and Far Away," *Teaching Fairy Tales* (Detroit: Wayne State University Press, 2019), 174.
8. Ibid., 176.
9. Ibid.
10. Ibid., 177.
11. Jennifer Nash, "Feminist Originalism: Intersectionality and the Politics of Reading." *Feminist Theory* 17, no. 1 (2016): 3.
12. Ibid., 5.
13. Ibid., 9.
14. Butler, *Gender Trouble*, viii.
15. "Introduction: Cinderella across Cultures," *Cinderella across Cultures: New Directions and Interdisciplinary Perspectives* (Detroit: Wayne State University Press, 2016), 5.
16. Butler, *Gender Trouble*, 4.
17. Ibid.
18. Pauline Greenhill and Jill Terry Rudy. "Introduction: Channeling Wonder: Fairy Tales, Television, and Intermediality," *Channeling Wonder: Fairy Tales on Television* (Detroit: Wayne State University Press), 13.
19. Maria Tatar, *Off with Their Heads! Fairy Tales and the Culture of Childhood* (Princeton: Princeton University Press, 1992), xxvi.
20. Jack Gould, "TV; Broadway: Rodgers-Hammerstein 'Cinderella' Offered." *New York Times,* 1 April 1957.
21. Ibid.
22. Ibid.

23. Jack Gould, "TV: 'Cinderella' in Sumptuous Revival: Costumes by Whittaker Make for Spectacle." *New York Times*, 23 February 1965.

24. Ibid.

25. Jack Gould, "Tedious Fairy Tale: Dancing 'Cinderella' Distorted to Meet Technical Requirements of TV." *New York Times*, 5 May 1957.

26. Gould, "TV: Broadway."

27. Martin Manalansan, *Global Divas: Filipino Gay Men in the Diaspora* (Durham: Duke University Press, 2003), 21.

28. Bliss Lim, *Translating Time: Cinema, the Fantastic, and Temporal Critique* (Durham: Duke University Press, 2009), 13.

29. Butler, *Gender Trouble*.

30. Flattened notions of prehistory and the glorification of certain historical periods may result in literalized violence. Cord J. Whittaker, along with fellow medievalists, has chronicled the perilous purposes to which white nationalists have put undifferentiated, de-historicized appeals to the Middle Ages. With vastly different stakes, these white nationalists are performing a similar rhetorical move as Baum in the preface to his "new" Oz tales: the manipulation of the historical record for self-serving effect. In this light, the alignment of a praiseworthy timelessness of the 1965 *Cinderella* with its "simpler, more medieval presentation" ought to give us pause (Patricia Sawin, "Things Walt Disney Didn't Tell Us [But at Which Rodgers and Hammerstein at least Hinted]: The 1965 Made-for-TV Musical of *Cinderella*," *Channeling Wonder: Fairy Tales on Television* [Detroit: Wayne State University Press, 2014], 108). With appeals to both the modern and the ageless capable of advancing imperialist or nationalist political aims, attachment to either category as a marker of *value* warrants suspicion and critical interrogation.

31. Robin Pogrebin, "Magical Find Excites TV Historians; 'Cinderella' Film Reflects An Emerging Medium." *New York Times*, 20 June 2002.

32. Jacqueline Cutler, "Reviving a 'Cinderella' That Charmed a Nation." *New York Times*, 4 December 2004.

33. Pogrebin, "Magical Find."

34. Ibid.

35. Muñoz, *Cruising Utopia*, 5.

36. Ibid., 1.

37. The Julie Andrews Archive, "Rodgers and Hammerstein's Cinderella (1957)." *YouTube*. 23 June 2019, https://www.youtube.com/watch?v=C1F4YhBOA14&t=96s.

38. Muñoz, *Cruising Utopia*, 1.

39. Ibid.

40. Ibid., 3.

41. Stacy Wolf, *Changed for Good: A Feminist History of the Broadway Musical* (Oxford: Oxford University Press, 2011), 9.

42. Ibid., 18.

43. The Julie Andrews Archive, "Rodgers and Hammerstein's Cinderella (1957)."

44. Ibid.

45. Ibid.

46. Ibid.

47. Sawin, "Things Walt Disney Didn't Tell Us," 115.

48. The Julie Andrews Archive, "Rodgers and Hammerstein's Cinderella (1957)."

49. Gould, "TV: Broadway."

50. Bart, "Impossible/It's Possible."

51. Ibid.

52. Special_Effect, "Rodgers and Hammerstein's Cinderella (1997 Film)."

53. Ibid.

54. Ibid.

55. James, "The Glass Slipper Fits."

56. Ibid.

57. Original Broadway Cast Recording, "'In My Own Little Corner' (Reprise)."

58. Ibid.

59. Original Broadway Cast Recording, "Impossible."
60. Ibid.
61. Ibid.
62. Sophia BP, "RODGERS AND HAMMERSTEIN'S CINDERELLA (Broadway)—Medley [LIVE @ The 2013 Tony Awards]."
63. Ibid.
64. Ibid., – 'Impossible' [LIVE @ CBSS Thanksgiving Parade]."
65. Brantley, "Gowns."
66. Pressley, "Cinderella."
67. Ibid.
68. The Julie Andrews Archive, "Rodgers and Hammerstein's Cinderella (1957)."
69. The Julie Andrews Archive, "Rodgers and Hammerstein's Cinderella (1957)."
70. Ibid.
71. Ibid.
72. Ibid.
73. Butler, xxiv.
74. Jack Halberstam, *The Queer Art of Failure* (Durham: Duke University Press, 2011), 2.
75. Freeman, *Time Binds*, xxiii.
76. Ibid., xxi.
77. Maria Nikolajeva, *From Mythic to Linear: Time in Children's Literature* (Lanham: Scarecrow Press, Inc., 2000), 9.
78. Ibid., 33.

BIBLIOGRAPHY

Bacchilega, Cristina. "Forward." In *Cinderella across Cultures: New Directions and Interdisciplinary Perspectives*, edited by Martine Hennard Dutheil de la Rochère, Gillian Lathey, and Monika Woźniak, xi–xiv. Detroit: Wayne State University Press, 2016.
Bart, Blair, II. "Impossible/It's Possible Lesley Ann Warren." YouTube. Video, https://www.youtube.com/watch?v=vDnTajjIL54&t=328s.
Brantley, Ben. "Gowns from the House of Sincere and Snark." *New York Times*, Mar. 3, 2013.
Butler, Judith. *Gender Trouble: Feminism and the Subversion of Identity*. New York: Routledge, 1990.
Caryn, James. "The Glass Slipper Fits with a 90's Conscience." *New York Times*, Oct. 31, 1997.
Chance the Rapper. "Zanies and Fools." Released July 2019. Track 22 on *The Big Day*, self-released, audio recording.
Cutler, Jacqueline. "Reviving a 'Cinderella' That Charmed a Nation." *New York Times*, Dec. 4, 2004.
Freeman, Elizabeth. *Time Binds: Queer Temporalities, Queer Histories*. Durham: Duke University Press, 2010.
Gould, Jack. "Tedious Fairy Tale: Dancing 'Cinderella' Distorted to Meet Technical Requirements of TV." *New York Times,* May 5, 1957.
———. "TV; Broadway: Rodgers-Hammerstein 'Cinderella' Offered." *New York Times,* Apr. 1, 1957.
———. "TV: 'Cinderella' in Sumptuous Revival: Costumes by Whittaker Make for Spectacle." *New York Times*, Feb. 23, 1965.
Greenhill, Pauline and Jill Terry Rudy. "Introduction; Channeling Wonder: Fairy Tales, Television, and Intermediality." In *Channeling Wonder: Fairy Tales on Television*, edited by Pauline Greenhill and Jill Terry Rudy, 1–21. Detroit: Wayne State University Press, 2014.
Halberstam, Jack. *The Queer Art of Failure*. Durham: Duke University Press, 2011.
"Introduction: Cinderella across Cultures." In *Cinderella across Cultures: New Directions and Interdisciplinary Perspectives*, edited by Martine Hennard Dutheil de la Rochère, Gillian Lathey, and Monika Woźniak, 1–24. Detroit: Wayne State University Press, 2016.

Joosen, Vanessa. *Critical and Creative Perspectives of Fairy Tales: An Intertextual Dialogue between Fairy-Tale Scholarship and Postmodern Retellings*. Detroit: Wayne State University Press, 2011.

The Julie Andrews Archive. "Rodgers and Hammerstein's Cinderella (1957)—Julie Andrews, Jon Cypher, Edie Adams." YouTube. June 23, 2019. Video, https://www.youtube.com/watch?v=C1F4YhBOA14&t=96s.

Lim, Bliss Cua. *Translating Time: Cinema, the Fantastic, and Temporal Critique*. Durham: Duke University Press, 2009.

Manalansan, Martin F., IV. *Global Divas: Filipino Gay Men in the Diaspora*. Durham: Duke University Press, 2003.

Muñoz, Jose Esteban. *Cruising Utopia: The Then and There and Queer Futurity*. New York: NYU Press, 2009.

Nash, Jennifer. "Feminist Originalism: Intersectionality and the Politics of Reading." *Feminist Theory* 17, no. 1 (2016): 3–20.

Nikolajeva, Maria. *From Mythic to Linear: Time in Children's Literature*. Lanham: Scarecrow Press, Inc., 2000.

Original Broadway Cast Recording. "Impossible." Track 7 on *Rodgers + Hammerstein's Cinderella*, Ghostlight Records, audio recording.

Original Broadway Cast Recording. "'In My Own Little Corner' (Reprise)." Released May 2013. Track 6 on *Rodgers + Hammerstein's Cinderella*, Ghostlight Records, audio recording.

Pogrebin, Robin. "Magical Find Excites TV Historians; 'Cinderella' Film Reflects an Emerging Medium." *New York Times*, June 20, 2002.

Pressley, Nelson. "'Cinderella,' Being What It Wants to Be." *Washington Post*, Nov. 19, 2015.

Sawin, Patricia. "Things Walt Disney Didn't Tell Us (But at Which Rodgers and Hammerstein at least Hinted): The 1965 Made-for-TV Musical of *Cinderella*." In *Channeling Wonder: Fairy Tales on Television*, edited by Pauline Greenhill and Jill Terry Rudy, 103–124. Detroit: Wayne State University Press, 2014.

Schacker, Jennifer. "Long Ago and Far Away: Historicizing Fairy-Tale Discourse." In *Teaching Fairy Tales*, edited by Nancy L. Canepa, 174–179. Detroit: Wayne State University Press, 2019.

Sophia BP. "RODGERS AND HAMMERSTEIN'S CINDERELLA (Broadway)—Medley [LIVE @ The 2013 Tony Awards]." YouTube. June 11, 2013. Video, https://www.youtube.com/watch?v=hcP1cV3nBZI.

———. "RODGERS + HAMMERSTEIN'S CINDERELLA (Broadway)—'Impossible' [LIVE @ CBSS Thanksgiving Parade]." YouTube. Dec. 1, 2013. Video, https://www.youtube.com/watch?v=w-lEAHwCaS4&list=RDw-lEAHwCaS4&start_radio=1.

Tartar, Maria. *Off with Their Heads!: Fairy Tales and the Culture of Childhood*. Princeton: Princeton University Press, 1992.

Wolf, Stacy. *Changed for Good: A Feminist History of the Broadway Musical*. Oxford: Oxford University Press, 2011.

Zipes, Jack. "The Triumph of the Underdog: Cinderella's Legacy." *Cinderella across Cultures: New Directions and Interdisciplinary Perspectives*, edited by Martine Hennard Dutheil de la Rochère, Gillian Lathey, and Monika Woźniak, 358–401. Detroit: Wayne State University Press, 2016.

II

(Re)Production: A Classic Tale Told Anew

Chapter Five

Queen of the Ashes

Daenerys Targaryen, Cinderella of the Apocalypse, and Her Mirror Prince in Game of Thrones

Loraine Haywood

The "Cinderella" fairy tale, like "Sleeping Beauty" and "Snow White," "enumerates experiences which pertain only to the female; she must undergo them all before she reaches the summit of femininity."[1] In the HBO television series *Game of Thrones*, Daenerys Targaryen is given a gown by her brother, Viserys, to meet a rugged style of Prince. In the game of thrones, her brother exchanges her body for an army to take back the crown of the seven kingdoms of Westeros for himself. Daenerys's life is intertwined with magic and sibling rivalry, and overshadowed by oedipal concerns. The many variations of the "Cinderella" fairy tale involve these themes in varying degrees, but the concern of the narrative involves her transformation. Cinderella rises from the ashes and transcends her degraded state.[2] Dany imitates this as a dark rise from the ashes of her husband's funeral pyre with three dragons—the magical power behind her conquest.

In the final episodes, at the pinnacle of Dany's phoenix-like rise to power, these fairy-tale motifs collide and unravel the magic spell that *Game of Thrones* had over viewers. As the castrated woman, the elusive happy ending in true Cinderella style does not materialize. The narrative does not allow her character to reconcile the oedipal conflict within her; there is no growth but instead regression. Becoming the dragon, she descends once again into the ashes from which her conquest was born. She has never been freed from her enchantment with the Iron Throne.[3] As her counterpart, Cinderella, The Prince who was Promised (Jon/Aegon), tries to metaphorically make the slipper fit—make her fit for the kingdom. But like the warnings of Cinderella's fairy godmother, Dany has forgotten her own cautionary tale in the oedipal struggle against the curse of becoming her father; like Cinderella at midnight, the bells have rung, and the spell is broken.

Game of Thrones acquires an uncanniness to fairy tale in its "separation from a familiar world,"[4] and its familiar content: magic, mythical beasts, "murder, mutilation, cannibalism, infanticide . . . incest."[5] The unfamiliar/familiar fantasy medieval setting tells a twenty-first-century version of "Cinderella" through Daenerys Targaryen. The dissatisfaction that some find in her ending demonstrates the lack of reward in the heroine's struggle. Dany aligns with Cinderella in the ideological belief that she "is worthy at the end to be exalted."[6] But the fairy tale loops back on itself and another Cinderella (Jon Snow) rivals her claim. Dany rises from the ashes only to be reclaimed by them as Queen. In this sense there is a return to the fairy-tale motifs of the inert beautiful woman in her death,[7] thus restoring "the patriarchal and puritanical code,"[8] not through marriage but by her castration.

Game of Thrones highlights the twenty-first-century obsession with apocalyptic destruction and its "trauma culture" seen in the devastation of King's Landing,[9] and its depiction that is reminiscent of 9/11. This culminates in the "Cinderella" fairy tale of Dany and her Prince at the ball and the dance with death where "viewers are captivated by the sublime image."[10] This is the spirit of the age and its obsession with the repetition of trauma. In Dany's death is a psychoanalytical engagement with the sublime at the summit of her femininity as post-mortem subject.

INTRODUCTION

Daenerys Targaryen is some type of Cinderella girl: an apocalyptic Queen for the twenty-first century. In the classic tales of "Cinderella," the formula is a transformation from ashes to throne as she marries the Prince and will become Queen over a utopian kingdom. This ideological utopia is achieved through the overcoming of obstacles to her exaltation as she conforms to the patriarchal mirror of her sublime body as object. This crescendo of exaltation is a pivotal moment in *Game of Thrones* in the death of Daenerys Targaryen. As Queen of the ashes, metaphorically the shoe does not fit: she is not fit for the kingdom. Jon Snow as her mirror Prince is the patriarchal voice of judgment and she dies conforming to the mirror image of his death at Castle Black. He is the prophesised traitor. Dany and Jon are trapped in the fate of the mirroring of their "Cinderella" story worlds. Their clash of ideologies results in the breaking of the magic spell over the kingdom, the belief in the notion that a Cinderella will arrive to fit the Western utopian dream.

Game of Thrones hosts ideological/moral contests (or conquests) for who could best fit the kingdom, subsuming believers (viewers) into the mirror of

Western democratic fairy tales. Film uses the sublime image much like the staged fascination with the beauty of Cinderella at the ball, her transformation from cinders and ashes to worthy bride. Taken to its zenith, as a work of art, film can become a pop culture phenomenon: *Game of Thrones* is one of these. Undoubtedly, two characters in this HBO series involve "Cinderella" narratives as a contest for who will fit the mold: Daenerys Targaryen or Jon Snow. The disappointment of viewers in the failure of either character to fulfill the rags-to-riches narrative is because "Cinderella" is a "loose trope" that has been applied as a prosthetic cultural support.[11] This engages with the capitalist dream entangled with the puritan logic that utopia exists in our current context. This is evidenced in Dany's ideological statements that she is building a better world, her vision of a utopian future. But the failure of Dany's utopian future, her Cinderella rise, is mirrored in the failure of Western democracy as utopia and the inherited madness seen in images of apocalyptic destruction, real and imagined.

Dany, as Queen of the Ashes, is subsumed into a twenty-first-century "Cinderella" narrative of apocalyptic destruction. The viewer is subsumed into her ideology of a fairy-tale reign as a benevolent ruler which did not eventuate. Her performance of violence in the destruction of King's Landing is a return to the ashes of the funeral pyre. Her death scene is the violence of fairy tale at its purest. Jack Zipes says that films that use fairy tale evoke an "imaginative gaze" with a perverse core.[12] Dany's "Cinderella moment" is to be trapped in another fairy tale where the gaze of patriarchy is a conjoining with the mirror Prince in a macabre dance of death.[13]

Game of Thrones involves the twenty-first-century fascination for images, an "enchanted screen" in the mirror world of sublime images and the castrated subject moving against fate and apocalypse.[14] To analyze the phenomenon of *Game of Thrones*, I am drawing on the critical work by Jack Zipes, Maria Tatar, and Armando Maggi on fairy tale and film. Although Bruno Bettelheim is a controversial choice, his work is an important contribution to the analysis of fairy tale and its psychoanalytic elements. In critical theory in film, ideology, and culture, Slavoj Žižek and E. Ann Kaplan are an essential lens with which to understand the filmic medium in the twenty-first century.

QUEEN OF THE ASHES, THE THRONE ROOM, AND THE END OF THE GAME OF THRONES

Willing herself into a fairy tale,[15] Daenerys Targaryen sits by the fire on Dragonstone on the eve of her destruction of King's Landing.[16] In her fairy-tale return to Westeros she is overcome by a tragic fate. She tells her tale of a broken heart as a clash between East and West in a comparative text with the concerns of the twenty-first century. East and West are political twins in a type of sibling rivalry for who best fits the geo-kingdom. Dany's rival Cinderella Jon Snow is a Western Messiah, with a covert identity—the Prince who was promised. He is loved, and she is the invader from the East. They typify and embody political dichotomies in twenty-first-century concerns of power struggles and the performance of violence to achieve that dominance. The framing of Dany's conquest and her attack on King's Landing is as a terrorist incursion rising from the East against the West causing an apocalyptic vision. Dany's coming to Westeros is "the dystopic tales . . . the cultural dichotomies of the barbarian and civilization."[17] Allen Feldman considers the "Civilization/Barbarian dichotomy . . . was closely followed by the wedding of history to patriarchal law" and the "gendered movement from feminized bereavement and social empathy to the masculine hierarchy of the lawgiver versus the lawbreaker, and the executioner versus the punished."[18] Dany as Queen does more than make the East-West contest analogy; it creates a feminized Other that promotes exceptionalism and the right to punish as masculine.

In the eerie desolation of the ruins of the Throne Room in King's Landing, both ash and snow fall as Daenerys Targaryen reaches out and touches the Iron Throne.[19] This fairy-tale moment echoes the enchantment held by the spinning wheel in the tale of "Sleeping Beauty." Jon/Aegon emerges from the same dark void following his Cinderella. As her mirror he descends the stairs looking like the Huntsman from "Snow White" and he does not disappoint. In the devastation of the Throne Room Jon confronts Dany with the horror of her actions, he says, "Have you been down there? There are children, little children burnt."[20] The utopian dream has turned to ashes and one of oppressive rule where she will decide "what is good."[21] Dany's actions do not mirror Jon's striving for a "better world than the shit one they have always known."[22]

Jon, who had been content to be the Queen's mirror and who would not accept the throne, is suddenly a woke Cinderella transformed into Aegon, the Prince who was Promised. In some sense of the enigma of this prophecy, their embrace traps them in the mirror; are they the Prince and Princess who were promised? The prophetic mirror is further emphasized when Jon embraces Dany. In the background is the circle of an empty window frame blasted by dragon fire. The Throne Room becomes synonymous with the ballroom where Dany and Jon are locked in a Disney-style romantic embrace, and true love's kiss is transformed into the sublime in the dance of death. Jon holds her close to his body and plunges the dagger into her heart. In the death embrace he lowers her to the ground while weeping.

This scene, like Dany's visions in the House of the Undying in season 2,[23] reveals her at "the summit of her femininity" as Cinderella.[24] In the beauty of her dead body,[25] she joins other fairy-tale mortified sublime bodies in "Snow White" and "Sleeping Beauty." Taken up by Drogon into the clouds, she passes into another realm, beyond the wall of language,[26] to the Real of death, or fairy-tale resurrection?

The Iron Throne, as enchanted object, is destroyed by Drogon (some viewers tried to find a reason this would happen, and fairy-tale enchantment is the answer). Viewers are left to grasp some sort of poetic plane in the ethereal image of a romantic transcendence as Drogon flies away with her body through the clouds. Dany's fairy-tale rise as Cinderella has ended and Jon/Aegon is banished in the return/rejection of the rightful King, to the Night's Watch where the outcasts of society perform a life-long penance for their crimes. Jon returns to his degraded state as outcast dressed in animal clothes, as a crow. Like Dany, Jon's Cinderella rise ends with her death. His transformation into Cinderella, the rightful King of the Seven Kingdoms, happens as Aegon and his banishment defy the viewer's wish of a fairy-tale resolution. Jon fulfils his Night's Watch vow as the sword in the darkness, and he fulfills the prophecy of the Prince who was promised by bringing the dawn (of a new age). Jon's Cinderella rise ends and disrupts fairy-tale endings by becoming a fall, back to the black, back to where he was killed and resurrected. He becomes the thing he despised: a traitor and a Queen-slayer. Following the journey of Messiahs and heroes, he journeys into the wilderness, beyond the wall into the land of dead things.

CINDERELLA AND HER MIRROR PRINCE: DANY AND JON

Bound by fate throughout the series, Dany and Jon have parallel lives that clearly involve the narratives, themes, motifs, types, and character building of "Cinderella." Both of their stories involve the mother who dies in childbirth that exposes them to oedipal concerns and sibling rivalry. The gown given to Dany by her brother is the "Cinderella" narrative of the female body that is displayed for attraction and male pleasure.[27] She is a commodity of exchange within the patriarchal order in the game of thrones, as Viserys wants an army in exchange for her marriage to Karl Drogo. Dany is also joined by a fairy-tale dwarf or imp,[28] an intelligent spinner like Rumpelstiltskin, "half benevolent and half harmful,"[29] and an underworld creature/advisor like one of the Seven Dwarfs.

In *Game of Thrones* the rival Cinderella is the Prince who was promised, Aegon Targaryen/Jon Snow. His story overlays with Biblical stories of Jesus as the immaculately conceived secret Son of God and the Virgin Mary, a Saviour who was promised, raised from the dead, or the dragon-slayer from the *Book of Revelation*.[30] As in Grimm's "Cinderella," Jon Snow's mother dies and he is brought up by a stepmother, Lady Catelyn Stark, who is really his aunt. Without the secret knowledge of his birth she hates him, playing the role of the jealous Queen, as she is told he is the illegitimate offspring of her husband, Ned Stark. Jon follows the "Cinderella" motifs of despised and displaced sibling who is transformed. He proves his worthiness in a journey of transcendence from a degraded state to become respected then despised in the Night's Watch. Jon is killed and resurrected sharing in magical transformation at the hands of a witch. Dany shares some of these motifs, but her magical ability to be the unburnt concerns the transformation of her body into the sublime body of Cinderella. She is often seen in images of cinders, ash, and fire in the literality of the "Cinderella" tale.

Dany is both associated with and exceeds the motifs and themes of the "Cinderella" fairy tale. In a parody of "Cinderella," she is magically bound to fire and the ashes. Dany magically rises from the ashes of her husband's funeral pyre with three dragons, earning her the title "mother of dragons."[31] In the temple of the Dosh Khaleen, she burns the Khals.[32] From their ashes and the destruction, she emerges, walking through fire and blood. In both scenes her body is magically transformed into a sublime body that resists burning and death. Throughout the series she demonstrates these magical abilities and shares nonhuman traits with her dragons.

Daenerys Targaryen's and Jon Snow's journeys mirror the "Cinderella" fairy tale without the fairy-tale ending. Throughout *Game of Thrones* Dany outmaneuvers sibling rivalry and has a sense of home that is tied to an enchantment with the Iron Throne and the specter of her father, Mad King Aerys II. After her father's assassination she is born on Dragonstone, where her mother dies in childbirth. Dany considers King's Landing as her birthright. Home and throne become synonymous with her drive to return to Westeros and take back what was stolen from her. Finding out that Jon is Aegon Targaryen does not diminish her right to rule in her eyes. He has a better claim, but she wants him to remain a ragged Cinderella. Jon would just remain her mirror Prince with her as Queen. The Cinderella contest between them in the revelation of Jon's birth causes a political rift. This contest ends with neither of them winning the throne or being exalted in any way.

Dany and Jon mirror Cinderella throughout the series. Their lives become so entangled it becomes uncanny. Dany is the image of the mother and life, while Jon is the twin of death seen in his battle scenes or death images—including himself as a return of the dead. They share an uncanny predilection with the portrayal of the gods of the ancient Greeks,[33] and they refuse to die or are resurrected. Theirs is a contest seen in life and death struggles for who will best fit the kingdom or outlive the other to take the throne.

As in the Brothers Grimm fairy tales that have moralistic religious themes, there is also a religious element: the prophecy of the Prince who was promised to bring the dawn. This augments the Cinderella contest through religious tales spun by practitioners who try to fulfill the prophecy with a Prince or Princess who was promised. This enigmatic prophecy weaves a magic spell over viewers who speculate upon, and are divided on, the identity of the Cinderella character.

THE BELLS: CINDERELLA OF THE APOCALYPSE, RECLAIMED BY THE ASHES OF TWENTY-FIRST-CENTURY FAIRY TALE

Dany has forgotten her own cautionary tale in the oedipal struggle against the curse of becoming like her father; like Cinderella at midnight, the bells ring,[34] and the spell is broken. King's Landing has been destroyed in the name of the father. In psychological terms it is the return of the repressed in human consciousness. This is the end of formulas that mirror the parables in fairy-tale endings and the satisfaction in the hero or heroine in that "victory is not over others but only over oneself."[35] In *Game of Thrones* there is no victory for Dany over the self. She exceeds her father, which is visually overlayed in dragon fire and wildfire igniting in the city. Dany's oedipal turn becomes inevitable as she returns to King's Landing and her inheritance where she is reclaimed by madness. Dany is locked in an oedipal failure to metaphorically kill the father within her. The ending of *Game of Thrones* engages with the primal father—the dead father as stronger, more powerful.[36] Thus, the ending that promised a Cinderella parable "from abuse and poverty to happiness and nobility,"[37] a rags-to-riches story of the heroine's reward turns to a psychological engagement with hysteria, terrorism, trauma, and the Real.

Psychoanalytically, the adaptation of the "Cinderella" tale that features Dany as Queen of the Ashes frames the continuing embedded trauma of 9/11 in film. Dany's vision for continuing conquest that will burn cities to the ground is reminiscent of the war on terror. However, the images of annihilation and destruction were particularly focused in the final episodes of *Game of Thrones*, as measured and mimetic representations of the 9/11 event and the consequent desire for the expansion of Empire. The episode "The Bells' offers the viewer something of a fairy-tale adaptation of 9/11. Zipes maintains that "literature and art cannot be fully understood without considering the socio-political-cultural context."[38] It is in the context of the 9/11 event that the episode becomes strangely familiar. Zipes considers that the uncanny "plays a significant role in the act of reading, hearing or viewing a fairy tale. . . . it separates the reader from the restrictions of reality from the onset and makes the repressed unfamiliar familiar once again."[39] The scenes in "The Bells" involve familiar images of 9/11 with fairy-tale elements. Dany flies her dragon over King's Landing, toward the Red Keep, as their shadow appears on the buildings below. The dragon fire explodes the buildings, rather than planes. Cersei and Jamie Lannister die in the rubble at the bottom of the destroyed towers when it collapses. The appearance of Arya Stark evokes well-known images of the event thus looping into twenty-first-century real and imagined tales of apocalypse.

Game of Thrones takes these twenty-first-century elements and portrays them through a medieval lens, in resolutions that engage with the fairy tale. Bran exemplifies the new technological fairy tale as a means of "socialisation of boys and girls [that] has shifted from the family to mass media."[40] This shift is mirrored in Bran as virtual King of the six kingdoms. He is an internet (Weirwood net) King who lives through the tree found in original *Cinderella* tales from long ago.[41] All interaction and warfare are now virtual (magic) as Bran returns to the tree to *see*. The new order or dawn in Bran's reign is the age of instantaneous, interactive history in the compression of time and space. Bran is a castrated traveller, a male Snow White, his inert body on display as King in a corpse chair. *Game of Thrones* mixes "Cinderella" gender roles and stereotypes, and like fairy tale does not question the role of the patriarchy in establishing order with the imp and Bran ruling the six kingdoms.

Viewers reacted to this ending of *Game of Thrones* in its lack of reward for the hero/heroine; because it was told within an accepted tradition in the violence of fairy tale, its magic motifs led to the logical expectation that it should end happily—for someone. The series transforms the "Cinderella" tale by transgressing the boundaries enforced by patriarchal and puritanical codes but then it restored them through female hysteria.[42] Cinderella's oedipal concerns and sibling rivalry are struggles against injustice and restoration that accept marriage to the Prince as a resolution. But the ending of *Game of Thrones* castrates the Cinderellas and the "Cinderella" narrative text that has, at a fundamental level, an expectation of growth. Dany and Jon represent the relationships of power in the twenty-first century in the sibling rivalry of East and West that polarizes the world. They are the twin realities of the geopolitical dance for dominance. They cannot share the Cinderella crown, but are instead entangled in a mirrored destiny. Jon understands that to be King is a hollow crown, because death is the void at its center,[43] while Dany believes she can fill this void.

Throughout the HBO series *Game of Thrones*, the journey with Dany in the Cinderella motif contains an ideological twist as the viewer is subsumed into her thralldom and power. *Game of Thrones* has revealed that twenty-first-century engagements with fairy tale exemplify the state of a deluded Western consciousness. In Western society the "Cinderella" fairy tale engages with the rags to riches dream of the masses as an ideology. This sustains the dream that the leader, particularly in Western democracies, strives for human equality and justice. Slavoj Žižek claims that "An ideology really succeeds when even the facts which at first sight contradict it start to function as arguments in its favour."[44] This paradox is at the heart of the rise of Dany in the mind of viewers. Her brutality and conquest are framed and elevated to the status of the dawn of a new age. Dany becomes the "Cinderella" story as a sacred text in the good benevolent ruler even though she is violent and brutal.

In the context of twenty-first-century filmic representations of "Cinderella," Armando Maggi considers that films involving millennial Cinderella such as *Maid in Manhattan*[45] or the *Princess Diaries*[46] treat the "Cinderella" text as sacred.[47] This involves a tripartite confluence between the literary Perrault/Grimm tales and Disney animated films installed as a type of "correct" version because of "the increasing globalization of our culture,"[48] its selling of democracy's utopian vision, and Westernization's prosperity narrative. "Cinderella" is therefore referenced as a type, within "formulaic narratives [that] resist their inevitable transformation."[49] Within this climate of the sacrosanct "Cinderella" story, *Game of Thrones* emerges as an avenue of resistance to formulas and narrative sacredness. This is like the folktale itself constantly evolving "the basic motif of the 'Cinderella' story (from rags to riches) may in fact take up radically different meanings according to the tale in which it appears."[50] *Game of Thrones* confronts the viewer with non-moralistic codes of understanding its world that challenge the superficial Western literary and Biblical traditions adopted in cultural, social, and political life. This makes it popular. But the spell of cultural pacification and investment in, and anticipation of, fairy-tale endings are ingrained in the ideologies and dreams of the West as Utopia. Viewers are disappointed and outraged when their hoped-for Cinderella within the fairy tale loops back on itself. Dany defeats Cersei, then she is reclaimed by the ashes, madness, and her mirror.

THE QUEEN'S MIRROR: PATRIARCHAL VOICE AND MADNESS

To understand the fairy tale's place in Western or globalized consciousness and the patriarchal grip over viewer expectation, it should be understood that "Cinderella," "Snow White," and "Sleeping Beauty" are all about the rise of the feminine within the confines of the mirror, coffin, or palace/place of domesticity. The world of women is bound up with feminine beauty, which is the "Cinderella" tale at its purist: adorned to catch a Prince in a mutual gaze. But the female is confined within the symbolic order of patriarchal rules and trapped in its gaze where "the feminist voice is silenced."[51] Zipes raises questions of Cinderella girls in systems that "lay traps for her in any game situation."[52] *Game of Thrones* has fairy-tale traps for Cinderella similar to the characters and situation in Disney's *Snow White and the Seven Dwarfs.*[53] The triad of older Queen, younger more beautiful rival, and a male mirror. This sets the rules of a contest for the throne and exultation in the kingdom. In *Game of Thrones* this triad is evidenced in Queen Cersei, Queen Daenerys, and her mirror Prince, Jon.

Game of Thrones plays with this triadic struggle. Cersei is told by a Witch, Maggy the Frog, that she will be Queen, and all her children will die.[54] Then comes the echo of the magic mirror: "but then comes another, younger, more beautiful, to cast you down and take all that you hold dear."[55] Cersei as "Wicked Queen" drives Tommen to suicide and she takes the crown. Her struggle with Daenerys is in the tradition of a fairy tale in a "female oedipal struggle."[56] However, this struggle is presided over by "the rules of the game,"[57] as reflected by Jon Snow's "patriarchal and puritanical code" that flows from honorable men that he admires and respects.[58]

Jon as mirror holds the phallus (symbolic power) and engages in symbolic communication and symbolic exchange as the empty gesture.[59] Jon continually makes empty declarations to Dany, calling her his Queen and giving reassurances of his loyalty. Dany has glimpsed and seen in Jon, her mirror Prince, her ideological self-image. He is the benevolent, good, and just ruler that she longed to be. But she cannot have an identity outside the mirror's gaze. She is overtaken by the same concerns as Cinderella in the ashes of the hearth; in the shadow of her father's rule, that is in the shadow of madness, and caught in the patriarchal mirror of Jon Snow.

This exchange is clearly demonstrated in Disney's *Snow White and the Seven Dwarfs*. The patriarchal voice resides in the mirror as an internalization of the King's rules, that causes madness for the Queen.[60] Jon's image as rightful King and citizen of Westeros, who has the respect of his soldiers and is admired for being a good ruler, competes with Dany's image of herself. The impact of his world is the reflection that crashes through her ambition and her need to be ruler of the Seven Kingdoms of Westeros. This breaking through from the imaginary world to the Real is similar to the fable "Fauna of Mirrors," where invaders, who are trapped behind mirrors, break through into the physical world which then erupts in violence.[61] In the ruins of the Throne Room in King's Landing, Jon steps through the mirror, suggested by the dark void he traverses walking down the stairs toward Dany. As her Cinderella reflection he kills her just as he had been killed; with a dagger to the heart, and betrayed. He partners her in the performance of the ideological dance, chosen by the spinning of the patriarchal voice (Tyrion—spinner and the father slayer) as unfit for the kingdom. Only marriage to death guarantees a place in the kingdom as postmortem subject. Dany's marriage to death with the mirror Prince makes her his dead reflection (he is a walking dead). In the horror of her death she emulates marriage to heroes in Greek tragedy and myths in the conflation of marriage and funeral rites such as Polyxena slaughtered on the grave of Achilles. Eric Neuman describes the bride dedicated to death as "the profound experience of the feminine, the marriage of doom recounted in innumerable myths and tales . . . [in] sacrifice[d] to a monster, dragon, wizard or evil spirit."[62]

Dany's death at King's Landing, as the mirror image of Jon's murder at Castle Black, is a type of compulsion (enchantment) which draws her to that place: a type of Freudian death drive.[63] Jon plays the role defined by the inscription on the cross at Castle Black, a traitor. Jon is claimed by the cross as an object signifying his transformation as an instrument of death (a sword in the darkness). Jon brings his world crashing through the mirror into the Throne Room, replicating his own murder: the knife through the heart, and the blood on the snow. Emulating Jon's Dire Wolf, Ghost, Drogon cries over Dany's body. The contest results in a transformation into the animal nature of their helpers: Dany becomes the dragon, flying through the clouds, and Jon becomes the wolf. He becomes a ghost, an ethereal wanderer in animal clothes (black crow).[64]

THE FAIRY-TALE LIKENESS AND *GAME OF THRONES*

Game of Thrones has all the magic, violence, and sex of a fairy tale.[65] It is consumed by viewers and criticized or acclaimed for various reasons. Some viewers criticize the adaptation for the lack of adherence to the doctrine of the books or wanted the series cleaned up; this included moral outrage concerning rape scenes.[66] This approach is similar to the situation of the Grimm Brothers who collected, revised and redacted folktales, and when asked by friends and colleagues to tone it down would do so but more often "made a point of intensifying violent episodes."[67]

As the Brothers Grimm's fairy tales became more popular, however, this attitude waned and toning down the tales for greater consumption for children was necessary to their commercial success. Tatar clams that in Brothers Grimm's *Nursery and Household Tales* "what appeared too crude or offensive for children's ears was eliminated . . . coarse, inelegant phrasing was polished and refined . . . in their editorial activities."[68] What survives in the fairy tale regardless of redaction is the reality of human struggle against injustice, trauma, violence, and death. If we accept *Game of Thrones* as fairy tale–like then the expectation is that by the story's ending those that have struggled receive reward, but this does not happen. These formulas for fairy-tale endings and the satisfaction in the hero or heroine is that "victory is not over others but only over oneself."[69] Dany's madness and Jon's banishment take on hard truths in the psychological and political realities of life.

Game of Thrones engages in fairy-tale reversals and distortions that subvert viewer expectation. Zipes describes Perrault's version of *Sleeping Beauty* as a tale of a sleeping woman who is sexually violated: "he approached trembling . . . and knelt down beside her . . . the enchantment having ended, the princess awoke."[70] He also points out that the Grimm Brothers added "the Kiss."[71] Zipes says "How is the princess to be saved? The act of resolution is a moral act, and it is apparent that the salvation of a sleeping princess in the Baroque period was secondary to the fulfillment of male sexual passion and power."[72] Jon violates Dany with a symbolic phallus while kissing her, lowers her body to the ground, and she is dead. Perhaps this is why George R. R. Martin gives the precautionary claim concerning his *Song of Ice and Fire* series that it is not a type of "Disneyland Middle Ages."[73]

The conflation and intertextuality in Western literary traditions in the elements of the fairy tale make comparisons easy. *Game of Thrones* certainly contains enough of the characters, settings, and tropes of the fairy tale to make a comparison. In some respects, it feels like a medieval quest romance in the dragon-slaying theme. *Game of Thrones,* like the fairy tale, has Wicked Queens, Dragons, giants, imps, and magic enchantments with some interchangeable fairy-tale gender roles. These tropes are reinforced through cinematography. As a fairy-tale suggestion through cinematography, Dany dismounts from her dragon at the top of the stairs. Her image is superimposed over her dragon, a visual symbol of her magical transformation into a flying destroyer. Like Sleeping Beauty, she has awoken from her own tale into another reality: the dragon Queen in all its terrifying elements of fire and blood. The release of the dragon in Dany is the crumbling of her ideology of a better world that can only be enacted by the Prince in patriarchal society. So, in Brothers Grimm's fairy tale of "Sleeping Beauty," the Prince brings a new dawn with a kiss that breaks the magic spell. This is Jon in the role of hunter, who realizes that to bring a new dawn will require the silencing of the feminine voice. His rescue is a political one, saving the seven kingdoms, and not of the fairy-tale type seen in "Cinderella" or "Snow White."

Hunters in fairy tale can be considered as "unconscious representation of the father."[74] This belief in the fairy-tale Hunter/father as rescuer has a deeper meaning—"he represents the subjugation of the animal, asocial, violent tendencies in man."[75] It is the patriarchal voice that instructs in the social moral rules of order, the symbolic order. The underlying violence of this fairy-tale world view provides a solution through the rescue of humankind from violent, often female, characters: Cinderella's stepmother and stepsisters, Snow White's stepmother/queen, and Maleficent in Disney's *Sleeping Beauty*.[76]

Although not often explored in the Western tradition of Perrault/Grimm/ Disney fairy tales of Cinderella, Francisco Vaz da Silva traces European fairy-tale versions of a "Dragon slaying Cinderella."[77] The plot of a Prince driven from home who sheds his rags and fights a dragon and drops a shoe is of interest as a portrait of a male Cinderella.[78] By recounting the types, motifs, and themes he demonstrates connections that were considered disparate characterizations of a "Dragon Slayer" with the "Cinderella" story.[79] The intertextual nature of the fairy tale thus alludes to the characterizations seen in *Game of Thrones*. The sharing of these types, motifs, and themes all revolve around Jon Snow. The law of three applies: the dragon has three heads and Jon is the third child of Rhaegar Targaryen. Dany and Jon share the essence of the dragon and are blood relations, told in fairy tales where "the dragon slayer and his victim are essentially one."[80]

Jon as dragon-slayer/hunter kills Dany as she reached her goal of the Iron Throne. The familiar fairy tales of "Cinderella," "Snow White," and "Sleeping Beauty" all concern the female and her reaching "the summit of her femininity."[81] Like Dany these tales usually involve female mortification, the body on display, losing none of its beauty under a magic spell, and sublime: "composed of some other substance."[82]

FAIRY TALE, THE SUBLIME, AND CASTRATION

Dany's body possesses qualities of the sublime. She inspires awe when she emerges from fire unburnt and unharmed by it. In this regard she is Queen of the Ashes—something Tyrion told her she wanted to avoid when taking King's Landing. It is her making of ashes that makes her "Cinderella" tale circular. The "Cinderella" tale is a tale of liberation from the ashes, but Dany has been reclaimed by them. The transfiguration of the "Cinderella" tale in *Game of Thrones* involves violent death in a "Cinderella" contest. Dany, as Cinderella, dies in the embrace of her Prince and the spell of her "Cinderella" story is broken for viewers. The story of Dany's transformation into a monster releases Jon's prophetic destiny and he does what he does best, and becomes the mirror Prince Aegon (the woke Cinderella). He is the dragon-slayer and slays the dragon. Jon both castrates Dany (she loses her power) and she becomes the holder of the phallus in the object of the dagger. Julius E. Heuscher considers that in some versions of "Cinderella," "the father reappears as the cruel, and maybe jealous castrator . . . cuts down with an axe the birdhouse or . . . the pear tree."[83] Jon symbolically cuts down Dany at the summit of her desire and enchantment. In this sublime movement in the dance of death is the sublime image of Cinderella where "dancing itself can be viewed as representing sexual arousal . . . and the foot slips into the slipper."[84] This "Cinderella" fairy tale double entendre engages a horrifying direct correlation to *Game of Thrones* in Dany's murder scene linking the dagger thrust into her body, and their sexual act.

As Cinderella, both Jon and Dany become the "the sublime object placed in the interspace between two deaths."[85] The viewer is at once traumatized and transfixed by the sublime body of Dany transported through the clouds, but it is Jon's castration by Tyrion that is the most surprising moment. Tyrion tells Jon when he is in prison that he is to be exiled and sent back to the

Night's Watch where he will father no children. Jon's body becomes a partial object and as a living dead he is exiled into the frozen world of the dead. Both Dany and Jon are in a sense castrated as a punishment for their incest.[86]

In the last season viewers have to grapple with characters that have been subsumed into fairy-tale narratives offering partial resolutions. *Game of Thrones* shares the fairy-tale world as dark entanglements in contests of power that involve the worst of human nature. They share in the violence, but fairy tales usually end with the death of the antagonist.[87] However, in *Game of Thrones* it is the protagonists, these dead Cinderellas, that join other fragmented bodies: Bran the castrated is made King and Tyrion is the "Hand of the King" the half-man, the dwarf.[88] These partial objects "cannot be assimilated into . . . narcissistic illusion[s] of completeness."[89] This notion of the fragmented body is also tied to castration anxiety and signals an enjoyment that must be refused.[90] Some viewers cannot find any type of resolution or closure in the ending of *Game of Thrones*; neither fairy-tale comparisons, nor the application of psychoanalysis to study the film can offer a solution. These are tools used in media that can explain and analyze the effect of the Real on the viewer as Dany's struggles end in death.

In the Brothers Grimm's tales, Cinderella overcomes sibling rivalry, oedipal entanglements, and resolves castration anxiety by restoring the patriarchal order, achieved through her feminine body. In Cinderella's sublime body, on display at the ball, she is transformed from ashes and cinders and rewarded with her marriage to the Prince. Dany's passage through fire witnesses many times as an escape or resurrection from the ashes in a phoenix-like rise ends when she is claimed by "the patriarchal resolution [which] is a coffin of another kind."[91] Her female mortification is paralleled in fairy-tale texts of "Snow White" and "Sleeping Beauty," bodies that retain their beauty and glory in the feminine body as a sublime body.[92] Dany becomes the embodiment of "the impossible thing, the sublime object."[93]

CONCLUSION

Game of Thrones can be typified like other violent adaptations as a "disturbing fairy-tale film."[94] Heuscher claims that "fairy tales are astonishingly sensitive to the trends of their times."[95] Under the spell of cultural pacification, twenty-first-century viewers are invested in fairy-tale endings in the ideologies and dreams of the West as Utopia. *Game of Thrones,* however, displays a brutal ideology that considers castration as a response to a world in need of correction. For viewers, this is not the ending that was promised or expected!

In the Throne Room in King's Landing, Dany walks toward Jon Snow recounting their childhoods; she says, "I was a girl who couldn't count to twenty and you were a bastard boy."[96] In other words, we made it! This is our Cinderella moment! However, this illusion melts away to her blood on the snow, emulating the opening of so many fairy tales; but it is also a brutal fulfillment of the dream of breaking the wheel. The ending of *Game of Thrones* is the failure of either character to fulfill the "Cinderella" narrative, thus ending the utopian dream. Does this signal that Western society's "Cinderella" era has ended? Perhaps *Game of Thrones* represents the Real Cinderella ending in twenty-first-century apocalyptic style by mirroring ecological, cultural, political, and societal collapse. To parallel reality, viewers are caught up in the game, swept up in the ideology of the hero, or following the great leader. They fear the creation of monsters used as weapons, seen in the Night King and his army, the tearing down of sacred trees, and the killing of indigenous inhabitants.

The brutality of Dany and Jon's tales end with a journey beyond the wall as the metaphor for death as foretold in Dany's visions. Death is beyond the wall of language (it is silent) outside the rules and social codes of the symbolic order. Dany's journey is the parallel/parody of romance that is brutal as she is swept up in the talons of her dragon. Jon's journey is beyond the literal wall outside the laws and rules associated with kingdoms or civilization in the symbolic order. He is finally worthy to follow his Uncle Benjen in a journey beyond the wall to the land of the dead.

Jon as the face of the patriarchal mirror became as "grim as death."[97] Dany, like Western society's "Cinderella" tale of utopia, has been reclaimed by the ashes of the twenty-first century. Her destruction of King's Landing aligns the tale with the contests of empire in twenty-first-century obsessions with apocalyptic visions. *Game of Thrones* highlights this obsession with the sublime image, and the repetition of trauma in the telling and retelling of violent tales. But like the telling of the oral folktale that is enlarged by the telling, retelling, and sharing, this story seems endless. Dany and Jon as mirrors share in the interchangeable twin realities of life and death, and this could make something impossible happen. Dany can be resurrected, like Jon, after being stabbed through the heart. If you believe in fairy tales, then once upon a time there was a dead girl taken to Volantis in the talons of her dragon, and given to a Red Witch . . .

NOTES

1. Bruno Bettelheim, *The Uses of Enchantment: The Meaning and Importance of Fairy Tales* (London: Penguin Books, 1978), 235.

2. Bettelheim, *The Uses of Enchantment: The Meaning and Importance of Fairy Tales*, 243.

3. Bettelheim, *The Uses of Enchantment: The Meaning and Importance of Fairy Tales*, 277.

4. Jack Zipes, *The Enchanted Screen: The Unknown History of Fairy Tale Films* (London: Routledge, 2011), 2–3, ebook.

5. Maria Tatar, *The Hard Facts of the Grimm's Fairy Tales* (Princeton: Princeton University Press, 2003; repr., Expanded Second Edition), 3.

6. Bettelheim, *The Uses of Enchantment: The Meaning and Importance of Fairy Tales*, 240.

7. Bettelheim, *The Uses of Enchantment: The Meaning and Importance of Fairy Tales*, 213.

8. E. Ann Kaplan, *Trauma Culture: The Politics of Terror and Loss in Media and Literature* (New Bruswick: Rutgers University Press, 2005), 25.

9. Kaplan, *Trauma Culture: The Politics of Terror and Loss in Media and Literature*, 1.

10. Slavoj Žižek, *Looking Awry: An Introduction to Jacques Lacan through Popular Culture* (Cambridge: MIT Press, 1991), 83.

11. Armando Maggi, "The Creation of Cinderella from Basile to the Brothers Grimm," ed. Maria Tartar, *The Cambridge Companion to Fairy Tales* (Cambridge: Cambridge University Press, 2014). 163.

12. Zipes, *The Enchanted Screen: The Unknown History of Fairy Tale Films*, 358.

13. Maggi, "The Creation of Cinderella from Basile to the Brothers Grimm," 150.

14. Zipes, *The Enchanted Screen: The Unknown History of Fairy Tale Films*.

15. Zipes, *The Enchanted Screen: The Unknown History of Fairy Tale Films*, 358.

16. *Game of Thrones,* season 8, episode 5, "The Bells" directed by Miguel Sapochnik, aired May 12 2019, on HBO.

17. Allen Feldman, "Ground Zero Point One," in *The World Trade Center and Global Crisis*, ed. Bruce Kapferer (New York: Berghahn Books, 2004), 31.

18. Feldman, "Ground Zero Point One," 31.

19. *Game of Thrones,* season 8, episode 6, "The Iron Throne," directed by David Benioff and D. B. Weiss, aired May 19, 2019, on HBO.

20. *Game of Thrones,* season 7, episode 3, "The Queen's Justice," directed by Mark Mylod, aired July 30 2017, on HBO.

21. Ibid.

22. Ibid.

23. *Game of Thrones,* season 2, episode 10, "Valar Morghulis," directed by Alan Taylor, aired 3 June 2012, on HBO, Blu-ray.

24. Bettelheim, *The Uses of Enchantment: The Meaning and Importance of Fairy Tales*, 235.

25. Slavoj Žižek, *The Sublime Object of Ideology* (London: Verso, 1989).

26. Slavoj Žižek, *How to Read Lacan* (New York: W. W. Norton & Co., 2007), 65.

27. *Game of Thrones,* season 1, episode 1, "Winter is Coming," directed by Tim Van Patten, aired April 17, 2011, on HBO.

28. *Game of Thrones,* season 5, episode 8, "Hardhome," directed by Miguel Sapochnik, aired May 31, 2015, on HBO.

29. Julius E. Heuscher, *A Psychiatric Study of Myths and Fairy Tales: Their Origin, Meaning and Usefulness*, Second ed. (Springfield: Charles C. Thomas, 1974), 266.

30. Rev. 20:1–3.

31. *Game of Thrones,* season 1, episode 10, "Fire and Blood," directed by Alan Taylor, aired June 19, 2011, on HBO, Blu-ray.

32. *Game of Thrones,* season 6, episode 4, "Book of the Stranger," directed by Daniel Sackheim, aired May 15, 2016, on HBO.

33. Max Lüthi, *The Fairytale as Art Form and Portrait of Man*, trans. Jon Erickson (Bloomington: Indiana University, 1984), 1.

34. *Game of Thrones.*

35. Bettelheim, *The Uses of Enchantment: The Meaning and Importance of Fairy Tales*, 127.

36. Žižek, *Looking Awry: An Introduction to Jacques Lacan through Popular Culture*, 24.

37. Maggi, "The Creation of Cinderella from Basile to the Brothers Grimm," 150.

38. Zipes, *The Enchanted Screen: The Unknown History of Fairy Tale Films*, ix.

39. Zipes, *The Enchanted Screen: The Unknown History of Fairy Tale Films*, 2.
40. Jack Zipes, *Breaking the Magic Spell: Radical Theories of Folk and Fairy Tales*, Revised and Expanded Edition ed. (Lexington: University Press of Kentucky, 2002), 195.
41. Zipes, *Breaking the Magic Spell: Radical Theories of Folk and Fairy Tales*, 194.
42. Kaplan, *Trauma Culture: The Politics of Terror and Loss in Media and Literature*, 25.
43. Žižek, *How to Read Lacan*, 70.
44. Žižek, *The Sublime Object of Ideology*, 49.
45. Wayne Wang, "Maid in Manhattan" (Kew: Shock Records, 2002), DVD.
46. Garry Marshall, "The Princess Diaries" (South Yarra: Buena Vista Home Entertainment, 2001), DVD.
47. Maggi, "The Creation of Cinderella from Basile to the Brothers Grimm," 163.
48. Maggi, "The Creation of Cinderella from Basile to the Brothers Grimm," 150.
49. Maggi, "The Creation of Cinderella from Basile to the Brothers Grimm," 163.
50. Maggi, "The Creation of Cinderella from Basile to the Brothers Grimm," 151.
51. Zipes, *The Enchanted Screen: The Unknown History of Fairy Tale Films*, 188.
52. Zipes, *The Enchanted Screen: The Unknown History of Fairy Tale Films*, 189.
53. David Hand and William Cottrell, "Snow White and the Seven Dwarfs," ed. David Hand (South Yarra: Walt Disney Company, 1937), DVD.
54. *Game of Thrones,* season 5, episode 1, "The Wars to Come," directed by Michael Slovis, aired April 12, 2015, on HBO.
55. Ibid.
56. Bettelheim, *The Uses of Enchantment: The Meaning and Importance of Fairy Tales*, 205.
57. Zipes, *The Enchanted Screen: The Unknown History of Fairy Tale Films*, 189.
58. Kaplan, *Trauma Culture: The Politics of Terror and Loss in Media and Literature*, 25.
59. Žižek, *How to Read Lacan*, 12.
60. Sandra M. Gilbert and Susan Gubar, *The Madwoman in the Attic: The Woman Writer and the Nineteenth-Century Literary Imagination* (Yale University Press, 1980), 40.
61. Jorge Luis Borges and Margarita Guerrero, *The Book of Imaginary Beings*, trans. Norman Thomas Giovanni (London: Vintage Publishing, 2014).
62. Erich Neumann, *Amor and Psyche* (New York: Princeton University Press, 1971), 62.
63. Slavoj Žižek, "'In His Bold Gaze My Ruin Is Writ Large'," in *Everything You Always Wanted to Know about Lacan (But Were Afraid to Ask Hitchcock)*, ed. Slavoj Žižek (New York: Verso, 1992), 260.
64. Lüthi, *The Fairytale as Art Form and Portrait of Man*, 136.
65. Tatar, *The Hard Facts of the Grimm's Fairy Tales*, 3.
66. Shiloh Carroll, "Tone deaf? Game of Thrones, showrunners and criticism," in *HBO's Original Voices: Race, Gender, Sexuality and Power*, ed. Victoria McCollum and Giuliana Monteverde (Abington: Routledge, 2018), 170–73.
67. Tatar, *The Hard Facts of the Grimm's Fairy Tales*, 5.
68. Tatar, *The Hard Facts of the Grimm's Fairy Tales*, 38.
69. Bettelheim, *The Uses of Enchantment: The Meaning and Importance of Fairy Tales*, 127.
70. Zipes, *Breaking the Magic Spell: Radical Theories of Folk and Fairy Tales*, 212.
71. Zipes, *Breaking the Magic Spell: Radical Theories of Folk and Fairy Tales*, 212.
72. Zipes, *Breaking the Magic Spell: Radical Theories of Folk and Fairy Tales*, 213.
73. "George R. R. Martin, Author of 'A Song of Ice and Fire,'" Series: Interview on The Sound of Young America, Bullseye, 2011, accessed 25 June 2019, https://www.maximumfun.org/sound-young-america/george-r-r-martin-author-song-ice-and-fire-series-interview-sound-young-america.
74. Bettelheim, *The Uses of Enchantment: The Meaning and Importance of Fairy Tales*, 205.
75. Bettelheim, *The Uses of Enchantment: The Meaning and Importance of Fairy Tales*, 205.
76. Clyde Geronimi, "Sleeping Beauty" (South Yarra: Walt Disney Company, 1959), DVD.

77. Francisco Vaz da Silva, "Cinderella the Dragon Slayer," *Studia Mythologica Slavica* 3 (2000): 187.
78. Ibid.
79. Vaz da Silva, "Cinderella the Dragon Slayer," 188.
80. Vaz da Silva, "Cinderella the Dragon Slayer," 189–90.
81. Bettelheim, *The Uses of Enchantment: The Meaning and Importance of Fairy Tales*, 235.
82. Žižek, *The Sublime Object of Ideology*, 134.
83. Heuscher, *A Psychiatric Study of Myths and Fairy Tales: Their Origin, Meaning and Usefulness*, 225.
84. Heuscher, *A Psychiatric Study of Myths and Fairy Tales: Their Origin, Meaning and Usefulness*, 225.
85. Žižek, *The Sublime Object of Ideology*, 145.
86. Jacques Lacan, *Feminine sexuality: Jacques Lacan and the ećole freudienne*, trans. Juliette Mitchell, ed. Jacqueline Rose and Juliette Mitchell (London: Macmillan, 1982), 76.
87. Tatar, *The Hard Facts of the Grimm's Fairy Tales*, 190.
88. *Game of Thrones*.
89. Dylan Evans, *An Introductory Dictionary of Lacanian Psychoanalysis* (London: Routledge, 2010), 135.
90. Evans, *An Introductory Dictionary of Lacanian Psychoanalysis*, 22.
91. Zipes, *Breaking the Magic Spell: Radical Theories of Folk and Fairy Tales*, 216.
92. Žižek, *The Sublime Object of Ideology*, 134.
93. Žižek, *Looking Awry: An Introduction to Jacques Lacan through Popular Culture*, 83.
94. Zipes, *The Enchanted Screen: The Unknown History of Fairy Tale Films*, 355.
95. Heuscher, *A Psychiatric Study of Myths and Fairy Tales: Their Origin, Meaning and Usefulness*, 157.
96. *Game of Thrones*.
97. Zipes, *The Enchanted Screen: The Unknown History of Fairy Tale Films*, 122.

BIBLIOGRAPHY

Benioff, David, and D. B. Weiss, dir. *Game of Thrones,* Season 8, episode 6, "The Iron Throne." Aired May 12, 2019, on HBO.
Bettelheim, Bruno. *The Uses of Enchantment: The Meaning and Importance of Fairy Tales.* London: Penguin Books, 1978.
Borges, Jorge Luis, and Margarita Guerrero. *The Book of Imaginary Beings.* Translated by Norman Thomas Giovanni. London: Vintage Publishing, 2014.
Carroll, Shiloh. "Tone Deaf? Game of Thrones, Showrunners and Criticism." Chap. 12 in *Hbo's Original Voices: Race, Gender, Sexuality and Power*, edited by Victoria McCollum and Giuliana Monteverde, 169–81. Abington: Routledge, 2018.
Evans, Dylan. *An Introductory Dictionary of Lacanian Psychoanalysis.* London: Routledge, 2010.
Feldman, Allen. "Ground Zero Point One." In *The World Trade Center and Global Crisis*, edited by Bruce Kapferer, 26–36. New York: Berghahn Books, 2004.
"George R. R. Martin, Author of 'A Song of Ice and Fire.'" Series: Interview on The Sound of Young America, Bullseye, 2011, accessed 25 June 2019, https://www.maximumfun.org/sound-young-america/george-r-r-martin-author-song-ice-and-fire-series-interview-sound-young-america.
Geronimi, Clyde. "Sleeping Beauty." South Yarra: Walt Disney Company, 1959. DVD.
Gilbert, Sandra M., and Susan Gubar. *The Madwoman in the Attic: The Woman Writer and the Nineteenth-Century Literary Imagination.* Yale University Press, 1980.
Hand, David, and William Cottrell. "Snow White and the Seven Dwarfs." South Yarra: Walt Disney Company, 1937. DVD.
Heuscher, Julius E. *A Psychiatric Study of Myths and Fairy Tales: Their Origin, Meaning and Usefulness.* Second ed. Springfield: Charles C. Thomas, 1974.

Kaplan, E. Ann. *Trauma Culture: The Politics of Terror and Loss in Media and Literature.* New Bruswick: Rutgers University Press, 2005.

Lacan, Jacques. *Feminine Sexuality: Jacques Lacan and the Ećole Freudienne.* Translated by Juliette Mitchell. Edited by Jacqueline Rose and Juliette Mitchell. London: Macmillan, 1982.

Lüthi, Max. *The Fairytale as Art Form and Portrait of Man.* Translated by Jon Erickson. Bloomington: Indiana University, 1984.

Maggi, Armando. "The Creation of Cinderella from Basile to the Brothers Grimm." In *The Cambridge Companion to Fairy Tales,* edited by Maria Tartar Cambridge: Cambridge University Press, 2014.

Marshall, Garry. "The Princess Diaries." South Yarra: Buena Vista Home Entertainment, 2001. DVD.

Mylod, Mark, dir. *Game of Thrones,* Season 7, episode 3, "The Queen's Justice." Aired July 30, 2017, on HBO.

Neumann, Erich. *Amor and Psyche.* New York: Princeton University Press, 1971.

Sackheim, Daniel, dir. *Game of Thrones,* Season 6, episode 4, "Book of the Stranger." Aired May 15, 2016, on HBO.

Sapochnik, Miguel, dir. *Game of Thrones,* Season 5, episode 8, "Hardhome." Aired May 31, 2015, on HBO.

——, dir. *Game of Thrones,* Season 8, episode 5, "The Bells " Aired May 12, 2019, on HBO.

Slovis, Michael, dir. *Game of Thrones,* Season 5, episode 1, "The Wars to Come." Aired April 12, 2015, on HBO.

Tatar, Maria. *The Hard Facts of the Grimm's Fairy Tales.* Princeton: Princeton University Press, 2003. Expanded Second Edition.

Taylor, Alan, dir. *Game of Thrones,* Season 1, episode 10, "Fire and Blood." Aired June 19, 2011, on HBO.

——, dir. *Game of Thrones,* Season 2, episode 10, "Valar Morghulis." Aired 3 June, 2012, on HBO.

Van Patten, Tim, dir. *Game of Thrones,* Season 1, episode 1, "Winter is Coming." Aired April 17, 2011, on HBO.

Vaz da Silva, Francisco. "Cinderella the Dragon Slayer." *Studia Mythologica Slavica* 3 (2000): 187–204.

Wang, Wayne. "Maid in Manhattan." Kew: Shock Records, 2002. DVD.

Zipes, Jack. *Breaking the Magic Spell: Radical Theories of Folk and Fairy Tales.* Revised and Expanded Edition ed. Lexington: University Press of Kentucky, 2002.

——. *The Enchanted Screen: The Unknown History of Fairy Tale Films.* London: Routledge, 2011. ebook.

Žižek, Slavoj. *How to Read Lacan.* New York: W. W. Norton & Co, 2007.

——. "'In His Bold Gaze My Ruin Is Writ Large.'" In *Everything You Always Wanted to Know about Lacan (but Were Afraid to Ask Hitchcock),* edited by Slavoj Žižek, 211–72. New York: Verso, 1992.

——. *Looking Awry: An Introduction to Jacques Lacan through Popular Culture.* Cambridge: MIT Press, 1991.

——. *The Sublime Object of Ideology.* London: Verso, 1989.

Chapter Six

Forgive Me Mother for I Have Sinned

Cinderella's Stepmother Meets Derrida's Forgiveness

Brittany Eldridge

The tale of "Cinderella" is by far "the best-known fairy tale, and probably also the best liked" due in part by Cinderella's escape from an abusive household.[1] It is the story of the underdog triumphing over their intelligent opponent. The evil stepmother is the mastermind behind all of Cinderella's torment. With stepmothers in fairy tales constantly persecuting their step-daughters, the stepdaughters take on "the role of the innocent martyrs and patient sufferers" and the stepmother is to "stand as an abiding source of evil."[2] These are set roles within the tales for the characters: the wicked stepmother and the innocent princess. Throughout the progression of the "Cinderella" tale from Charles Perrault's 1697 "Cendrillon" to the Disney film adaptations, the story of Cinderella retains "the same or very similar constituents," but "the outcomes differ profoundly."[3] The roles are similar, but the outcomes and characters are becoming less concrete as the representation of female characters change in film adaptations. The adaptation of the "Cinderella" tale into the 2015 film *Cinderella* (produced by Walt Disney Pictures) shows the development of both Lady Tremaine and Cinderella, along with their relationship, through the conceit of forgiveness. Forgiveness as represented in the 2015 film is shown through the *act* of forgiving. Cinderella forgives her mother for dying and her stepmother for abusing her; however, this work discusses the relationship of Cinderella and her stepmother, not the comparison of the stepmother to the birth mother. Therefore, the focus is on the forgiveness Cinderella presents to her stepmother at the end of the film as Cinderella explicitly states that she forgives her stepmother.

Forgiveness is a central aspect to the 2015 film *Cinderella*. Forgiveness is an act of kindness from one person to another and helps to maintain various types of relationships, such as the relationship of a child and their parental figure. This specific relationship requires constant acts of forgiveness from both parties, as "parent-child relationships inevitably face conflict. Sometimes the parent is the person who exacerbated the conflict or caused the rupture in the relationship with [the] child."[4] The parent and child must then fix this rupture in the relationship by the use of forgiveness. Children "are dependent on their parents, physically and emotionally," therefore an establishment of a positive relationship should take place.[5] Forgiveness aids in this establishment. For there to be a positive relationship, children need to "learn to forgive and ask for forgiveness. Forgiveness is especially helpful emotionally, because it helps people let go of hurt and bitterness, and promotes positive regard, compassion, and sympathy."[6] Both the child and parent must learn to be forgiving to promote a sympathetic and compassionate relationship. A child forgiving their parental figure occurs within Disney's *Cinderella* (2015), as Cinderella forgives not only her biological mother for dying, but also her stepmother for her wicked deeds. The forgiveness of the stepmother is a pivotal point at the end of the film. During this time, Cinderella is freed from her stepmother and her oppression. Does this forgiveness promote a compassionate relationship, or is it a manipulation tactic? Is Cinderella's forgiveness pure forgiveness?

What defines forgiveness? Jacques Derrida defines forgiveness as something that "*should* remain exceptional and extraordinary, in the face of the impossible: as if it interrupted the course of historical temporality."[7] Forgiveness is a concept that can only exist if it is an extraordinary measure. A person should not expect forgiveness. Pure forgiveness is "unconditional," and must have "no meaning, no finality, even no intelligibility."[8] The function of Derridean forgiveness is that it has no true meaning. Pure forgiveness is not an understandable concept. It has to be exceptionally extraordinary, and it should not be a logical conclusion. Forgiveness should not be a means to an end, but in *Cinderella* that is the purpose of the forgiveness presented. The type of forgiveness that does occur is politically motivated. Pure forgiveness is attainable in the political realm through a sovereign figure who pardons the guilty allowing the forgiveness to remain pure, but as will be shown, this is not the case in *Cinderella*. So, does this forgiveness presented promote a compassionate relationship, or is it a manipulation tactic? By looking at *Cinderella*'s depiction of the stepmother and Cinderella's relationship, this chapter will prove Cinderella's forgiveness is politically motivated, making Cinderella nothing more than a good politician.

FORGIVENESS

To understand Cinderella's action of forgiveness when she leaves her step-mother, and to discern whether or not it is pure or political, there has to be a clear understanding of forgiveness. Derrida clearly states in "On Forgiveness" that "there is no limit to forgiveness, no *measure*, no moderation."[9] Forgiveness can be freely given, but that does not mean it should be common. Pure forgiveness is not an everyday occurrence and is not a normal action between two people. Pure forgiveness is exceptional. Forgiveness cannot be expected; it should be a rarity and be unconditional. Pure forgiveness should be seen as impossible as "forgiveness forgives only the unforgivable."[10] Forgiveness in its purest form is not an everyday phenomenon. The victim has to forgive the "unforgivable." This unforgivable act that Derrida speaks of is equivalent to that of a "mortal sin."[11] With Derrida's reliance on religion to show such an act of violation within a relationship, a discussion of mortal sin and the Ten Commandments will further aid in understanding the abusive relationship between Lady Tremaine and Cinderella.

A mortal sin within Catholicism is seen as horrendous because it is when a person violates one of the ten rules written by God. These ten rules were given to the people by Moses as he went to converse with God on Mt. Sinai. These ten rules are a guide within the Judeo-Christian tradition on how to live a sinless life. A mortal sin within Catholicism is "sin whose object is grave matter and which is also committed with full knowledge and deliberate consent."[12] The "grave matter" is the Ten Commandments, making mortal sin a conscious and deliberate violation of one, or more, of the Ten Commandments. The violation of the Ten Commandments is a mortal sin because a person is disobeying God. That is the type of act that only pure forgiveness can forgive. Derrida uses this as an example because this sin is a defiance of a God. This "unforgivable" act is imperative to understand as it shows how atrocious an act must be in order for forgiveness to emerge. Before forgiveness can occur, an unforgivable evil must present itself. In order for this unforgivable evil to transpire, the type that "would make forgiveness emerge," a violation of intimacy must occur.[13] The unforgivable evil arises because of a betrayal of intimacy and is a mortal sin. Within the most intimate of moments, hatred has to cause the unforgivable evil that is required for forgiveness to be able to come to fruition. The guilty must have a close relationship to the victim, physically and emotionally. A betrayal of a close friend or family member, when one of them commits unforgivable evil toward the victim, this is the only way for forgiveness to come about.

An unforgivable evil (betrayal) must emerge and be enacted upon by a close friend or family member. Pure forgiveness must be extraordinary, and in order for it to be extraordinary the evil enacted upon must be unforgivable. Pure and unconditional forgiveness can have no real meaning. Forgiveness is madness.[14] Pure forgiveness is so extraordinary that it should appear as madness when given. A person would have to be mad in order to forgive the unforgivable. Within the madness of forgiveness, there are two parties that must be involved, the guilty and the victim. The victim is the only singularity that "has the right to forgive."[15] The victim of the unforgivable act has to forgive not just the guilty party but also forgive "the fault" (the action of betrayal) and "the guilty."[16] The victim has to forgive the guilty and the unforgivable evil that the guilty party enacts on. The victim has to forgive the person and the action.

The action of forgiveness has to be impossible and therefore the act that has been committed must be unforgivable, such as a mortal sin. The act of pure forgiveness cannot be used for any purpose outside of the impossible act of forgiving. Forgiveness cannot be an act of reconciliation: "forgiveness does not, it should never amount to a therapy of reconciliation."[17] The forgiveness has to be a "gracious gift" bestowed upon the guilty party.[18] The act of reconciliation causes the forgiveness to no longer be pure as it has an ulterior motive, to reconcile. Reconciliation changes the forgiveness into "ordinary forgiveness which is anything but forgiveness."[19] There is nothing impossible or extraordinary about ordinary forgiveness. This type of forgiveness is seen every day and is used for reconciliation between parties. The moment reconciliation begins, there is another motive to the forgiveness. The very moment the victim begins to process, to understand "the criminal, as soon as she exchanges, speaks, agrees with him, the scene of reconciliation has commenced, and with it this ordinary forgiveness which is anything but forgiveness."[20] The moment the victim speaks with the guilty about the fault, there is a form of reconciliation that begins. When reconciliation begins, the forgiveness becomes ordinary:

> each time forgiveness is at the service of a finality, be it noble and spiritual (atonement or redemption, reconciliation, salvation), each time that it aims to re-establish a normality (social, national, political, psychological) by a work of mourning, by some therapy or ecology or memory, then the "forgiveness" is not pure—nor is its concept.[21]

Derrida means that unless forgiveness is essentially unmotivated/without gain, it is not pure, because there is a motive behind the forgiveness such as atonement or a political agenda. If forgiveness has a motive, then it is not pure as there is a selfish gain when presenting such forgiveness. The forgiveness is focusing on the victim's personal agenda and no longer on the act of forgiving. The forgiveness becomes selfish.

Even with reconciliation, there is another way for forgiveness to occur. This forgiveness is not ordinary forgiveness; Derrida claims it is another form of pure forgiveness. This other form of pure forgiveness that can emerge is through the transformation of the guilty party. For forgiveness to maintain its maddening status of extraordinary, there needs to be a form of "repentance and transformation of the sinner."[22] Through transformation, the guilty is no longer the same as they once were. This type of forgiveness has been named "conditional forgiveness."[23] A conditional forgiveness can be given if there is a "recognition of the fault . . . repentance . . . [and] the transformation of the sinner who then explicitly asks forgiveness."[24] The guilty party has to have thought about their actions and come to realize their own wrongdoing. Through the transformation, the person asking forgiveness is then "no longer guilty through and through, but already another, and better than the guilty one. To this extent, and on this condition, it is no longer the *guilty as such* who is forgiven."[25] Conditional forgiveness can only occur through the transformation of the guilty. If reconciliation has begun, then the transformation of the guilty party is the only way that pure forgiveness can still arise.

A third and final way for pure forgiveness to occur even if "conditional" forgiveness cannot is through a monarch. Derrida theorizes that "the absolute monarch, by divine right, can pardon a criminal" because "the sovereign [can] pardon only where the crime concerns himself."[26] The absolute monarch, the singular head of a State, can forgive crimes committed. This forgiveness can only exist if the crime committed involves the monarch as a victim. There is one specific crime that the monarch can forgive, and no other. Derrida claims the only type of crime that the monarch can forgive is one of "absolute victimization."[27] The definition given by Derrida of "absolute victimization" is a depravation of "life, or the right to speak, or that freedom that force and that power which *authorises*."[28] The unforgivable act that the monarch can forgive is the act of absolute victimization. This absolute victimization occurs when the victim cannot voice their defense, or opinions, or forgiveness. When the forgiveness of this act of oppression is presented, it presumes an act of sovereignty. This role of sovereign could be "a strong and noble soul, but also a power of State."[29] It can be given by a person who is noble or by an actual monarch/sovereign of state. The forgiveness by a sovereign can be seen as pure, but only if the forgiveness involves the act of absolute victimization. This forgiveness can involve the power of the monarch as a role, but the forgiveness cannot be a show of power. Pure forgiveness when in relation to the sovereign has to be presented as "*unconditional but without sovereignty.*"[30] It has to be a forgiveness that surpasses the power of the monarch. Separating the power of sovereignty from the forgiveness is a "difficult task," but one that is "necessary and apparently impossible" as "*unconditionality* and *sovereignty*" are difficult to dissociate.[31] Disassociating the unconditionality of forgiveness and the sovereignty that comes into play during the forgiveness is a task that Derrida sees as impossible. A sovereign has to put aside their affirmation of power in order to present pure forgiveness.

Pure forgiveness is possible. It has conditions to aid in its purity, along with different opportunities to continue to present other types of pure forgiveness if the original conditions are violated. Pure forgiveness can give way to conditional forgiveness or the forgiveness by an absolute monarch. In *Cinderella* (2015), there is no pure forgiveness presented, even with the many variations that had a chance to present themselves. Lady Tremaine is cruel and does commit heinous acts against Cinderella. The stepmother even victimizes Cinderella through the act of absolute victimization. Lady Tremaine causes Cinderella unbelievable amounts of grief, but the stepmother is not the only one who faults in the interaction between the two. Cinderella has the chance to present pure forgiveness and does not. She is politically motivated to present the forgiveness, so she can maintain the image of a kind ruler. Cinderella uses her new status in society to present the forgiveness to her stepmother. The forgiveness is a show of power.

THE SINISTER STEPMOTHER:
LADY TREMAINE'S TRIALS AND TRIBULATIONS

Derrida's pure forgiveness has a chance to exist within the film *Cinderella* (2015), as Cinderella has the opportunity to present the forgiveness after the first sin of the stepmother, but Cinderella waits until there is a shift in power within their relationship before presenting this forgiveness, making the forgiveness impure as there is motive. Derrida creates many opportunities for forgiveness within the various parameters he sets. Cinderella has an ample amount of time to present pure forgiveness to Lady Tremaine. She does not. Cinderella is motivated by her role as queen to present forgiveness. The forgiveness becomes a show of power as she finally ranks higher than her abusive stepmother. In "human societies, some individuals wield great power over others."[32] Lady Tremaine has great power over Cinderella as her stepmother, thus ranking Lady Tremaine above Cinderella in the hierarchy. This comprehension of the household's hierarchy is important in understanding the relationship between Lady Tremaine and Cinderella. Lady Tremaine is dominant because "human social hierarchies are dominance hierarchies."[33] With the dominance of Lady Tremaine, the relationship becomes a power struggle between the two. The forgiveness may be part of the story plot, but it is not pure forgiveness because of the constant motivation for power. The forgiveness presented is a ploy used for political gain in the social hierarchy on Cinderella's behalf. Based on the parameters set by Derrida, the forgiveness presented by Cinderella to her stepmother Lady Tremaine is not pure.

The forgiveness has a chance to be pure within the first few transactions between Lady Tremaine and Cinderella. Lady Tremaine and Cinderella develop an abusive relationship the moment Cinderella's father leaves the house. For forgiveness to occur, by Derrida's standards, one of the two will have to violate the most "intimate of intimacy" or one of the Ten Commandments.[34] Lady Tremaine wants to rid herself of Cinderella. The stepmother wishes to "advance her own daughters," and Cinderella hinders this advancement.[35] Lady Tremaine's main goal during the film is to "acquire advantageous marriages for [her] two daughters."[36] With this goal in mind, Lady Tremaine takes advantage of her time as the only parental guardian. As Cinderella's father leaves for his business trip, Lady Tremaine offers comfort to the child. She calls her "Ella dear" and opens her arms to invite the child to sit beside her.[37] She embraces Cinderella and wipes away the child's tears. Her tone is that of a mother with her child as she soothes Cinderella: "Now, now, musn't blub."[38] These are the compassionate words that she uses toward her stepdaughter, but the tone becomes false as the conversation continues. Cinderella calls Lady Tremaine "stepmother." The words to come from Lady Tremaine's lips are kind as she begins to correct Cinderella: "you needn't call me that."[39] With the comforting tone Lady Tremaine uses, the audience expects for her to be endearing in her response. She is not. Lady Tremaine tells Cinderella: "Madam will do."[40] The tone is no longer of a caring mother, but a sickly-sweet falsity that Lady Tremaine uses to her advantage. She catches Cinderella off guard with her change in tone. This is a violation of an intimate moment, which Lady Tremaine follows up by manipulating the child with Cinderella's permanent move to the attic. This is a power move by Lady Tremaine. She is showing to Cinderella that she is in charge. In the household, Lady Tremaine ranks higher than Cinderella because she has a "positional advantage" as her role of stepmother, allowing her to have control over Cinderella.[41] With this new power, Lady Tremaine demeans Cinderella to isolate the child and neutralize the threat to her biological daughters.

The isolation is the start of the torments that Cinderella endures. This isolation and constant belittling of the child begins to manipulate Cinderella into seeing herself as other, as "merely a creature of ash and toil."[42] Lady Tremaine is jealous of Cinderella because her own biological daughters lack "accomplishment in any art."[43] This makes Drizella and Anastasia harder to marry off. Lady Tremaine does not want the child to call her stepmother or mother as that would allow an emotional connection, and Lady Tremaine only sees Cinderella as a threat to her daughters. Lady Tremaine isolates the child as she would a threat. Cinderella threatens Lady Tremaine's ability to find advantageous marriages for her daughters because she is talented and beautiful.[44] Lady Tremaine wants her daughters to find advantageous marriages, but Cinderella presents as a threat with her skills and beauty. This

competition between the stepmother and her stepchildren is a common occurrence as "women [strive] against women because they [wish] to promote
their own children's interest over those of another union's offspring."[45] Lady
Tremaine's motivation is to procure marriages for her daughters, but Cinderella's mere existence threatens her daughters' chances. Lady Tremaine begins her tyrannical cruelty by isolating Cinderella, allowing ample opportunities for Lady Tremaine to promote her daughters. Christy Williams writes
in her essay, "Who's Wicked Now": "Thus, cruelty to her new husband's
biological children would be a way to ensure survival for her own biological
children."[46] Cinderella is a threat as she is likely to have an advantageous
marriage due to her beauty and talents, creating competition between Cinderella and her new stepsisters. The stepmother often finds "herself and her
children in competition—often for scarce resources—with the surviving offspring of the earlier marriage" who appear "to threaten her own children's
place."[47] Cinderella's stepmother sees this competition for resources as a
threat to her daughters. Lady Tremaine is then cruel to Cinderella so she can
eliminate her daughters' competition for the one scarce resource she is focused on, an advantageous marriage. By using her positional power to her
advantage, Lady Tremaine is able to demean Cinderella and isolate her from
society.

Lady Tremaine wields her power because of this constant competition her
biological daughters are in with Cinderella for advantageous marriages. Lady
Tremaine's villainous acts toward Cinderella are then motivated by her desire to protect her biological daughters. Lady Tremaine's solution is to find
Drizella and Anastasia advantageous marriages. For Lady Tremaine to rid
herself of the competitor that lives in her home, she has Cinderella call her
"madam," to show the separation that Lady Tremaine desires. By separating
Cinderella from her stepfamily, Lady Tremaine does not make an emotional
connection and continues to see Cinderella as a threat. Lady Tremaine separates Cinderella from the family by moving the child to a secluded part of the
house and forcing Cinderella to be the only servant. Lady Tremaine dismisses the household in order to keep the family financially stable.[48] Cinderella replaces the servants and "her stepmother and stepsisters ever misused
her. By and by, they considered Cinderella less a sister than a servant, and so,
Cinderella was left to do all the work."[49] The film explicitly states that the
family begins to see Cinderella as more of a servant than a family member.
She is the only servant, which adds to the isolation aspect of Cinderella's
torment. Since the stepfamily treats her as a servant, this causes Cinderella to
appear lower in station and "those occupying lower positions in these power
hierarchies have . . . diminished access to desired and desirable goods."[50]
Cinderella's diminished access allows for Drizella and Anastasia to become
more viable candidates for marriage as they have a higher station in society
than their lowly stepsister. The cruelty of the stepmother can be because of

the competition for resources within the household. In the case of Cinderella and her stepsisters, they are in competition for advantageous marriages. By forcing Cinderella to do the chores around the house and treating her as a servant, it only adds to the separation of the family from Cinderella; in turn, this isolates Cinderella further. Cinderella begins to see herself as a servant and nothing more. Lady Tremaine has the child believing that the stepmother has the power in the social hierarchy of the household.

According to Derrida's definitions, Lady Tremaine's assertion of power in the intimate moment that she shares with Cinderella is a violation of intimacy and is as bad as a mortal sin. Lady Tremaine's nefarious treatment of Cinderella is only the start of her terrible actions. Cinderella sleeps by the fire in order to stay warm at night because the attic is too cold.[51] The stepsisters and Lady Tremaine give the child a nickname of "Cinderella" during a scene where Cinderella is covered in ashes because of her sleeping arrangements. They see her covered in ashes and begin to call her cruel names. By no longer calling her by her birth name, Ella, but by a cruel nickname, they further isolate and demean the child. These acts are not sins, but Derrida claims these types of acts are just as horrendous as a violation of the Commandments. The acts of the stepmother violate the intimacy of Cinderella and Lady Tremaine's relationship. Lady Tremaine then, theoretically, sins.

Lady Tremaine does violate one of the Ten Commandments later on in the film. Toward the end of *Cinderella* (2015), the stepsisters have just tried on the glass slipper, and failed. Lady Tremaine is saying goodbye to the Captain of the Guard and the Grand Duke, but before they leave, Cinderella's singing can be heard from up above. The Captain asks Lady Tremaine: "Madam, there is no other maiden in your house?" Lady Tremaine responds with her blatant lie: "No."[52] The sin is committed once Lady Tremaine lies and this only adds to her wrongdoing. She breaks the commandment: "Thou shalt not bear false witness against thy neighbour."[53] Lady Tremaine's lies are what cause her to sin. This allows another chance for Cinderella to present pure forgiveness to Lady Tremaine. The ability to present the forgiveness has been available to Cinderella from the moment the word "madam" comes from Lady Tremaine's mouth.

Lady Tremaine not only violates an intimate moment, she does violate one of the Ten Commandments in relation to Cinderella; therefore she mortally sins. Lady Tremaine lies to the guards when they ask her if there is anyone else living in the house. The guards are in search of the foot that fits the glass slipper. Lady Tremaine at first tells them no one else resides in the house. She only corrects herself when she is caught in the lie as the Captain of the Guard reveals Cinderella in the attic. Lady Tremaine's excuse, Cinderella is "no one of importance."[54] The stepfamily has completely separated themselves from Cinderella. Lady Tremaine sees her as an agent of her demise. This treatment of Cinderella is considered a mortal sin; therefore,

Lady Tremaine does commit an unforgivable act, which permits an opportunity for "pure" forgiveness.

Cinderella supposedly forgives all of Lady Tremaine's villainy. This forgiveness has many chances to present itself in the film, but Cinderella waits until the end of the film to present it. This waiting creates impure forgiveness as there is a scene of reconciliation between Cinderella and Lady Tremaine before Cinderella presents forgiveness to her stepmother. The scene commences as Cinderella searches the attic for the hidden glass slipper. Lady Tremaine is waiting for her with the slipper in her grasp. Lady Tremaine asks for the story that compliments the glass slipper, but she does not give Cinderella a chance to respond as she begins telling her story:

> Once upon a time there was a beautiful young girl, who married for love and she had two loving daughters. All was well. But one day, her husband, the light of her life, died. The next time, she married for the sake of her daughters, but that man too was taken from her—and she was doomed to look every day upon his beloved child. She had hoped to one day marry off one of her beautiful, stupid daughters to the prince, but his head was turned by a girl with glass slippers. And so, I lived unhappily ever after. My story would appear to be ended.[55]

Lady Tremaine gives new and informative detail about her story, informing Cinderella of her motives behind her cruelty. This is the start of the reconciliation scene between the two characters as Cinderella begins to "understand the criminal."[56] As the conversation continues, Lady Tremaine shatters Cinderella's glass slipper, causing Cinderella to exclaim: "Why are you so cruel?"[57] Lady Tremaine is so vile in her treatment of Cinderella that her response is explosive: "Why? Because you are young, and innocent, and good. And I—"[58] Lady Tremaine never finishes this sentence. She gives Cinderella a look of disdain before slamming the attic door behind her, locking Cinderella away.[59] This interaction allows for Cinderella to begin to understand Lady Tremaine's motives for her villainy. It is also a show of Lady Tremaine's power in the relationship as she locks the child away. Lady Tremaine is able to do this because "the lower one's status, the less control one has."[60] Lady Tremaine has the highest status in the house and Cinderella has the lowest. Due to this hierarchy, Lady Tremaine can lock Cinderella in the attic after the scene of reconciliation.

The scene of reconciliation that commences changes the forgiveness from pure to ordinary and it is also a show of power from Lady Tremaine as she locks Cinderella away. Ordinary forgiveness is not real forgiveness.[61] Within this scene, the victim begins to understand the criminal. As soon as the victim "exchanges, speaks with [the guilty], the scene of reconciliation has commenced."[62] The reconciliation commences in the attic when Lady Tremaine delivers her monologue and describes the motivations behind her crimes against Cinderella. With the reconciliation, the forgiveness becomes motivated; and forgiveness should never have a motive. The reconciliation occurs because Cinderella aims to "re-establish a normality" within the social constructs of the household by trying to establish an understanding of her stepmother's cruelty.[63] Cinderella is trying to regain her status as a daughter within the household, instead of a servant by understanding her stepmother's cruelty toward her. The scene of reconciliation is a show of the power dynamics in the relationship between Cinderella and Lady Tremaine. This scene of understanding makes the forgiveness not pure, nor its concept.[64] The ability for pure forgiveness is no longer possible through the first method which Derrida describes because of this scene.

With the scene of reconciliation, the forgiveness becomes ordinary. This does not mean pure forgiveness is impossible, there still remains two chances for the forgiveness presented to be pure in *Cinderella* (2015). One of the other means is through the transformation of the guilty party. There needs to be a "repentance and transformation of the sinner."[65] Lady Tremaine does not transform. She is cruel to Cinderella even at the bitter end. In the second to last interaction between Lady Tremaine and Cinderella, Lady Tremaine is her cruelest as she tries to reestablish her position of power within their relationship. The Captain of the Guard finds Cinderella in the attic, proving that Lady Tremaine has lied about having another lady in the house. Lady Tremaine calls Cinderella "no one of any importance" as she introduces her to the Captain of the Guard.[66] The Captain of the Guard requests Cinderella presents herself to the King (once the prince) and try on the glass slipper. Lady Tremaine immediately interjects: "I forbid you to do this."[67] Lady Tremaine is trying to remain in command of Cinderella, but she fails as the Captain of the Guard has a higher rank in society, and therefore, the most power in the room. He forbids Lady Tremaine to forbid Cinderella. He asks Lady Tremaine: "Who are you to stop the officer of a king? Are you an empress, a saint, a deity?"[68] This is the first moment Cinderella sees someone demean Lady Tremaine. She sees her stepmother's inability to cause further harm. Lady Tremaine declares that she is "her mother," as a strategic way of trying to reestablish her dominance over Cinderella.[69] Cinderella is able to gain control in the relationship as she calmly tells Lady Tremaine that "she has never been, nor never will be" her mother.[70] Lady Tremaine does not take this disobedience lightly as she grasps Cinderella's arm before the child can flee. Lady Tremaine hatefully hisses to Cinderella: "Just remember who you are, you wretch."[71] These are the final spoken words of Lady Tremaine. Cinderella leaves the attic, never to return, and the door closes on Lady Tremaine as it symbolically shows the shift in power. Lady Tremaine is alone in the attic with the door shut, a symbolic mirroring of how she imprisons Cinderella in the same room. After the following scene with the king, Cinderella is about to leave her childhood home and she looks up to Lady

Tremaine and states: "I forgive you."[72] Cinderella says this in front of the king, her soon-to-be husband, and his Captain of the Guard. The power in the room shifts as Lady Tremaine is no longer the highest-ranking member of society in the room: "those further down the hierarchy fear and tear with deference those higher [in] the hierarchy."[73] With Lady Tremaine now being lower in the social hierarchy than Cinderella, she has a fear of the child she once ruled over. Cinderella's forgiveness is a show of power, and not pure forgiveness. As the narrator begins to describe the epilogue of the film, they too see that the forgiveness is not from a pure place: "forgiven or not, Cinderella's stepmother and her daughters would soon leave."[74] Cinderella presents forgiveness, but not even the narrator agrees that the forgiveness is true. Cinderella uses this final moment to show her newly gained political power within the hierarchy. She presents the forgiveness because she now holds the power in her relationship with Lady Tremaine. Lady Tremaine does not change in this film, but Cinderella does the moment she is given power.

Lady Tremaine does not go through a transformation. Cinderella has an opportunity to present pure forgiveness to Lady Tremaine, regardless of the transformation of the sinner. The final way for any type of pure forgiveness to emerge is through the powers of a monarchical figure. The "absolute monarch, by divine right, can pardon a criminal," but the monarch can only pardon if the crime "concerns" him/herself.[75] The only crime that the monarch can forgive, the one that concerns him/herself, is the crime of "absolute victimization."[76] Lady Tremaine does commit this crime when she locks Cinderella away in the attic. Cinderella cannot speak or testify against Lady Tremaine as she is locked away in a room with no escape. Lady Tremaine takes away Cinderella's ability to testify and to speak out against the crimes of Lady Tremaine.[77] This absolute victimization allows Cinderella to produce pure forgiveness as a monarchical figure. She is given this ability once she agrees to marry the new king. Cinderella does go through an elevation in status and rises above her stepmother before she leaves the home. The elevation of status allows for those who are "higher up [in] the hierarchy" to have "the power to arbitrarily interfere with the life of those further down the hierarchy."[78] Lady Tremaine was the matriarch of the household and the one who held the power. When Cinderella is taken away to marry the king there is a change in the household's power dynamic. Cinderella becomes the matriarch of the kingdom and the household. The change in power within the relationship is imperative as it is the reason Cinderella forgives her stepmother: "forgiving is actually a sign of strength."[79] Cinderella presents the forgiveness as she acquires new power in the social hierarchy. This forgiveness is a sign of her newly obtained political power. Cinderella becomes a queen, but her status as queen does not mean that her forgiveness is pure. Cinderella has an elevation in status when the king decides to marry her, but she still has a scene of reconciliation with her stepmother before she presents the forgiveness. The timing of Cinderella's forgiveness shows she has a political motive and the forgiveness is not, and can never be, pure. Cinderella finds a way to escape the abusive relationship she is in. This abusive environment teaches "that the person who uses force against others is the winner."[80] Cinderella gains her power and uses it as a way to show her stepmother that she won. With Cinderella's political career at stake, she presents the forgiveness to maintain her image. Cinderella is the "martyr" of her tale and a "patient sufferer."[81] If she were not to present forgiveness to her stepmother, she would no longer be the good-hearted and benevolent Cinderella. Her reign would not be "fair and kind" if it started with Cinderella banishing her stepfamily outright.[82] Essentially, Cinderella banishes her stepfamily through the implementation of a subtle fake forgiveness. So, Cinderella presents a false forgiveness to her stepmother in order to maintain her image as a compassionate queen. The stepmother sees past the false forgiveness. Lady Tremaine flees the country with her daughters because she knows that Cinderella could exact revenge on the family. Cinderella becomes more of a threat because of her new social status. Cinderella now has the power within her relationship with Lady Tremaine. Cinderella's forgiveness is not pure. It is politically motivated.

There is an availability for forgiveness to be pure in *Cinderella* (2015) as soon as Lady Tremaine violates the intimacy between Cinderella and herself. Lady Tremaine goes above and beyond as she also commits a mortal sin. The forgiveness Cinderella presents for these crimes has the chance to be pure. The timing of the forgiveness is what shows Cinderella's political motive. It occurs after a scene of reconciliation; and there is a social motive behind the reconciliation with a political motive behind the forgiveness that follows. Cinderella does not forgive Lady Tremaine until the end of the film because Cinderella does not have the upper hand in the relationship. Cinderella still ranks below her stepmother in station and remains reliant on her physically and emotionally until the king comes for her. Cinderella learns from her abusive relationship with Lady Tremaine that "power and strength keep you safe."[83] Cinderella is not safe from her stepmother until she holds power in the relationship. At the end of the film, Cinderella has the power of a dominant figure in the social hierarchy, authorizing her to present the false forgiveness as a show of this new power.

THE SINS OF CINDERELLA: CINDERELLA'S CRIMES

Forgiveness is a tool used in relationships to maintain a positive and compassionate relationship. Children need to learn to forgive as it is helpful emotionally and promotes this compassion within the relationship.[84] Forgiveness can also be used as a tool to show who holds the power in the relationship.

This manipulation tactic occurs during *Cinderella* (2015). The forgiveness Cinderella presents has political motivation and is a tactic to manipulate the general populace into believing that Cinderella is a kind and benevolent ruler. The relationship between Cinderella and Lady Tremaine is one based on power. Lady Tremaine asserts her power over Cinderella for the majority of the movie through her abuse. Cinderella constantly struggles to fight for her own sovereignty. Cinderella presents the forgiveness as a means of political gain. The forgiveness is selfish.

Although Lady Tremaine never receives pure forgiveness, she may have the right to forgive. Cinderella violates more than one Commandment during her time with her stepmother. Cinderella is in an abusive relationship with Lady Trermaine and Cinderella is reliant on her stepmother to care for her, as any child would want. Lady Tremaine does hold the role of Cinderella's mother, even though the relationship is not biological. This does not mean that Lady Tremaine has a right to abuse the child, only that this is their relationship. The Commandment that Cinderella violates is: "honour thy father and thy mother."[85] Cinderella disobeys her stepmother by going to the ball and dishonors Lady Tremaine by giving the stepmother false forgiveness. Lady Tremaine explicitly tells Cinderella that she "shall not go to the ball."[86] The famous scene of Cinderella's dress transformation follows with the help of her fairy godmother, and then Cinderella disobeys her stepmother and goes to the ball. It is a rebellious action. This inability to follow her stepmother's orders is then accompanied by Cinderella's lie. An omission of facts is a form of lying. Cinderella lies by omission as her stepsisters and stepmother talk about the "mysterious" princess who attended the ball and Cinderella does not present the information that this mystery princess is, in fact, her.[87] Cinderella lies and does not honor her parental figure. She commits a mortal sin and is thus a guilty part within her tale. Cinderella is not at fault for the abusive relationship. This is merely a discussion on how she is not as innocent of a character as she has been presented in the past. This violation of one of the Commandments then gives Lady Tremaine a chance to present pure forgiveness to Cinderella.

Lady Tremaine never forgives nor presents forgiveness to Cinderella. Lady Tremaine does not see herself as a faulty party, but as a victim. She only wants to better her daughter's lives, and although she does so in an abusive way and fails in her task, she was trying to be a good mother to her two biological daughters. Cinderella is a threat to Lady Tremaine's children and her monologue shows how she believes she and her biological family will live "unhappily ever after" because of Cinderella.[88] Lady Tremaine does have the ability to forgive Cinderella. Lady Tremaine is also a victim in their relationship. The abusive relationship between the two characters makes them both victims and faulty parties. Cinderella presents forgiveness, even though it is not pure. Lady Tremaine does not, nor does she have any desire, to forgive Cinderella.

Lady Tremaine does not forgive Cinderella, nor is she ever expected to, as she sees Cinderella as such a threat that she flees the country. When Cinderella becomes a monarchical figure, she uses this new political power to her advantage. Cinderella occupies a higher position in the hierarchy and uses this position of power to "diminish her stepfamily's access to desirable goods."[89] The desirable goods in the stepfamily's case can be seen as the home they reside in, the advantageous marriages Lady Tremaine desperately wants for her daughters, and the ability to remain in the kingdom without fear of punishment. Cinderella has the chance to present pure forgiveness to Lady Tremaine through most of the film, but she waits until the moment the power in the relationship shifts. When the power shifts in the relationship, Cinderella presents the false forgiveness.

During the entirety of the film, Lady Tremaine uses her position of power within her relationship with Cinderella to isolate the child. Lady Tremaine subdues the threat by implementing her power of status when it comes to her relationship with Cinderella. As Cinderella is about to marry the king at the end of the film, she now holds a higher position in society than her stepmother. She uses her new political power to belittle her stepmother through the use of forgiveness. Cinderella finally ranks higher than her stepmother in the social hierarchy. Cinderella uses her new political power to forgive her stepmother, only so she can maintain the political image of being "fair and kind."[90] The use of political power is what makes the forgiveness fake. As a sovereign "what makes the 'I forgive you' sometimes unbearable or odious, even obscene, is the affirmation of sovereignty."[91] Cinderella is about to become a queen with her upcoming nuptials to the king. Cinderella only forgives her stepmother once she attains a more powerful station in society. She uses her newfound sovereignty to affirm her power over her stepfamily. A sovereign has to put aside their affirmation of power in order to present pure forgiveness. Cinderella does not do this. She enacts political forgiveness, not pure forgiveness, to keep her abusive past from blemishing her new role as queen. The forgiveness Cinderella presents does not promote a compassionate relationship as Lady Tremaine and her daughters flee the country after Cinderella's rise to power. The forgiveness is a manipulation tactic. Cinderella uses her power as a monarch to manipulate the public with her false forgiveness. Cinderella's forgiveness is not pure, but a means to an end. She implements forgiveness as a show of power and a warning to her stepmother: Cinderella is in charge now.

NOTES

1. Bruno Bettelheim, *The Uses of Enchantment: The Meaning and Importance of Fairy Tales* (New York: Random House, 1975), 236.

2. Maria Tatar, *The Hard Facts of the Grimms' Fairy Tales* (Princeton: Princeton University Press, 1987), 141.

3. Ruth Bottigheimer, *Grimms' Bad Girls and Bold Boys: The Moral and Social Vision of the Tales* (New Haven: Yale University Press, 1987), 35.

4. Daniel Siegel and Mary Hartzell, *Parenting from the Inside Out: How a Deeper Self-Understanding Can Help You Raise Children Who Thrive* (New York: Penguin Group, 2003), 185.

5. Maria Nikolajeva, *The Rhetoric of Character in Children's Literature* (Lanham: Scarecrow, 2002), 116.

6. Zipora Shechtman, *Treating Child and Adolescent Aggression through Bibliotherapy* (New York: Springer, 2009), 55.

7. Derrida, "On Forgiveness," *On Cosmopolitanism and Forgiveness*, translated by Mark Dooley and Michael Hughes (London: Routledge, 2001), 32.

8. Ibid., 45.

9. Ibid., 27.

10. Ibid., 32.

11. Ibid., 32.

12. "The Gravity of Mortal and Venial Sin," *Catechism of the Catholic Church*, Second editon (Washington D.C.: Libreria Editrice Vaticana), 455.

13. Derrida, "On Forgiveness," 49–50.

14. Ibid., 45.

15. Ibid., 44.

16. Ibid., 39.

17. Ibid., 41.

18. Ibid., 44.

19. Ibid., 49.

20. Ibid., 49.

21. Ibid., 31–32.

22. Ibid., 44.

23. Ibid., 34.

24. Ibid., 34–35.

25. Ibid., 35.

26. Ibid., 45–46.

27. Ibid., 58.

28. Ibid., 58–59.

29. Ibid., 59.

30. Ibid., 59.

31. Ibid., 59.

32. Lorenzo Del Savio and Matteo Mameli, "Power Hierarchies and Social Status: On the Normative Significance of Social Epidemiology," *The American Journal of Bioethics* 15, no. 3 (2015): 52.

33. Ibid., 53.

34. Derrida, "On Forgiveness," 49.

35. Bettelheim, *The Uses of Enchantment: The Meaning and Importance of Fairy Tales*, 249–50.

36. *Cinderella*, directed by Kenneth Branagh (Walt Disney Pictures, 2015).

37. Ibid.

38. Ibid.

39. Ibid.

40. Ibid.

41. Del Savio and Mameli, "Power Hierarchies and Social Status," 52.

42. *Cinderella*, Branagh.

43. Ibid.

44. Ibid.

45. Marina Warner, *From the Beast to the Blonde: On Fairy Tales and Their Tellers* (London: Vintage Random House, 1995), 238.

46. Christy Williams, "Who's Wicked Now? The Stepmother as Fairy-Tale Heroine," *Marvels & Tales: Journal of Fairy-Tale Studies* 24, no. 2 (2010): 260.

47. Warner, *From the Beast,* 213.

48. *Cinderella,* Branagh.

49. Ibid.

50. Del Savio and Mameli, "Power Hierarchies and Social Status," 52.

51. *Cinderella,* Branagh.

52. Ibid.

53. "Exodus," 20:16, *The Holy Bible* (Nashville: Thomas Nelson Publishers, 1989).

54. *Cinderella,* Branagh.

55. Ibid.

56. Derrida, "On Forgiveness," 49.

57. *Cinderella,* Branagh.

58. Ibid.

59. Ibid.

60. Del Savio and Mameli, "Power Hierarchies and Social Status," 52.

61. Derrida, "On Forgiveness," 48.

62. Ibid., 49.

63. Ibid., 32.

64. Ibid.

65. Ibid., 44.

66. *Cinderella,* Branagh.

67. Ibid.

68. Ibid.

69. Ibid.

70. Ibid.

71. Ibid.

72. Ibid.

73. Del Savio and Mameli, "Power Hierarchies and Social Status," 52.

74. *Cinderella,* Branagh.

75. Derrida, "On Forgiveness," 45–46.

76. Ibid., 58.

77. *Cinderella,* Branagh.

78. Del Savio and Mameli, "Power Hierarchies and Social Status," 53.

79. Shechtman, *Treating Child and Adolescent Aggression,* 77.

80. Ibid., 75.

81. Tatar, *Hard Facts,* 141.

82. Branagh, *Cinderella.*

83. Shechtman, *Treating Child and Adolescent Aggression,* 75.

84. Ibid., 55.

85. "Exodus," 20:12.

86. *Cinderella,* Branagh.

87. Ibid.

88. Ibid.

89. Del Savio and Mameli, "Power Hierarchies and Social Status," 52.

90. *Cinderella,* Branagh.

91. Derrida, "On Forgiveness," 58.

BIBLIOGRAPHY

Bettelheim, Bruno. *The Uses of Enchantment: The Meaning and Importance of Fairy Tales.* New York: Random House, 1975.

Bottigheimer, Ruth B. *Grimms' Bad Girls and Bold Boys: The Moral and Social Vision of the Tales.* New Haven: Yale University Press, 1987.

Branagh, Kenneth. *Cinderella.* Walt Disney Pictures, 2015.

Del Savio, Lorenzo, and Matteo Mameli. "Power Hierarchies and Social Status: On the Normative Significance of Social Epidemiology." *The American Journal of Bioethics* 15, no. 3 (2015): 52–53.

Derrida, Jacques. "On Forgiveness." In *On Cosmopolitanism and Forgiveness,* translated by Mark Dooley and Michael Hughes, 25–60. London: Routledge, 2001.

"Exodus," 20:16. In *The Holy Bible.* Nashville: Thomas Nelson Publishers, 1989.

"The Gravity of Mortal and Venial Sin." In *Catechism of the Catholic Church,* Second edition, 454–58. Washington D.C.: Libreria Editrice Vaticana.

Nikolajeva, Maria. *The Rhetoric of Character in Children's Literature.* Lanham, Md.: Scarecrow, 2002.

Shechtman, Zipora. *Treating Child and Adolescent Aggression through Bibliotherapy.* New York: Springer, 2009.

Siegel, Daniel J., and Mary Hartzell. *Parenting from the Inside Out: How a Deeper Self-Understanding Can Help You Raise Children Who Thrive.* New York: Penguin Group, 2003.

Tatar, Maria. *The Hard Facts of the Grimms' Fairy Tales.* Princeton: Princeton University Press, 1987.

Warner, Marina. *From the Beast to the Blonde: On Fairy Tales and Their Tellers.* London: Vintage Random House, 1995.

Williams, Christy. "Who's Wicked Now? The Stepmother as Fairy-Tale Heroine." *Marvels & Tales: Journal of Fairy-Tale Studies* 24, no. 2 (2010): 255–71.

Chapter Seven

Tiana Can't Stay Woke

Reassessing the "Cinderella" Narrative in Disney's
The Princess and the Frog

Camille S. Alexander

In an era of being woke, fairy tales like "Cinderella," both the Perrault and Brothers Grimm version, and "The Frog Prince" fall short of this contemporary pop culture identifier. Regardless of the version of the story or the depiction of the protagonist, fairy princesses seem weaker than woke. These characters are perpetual victims, in one form or another; are dependent; and lack the self-awareness indicative of being woke. The term was first used within a sociocultural framework referencing the African American lexicon by late cultural critic William Melvin Kelley (1937–2017) in a 1962 article. *Merriam-Webster* notes that the phrase "stay woke" was likely transformed "into a byword of social awareness"[1] in Erykah Badu's song "Master Teacher."[2] The song, credited to Badu, was written by Georgia Anne Muldrow, who duets the piece with Badu. Elijah C. Watson's interview with Muldrow revealed that the tone of the song changed from its original "psychedelic, futuristic funk" to a "more minimal and subdued" form—much like "an African chant."[3] The use of an African chant tone is significant as it transports the listener from the contemporary US, where African Americans remain marginalized, to an African homeland in which Blacks were free of the impositions of a post-chattel slavery society. The song's lyrics use the term "I stay woke" to indicate a state of awareness, whether social, cultural, historical, political, racial, gendered, or self—that the speaker "attained the self she was searching for."[4] However, Muldrow notes that the original refrain was "I'd stay woke," implying "that she's still searching, striving for that new self."[5] The combination of lyrics that raise Black Diaspora cultural

awareness in the West with a smooth, R&B/hip-hop beat—one paying homage to an African homeland—cements the term "woke" in contemporary
African American lexicon and, according to Watson, is an example of "the
continual mishandling of blackness" as the term has been appropriated into
mainstream culture, thus losing much of its original intent and potency.[6] The
term "woke" is particularly relevant when assessing the efficacy of Disney's
first and only African American princess, Tiana, who is also a Cinderella
character.

Cinderella characters are devoid of all forms of awareness, weak-willed,
preternaturally upbeat given their socioeconomic marginalization, and un-
willing to fight for their own survival, opting instead to be "saved" by a fairy
godmother, handsome prince, or a combination of the two rather than acting
out of self-preservation. Based on Cinderella, either by Perrault or the
Grimm Brothers, these characters are protagonists in rags-to-riches stories
with gendered connotations as the main character's focus is on marrying a
prince, transforming her from, for example, a maid to a princess. Disney's
The Princess and the Frog[7] attempts to restructure the rags-to-riches, Cinderella narrative simply by introducing an African American princess into the
Cinderella role. The movie is a mashup of "Cinderella" and "The Frog
Prince" with the inclusion of an African American princess to give the animated film the appearance of being more woke. While the inclusion of an
African American female protagonist in the Cinderella role might seem to be
someone who would "stay woke," an analysis of this film reveals that the
term cannot be used in relation to Tiana, who fails to employ elements of
being woke in her daily life. Essentially, whether a Cinderella character is
depicted as a woman of color or not, she can never be woke, get woke, or
stay woke. *The Princess and the Frog*, which is imbued with the rags-to-
riches theme, attempts to portray a Cinderella character who is woke, using
her work ethic and dedication to fulfill her father's dream of opening a
restaurant as indicators of her self-awareness. However, the reality is that the
character remains a tiresome depiction of the overly-optimistic girl consis-
tently at the whim of others—whether the other is her deceased father who
longs to open a restaurant; her mother, who wants her to find her Prince
Charming; or the Fenner brothers, who deny her the opportunity to become
the proprietor of her own business. While Tiana is not as weak as the typical
Cinderella, she, like the original, cannot stay woke. This iteration of Cinderella seems novel because Tiana is African American, independent, and actively working toward a life goal. However, Tiana lacks true self-awareness,
unable to separate her dream from her father's. Tiana differs from other
Cinderella characters in her ability to survive independently. However, this
trait is inadequate and does not distinguish her completely from the fantasy
and fairy tale indicative of the Cinderella trope as, in the end, she opts to
place emphasis on a relationship over regaining her human form and fulfill-

ing her dream of owning a restaurant. Finally, the movie fails to stay woke by refusing to acknowledge that Tiana is black. Given the period (1920s) and the location (New Orleans), it seems unrealistic to avoid the topic of race, yet the film never mentions the subject directly. Although Tiana is black, hard-working, and independent, she cannot stay woke.

Disney's *The Princess and the Frog* (hereafter *PTF*) is a contemporary take on "The Frog Prince," or "Iron Heinrich" (*Der Froschkönig oder der eiserne Heinrich*), the first story in the Grimm Brothers' collection *Kinder- und Hausm ä rchen*.[8] Based loosely on E. D. Baker's novel *Tales of the Frog Princess*,[9] Disney's version of the tale is set in New Orleans and the bayous of Atchafalaya Basin. Unlike both the Grimm Brothers and Baker version, Disney's protagonist is a young, working-class, African American woman named Tiana. Set in the post-WWI 1920s, *PTF* captures the music of the Jazz Age and the hopes of the post-war years without referencing the movie's key element: race. Scott Foundas of *The Village Voice* observed that *PTF*, "for all its superficial innocuousness . . . is the most insidious" of the Disney films "because it comes packaged as an all-ages entertainment."[10] Cassandra Stover postulates that later Disney films, representing a "New Wave" in the depictions of minority characters in animation, can be "problematic in vari- ous ways," representing "unprecedented attempts by Disney to broaden their market appeal towards postmodern diversity while catering to the new expec- tations of its female audience."[11] The film avoids race and the American political landscape in the WWI years, when the film begins, and in the 1920s, which is the historical setting for the majority of the film, while perpetuating a "racial fantasy . . . of a 'post-racial' era, in which African Americans are present yet absent and race is implicit yet unaddressed."[12] This representa- tion is problematic—particularly for younger viewers—because it promotes an attitude that race is no longer an issue in the US, meaning that, as these young viewers age into America's systemically racist society, they will do so with the firm belief that racism, systemic and interpersonal, are no longer relevant because there was once an African American Disney princess.

Avoiding race leaves much unsaid and a significant historical gap as, in the 1920s, neither Louisiana nor any southern state provided a safe or ideal location for African Americans. Ajay Gehlawat observes that this period referred to as the "Jazz Age" was also "the advent of many racist policies as well as the reestablishment of the Ku Klux Klan."[13] In an early scene in the film, a newspaper headline announcing the election of Woodrow Wilson, who was known for his "personal racism and the policies of racial segrega- tion he enacted during his tenure in office,"[14] is prominent. Jennifer L. Bark- er notes that "the likelihood of Disney making a children's movie that ad- dresses the racial realities of the Deep South in the 1920s is something that will undoubtably never happen."[15] Essentially, this is a children's film; how- ever, race could have been addressed in a more realistic manner, first by simply having Tiana acknowledge that she is black. The film depicts the typical, Cinderella rags-to-riches narrative, replacing the singing domestic worker longing for her prince with a singing young woman with aspirations of owning a high-end French cuisine restaurant and jazz club. While Tiana manages to achieve her goals, the troubling avoidance of race, by Tiana and every other character, adds another layer to the Disney fantasy. *PTF* acknowledges the limitations society places on women while ignoring racial discrimination. As a result, Tiana lacks self- and social awareness—the keystones of being woke.

PTF has been described as "a predictable attempt to cash in on the contemporary Obama-esque, color-blindish liberal landscape."[16] Watching the meteoric rise to power of a little-known state senator turned US senator from Illinois, who was also the product of an interracial marriage between a white midwestern woman and a Kenyan man, and quite an intellectual in his own right, was a turning point in US history that was perhaps not seen since the days of another famous Illinoisan, Abraham Lincoln. The Obama rags-to-riches story depicted in the media, replete with an attractive, professional African American wife and two lovely little girls, set the tone for a new age in American history—the Age of Obama, which was characterized by black excellence and over-achievement. Given the impact of Obama's presidency on the entire country, it was in Disney's pecuniary interests to promote African American life in a feature animated film, representing not so much a "New Wave" as a new source of revenue. The result was *PTF*, which initially began with some cultural misinformation, requiring the input of both the NAACP and Oprah Winfrey, among others.[17] In an interview, Disney's chief creative officer John Lasseter stated, "we didn't want to do anything that might hurt anybody so we worked with a lot of African American leaders."[18] However, it is important to note that in the process of consulting African Americans, no black intellectuals, such as bell hooks, who is also the author of several successful children's books and a critical race theorist, were consulted by the Disney Company or writers, Musker and Clements. This omission is telling as it reflects either Disney's cluelessness or the company's emphasis on audience pleasing for profit. One element of this attempt at pleasing an audience for profit manifests itself in Tiana's hard-work mantra and the fact that this attitude is largely based on fulfilling a dream posed by her father before his untimely death.

Early in the film, Tiana's father, James, is introduced. He is depicted in the family's small, shotgun home, set among the other homes of New Orleans's working class—or perhaps working poor. The family home is a sharp contrast to the Garden District home of the La Bouffs—the employers of Tiana's mother, Eudora, a *de facto* nanny to the family's spoiled child, Charlotte (Lottie), who is also Tiana's best friend. Lauren Dundes and Madeline Streiff observe that "Disney emphasizes Tiana's family's lower status . . . by never mentioning their last name,"[19] whereas the La Bouff family name is prominent in the film. Emphasis is placed on James as the head of the family but also as a loving and involved parent; he is Tiana's mentor in her culinary endeavors and her instructor in the kitchen. Using James's character as Tiana's cooking teacher is an interesting twist as taking this direction de-feminizes cooking, which is typically seen as "woman's work." James's culinary endeavors and his dream of owning a restaurant—one with tablecloths and a full staff rather than a greasy spoon—demonstrates the film's awareness of the "New Negro," or "African-Americans who were considered more refined, educated, sophisticated, and involved in the political process."[20] Barker notes that "[i]n terms of Black stereotypes, [Tiana] is the antidote to the 'lazy Negro,'"[21] a categorization propagated in the latter half of the nineteenth century by segregationists and supporters of Jim Crow.

While James makes a positive contribution to the film, at some point in the narrative the lines between his dream and Tiana's become blurred as the goal of owning a restaurant was initially his. This blurring raises questions, such as whether owning a restaurant is really Tiana's dream or whether she is pursuing this dream to honor her father. James dies early in the film, likely in WWI indicated by a picture of him in uniform and a medal on Tiana's dresser, and "[h]er quest to please her father is transparent."[22] Juliana Garabedian has a positive view of Tiana's dream of restaurant ownership, noting that *PTF* depicts "the female lead trying to break out of her gender role and follow her own path rather than the one defined for her."[23] While Garabedian makes a valid point from a feminist perspective, this view is problematic because of the presence of underlying racial issues—that while this trope is easily applied to white women, for women of color the option of following one's own path has not been so much a choice as a necessity for survival. In addition, the ambiguity of the origin of Tiana's goal is problematic when attempting to determine whether Tiana is woke as she does not seem aware of the answer. Tiana is following her father's dream, begging the question of whether she has her own. A character who does not understand her needs— whether the direction her life takes is the result of her own desires or her father's—cannot be considered woke as she lacks the self-awareness to formulate an answer.

Georgia Anne Muldrow notes that to be woke is "understanding what your ancestors went through. Just being in touch with the struggle."[24] Tiana understands that her father worked hard, but her understanding of James's struggles is limited. In a scene with Dr. Facilier, the Shadow Man, he reminds her that James worked hard, using this emotional appeal to win Tiana over and fulfill his dreams of stealing the La Bouff family's wealth. James's death in WWI is also an indicator of his willingness to sacrifice for family and country, which is intriguing as the US, circa the WWI era, was racially hostile and plagued by Jim Crow laws, which are carefully sidestepped in the film. Tiana is aware of her father's strength and accomplishments, elevating him to hero status in the film, but she seems unaware of her status as a black, working-class, young woman in the Jim Crow South. Like the original Disney Cinderella, she works almost twenty-four hours a day—backbreaking work as a waitress in two restaurants—reinforcing common stereotypes about professional black women. The film repeats racially-coded and gendered stereotypes that professional black women are "so busy working [that they do] not focus on building a relationship and family."[25] Tiana has a surface understanding of her father's life and struggles and an even more tenuous understanding of her mother's. The film makes no mention of Tiana's biological ancestors, further limiting her access to their knowledge and wisdom. Toni Morrison notes that in black writing, "[t]here is always an elder"—a "sort of timeless people whose relationships to the characters are benevolent, instructive, and protective, and they provide a certain kind of wisdom."[26] Both James and Eudora as well as Mama Odie, the 197-year-old voodoo practitioner who lives in the bayou, provide some element of the ancestral connectedness needed to develop a sense of self-awareness, but they do not provide enough to Tiana. There are no older black adults in the film guiding Tiana with a firm and affectionate hand, thus making the character seem rootless, drifting, and unable to stay woke.

In addition to lacking self-awareness, Tiana also lacks an awareness of the society she occupies and how this directly impacts her as a black woman. The headline announcing Wilson's election at the beginning of the film seems innocuous, but it announces a new age in discriminatory policies that impacted African Americans more than any other group. Tiana and her family live in a black, working-class area of New Orleans while the La Bouffs live in the Garden District, yet no mention is made in *PTF* about their divergent socioeconomic and social statuses. Eudora works for the La Bouffs as a seamstress, which is a professional position with some status, yet her job also entails entertaining Lottie with stories about princesses kissing frogs who become handsome princes. Tiana and Lottie are described in the film as best friends, but neither Tiana nor Lottie seem aware of the differences between them, including race. Neal A. Lester notes that "Disney's fantastical design would have us believe that a poor black girl and a rich white girl in 1920s New Orleans can remain best friends without external social disapproval or scrutiny."[27] Sarita McCoy Gregory contends that while "Tiana and Lottie remain friends throughout the movie, the audience" becomes attuned to the "distance between them wrought by race, class, and" the passing of many years[28] since they first listened to Eudora tell the story of the frog prince as children. The distance between the two becomes clearer as they age into young adulthood.

While Lottie dreams of becoming a princess by marrying a prince, Tiana's dreams do not extend beyond the service industries. Unlike other Disney princesses, who "remain 'happily ever after' in the ivory towers of fairyland bliss," "Tiana aspires for a career in the service industry."[29] Tiana's "'dreams of success as a restaurateur are constantly framed in terms of actual cooking, an occupation . . . historically connected with black women."[30] Foundas notes, "that Disney's first black 'princess' lives in a world where the ceiling on black ambition is firmly set at the service industries."[31] This observation is troubling because "Tiana and her neighbors seem downright sip-a-dee-doo-dah happy about"[32] their limited social status and economic opportunities in the film. The film's troubling avoidance of racial issues in the US cannot help but create a protagonist who is not woke as the plot implies that there is nothing to be woke about. Tiana cannot stay woke because the film creates a fantasy land in which there are no social issues necessitating her being woke at all. Nic Stone notes that to be black in America means experiencing "dehumanizing experiences" almost daily—and this observation is in the post-racial, post-Obama era.[33] To have been black in America in the early 1900s must have raised inexplicable feelings of frustration that *PTF* simply does not convey. The only character to express frustration with his limitations is Dr. Facilier, and he is a thief and a con artist, reinforcing stereotypes of black men, which are "hard to fight against because they are so all-encompassing and systemic in nature."[34] James's death early in the film combined with the fact "that the other black males are either physically challenged, illiterate and old, or engaged in criminal voodoo activity also raise serious questions about Disney's construction of African-American maleness."[35]

When Dr. Facilier gives Tiana the option of betraying Naveen to regain her human form and fulfilling her dream of owning her own restaurant, initially, the audience is left wondering which she will choose: love or her dream? In typical Disneyesque fashion, Tiana does not experience an extended pause as she quickly opts for saving Naveen, which means that she will likely remain a frog and never attain her dream of entrepreneurship. Disney glosses over the gendered connotations of this option as, yet again, a woman is asked to decide between her goals and a man, thus reaffirming the narrative of the "only" choice for a woman is male companionship. As Tiana is a black woman, this predicament is even more troubling as she is not only economically but physically impeding herself. If she chooses love, she will remain a frog, which means that she will never open her restaurant. In *PTF*, Disney promotes the same tiresome narrative that it always has: once a girl finds her prince, every problem is instantly resolved. There is no need for a woman to look beyond social and familial strictures dictating that finding the right man is the optimal result.

Like other contemporary Disney princess tales (*Aladdin, Mulan, Pocahontas 2*), Tiana's romance with Prince Naveen of (imaginary) Maldonia develops over time, replacing the traditional Cinderella story of love at first sight or waking up in love as in *Sleeping Beauty*. The deceleration of the typical princess romance in *PTF* does little to demonstrate that Tiana is woke as emphasis is placed, not on Tiana, but on her relationship with a prince, who can best be described as a "scrub."[36] Dundes and Streiff describe Prince Naveen "as a ne'er-do-well and playboy who is broke because he has been cut off by his family."[37] Naveen is spoiled, lazy, inept, and a bit cowardly as he "is the only Disney prince who fails to even *try* to take on the malefactor Dr. Facilier who tricks him."[38] When Naveen and Tiana are, as frogs, lost in the bayou, Naveen distinguishes himself as the laziest Disney prince in animation history as he plays the guitar while Tiana steers them through the water, moving branches out of their way, and generally taking care of this man-baby just as his servants likely did. Tiana's enthusiastic whistle-while-you-work attitude is a sharp contrast to Naveen's sing-while-others-work-for-you predisposition. Through the film, Naveen relies on Tiana to save him, to protect him, to help him, and this does not change as, at the end of the film, Naveen moves from relying on Tiana as a friend to "reliance on his wife."[39] From his first interaction with Tiana, when he is a frog begging Tiana to kiss him and restore his human form, Naveen is mildly offensive, raising questions about Disney's goals with having its first African American princess courted by a "scrub." Naveen "fails to possess *any* characteristic that makes him notably worthy, heroic, or memorable," so why is he Tiana's love interest and why does she eventually fall in love with and marry him?

While Naveen's "unconventional auxiliary role and lack of stellar qualities offer further evidence of the alternative narrative for princess of color"[40] in the Disney universe, his shortcomings also suggest that Tiana, in ultimately choosing to love this weak and inept man, is not woke. While Damon Young jokingly suggests that being woke means that one is "so awake that your 'third eye' [sees] things that aren't there,"[41] he also notes that "to be woke . . . is to recognize and reject the damage power inflicts on the most vulnerable."[42] Tiana seems only marginally aware of the ramifications of Naveen being a prince in the decade following WWI. Somehow, it escapes Tiana's notice that Naveen is the member of a social class responsible for both her status and, by extension, her father's untimely death in WWI. Instead, when she first meets him, Tiana is willing to kiss a talking frog, who claims to be a prince, so that she can, with the financial help of this prince, buy her restaurant. She never questions why he is a prince—essentially who had to die or suffer for him to gain his position—or the origin of the money he will use to pay her in return for this kiss. As their romance develops, Tiana seems more focused on their relationship than anything else. Even the possibility of owning her restaurant, when offered by Dr. Facilier, does not have the outcome of turning Tiana's attention away from Naveen as Dr. Facilier hoped.

Another troubling element of *PTF* encouraging Tiana "to stay asleep"[43] is the avoidance of race in the film. While race is certainly a relevant topic to the film—particularly as Disney marketed Tiana as the first African American princess—there seems to have been little effort to depict Tiana as a woman of color who is keenly aware of the impact of her racial affiliation on her socioeconomic status. Charania and Simonds take a divergent approach, noting that Tiana "seems cognizant of her subaltern place in society, but determined to fight for her goals."[44] One might question where exactly in the film does Tiana seem aware of her "subaltern place in society" and whether this is coded language for "servant" or "black." The avoidance of race in *PTF* raises questions about whether Tiana is woke.

There are many definitions of the term "woke," such as "to be angry"[45] or to have "racial awareness."[46] Tiana is rarely angry in the film, which, had it been more prominent, would likely have perpetuated the "angry black woman" narrative used to sideline black women who refuse to be reduced to subaltern status or silenced about their marginalization. Of the many definitions for the term "woke" available, Watson gives what is perhaps the most critical and relevant one, noting that "[t]o be woke is to be black."[47] One might question when and where in *PTF* Tiana gives the slightest inkling of acknowledging that she is black. Turner notes that the "film represents a complex moment in a culture steeped in political correctness and an adherence to the politics of colorblindness."[48] To accomplish this task, a connection is made "between blackness and a strong work ethic."[49] The use of Tiana's work ethic as a marker for the "positive" side of being black is problematic because it also distracts from other elements of African American culture and experiences. McCoy Gregory contends that Tiana is "exceptional in that she does not partake in any distractions, including dancing, which was a ritual among blacks."[50] This theory is supported by research into the roots of dancing among black New Orleanians, dating back to the times of American chattel slavery. Although dancing is an important element to black culture—both on the African continent and in the diaspora—it is not the only element. Therefore, this theory seems steeped in the same colorblindness that it claims to reject. Tiana fails to stay woke because she is a black woman who does not seem to understand that she is black or what that means—either to her as an individual or to her community.

Throughout the film, there are a few markers to remind the audience that Tiana is black. For example, Eudora works as a seamstress and surrogate nanny for the La Bouff family while James is a laborer. While Lottie wiles away her days in the family's Garden District mansion dreaming of her future prince, Tiana works two jobs as a waitress. One might ask why a young woman as intelligent as Tiana submits to manual labor so willingly when, with some encouragement and support, she could have been a university student or a trained professional, and not in the service industry. When the Fenner Brothers, the real estate agents who first agree to take Tiana's deposit on the building for her restaurant, renege on the deal, it is because "A little woman of [her] . . . background . . . would have had her hands full trying to run a big business like that." While Tiana is aware that she has been outbid on the property, she does not connect the Fenner Brothers comment about her "background" to her race. This comment, in conjunction with mentioning that she is a "little woman" places emphasis on Tiana as a black woman; yet, in the entire interaction, Tiana is only cognizant of losing her restaurant. This interaction takes place at Lottie's masquerade ball, which she and Big Daddy throw to welcome Prince Naveen to New Orleans. Tiana, who is supposedly Lottie's best friend, attends the ball dressed like another servant, and she is also there as cook, having made her "man-catching beignets" at Lottie's request. One might question whether Lottie would have asked a white best friend, regardless of her culinary talents, to cook for her party and attend as a servant rather than a guest. McCoy Gregory notes that black women functioned as "an invisible workforce in the private sphere, primarily in the capacity of cooks" and other domestic workers.[51] In addition, food is used in the film "to mitigate the presence on screen of" Disney's "first African American female protagonist . . . making her more acceptable to mainstream audiences."[52] To that end, "connecting food with specific racial and ethnic identities can also be employed to express and negotiate cultural tensions."[53] Yet, throughout these events, Tiana does not seem to identify race as the critical factor. While the majority American viewing public may be colorblind, making the first African American Disney princess blind to her own color is troubling.

Tiana seems willfully asleep regarding race. There are no discussions of prejudice, black experiences, or any other racial topics. The film suggests that James dies in WWI, but in 1919, the US experienced one of its greatest public events of racial profiling leading to violence: Red Summer. In this particularly disturbing event, which spanned much of 1919, African American soldiers in US military uniforms were violently attacked by angry white mobs in public for wearing their uniforms—markers of serving their country. *PTF* implies that James died in the war, but he could have been murdered during Red Summer. Here, Disney makes a fatal flaw, contributing to a narrative of racial uplift that simply did not exist at the time. While the film cannot be set in the 1920s and express the anger and frustration of the latter half of the twentieth century that many African Americans had toward fighting for a country that neither valued their service nor their lives as civilians,[54] it could have done a better job of portraying the realities of the time. As a result, Tiana honors James as a hero, placing his photograph and medal on her dresser; however, she does not seem cognizant of the social events that make this image of her black father dressed as an American soldier problematic. Therefore, in this scene as in the rest of the *PTF*, Tiana stays asleep—almost willfully choosing to avoid the topic of race and focusing her psychological, emotional, and physical energy on obtaining her restaurant. Tiana's inability to stay woke shines through in a film that is marketed as addressing the experiences of a young black woman.

Throughout Disney's *The Princess and the Frog*, it would not escape a woke audience member's notice that Tiana's view of the world is myopic—centered on achieving her goal of owing a restaurant—and only slightly derailed by romance with a handsome and broke prince and occasionally interrupted by an inordinate amount of singing. There are no discussions of race, as if the image of a young black woman on film—granted, one who spends the majority of said film in "greenface"[55]—is enough to mitigate the character's colorblindness and inability to stay woke. Georgia Anne Muldrow observed that for people of the African Diaspora, "[t]here was no year where the fight wasn't going down."[56] The concept of staying woke is inextricably linked with black struggle in the West. This is not an experience that can be set to music or mitigated by depicting a black female character with a "can do" attitude. If hard work and perseverance were the only traits needed for black achievement, Tulsa, Oklahoma's Greenwood District would still be the Black Wall Street, Ferguson would never have occurred, and Watts would be a booming neighborhood instead of the setting of riots that left it socially and economically damaged and underdeveloped decades later. The issue with Disney's depiction of Tiana is that it is an attempt to pacify black audiences while failing to remind white audiences that there are links in a long chain of people and events that contributed to this young woman's plight—not her transformation into a frog, but the socioeconomic factors that took her father away, that make owning a high-end restaurant in 1920s New Orleans an unreachable dream, that hamper her ability to find a life partner who is as dedicated as she is. In *The Princess and the Frog*, it is far less complicated to have Tiana stay asleep because, if she were woke, she would see that her life hangs in a more precarious position that she imagined and that, regardless of how hard she works or how loudly she sings, there are no viable solutions. In the end, dreams for young black women with ambitions do not "really come true in New Orleans" and the black diaspora in the West continues to be "almost there." Staying woke is not simply "racial awareness"[57] or to be "slightly aware of the way systemic racism and marginalization function."[58] To be woke is to be like "the canaries in [the] coalmines, alerting [other blacks] to dangers [they] might be too drowsy to see."[59] According to Watson, "being woke isn't fucking fun,"[60] and Princess Tiana is definitely having too much fun to be woke.

NOTES

1. "Stay Woke," *Merriam-Webster*, last modified 2020, https://www.merriam-webster.com/words-at-play/woke-meaning-origin.
2. "Master Teacher," Track #8 on *New Amerykah Part One (4th World War)*, Motown Record Company, L. P., 2008. Erykah Badu and Georgia Anne Muldrow, 2008.
3. Elijah C. Watson, "The Origin of Woke: How Erykah Badu and Georgia Anne Muldrow Sparked the 'Stay Woke' Era," *Okayplayer*, February 27, 2018, https://www.okayplayer.com/originals/georgia-muldrow-erykah-badu-stay-woke-master-teacher.html, par. 25.
4. Watson, par. 28.
5. Ibid.
6. Watson, par. 33.
7. *The Princess and The Frog*, directed by John Musker and Ron Clements (2009; Burbank, CA: Buena Vista Home Entertainment, Inc., 2019), DVD.
8. The Brothers Grimm, "The Frog Prince or Iron Heinrich" ["*Der Froschkönig oder der eiserne Heinrich*"], in *Children's and Household Tales* [*Kinder-und Hausmärchen*] (Berlin: In Der Realschulbuchhandlung, 1812).
9. E. D. Baker, *Tales of the Frog Princess* (London: Bloomsbury Publishing, 2002).
10. Scott Foundas, "Disney's Princess and the Frog Can't Escape the Ghetto," *The Village Voice*, November 24, 2009, https://www.villagevoice.com/2009/11/24/disneys-princess-and-the-frog-cant-escape-the-ghetto/, par. 6.
11. Cassandra Stover, "Damsels and Heroines: The Conundrum of the Post-Feminist Disney Princess," *LUX: A Journal of Transdisciplinary Writing and Research from Claremont Graduate University* 2, no. 1 (2013): 5.
12. Ajay Gehlawat, "The Strange Case of 'The Princess and the Frog': Passing and the Elision of Race," *Journal of African American Studies* 14, no 4 (December 2010): 429.
13. Gehlawat, 420.
14. Ibid.
15. Jennifer L. Barker, "Hollywood, Black Animation, and the Problem of Representation in *Little Ol' Bosko* and *The Princess and the Frog*," *Journal of African American Studies* 14 (2010): 493.
16. Moon Charania and Wendy Simonds, "The Princess and the Frog," *Contexts* 9, no. 3 (Summer 2010): 69, https://journals.sagepub.com/doi/abs/10.1525/ctx.2010.9.3.69.
17. Barker, 482.
18. Sarah E. Turner, "Blackness, Bayous and Gumbo: Encoding and Decoding Race in a Colorblind World," in *Diversity in Disney Films: Critical Essays on Race, Ethnicity, Gender, Sexuality and Disability*, ed. Johnson Cheu (Jefferson, NC: McFarland & Company, 2014), 84.
19. Lauren Dundes and Madeline Streiff, "Reel Royal Diversity? The Glass Ceiling in Disney's Mulan and Princess and the Frog," *Societies* 6, no. 35 (2016): 8.
20. Gene Jarrett, "Who Was the 'New Negro'? Questions for Black History Month," *BU Today*, February 21, 2008, http://www.bu.edu/articles/2008/who-was-the-new-negro-questions-for-black-history-month/, par. 4.
21. Barker, 494.
22. Dundes and Streiff, 7.
23. Juliana Garabedian, "Animating Gender Roles: How Disney Is Redefining the Modern Princess," *James Madison Undergraduate Research Journal* 2, no. 1 (2014): 23.
24. Watson, par. 5.
25. Rebecca Wanzo, "Black Love Is Not a Fairytale," *Poroi* 7, no. 2 (2011): 5.
26. Toni Morrison, "Rootedness: The Ancestor as Foundation," in *The Norton Anthology of African American Literature*, ed. Henry Louis Gates, Jr. and Nellie Y. McKay, second edition (New York: W. W. Norton & Company, 2004), 2289.
27. Neal A. Lester, "Disney's *The Princess and the Frog*: The Pride, the Pressure, and the Politics of Being a First," *The Journal of American Culture* 33, no. 4 (December 2010): 302.
28. Sarita McCoy Gregory, "Disney's Second Line: New Orleans, Racial Masquerade, and the Reproduction of Whiteness in *The Princess and the Frog*," *Journal of African American Studies* 14 (2010): 445.

29. Lester, 295.

30. Fabio Parasecoli, "A Taste of Louisiana: Mainstreaming Blackness through Food in *The Princess and the Frog*," *Journal of African American Studies* 14 (2010): 450.

31. Foundas, par. 7.

32. Ibid.

33. Nic Stone, "To Be Black and #Woke Is to Be in a Rage All The Time," *Huffington Post*, August 9, 2018, https://www.huffpost.com/entry/opinion-mike-brown-rage-racism_n_5b6992cee4b0de86f4a52959, par. 7.

34. Barker, 486.

35. Lester, 301.

36. The term "scrub" is used in reference to the TLC song "No Scrubs" (1999) from the album *FanMail*. The first verse includes the lyrics "Always talkin' 'bout what he wants and just sits on his broke ass." This is an apt description for the unemployed, homeless, financially unstable Naveen.

37. Dundes and Streiff, 11.

38. Dundes and Streiff, 11.

39. Ibid.

40. Ibid.

41. Damon Young, "In Defense of Woke," *New York Times*, November 29, 2019, https://www.nytimes.com/2019/11/29/opinion/woke-impeachment-trump.html, par. 6.

42. Young, par. 12.

43. Stone, par. 6.

44. Charania and Simonds, 70.

45. Stone, par. 7.

46. Young, par. 6.

47. Watson, par. 1.

48. Turner, 83.

49. McCoy Gregory, 446.

50. Ibid.

51. McCoy Gregory, 444.

52. Parasecoli, 451.

53. Ibid.

54. The Geto Boys "Fuck a War" from their album *We Can't Be Stopped* (1991) provides an admirable example of African American frustration with blacks fighting for the US, which, to this day, maintains black subaltern status socially, economically, and in education through biased policies.

55. Esther J. Terry, "Rural as Racialized Plantation vs Rural as Modern Reconnection: Blackness and Agency in Disney's *Song of the South* and *The Princess and the Frog*," *Journal of African American Studies* 14 (2010): 470.

56. Watson, par. 5.

57. Young, par. 6.

58. Stone, par. 7.

59. Young, par. 15.

60. Watson, par. 35.

BIBLIOGRAPHY

Badu, Erykah, and Georgia Anne Muldrow. "Master Teacher." Track 8 on *New Amerykah Part One (4th World War)*, Motown Record Company, L. P., 2008, CD.

Baker, E. D. *Tales of the Frog Princess*. London: Bloomsbury Publishing, 2002.

Barker, Jennifer L. "Hollywood, Black Animation, and the Problem of Representation in *Little Ol' Bosko* and *The Princess and the Frog*." *Journal of African American Studies* 14 (2010): 482–498.

Charania, Moon, and Wendy Simonds. "The Princess and the Frog." *Contexts* 9, no. 3 (Summer 2010): 69–71. https://journals.sagepub.com/doi/abs/10.1525/ctx.2010.9.3.69.

Dundes, Lauren, and Madeline Streiff. "Reel Royal Diversity? The Glass Ceiling in Disney's Mulan and Princess and the Frog." *Societies* 6, no. 35 (2016): 1–14.

Foundas, Scott. "Disney's Princess and the Frog Can't Escape the Ghetto." *The Village Voice*, November 24, 2009. https://www.villagevoice.com/2009/11/24/disneys-princess-and-the-frog-cant-escape-the-ghetto/.

Garabedian, Juliana. "Animating Gender Roles: How Disney Is Redefining the Modern Princess." *James Madison Undergraduate Research Journal* 2, no. 1 (2014): 22–25.

Gehlawat, Ajay. "The Strange Case of 'The Princess and the Frog': Passing and the Elision of Race." *Journal of African American Studies* 14, no. 4 (December 2010): 417–431.

Geto Boys. "Fuck a War." Track 9 on *We Can't Be Stopped*. Rap-a-Lot Records, 1991, CD.

Grimm, The Brothers. "The Frog Prince or Iron Heinrich" ["*Der Froschkönig oder der eiserne Heinrich*"], in *Children's and Household Tales* [*Kinder-und Hausmärchen*]. Berlin: In Der Realschulbuchhandlung, 1812.

Jarrett, Gene. "Who Was the 'New Negro'? Questions for Black History Month." *BU Today*, February 21, 2008. http://www.bu.edu/articles/2008/who-was-the-new-negro-questions-for-black-history-month/.

Lester, Neal A. "Disney's *The Princess and the Frog*: The Pride, the Pressure, and the Politics of Being a First." *The Journal of American Culture* 33, no. 4 (December 2010): 294–308.

McCoy Gregory, Sarita. "Disney's Second Line: New Orleans, Racial Masquerade, and the Reproduction of Whiteness in *The Princess and the Frog*." *Journal of African American Studies* 14 (2010): 432–449.

Merriam-Webster. "Stay Woke." Last modified 2020. https://www.merriam-webster.com/words-at-play/woke-meaning-origin.

Morrison, Toni. "Rootedness: The Ancestor as Foundation." In *The Norton Anthology of African American Literature*, edited by Henry Louis Gates, Jr. and Nellie Y. McKay, second edition, 2286–2290. New York: W. W. Norton & Company, 2004.

Parasecoli, Fabio. "A Taste of Louisiana: Mainstreaming Blackness through Food in *The Princess and the Frog*." *Journal of African American Studies* 14 (2010): 450–468.

The Princess and The Frog. Directed by John Musker and Ron Clements. USA: Buena Vista Home Entertainment, Inc., 2019. DVD.

Stone, Nic. "To Be Black and #Woke Is to Be in a Rage All The Time." *Huffington Post*, August 9, 2018. https://www.huffpost.com/entry/opinion-mike-brown-rage-racism_n_5b6992cee4b0de86f4a52959.

Stover, Cassandra. "Damsels and Heroines: The Conundrum of the Post-Feminist Disney Princess." *LUX: A Journal of Transdisciplinary Writing and Research from Claremont Graduate University* 2, no. 1 (2013): 1–10.

Terry, Esther J. "Rural as Racialized Plantation vs Rural as Modern Reconnection: Blackness and Agency in Disney's *Song of the South* and *The Princess and the Frog*." *Journal of African American Studies* 14 (2010): 469–481.

Turner, Sarah E. "Blackness, Bayous and Gumbo: Encoding and Decoding Race in a Color-blind World." In *Diversity in Disney Films: Critical Essays on Race, Ethnicity, Gender, Sexuality and Disability*, edited by Johnson Cheu, 83–96. Jefferson, NC: McFarland & Company, 2014.

Wanzo, Rebecca. "Black Love Is Not a Fairytale." *Poroi* 7, no. 2 (2011): 1–18.

Watson, Elijah C. "The Origin of Woke: How Erykah Badu and Georgia Anne Muldrow Sparked the 'Stay Woke' Era." *Okayplayer*, February 27, 2018. https://www.okayplayer.com/originals/georgia-muldrow-erykah-badu-stay-woke-master-teacher.html.

Young, Damon. "In Defense of Woke." *New York Times*, November 29, 2019. https://www.nytimes.com/2019/11/29/opinion/woke-impeachment-trump.html.

Chapter Eight

Predestination or the Rediscovery of Agency

Christian Jiminez

This chapter examines three contemporary versions of the "Cinderella myth" through Ron Howard's *Cinderella Man* (2005), Eninem's "Cinderella Man" (2005), and Kenneth Branagh's *Cinderella* (2015). It looks at how many *modern* "Cinderella" stories have come to be represented from the early 2000s to the present; in particular, how white heroism and masculinity are framed in highly similar ways whatever the actual genre. This chapter will treat these adaptations as responding mainly to Charles Perrault's version of the "Cinderella" myth. While numerous versions of "Cinderella" are available, Bonnie Cullen finds Perrault's version to be dominant. Even though major parts of Perrault's version, such as glass slippers and metamorphic creatures, are not used in some adaptations, performers, writers, and directors tend to use much of the plot (the wicked mother, the kind king, a godmother, etc.) to structure their revisions. While minimizing the supernatural aspects of past Cinderella stories, *Cinderella*, "Cinderella Man," and *Cinderella Man* nevertheless limit agency greatly.

Many scholars note that gender is used in problematic ways in the "Cinderella" myth. There has been some mention of how "Cinderella" as a story is used in sports including sports films,[1] but there is no in-depth discussion of race and Cinderella in either Howard's or Branagh's films.[2] The literature on Eminem analyzes race, but there is little discussion of how "Cinderella"-as-myth is specifically deployed.[3] One might object that the Branagh version is set in an explicitly fantastic space. However, the fantasy elements in Branagh actually make it more necessary to examine it carefully. The utopian space these texts imagine is one where nonwhites are free to be consumers or even helpers, but happiness and power are reserved mainly for the white heroes.

MYTH VERSUS NATURE

The method utilized in this chapter draws on Barthes's notion of myth. For Barthes virtually all of human life is already mythologized. The task of a critic is to unveil the mythic elements of a myth as fictional, as not in nature: "Myth is not defined by the object of its message, but by the way in which it utters this message: there are formal limits to myth, there are no 'substantial' ones."[4] In other words, the story of "Cinderella" is not of a pretty girl winning a prince. As we shall see, gender and race are flexible but the essence of the myth is that of an underdog a modern audience can identify with. The problem is that the "underdogs" in question turn out to be remarkably similar to one another: a beautiful, athletic white man or woman who often already has a good deal of money and power.

The "Cinderella" myth is often criticized at a direct level. Because Cinderella is usually a woman, the myth tries to impose an unreal standard of beauty. According to Barthes, myth engenders

> history into nature. . . . [I]n the eyes of the myth consumer, the intention, the adhomination of the concept can remain manifest without however appearing to have an interest in the matter: what causes mythical speech to be uttered is perfectly explicit, but it is . . . frozen into something natural: it is not read as a motive, but as a reason.[5]

What is contingent (princes picking wives) is turned into "nature" (princes naturally should pick their wives). But history might have gone in another direction where princesses have the power to choose their husbands. The story is of a man seeking a wife—but the woman has the power. However, one should note Barthes errs in seeing myths as being virtually unchanged. For Barthes, myths just are tools of a ruling class. While he allows that sometimes myths may step outside this framework, all myths for the most part confirm the status quo. Only one case here addressed wholly confirms Barthes's argument. Eminem's myth can be labeled reactionary but the other versions of "Cinderella" are more mixed. Both *Cinderella Man* and *Cinderella* contain both liberal and reactionary elements.

Of the three texts, only Eminem frames agency in a reactionary manner. Though textually he gives some credit to God, the agent is the person as performer. There is no outside force. However, Howard and Branagh are more equivocal. Howard shows Irish boxer James Braddock as being both driven by spiritual and political forces—Braddock represents a Christ-like figure. Branagh is in between these two extremes. While the viewer sees "magic" being done by the fairy godmother, almost all agency is attributed to the character of Cinderella. Branagh explicitly wanted to avoid making Ella appear "passive."[6] This runs against Barthes's argument since we might expect the texts to explicitly have agency attributed to some superstition or authority figure. Myths thus have somewhat more flexibility than Barthes allows. Still, these texts present themselves as "natural" and having no ideological motive even when they do.

CINDERELLA MYTH

Using these three texts as a sample, one can assume the modern "Cinderella" myth as a story must contain two elements: one is that the Cinderella-figure, male or female, is obscure. Secondly, the Cinderella-figure gains massive wealth and fame through cunning and guile. Most versions of the "Cinderella" myth do contain an explicit moral message so the rags-to-riches story is not seen merely as the Cinderella-character seeking gain. The move from obscurity to fame and riches is a reward for the person's extraordinary virtue. As Andrew Lang notes, "a fundamental idea of 'Cinderella' is . . . a person in a mean or obscure position, [who] by means of supernatural assistance, makes a good marriage."[7] However, marriage does not come up at all in "Cinderella Man." *Cinderella Man* is about the marriage of James Braddock, but Braddock is married at the beginning and stays with the same woman. Only in the Branagh version is marriage as a means of escaping poverty part of the main story. Hence while limiting feminism has often been an attribute of most "Cinderella" myths, these myths do not make it necessary that the Cinderella figure be married.

The "Cinderella" myth in *Cinderella Man* slightly changes the expected plot. Instead of rags-to-riches it is riches-to-rags-to-riches (again). Braddock begins by being somewhat famous—though known mainly to locals in his home in Hoboken. He unfortunately put too much of his money in a bad investment in the 1920s and like many was devastated by the stock market crash. Braddock meets Mike Wilson who like Braddock also tried to become a small-time capitalist. Whereas Braddock still has faith in the system, Wilson is wholly disillusioned and an anti-capitalist. To Wilson: "This governments dropped us flat. We need to organize, you know? . . . Fight back."[8] Braddock responds: "Fight? Fight what? Bad luck? Greed? Drought?"[9]

Usually, an adaptation will create a composite character to save time and compress events. But in *Cinderella Man*, Wilson symbolizes the Americans completely disillusioned; Wilson is not a real person but a mythic construct. Braddock's answer shows the film's debt to the fairy-tale genre. Instead of the specific policies that led to the Depression, Braddock attributes the large-scale events to all-too-human motives ("bad luck" and "greed"). The film avoids any detailed examination of the politics of the Depression. However, Howard is not saying that the Cinderella-hero should be passive. Braddock is hurt early on injuring his hand and his career appears finished. Wilson helps

Braddock as they work on the docks but it seems both are fated for poverty and even starvation. The moralistic subtext is explicit as with Perrault's version. When one of Braddock's children steals, he chides him. Even in desperate times, he says, stealing is wrong. His manager, Joe Gould, is sympathetic—though Braddock is a good fighter he has bad habits. However, Gould returns with an amazing offer: Braddock can fight a much better fighter. The film looks to be a simple boxing biopic but Howard adds complicating events. Wilson becomes drunk and leaves his wife to try to organize some local workers. When attempting to find him, Braddock comes across a shantytown and is stunned as the police brutally beat and kill some of the poor men. The police justify themselves in needing to suppress "commies."[10] Braddock is in shock; but instead of being disillusioned, he is inspired to win against heavyweight contender John "Corn" Griffin.

Braddock's battle is framed as a spiritual war. The priest, Father Rorick, notes the parishioners are praying for Braddock: "They all think that Jim's fighting for them."[11] Braddock, the local hero, now symbolizes a nation that needs to believe the humble, everyman, even in the most difficult circumstances, can win. When reporters ask what Braddock is fighting for, he responds simply: "milk."[12] Braddock is not interested in fame or fortune but simply wants to buy enough to feed and clothe his family. Johnston embodies Perrault's wicked stepmother, but also is the symbol of the bad, evil capitalist. Instead of taking pity and letting Braddock fight even with his injury, he wants an uninjured boxer who can put on a show for the audience. Braddock, outraged, pleads:

> Come on, Mr. Johnston, no contest? I broke my hand. Okay? It's legit. You don't see me crying about it. I don't see what you got to complain about. I still went out there, I still put on a show. I did what I could do. You know, we did that boondock circuit for you . . . me and Joe. Remember? I didn't quit on you. And I didn't quit tonight. I didn't always lose. I won't always lose again.[13]

Braddock, like the typical female Cinderella, is naïve. He thinks his moral qualities matter. But Johnston has no morals and only cares for himself.

Howard spends considerable energy to make sure the audience believes they are in the 1930s, from costumes to hairstyles to slang. He made a short documentary on the subject before the 2005 film.[14] Russel Crowe, who portrays Braddock, trained with Angelo Dundee, who worked with black boxers Mike Tyson and Ali. Crowe is therefore legitimized by men who worked with the best—who were often African American. Yet, cleverly, the film omits Braddock's final fight which was with Joe Louis, a black boxer, to avoid the subject of race.[15] In essence, Howard crafted a parable about (the white working) class. To Howard:

> What was   really shocking to me were the images of poverty [during the
> Depression] in big cities. Whenever you'd see poor straggling kids with the
> New York City skyline in the background, or you'd see these men, still
> dressed in their business suits but standing in a breadline, it was as least as
> devastating as the Okies with all their stuff packed on a Model T. I wanted to
> remind people that the working poor existed then, and we have it today. . . .
> We're not in a depression, thank God, but I think it's crossing our minds that
> something could happen . . . for the worse. [16]

The white male audience can be reassured that despite the gender flexibility
inherent in the title, Braddock controls his family. When Mae sends some of
their children to relatives because they lack money, Braddock responds as-
sertively: "You don't make decisions about our children without me." [17]
While Mae is shown as tough and fierce, James Braddock is the undisputed
head of the household.

Moreover, the script adds lines to make sure the audience knows Braddock is not just a man but a masculine man ("I broke my hand. . . . You don't
see me crying about it"). [18] As Braddock wins more and more victories,
Johnston is forced to allow him to box. However, when Braddock has the
possibility of facing Max Behr (Craig Bierko), who has literally killed several men in the ring, Johnston reasserts himself. The Cinderella-Man legend is
"shit." [19] It means nothing. Baer will kill Braddock and the natural order will
reassert itself. Or—as Howard hints—the improbable, the impossible, "the
magical" may happen and Jim will win. [20]

Johnston forces Braddock to see a documentary film of Baer's latest fight
and see for himself a man be killed. As the (fictional) film plays, the (actual)
film intercuts to Braddock imagining Wilson being killed. Braddock is shak-
en, but not necessarily by the film; instead, it is the guilt that Wilson has died
that disturbs him. Braddock mocks Johnston asking, "you're telling me
something?" [21] He continues:

> Like, what, boxing is dangerous, something like that? You don't think working
> triple shifts and at night on a scaffold isn't just as likely to get a man killed?
> What about all those guys who died last week living in cardboard shacks to
> save on rent money just to feed their family, cause guys like you have not quite
> figured out a way yet to make money off of watching that guy die? But in my
> profession—and it is my profession—I'm a little more fortunate. [22]

Boxing is a cruel and capitalistic sport. But it does give Braddock the means
to save his family. It also supports men like Johnston, whose profession is
profiting from men like Braddock. But Braddock defiantly turns the table,
noting that a man like Johnston would never survive in his world. The
(white) world of the boxing ring is a utopian space where Braddock can gain
justice and affirm white working-class spirituality. In real life, Baer was
Jewish and fought a Nazi boxer. All this is excluded by Howard. [23] The evil

of the system is located in individual men like Johnston. But Howard also chooses to demonize Baer who, in reality, cried over the murders that happened. Baer as a fighter towers over Crowe and clearly seems physically dominant. Braddock is being tested, not just as a man but a husband and father.

Howard uses certain stylistic elements of sports films to add a religious dimension to the fairy tale. At a promotional event, Braddock pleads for Baer to stop boasting he will kill him: "You're upsetting my family, particularly my wife."[24] Baer responds by threatening him: "Listen, Braddock. I'm asking you sincerely not to take this fight. Now, you seem like a decent fellow. People admire you. I really don't want to hurt you. It's no joke, pal. People die in fairy tales all the time." Baer has a voracious appetite for sex and murder. However, not just male toughness but also the "Cinderella" virtues of fortitude and fidelity are needed to win. Despite eliminating overt supernatural aspects, Howard reintroduces them through "angels" guiding Braddock from Mae to Wilson to his ultimate redemption in the ring. While not radical, it reaffirms the *Rocky* story line but with less use of racial metaphors of black and white fighters hurting one another for fame and money. In the end, Braddock triumphs and Wilson's spirit is reaffirmed: the common man wins. David has beaten Goliath. The Depression is conquered and Braddock goes to war to fight for his country. Mae and Braddock buy a house and live together happily.

White masculinity is normatively portrayed as tough and yet decent. It has to be powerful enough to assert itself physically but have elements Americans *want* to believe a hero has—compassion, fortitude, decency. The film intentionally plays

> the image of Crowe as an aggressive advocate for the common man . . . Despite his profession as a boxer, Braddock is portrayed as a gentle and compassionate, yet strongly determined, man of his word. . . . [O]nce he establishes himself as financially successful, he immediately returns his relief money to the unemployment board. As much as fighting is integral to this man's identity, Braddock's aggression functions primarily as a vehicle for his family's survival. He tells a press reporter that he is "fighting for milk," but as the narrative progresses, it becomes clear that his greater mission is to inspire a nation worn down by the tragedies of the Great Depression.[25]

Similarly, Roger Ebert sees the film as an allegory about Americanism. As he notes, despite Crowe being

> a tough customer, known to get in the occasional brawl [in real life]. . . . neither he nor anyone else in a long time has played such a nice man as the boxer Jim Braddock. You'd have to go back to actors like James Stewart and Spencer Tracy to find such goodness and gentleness. Tom Hanks could handle the assignment, but do you see any one of them as a prizefighter? . . . What is

remarkable during both the highs and the lows is that Braddock, as Crowe plays him, remains level-headed, sweet-tempered and concerned about his family above all. Perhaps it takes a tough guy like Crowe to make Braddock's goodness believable.[26]

Ebert does not mention race but the argument is implicit. Braddock's whiteness does not come up because equally compelling forms of black heroism like Joe Louis's or Jackie Robinson's are not shown or mentioned. Only one fight is shown where Braddock faces a black man, and the black man seems physically much more capable than Braddock. Thus race is cleverly both present and absent in the film.

What Howard wants us to believe is that Braddock is fighting for his family and nation. The gendering of toughness, ironically, has to be extreme in order for Crowe's Braddock to avoid even the hint of homoeroticism that sometimes comes up in similar films like *Fight Club* where men strip down to fight. Braddock is fated to be bloodily tested to achieve redemption for an entire nation.

EMINEM AND "CINDERELLA MAN"

In extreme contrast, Eminem makes use precisely of the racial metaphors the film *Cinderella Man* tries to minimize. The song "Cinderella Man" is explicitly based on the film and was released in 2010. However, Eminem does not make any sustained comparison between himself and Braddock except that both are incredibly tough and have gone through many trials.

The song's focus is on "Cinderella," but some background is needed to understand why Eminem invokes the tale at all so late into his career. A history of rap, even a short one, is not possible here. It will merely be posited that as a genre, hip hop is predominantly African American. When Eminem made his debut in 1996, he had little success. Kajikawa notes how his first album, *Infinite*, is largely derivative of New York rap (Eminem notably is from Detroit). He says:

> what gives these tracks an even more distinctive New York flavor is the way that the interlocking snare- and kick-drum beats appear to be set to a swinging scale of sixteenth-note triplets—a common practice for New York hip hop producers of this era, including Ski Beatz, Q-Tip, Premier, and Lord Finesse. Thus, the tracks on *Infinite* share the same groove, the same feel, with numerous New York–based rap albums of the time.[27]

Cinderella is name dropped by Nas in his first album, *Illmatic*, widely considered the best rap album of the 1990s. While Nas does invoke the "Cinderella" myth, he only uses it for a few lines. But it is important to note a black rapper made the first hip-hop blurring of gender through the creation of a male Cinderella.

After working with Dre in the late 1990s, Eminem changed his persona and invented an alter ego, "Slim Shady." It would be Eminem/Slim Shady who would be sold to the masses. His lyrics are often heteronormative, homophobic, and denigrate women; being poor and a member of the working class, Eminem has some legitimate claim that he is not a suburban outsider. But in songs like "White America" he notes that his race allowed him a level of success not easily attained by African Americans. Eminem's "Cinderella" reconfiguring is not just the rags-to-riches story but also his receiving legitimacy from an older figure, Dre. Eminem admits that it is "obvious to me that I sold double the records [of any black rapper] because I'm white . . . I truly believe I have a talent, but at the same time I'm not stupid. I know . . . being produced by Dre made it . . . acceptable for white kids to like me."[28] Dre's blackness gives Eminem's whiteness, paradoxically, an invisibility it might not have. As Armstrong notes, Eminem benefits from his whiteness. To Armstrong:

> He accomplishes a self-conscious parody of rap's racially based ethnicity. [. . .] In [the song] "White America" (Eminem, *The Eminem Show*), he infers: "Let's do the math, if I was black, I would not have sold half." It's pointless to impugn Eminem's motivations as a rapper because Eminem wittily exults in his own selfish . . . expropriation of black music.[29]

In essence, Eminem repeatedly admits to the charge—he is a white man exploiting his position.

Eminem has a fairy-like godmother in Dre, who discovered his talent. Once allowed to express himself, he gained his fame through merit. But as he admits, his skin color has always been crucial for white listeners. As Hess points out, "black artist-executives assert their control even as they market white artists to white listeners."[30] However, by the early 2000s, some parts of the fairy tale were being questioned. Recordings surfaced where he uses derogatory racial slurs. Eminem presents himself as "color-blind," but his lyrics show he was *always* very color-conscious. By the mid-2000s, Eminem needed to reinvent himself. On the one hand, Eminem had always used aspects of the Cinderella story. But like the film *Cinderella Man*, in his song by the same name he adds a spiritual dimension. But there are major differences. In *Cinderella Man*, the fairy tale is bestowed on Braddock as a journalist dubs him Cinderella. Alternatively, Eminem calls *himself* Cinderella Man.

Whereas Howard documents how Braddock became famous, Eminem actively participates in the myth to promote himself. But Eminem does use the film's trope that Braddock has been chosen by God. The importance of the "Cinderella Man" lyrics lie in what they say about Eminem as he faces a skeptical public. He begins by admitting that he has drunk so much and taken so many drugs he should be dead. But he lives. The chorus then makes this Christ-metaphor explicit by singing a refrain of *Amen*. While Braddock was a serious Irish Catholic, Eminem has no real attachment to religion. But later lines emphasize that God has played a role in saving him. On the one hand, he thanks God. But he also thanks the "hair on [his] nuts."[31] In other words, his male toughness is why he is still alive.

The masculinity represented in "Cinderella Man" is tough and thoroughly heteronormative. The nod to God is also not entirely superficial. A few lines later, Eminem references Proof, a black childhood friend and member of D12 who died in 2006. Like Mae or Wilson, Proof is an angel for Eminem to lean on. The song celebrates love (God, a friend who has passed) and yet boasts and exults in hatred. The lyrics are sexist and homophobic. An additional problem is that the "Cinderella" myth teaches a moral lesson. But aside from a hokey don't-give-up-on-your-dreams narrative, Eminem's basic message is for listeners to not be overly troubled about cultural appropriation, sexism, and homophobia. The moralistic subtext of the Perault "Cinderella" version is deliberately suppressed; if anything it is inverted. "Cinderella Man" is, ultimately, a shallow and repetitious restatement of the "Cinderella" myth without any pretense of a moral subtext. In the end, the "Cinderella" myth is cynically used to justify Eminem making himself wealthy. Eminem pushes his masculinity to an extreme to assure his fans he is normative, heterosexual, patriotic, and tough. While sharing the structure of the film, "Cinderella Man" empties its message and simply narrows the "Cinderella" story. For Eminem, the "Cinderella" trope is about a cunning person triumphing over seemingly impossible odds. The song forces listeners to recognize that the core of the myth has no real moral. The moral elements are ones its audience impose on it rather than something implicit.

DISNEY AND CINDERELLA

The final case, Disney's *Cinderella*, was released in 2015. In the film, Branagh presents a myth with only some supernatural aspects. *Cinderella* begins with Ella losing her mother but with a caring father to console her. However, after his father remarries to Lady Tremaine, he dies and Cinderella is turned into a servant to Tremaine and her daughters. Ella meets the prince, unknown to her, early on. Kit is out hunting when he and Ella encounter one another. Kit justifies his hunting a stag because "we're hunting you see. It's what's done."[32] Ella disputes him and says, "just because it's done, doesn't mean it's what should be done."[33] From there, the film follows the traditional Disneyfied story. Ella hears about the ball and intends to go. Before the ball, the sisters discuss their strategy. One sister says to Ella that "all men are fools, that's what mamá says. The sooner you learn that the better."[34] Ella rejects that viewpoint, however, and still looks at love romantically. Despite doing all her chores, Lady Tremaine sabotages her effort and her stepsisters destroy her dress. Ella's fairy godmother (Helena Carter) helps her. She is given a coach, a magical dress, and slippers but is warned they will have power only for a limited time. She comes to the ball and the prince falls in love. She is forced to flee and Kit searches for her using the slippers left behind.

Before the ball, the film cross-cuts to Kit training as a fencer and learning lessons from his father who is dying; his father (Derek Jacobi) insists he marries someone who will be good for the whole kingdom. Despite being recommended he marry a foreigner, Kit thinks "I believe we need not look outside our borders for strength or guidance. What we need is right before us, and we need only have courage and be kind to see it," an obvious allusion to Ella.[35] Whereas past versions had the prince order women to try on slippers, the 2015 version merely says "[the King] *requests* that she [the owner of the slipper] presents herself at the palace. Whereupon, if she be *willing*, he will, forthwith, marry her" (emphasis added).[36] Every woman in the kingdom tries the slippers but the wearer proves elusive. Overcoming several obstacles, Ella and the prince finally reunite.

While Howard and Eminem rely on a spiritual reading of "Cinderella," Branagh leans instead on the sheer textuality of the myth. The prince is played by *Game of Thrones* actor Richard Madden, who played Robb Stark, the king of the North in the kingdom of Westeros.[37] Kit—which is the first name of another *Game of Thrones* actor, Kit Harrington—also enjoys sword-play. So does Robb, played by Nonso Anozie, who was also on *Game of Thrones* playing pirate Xaro Xhoan Daxo, who is white in the source novel. As with Xaro, Anozie plays "Captain" as a clever, intelligent observer of power. Anozie is the only black character in the film, and Jacobi is openly queer. Even though all the versions analyzed are heteronormative, homosexuality as such is not demonized in *Cinderella*. It is simply unmentioned unlike in Eminem's lyrics, where it is castigated repeatedly.

What stands out the most is how much Branagh makes use of intertextual links between the film and actors. Lily James is known for her *Downton Abbey* character, Lady Rose. In that series, the story of Rose is one of a selfish girl maturing to a less self-centered adult aiding others. Blanchett plays Queen Elizabeth in several films. Skarsgård has also played a number of leading roles in British films including *King Arthur*. Branagh casts actors who have played monarchs or are well known to British audiences despite their ethnicity not being purely British. But these intertextual hints create some problems. Since Ella is benign from the beginning, Branagh does not lean entirely on the intertextual link audiences must make. As Rebecca-Anne

Rozario notes, Branagh's Ella is much more physically and powerfully adept than previous versions:

> Cinderella's mother's workbox . . . [has] spools of threads, bird bobbins . . . and a book-shaped drawer for ribbons and other odds and ends. . . . It sits beside her mother even as she dies and is so imbued with her presence that Cinderella's stepmother is anxious to have it taken from the room, giving it to Cinderella that she may be useful and occupied. . . . Cinderella turns her tools to good use in remaking her mother's dress for the ball.[38]

The dress ultimately shows Ella using her actual physical strength as much as her beauty.

The godmother's magic is critical in the later stages of the narrative, but Ella is presented as highly agentic from the beginning. This presents a contradiction the narrative never solves. If Ella is intelligent and hard-working enough, why does she bother to stay with such wicked siblings? This key contradiction is never explained. She simply suffers and waits for the ball and for the prince to see her and fall in love. There is also a major difference beyond textuality with prior versions. Branagh does not rely on Christian myths as much as Howard or Eninem. Some of this is due to the stronger secular setting in Britain. It may also be some inherent problems with the live action format. For example, Sarah Whitfield argues the film is marred because James's body cannot match the animated version.[39] Although Ella is beautiful and thin, James is not able to replicate the other-worldly quality of an animated body.

Branagh also does not rely on changes in consciousness. In *Cinderella Man*, Braddock sees ghosts because his body is pushed to an extremity with his mind in between states of consciousness.[40] In *Cinderella*, though, the film mainly concentrates on the mise en scene to immerse the viewer. Critics have largely dismissed this. Rozario argues that "Lily James's own sartorial style does not significantly inform . . . the character."[41] While the audience sees Ella walking in the magic slippers, they had to be added in post-production. The actual shoes were impossible to walk in. Rozario attributes Branagh's composition mainly to product placement. With shoes being sold after the film's release, "albeit with a high price tag. A Cinderella-esque fascination with designer shoes" was artificially emphasized.[42] To Hilary Neroni, Branagh's attempt to give Ella agency is simply a red herring. To her: "Rather than undermining the ideological link between beauty and biology, such proclamations work to solidify the average woman's belief in keeping up the rituals of beauty (such as wearing make-up, shaving, or dieting)."[43] She adds:

> When Cinderella (Lily James) arrives at the ball in this and most versions, everyone turns to stare at her and is dazzled by her beauty . She walks or floats

through the ball and the crowd parts while staring at her, and the prince
(Richard Madden) meets her on the dance floor . . . Cinderella's symbolic
identity is defined completely by how others, and this means everyone in the
kingdom, looks at her. And while the Prince might look quite handsome, he is
not defined by how they are looking at him, and he clearly takes up the
position of the one looking.[44]

But Neroni is not able to answer why the story even bothers then to elevate
Ella to the role of co-ruler. In the other Disney versions, Ella may be the wife
of the king, but there is no suggestion she will rule with the king.[45] Although
Allison Craven concedes Branagh has changed the plot slightly, she criticizes
the film as nothing more than another Disney effort "to make fairy tale seem
more like reality or, conversely, squeeze reality into fairy tale in the quest
for the profits of elevating the glass slipper."[46]

Cinderella as a film was very profitable and does fit the mold of Disney
turning its animated works into live-action features. However, Disney trying
to "make [the] fairy tale seem more like reality" seems strange. Craven notes
that the rulership twist occurred only in this particular adaptation. Other
directors may choose to not follow Branagh with how he frames the story. It
might be read as just a marketing gimmick. However, "Cinderella" should be
looked at contextually. In *Cinderella Man*, a white woman plays mainly the
role of helper. In "Cinderella Man," women are reduced mainly to whores or
objects of humor. But Ella does have power. The problem turns to what this
power means. Branagh gives a female-empowerment film but one without
any real politics. Just what Ella will do with her power is never clearly stated
and dodges what is manifestly there. As Richard Dyer notes, white discourse
"implacably reduces the non-White subject to being a function of the White
subject."[47] Branagh does some things to resist this tendency but like so many
past versions, even ones with a male Cinderella, *Cinderella* is a story about
white heroism that does not allow nonwhites a chance to be the hero.

CONCLUSION

Cinderella Man, "Cinderella Man," and *Cinderella* are fascinatingly polar-
ized as religious and secular versions of Perrault's "Cinderella." But the
central conceit is identical—a white hero (Crowe, Eminem, James) triumphs
without allowing for other forms of diversity. These are universal messages,
but the affirmation through careful exclusion of troubling historical events
guarantees they are aimed at only a rather narrow part of the modern audience in the West. Agency is often attributed to the white hero or heroine who
through sheer self-effort manages to overcome impossible odds. While the
attribution of agency itself is not racist, there are racially exclusionary aspects in the way the "Cinderella" myth has been transformed.

NOTES

1. Andrew C. Billings, Michael L. Butterworth, and Paul D. Turman, *Communication and Sport: Surveying the Field* (New York: Sage, 2018).

2. Tracy McVeigh, "Kenneth Branagh's Corseted Cinderella Fails the *Frozen* Test, Critics Say," *Guardian*, 1 Jan. 2015, https://www.theguardian.com/film/2015/mar/21/cinderella-disney-branagh-fails-frozen-role-model-test; Sarah Whitfield, "'For the First Time in Forever': Locating Frozen as a Feminist Disney Musical," *The Disney Musical: Critical Approaches on Stage and Screen from* Snow White *to* Frozen, (New York: Bloomsbury, 2017), 221–38.

3. Edward G Armstrong, "Eminem's Construction of Authenticity," *Popular Music and Society* 27.3 (2004): 335–55.

4. Roland Barthes, *Mythologies*, (New York: Paladin, 1973), 109.

5. Ibid., 129.

6. McVeigh, "Kenneth Branagh."

7. Andrew Lang qtd. in Victoria Anderson, "Investigating the Third Story: Bluebeard and Cinderella in Jane Eyre," *Horrifying Sex: Essays on Sexual Difference in Gothic Literature* (Jefferson, NC: McFarland, 2007), 111.

8. *Cinderella Man*, directed by Ron Howard (Universal Studios, 2005).

9. Ibid.

10. Ibid.

11. Ibid.

12. Ibid.

13. Ibid.

14. Dave Zirin, "Crass Slipper Fits Cinderella Man," *Visual Economies of/in Motion: Sport and Film* (New York: P Lang, 2006), 196.

15. Ibid., 199.

16. Ron Howard qtd. Ibid., 196.

17. *Cinderella Man*, Howard.

18. Ibid.

19. Ibid.

20. Ibid.

21. Ibid.

22. Ibid.

23. Zirin, "Crass Slipper," 198–99.

24. *Cinderella Man*, Howard.

25. Michael DeAngelis, "Cinderella Man: Russell Crowe as Il Diva," *Camera Obscura* 23.67, (2008): 62.

26. Roger Ebert, *Roger Ebert's Movie Yearbook 2009* (Kansas City: Mcmeel 2009), 108.

27. Loren Kajikawa, "Eminem's 'My Name Is': Signifying Whiteness, Rearticulating Race," *Journal of the Society for American Music* 3.03 (2009): 345.

28. Anthony Bozza, Whatever You Say I Am: The Life and Times of Marshall Mathers (New York: Crown Publishers, 2003).

29. Edward G. Armstrong, "Eminem's Construction of Authenticity," *Popular Music and Society* 27.3 (2004): 343.

30. Mickey Hess, "Hip-Hop Realness and the White Performer," 386.

31. Eminem, "Cinderella Man," *Critical Studies in Media Communication* 22.5 (2005): 372.

32. *Cinderella*, directed by Kenneth Branagh (Walt Disney Studios: 2015).

33. Ibid.

34. Ibid.

35. Ibid.

36. Ibid.

37. Sophie Schillaci, "Disney Casts *Game of Thrones* Actor as Cinderella's Prince," *The Hollywood Reporter*, 8 May 2013. https://www.hollywoodreporter.com/news/cinderella-game thrones-richard-madden-519557.

38. Rebecca-Anne C. Rozario, *Fashion in the Fairy Tale Tradition: What Cinderella Wore* (London: Palgrave Macmillan, 2018).

39.	Sarah Whitfield, "For the First Time in Forever."

40.	Bruce Babington, *The Sports Film: Games People Play* (New York: Wallflower Press, 2014), 48.

41.	Rozario, *Fashion*, 46.

42.	Ibid, 181.

43.	Hilary Neroni, *Feminist Film Theory and Cléo from 5 to 7* (London: Bloomsbury Publishing, 2016), 102.

44.	Ibid., 103.

45.	Allison Craven, "Once Upon a Dream Once More: Beauty Redacted in Disney's Re-adapted Classics," *Debating Disney: Pedagogical Perspectives on Commercial Cinema* (Lanham: Rowman & Littlefield, 2016), 187–98.

46.	Ibid., 195.

47.	Richard Dyer qtd. Elspeth Tilley, *White Vanishing: Rethinking Australia's Lost-in-the-Bush Myth* (Amsterdam: Amsterdam Publishers, 2012).

BIBLIOGRAPHY

Anderson, Victoria. "Investigating the Third Story: Bluebeard and Cinderella in Jane Eyre." *Horrifying Sex: Essays on Sexual Difference in Gothic Literature*, edited by Ruth Bienstock Anolik. Jefferson, NC: McFarland, 2007, 111–21.

Armstrong, Edward G. "Eminem's Construction of Authenticity." *Popular Music and Society* 27, no. 3 (2004): 335–55.

Babington, Bruce. *The Sports Film: Games People Play*. New York: Wallflower Press, 2014.

Barthes, Roland. *Mythologies*, trans. Annette Lavers. New York: Paladin, 1973.

Bellas, Athena. *Fairy Tales on the Teen Screen: Rituals of Girlhood*. New York: Palgrave MacMillan, 2017.

Billings, Andrew C., Michael L. Butterworth, and Paul D. Turman. *Communication and Sport: Surveying the Field*. New York: Sage, 2018.

Bozza, Anthony. *Whatever You Say I Am: The Life and Times of Marshall Mathers*. New York: Crown Publishers, 2003.

Cinderella. Dir. Kenneth Branagh. Lily James, Cate Blanchett, and Richard Madden. Walt Disney Studios, 2015.

Cinderella Man. Dir. Ron Howard. Russell Crowe, Renée Zellweger, Craig Bierko, Paul Giamatti. Universal Studios, 2005.

Craven, Allison. Once Upon a Dream Once More: Beauty Redacted in Disney's Readapted Classics." *Debating Disney: Pedagogical Perspectives on Commercial Cinema*, edited by Douglas Brode and Shea T. Brode. New York: Rowman & Littlefield, 2016, 187–98.

Cullen, Bonnie. "For Whom the Shoe Fits: Cinderella in the Hands of Victorian Writers and Illustrators." *The Lion and the Unicorn* 27, no. 1 (2003): 57–82.

DeAngelis, Michael. "Cinderella Man: Russell Crowe as Il Diva." *Camera Obscura* 23, no. 67 (2008): 47–67.

Ebert, Roger. *Roger Ebert's Movie Yearbook 2009*. Kansas City: McMeel.

El Shaban, Abir. "Gender Stereotypes in Fantasy Fairy Tales: Cinderella." *Arab World English Journal for Translation & Literary Studies* 1, no. 2 (2017): 123–37.

Eminem. *Recovery*, Interscope/Aftermath, 2010.

Hess, Mickey. "Hip-hop Realness and the White Performer." *Critical Studies in Media Communication* 22, no. 5 (2005): 372.

Holston, Kim R., and Tom Winchester. *Science Fiction, Fantasy and Horror Film Sequels, Series and Remakes*. Volume 2. Jefferson, NC: McFarland, 2018.

Kajikawa, Loren. "Eminem's 'My Name Is': Signifying Whiteness, Rearticulating Race." *Journal of the Society for American Music* 3, no. 3 (2009): 341–63.

Kenner, Rob. "13 Ways of Looking at a White Boy," *Vibe*, June/July 1999, 117–18, 120, 122.

McVeigh, Tracy. "Kenneth Branagh's Corseted Cinderella Fails the *Frozen* Test, Critics Say." *Guardian*, 1 Jan. 2015. https://www.theguardian.com/film/2015/mar/21/cinderella-disney-branagh-fails-frozen-role-model-test.

Nelson, George. *Hip Hop America*. New York: Viking, 2005.

Neroni, Hilary. *Feminist Film Theory and Cléo from 5 to 7*. London: Bloomsbury, 2016.

Osorio, Kim. *Straight from the Source: An Expose from the Former Editor in Chief of* The Source. New York: Simon & Schuster, 2008.

Perrault, Charles. *Cinderella, Or the Little Glass Slipper*. 1698. https://fairytalez.com/cinderella-little-glass-slipper-2/.

Rozario, Rebecca-Anne C. *Fashion in the Fairy Tale Tradition: What Cinderella Wore*. New York: Palgrave Macmillan, 2018.

Schillaci, Sophie. "Disney Casts *Game of Thrones* Actor as Cinderella's Prince," *The Hollywood Reporter*, 8 May 2013. https://www.hollywoodreporter.com/news/cinderella-game-thrones-richard-madden-519557.

Tilley, Elspeth. *White Vanishing: Rethinking Australia's Lost-in-the-Bush Myth*. Amsterdam: Amsterdam Publishers, 2012.

Verstegen, Ian. "Eminem and the Tragedy of the White Rapper." *The Journal of Popular Culture* 44 (2011): 872–89.

Whitfield, Sarah. "'For the First Time in Forever': Locating *Frozen* as a Feminist Disney Musical." *The Disney Musical: Critical Approaches on Stage and Screen from* Snow White *to* Frozen, edited by George Rodosthenous. London: Bloomsbury, 2017.

Zirin, Dave. "Crass Slipper Fits Cinderella Man." *Visual Economies of/in Motion: Sport and Film*, edited by C. Richard King and David J. Leonard (New York: Peter Lang, 2006, 195–202.

Zipes, Jack. *Breaking the Magic Spell: Radical Theories of Folk and Fairy Tales*. Lexington: Kentucky University Press, 2002.

Chapter Nine

Deaf Cinderella

The Construction of a Woke Cultural Identity

Carolina Alves Magaldi and Lucas Alves Mendes

The magnificent ball started and, upon meeting Cinderella for the first time, the prince was . . . relieved. That is the climactic moment in the Brazilian children's book *Deaf Cinderella* (*Cinderela Surda*, in the Portuguese original), the first published narrative written in Portuguese as well as SignWriting. On the surface, the fact that both Cinderella and the prince are deaf is a happy coincidence. However, the story resonates centuries of struggle from members of the deaf community, who were considered incapable of learning up to two hundred years ago, and unable to study in their own sign languages until the second half of the twentieth century in most of the globe. We argue that since the book in question is the first ever published in Brazilian Sign-Writing, it constitutes a landmark moment for deaf culture and language, raises awareness about aspects of deaf history and education, and contributes to constructing a woke cultural deaf identity among its target audience, which includes deaf children, their teachers, and family members.

In order to fully comprehend the impact of such narrative, we will present briefly the recent changes and improvements in inclusion and deaf studies, as well as their impacts on the narratives that are being produced in literature, film, TV and comics. Apart from the book itself, we will draw from the critical work by Itamar Even-Zohar (1997) and André Lefevere (2004). The Polysystem Theory, proposed by Itamar Even-Zohar (1997), will help us comprehend how this new version of "Cinderella" relates to the traditional tale and how it situates itself as the center of a new (woke) polysystem. Lefevere introduces the notion of rewriting as indistinguishable from manipulation in order to problematize the concept of translation, as well as adaptations, textbook collections and so forth. This perspective will shed light on how the original text was manipulated not only to accommodate deaf characteristics, but also to construct a woke culture surrounding that uniqueness. The book is relevant, both as a symptom of the cultural and political changes taking place in the deaf community and as a contribution to crafting its own cultural identity, following centuries of having decisions made by hearing individuals who viewed deaf people as lesser, or even as incapable of learning. This is significant because the late twentieth and early twenty-first century have been the first moment in which deaf community has gained narrative and political representation, finally being welcomed to the ball.

DEAF CULTURE GLOBALLY AND ITS NARRATIVE IMPACTS

Given the relevance of the work here studied to the deaf community in Brazil, it is vital that we highlight some of the landmarks regarding the legitimization of deaf culture and sign language education globally as well as in the country. Between the 7th and the 10th of June 1994, representatives of eighty-eight countries gathered in Salamanca to discuss educational parameters to those who, at the time, were called special needs individuals. Such an event represented a significant step forward to deaf education, since it distanced itself from oral-based methodologies, respecting the unique aspects of deaf culture, languages, and identities.

The 21st article of the Salamanca Statement says:

> Educational policies should take full account of individual differences and situations. The importance of sign language as the medium of communication among the deaf, for example should be recognized a provision made to ensure that all deaf persons have access to education in their national sign language. [1]

Another event of great significance to the official status of sign languages was the XII Seminar of the International Association for the Development of Intercultural Communication in Recife, Brazil, in 1987. According to Hildo Honório de Couto, "the event recommends to the United Nations taking necessary measures aiming at adopting and applying a universal declaration of linguistic rights." [2] This declaration was of the utmost importance to the development of Brazilian Sign Language studies as well as of several indigenous languages in the country.

In Brazil, those landmarks slowly started a process of legitimization of the cultural and linguistic characteristics of the deaf population. Its history, however, dates much further back, and may be easily confused with the trajectory of the National Institute of Deaf Education (INES, in Portuguese). Founded in 1857 by Dom João II, the institute focused on the French Sign Language since the emperor had invited Ernest Huet, a French deaf professor, to found a school specializing in deaf education. The classes, taught in

French Sign Language, caused a linguistic encounter with the sign language already used by the students, culminating in the Brazilian Sign Language— currently, Libras. This may explain why, in the *Deaf Cinderella* narrative, the French Sign Language is highlighted to its young readers.

Such work was not standard practice at the time, given that oral-based practices were prioritized since the Milan Congress of 1880. However, the sign-based system of the institute remains fully functional to this day, offering K–12 education as well as a Bilingual Pedagogy undergraduate course (Libras-Portuguese). Despite such resilient work, the law that formalizes the training of sign language professionals and the inclusion of deaf students only came into existence in 2005. The decree 5626 establishes the creation of courses in sign language linguistics, in order to train teacher of junior high and high school levels as well as bilingual pedagogy for the elementary school level. The sign language instructor position was also created to address the preexisting demand, as well as the creation of the official exam to interpreters. These measures helped shape a deaf community that made full use of its sign languages, experimented with SignWriting, and were ready to demand greater representation in narratives. This constituted a global phenomenon spanning literature, film, and television productions, as well as theatrical ones.

As an example, the TV show *Switched at Birth* not only has deaf main characters (most of whom are played by deaf actors) but was also the first television production to have subtitles for the American Sign Language (ASL) conversations. That is a significant change from having only stereotypical secondary characters who happened to be deaf, and by allowing them to speak for themselves. The show also included an episode shot entirely in ASL. The production has another element in common with the children's book here analyzed: the woke elements, such as explanations on the nature of deaf education, bilingual programs, why some deaf individuals are comfortable speaking orally while others are not, and so on. The Deaf West theatrical production of *Spring Awakening* relies on similar elements. The research group Prisma, led by the authors of this chapter, has dedicated an entire project to that production, given its unique bilingual characteristics. In the play, the musical is not only performed in English and ASL, but the visual nature of the American Sign Language is incorporated into the choreography, giving it a new layer in intersemiotic translation. It is also one of the few musicals available to deaf actors and audience.

These efforts are not limited to the US or to English speaking countries. The Japanese manga and anime *Koe no Katachi* (*A Silent Voice*) tells the story of a young deaf girl, bullied at school, and the road to redemption of her former bully years later. It was largely successful in Japan and abroad and it is worth noticing that foreign editions, such as the one printed in Brazil, include footnotes to explain the use of the Japanese Sign Language in its illustrations. Such instructions denote not only the inclusion of deaf characters, but also a newly constructed respect for deaf culture. It is in this sense of cultural and narrative representation that we may now dedicate ourselves to presenting the children's book *Deaf Cinderella*.

THE BRAZILIAN DEAF CINDERELLA

Brazil currently has approximately 10 million people who are either deaf or hard of hearing.[3] Apart from the medical definition of not being able to hear sounds under 24db, another distinction has emerged, which is largely linked to cultural identities. By this definition, *deaf* individuals would be those who communicate in Brazilian Sign Language (Libras), while *hearing impaired* would be those who have Portuguese as their primary language of instruction. This distinction highlights the importance of the sign language as an identity construction, and also establishes the role of the educational system in differentiating the two cultural categories. It is worth mentioning that it is possible to refer to hearing individuals who speak Brazilian Sign Language and are part of the community as *non-deaf* people, rather than *hearing* ones.

However, the possibility of having a school experience in sign language is quite recent to most deaf Brazilians, especially if they were born away from the southeast of the country. This scenario began to change with the National Plan for Education, created in 2014, which aimed at including underrepresented groups in the school environment throughout the country. However, higher education remained a distant dream for most deaf Brazilians. Until 2014 there was no national high school exam in sign language, and most candidates resorted to legal means to guarantee an interpreter. In 2015 and 2016, with the creation of the exam in Libras, an average of three thousand students submitted requests to video exams and interpreters a year. It is also worth pointing out that the essay topic of the 2017 edition of the exam was deaf education, which took most teachers and candidates by surprise, given the specific nature of the theme.

It was in this context that a group of teachers and researchers gathered to write *Deaf Cinderella*. The team was led by Lodenir Becker Karnopp, a professor at the Federal University of Rio Grande do Sul. She has published, alongside Ronice Müller Quadros, the book *Brazilian Sign Language—Linguistic Studies* (*Língua Brasileira de Sinais—Estudos linguísticos*, in the Portuguese original), which presents morphological, phonological and syntactic characteristics of the language, a landmark in linguistic studies in the country. The second member of the team, Carolina Hassel, is an assistant professor at the Federal University of Rio Grande do Sul and has conducted research into deaf education and culture, as well as taught at K–12 level. The third and final member of the group is Fabiano Souto Rosa, who teaches sign language at the Federal University of Pelotas.

The story they chose to (re)narrate begins with Cinderella's difficult life. The beleaguered heroine learns sign language in the streets of Paris; suffers the loss of her father; and experiences harsh treatment she received from her stepmother and stepsisters, who are barely capable of communicating with her, given that they only knew a few signs. This initial passage shows both their disregard to Cinderella's unique culture and their desire to keep her as a maid in their home, signing only the matters related to cleaning and tidying up. The book narrates the invitations to the ball and Cinderella's initial lack of permission to attend in similar fashion to the original fairy tale, with the exception of the fairy godmother. She has little attention in the book, but she can sign and communicate with Cinderella, giving her a pink dress and gloves, symbolizing the connection between deaf culture and hand movements. The ball itself is the magical moment of the fairy tale in any version. This time, the prince announces to Cinderella that he is also deaf, and they connect immediately with one another. The prince, however, had learned French Sign Language through formal instruction with a historical figure: Charles-Michel l'Épée.

In the early eighteenth century, l'Épée was born in Versailles, France, to a wealthy family. He took it upon himself to learn sign language when he started the religious tutoring of two deaf girls, having then the first contact with what would become the French Sign Language. At the time, deafness was commonly seen as divine punishment, and deaf people were usually thought of as incapable of learning. His efforts attracted attention of all the deaf community and in 1775 led to the creation of the Institution Nationale dê Sourds-Muets in Paris. With l'Épée's passing in 1789, the monk Sicard took over his work, but faced numerous political problems in revolutionary France including being arrested.

In *Deaf Cinderella*, l'Épée has an important role as he is the one who teaches French Sign Language to the prince. Bringing a historical character into the narrative also works toward recognition from the deaf community and professionals in the fields of deaf education, sign language studies, and linguistics. In the book, l'Épée teaches French Sign Language to a deaf prince who goes through a process of formal, school-based training. Cinderella, on the other hand, goes through a process of language acquisition by means of contact with other deaf individuals who speak sign language in the streets of Paris. Despite the difference in methods, Cinderella and the prince show no difficulties in communicating with one another. In real life, the more likely scenario would be for differing accents to have developed, different signs to indicate the same ideas of objects, and notable syntactic distinctions.

Despite the book being based on a traditional, well-known tale, a few narrative instruments were adopted in order to reach a more inclusive audience. This audience comprises of members of the deaf community, parents of deaf children, and teachers. The authors, right at the beginning of the story, highlight Cinderella's difficulty in communicating with her stepmother and stepsisters, since she is deaf and the other members of the household show no interest in learning sign language and leave the young girl isolated in her own home. Moreover, upon leaving the ball, Cinderella loses not her shoe, but her glove, which draws focus to the hands and their vital role in communication for deaf individuals. The matter of the glove only fitting the future princess remains the same as in the traditional story.

Two other differences are marked by absence: there is little emphasis on the meeting between Cinderella and the Fairy Godmother, who can speak French Sign Language and communicates easily with the girl. The fact that Cinderella follows her rules perfectly proves the efficacy in communication. The magical aspect of the encounter is, however, of little consequence to this new version of the tale. Another absence lies in the fact that at no point it is mentioned that the prince is deaf. At the ball, both he and Cinderella are immensely relieved to meet another deaf person; but it is unclear how he would have communicated with the other guests, or why the girls who intended to become his brides were unaware of such fact.

Linguistically speaking and design wise, the book was created in a bilingual layout, Libras-Portuguese, in the following pattern: on the left page, the authors include the text in SignWriting, with the Portuguese version underneath; illustrations are included on the right-hand side. SignWriting is a writing system created by North American Valerie Sutton in 1974 as a means of registering dance choreography. The system, however, caught the attention of sign language researchers in Denmark, where Sutton provided material and adapted the technique so that it could register any sign language in writing. The classic system used on the book is not the only form of writing sign languages in Brazil and it is still building popularity. However, it is highly useful in understanding signs and their phonological distinctions— hand configuration, placement, palm direction, movement and non-manual expressions[4]—thus stimulating the learning and register of sign languages.

On the back cover of the book there is an illustration of the authors with their respective signs expressed in SignWriting, another innovative aspect of the work. The use of such a writing system is of great importance to the register of sign languages, because it reveals the phonological aspects that facilitate the understanding and learning processes of such languages. In this system, the signs realized in the neutral space (in front of the speaker) do not have assigned placing. All of the others have specific representations, such as shoulders, head, and thorax. Hand configurations carry greater iconicity, which facilitates learning by tracing fingers and using two colors. White represents the palm of the hand and black represents the back of the hand. The movements are included by using arrows. Non-manual components, such as facial expressions, are represented by circles with traits that symbolize the eyes, mouth or eyebrows.

Apart from phonological parameters, SignWriting also represents the manner in which the hands interact with each other or with other body parts, with symbols meaning catching, hitting, brushing, among others.

According to Dallan (*apud* Daniela R. Cury):

> Learning sign languages allows the students greater symbolic exchanges, making it possible to increase their cognitive skills, given that they are writing in their own language. Besides, in his research, Dallan (2010) realized that learning sign writing improved the use of sign languages: "by learning more, they started to speak more fluently in signs."[5]

Therefore, we may comprehend the importance of SignWriting in terms of identity construction to a deaf student, because they will write and learn in the same language—as opposed to having Libras as an oral language and Portuguese as a written one. According to Cury, up to the 1970s, sign languages were considered non-written languages. Illustrations such as the ones found in the *Iconographia dos Signaes dos Surdos Mudos* by Basílio José da Gama (1875), were seen as non-written languages. In *Iconographia*, the author, a deaf student at INES, described signs and illustrated them with hand drawings and arrows. Such work has great historical importance, but does not amount to writing, and certainly did not evolve to the point of producing literary narratives.

The process of including sign languages and SignWriting in popular culture is relevant not only for educational purposes and cultural visibility, but also for the cognitive and social development of deaf individuals. For hearing people, contact with languages begins even before birth, and continues extensively in the first infancy. In the case of deaf babies born in hearing families, however, the most common scenario is of language deprivation, in which the child will only gain access to a language when they start formal education. As a result, a large portion of deaf children will only acquire or learn their first language when hearing children already have an extensive use of their mother tongue and are in the process of being alphabetized in such language.

There is an even more disheartening scenario when the language that the child is placed in contact with is the written form of the oral language spoken in their country of region, in our case, the Portuguese language. This approach has several complex consequences, given that the written Portuguese language is not meant for day-to-day interactions, does not represent their visual perspective of the world, and cuts them from building a connection with their communities. There is even the distinction, mentioned earlier, between deaf people, who communicate in sign languages and are part of their culture, and the hearing impaired, who have Portuguese as their main means of communication.

Thus, a large portion of the deaf community show animosity and frustration toward the Portuguese language, in a process similar to formerly colonized populations toward the colonizer's languages. This is why it is so remarkable that the *Deaf Cinderella* book chose to tell the story in Portuguese and in SignWriting. The book builds the prestige of sign language while maintaining a partnership with the official language of the country, which will invariably be a part of its citizen's lives, regardless of being hearing or deaf.

DISCUSSING REWRITING

In order to understand how *Deaf Cinderella* changed the classical tale, we turn to the concept of rewriting, by Andre Lefevere. He utilizes such concepts to study translations, adaptations, textbook compilations and so on. In his studies, it is highlighted that the process of rewriting is done by "professional readers" who reconstruct a piece in a new shape or environment, communicating it to other readers.[6]

Translating a work into a new language is the primary form of such rewritings, but it also includes adapting to a new audience, age group or cultural community, or illustrating and revisiting a classical piece. All of these forms are accomplished by the piece here studied. The interlingual translation part of the process is realized by the connection between Portuguese and SignWriting, which increases the popularity of the technique and keeps the two languages in contact. That is a relevant aspect both to hearing children and teachers who will have an opportunity to be in touch with a sign language in written form, as well as for deaf students and scholars, who will have contact with Portuguese in a context in which the language is not being imposed on them, or coming to forcibly replace Libras. Another aspect of rewriting comes in the form of adaptation to a new audience and cultural community, given that the original story depends on communication (Cinderella and the Fairy Godmother, Cinderella and the Prince) and has its climatic moment on a ball, an environment commonly associated with entertainment for hearing people. The solutions found by the rewriters do not erase such elements but find ways not to alienate the target audience of deaf children.

The final element of rewriting in *Deaf Cinderella*, the illustrations, are remarkably simple for a current narrative meant for children. Carolina Hassel, the illustrator, pointed out in an interview that she was particularly careful in not making one character more beautiful or uglier that the others, not even Cinderella. She highlighted that children's books usually associate ugliness with evil characters and wrongdoing, and that she was not comfortable reinforcing such parameters. This mentality shows that the authors and illustrator are aware of their role in the children's book system as a whole, and not only as a narrative for deaf children.

Andre Lefevere also contributes to the understanding of the narrative by crafting the concept of patronage and its role in shaping rewritings.[7] He discusses how people and institutions fund and foster the processes of rewriting, encompassing three components: ideology, economics and status. The ideological aspect affects the choices made on what to rewrite and how to go about it. In the case of *Deaf Cinderella*, there is a deep connection of the people involved in rewriting the book and deaf culture and communities. This impacts the choice of classical tale retelling, granting access to a marginalized community; and the construction of a visual narrative, through illustrations and SignWriting.

The economical dimension affects how rewriters make a living. In this case, all of the authors and illustrators have advanced degrees in linguistics and are college professors, which allows them to combine their research with the artistic endeavor of rewriting a classical fairy tale. The final element is status, which grants prestige or recognition. Becoming the authors of the first ever book published in SignWriting in Brazil certainly works to that effect. Another aspect of Lefevere's work is that he divides the types of patronage into undifferentiated, when all three elements are linked to the same institution (usually a characteristic of totalitarian regimes), or differentiated, when the three instances of patronage function independently, with a few instances in which the economic factor operates separately from the other two, as in the case of a few best sellers. Not only *Deaf Cinderella*, but also quite a few literary, audio-visual and theatrical productions involving deaf themes, characters and actors. The three instances of patronage have been connected with prestige, economic success and an inclusive ideology walking hand in hand.

It is also worth discussing the consequences of placing the classical tale of "Cinderella" in a new environment. Itamar Even-Zohar helps us comprehend the consequences of this change through his Polysystem Theory.[8] Based on his concept, cultural goods are connected to each other within systems that are hierarchical, dynamic and flexible. It is possible to notice the matter of hierarchy in literature by means of establishing canons—always mediated by instances of legitimization and patronage, as discussed before. In the *Deaf Cinderella* story, we have, for instance, a more central position than the original tale, because of the involvement of academic research. The question of flexibility also related to the university aspect of it, given that the same cultural and artistic work may be included in two or more systems. In our case, the book is part of a school system, academic research, and a children's literature system as well.

The dynamic aspect is probably the most fascinating one to understand the process of rewriting. It functions on the premise that the inclusion of a new work changes the interpretation and the relative standing of all the others, akin to the beginning of a pool game: you may aim at one of the balls, but all the others will have their positions changed as well. One clear example is when an artist reaches a degree of success with one piece and all of their previous works are revisited by instances of legitimization. In our case, the successive rewritings of the "Cinderella" story made it easier for a new approach to be well received, something that would probably not have happened with an equally well-known story that had been less experimented with.

The concept of systems is nothing new to the study of cultures and literatures, of course; Even-Zohar himself acknowledges that much in his epigraphs are dedicated to key researchers of the Russian formalism movement. His contribution is derived from the silencing of a key aspect of formalism: the historical dimension of their studies. The fathers of structuralism were deeply concerned with the historical aspect of a cultural or literary analysis, but that characteristic was all but forgotten when the movement was reinterpreted in the West, due to the prevalence of Saussure's chess table interpretation of structuralism. Through Even-Zohar's work, the chronological and historical aspects of a system come back into focus. This helps us comprehend that the *Deaf Cinderella* book is not only a product of the post-Salamanca/post-5626 decree world, but that it also retraces its historical heritage, going back to l'Épée and jumping past the Milan Congress in establishing the roots of deaf education. Another aspect of Even-Zohar's work that proves useful to understanding the rewriting of *Deaf Cinderella* is his concept of repertoire.[9] Instead of simply including a list of works produced by a certain group, country, language or culture, he considers that each work may function both as a cultural good and as a cultural tool.

The existence and role of cultural goods is commonplace in cultural and social studies. However, they are usually perceived as separate products of an infrastructure that generated and consumed them. In Even-Zohar's work, cultural goods such as the book here studied are instead perceived as cultural tools: elements of a given culture that function with specific purposes. In this case these involve popularizing SignWriting, discussing elements of deaf history and culture, and registering a story that was already part of deaf communities. The fact that it consists of a rewriting is also contemplated in the discussion, given that Even-Zohar's work perceives translations and rewritings, in general, as more prone to occupy a central position in literary polysystems when a system is young, peripheral or weak. In our case, the new advent of SignWriting and the exceedingly young school systems that are inclusive and bilingual may help explain the choice, the narrative, and the central position of the first book ever published in Libras SignWriting. The fairy tale becomes in this sense both traditional and innovative: certainly well-known, but with meaningful twists.

The process of rewriting and publishing *Deaf Cinderella* is, therefore, carefully designed with the purpose of contributing to the scholarly development and social inclusion of the deaf communities in Brazil. As Even-Zohar points out: "The people who were engaged in great intensity in making new repertoires, both 'idea-makers' and 'culture entrepreneurs,'" have always had in view some vision of improving the situation of the group for whom they targeted their repertoire inventions."[10]

This may be noticed in the presentation of the text, which states:

> We do not know who told this story for the first time. It has been retold among the deaf and we decided to register and divulge this beautiful text. Most people know the classical story of Cinderella. Our goal here is to retell this story from another culture, a deaf culture. Therefore, this book was constructed from a visual experience, with images, with the text rewritten within a deaf culture and identity and in written signs, also known as SignWriting. We have utilized the sign writing so that literary classics could also be read by deaf people.[11]

The statement made by the authors makes it clear that their purpose of telling a new version of Cinderella was based upon a larger project that intended to make SignWriting more visible and popular, contributing to more deaf children having access, in their own language, to the same literary classics as hearing kids. And, since the book was meant for both parents and teachers as well, the information regarding deaf culture and history contribute to a larger goal of constructing a woke deaf culture in Brazil.

FINAL THOUGHTS

The choice of the "Cinderella" story with the purpose of building a woke narrative has significant peers in currently Brazilian literature. A LGBTQ+ Cinderella is the most popular and acclaimed short story rewriting of the *Over the Rainbow* collection. This includes a transvestite version of the Fairy Godmother and a mental health battle fought by the miserable protagonist, who in the classical stories either suffers in silence or with the companionship of animals. Cinematically there is *Cinderela Pop*, with teen star Maisa Silva (although the last name is unnecessary to any Brazilian girl under the age of 18), who plays a struggling DJ having to deal with her father's infidelity with a wicked woman and her new life with her twin stepsisters. Far from being a revolutionary story, it illustrates that the classic fairy tale is still the most prominent one in empowered and woke versions to young Brazilians of underrepresented groups. In the case of the deaf community that has been discussed here, the *Deaf Cinderella* story is part of a long list of recent conquests in deaf and bilingual education, legal victories and unprecedented access to higher education, which will undoubtedly craft a new understanding of deaf Brazilian identity. It is written primarily in a language that is still unknown to most, including members of their own culture. It brings historical characters like l'Épée that are obscure to the majority of non-researchers, and it also contributes constructing to a society in which those elements will no longer be novel or exotic.

NOTES

1. Unesco, *The Salamanca Statement and Framework for Action on Special Needs Education: Adopted by the World Conference on Special Needs Education* (Salamanca: Unesco, 1994), https://unesdoc.unesco.org/ark:/48223/pf0000098427.
2. Hildo Couto, *Honório de. Ecolinguistica* (Thesaurus Editora, 2007), 392.
3. Alana Gandra, "País tem 10,7 milhões de pessoas com deficiência auditiva, diz estudo," Agência Brasil, 10 October 2019, http://agenciabrasil.ebc.com.br/geral/noticia/2019-10/brasil-tem-107-milhoes-de-deficientes-auditivos-diz-estudo.
4. Ibid.
5. Ronice Muller de Quadros and Lodenir Becker Karnopp, *Língua de sinais brasileira* (Porto Alegre: Artmed, 2004).
6. André Lefevere, *Translation/History/Culture* (Shanghai: Shanghai Foreign Language Education Press, 2004).
7. Ibid.
8. Itamar Even-Zohar, *Polysystem Studies* (Tel Aviv: Tel Aviv University Press, 1997).
9. Itamar Even-Zohar, *Interferência nos Polissistemas Literários* (Juiz de Fora: Revista Ipotesi, 2018).
10. Itamar Even-Zohar, *Interferência nos Polissistemas Literários*, 2.
11. Carolina Hassel, Lodenir Karnopp, and Fabiano Rosa, *Cinderela Surda* (Canoas: Editora da Ulbra, 2018).

BIBLIOGRAPHY

Brasil, Lei n.13.005, de 25 de junho de 2014. "Aprova o Plano Nacional de Educação—PNE edá outras providências." *Diário Oficial da União*, Brasília, DF., 26 jun. 2014. Accessed February 3, 2020. https://www.planalto.gov.br/ccivil_03/_ato2011-2014/2014/lei/l13005.htm.
Brasil, Presidência da República. Lei n. 10.436, de 24 de abril de 2002. "Dispõe sobre a Língua Brasileira de Sinais—Libras e dá outras providências." In: *Casa Civil, Subchefia para Assuntos Jurídicos*. Diário Oficial da União, Brasília, 2002. Accessed February 3, 2020. http://www.planalto.gov.br/ccivil_03/leis/2002/l10436.htm.
Couto, Hildo. *Honório de. Ecolinguistica*. Thesaurus Editora, 2007.
Cury, Daniela Ramalho. *Escrita de sinais: concepções de educadores Surdos e ouvintes*. Campinas: Unicamp, 2016.
Even-Zohar, Itamar. Interferência nos Polissistemas Literários Dependentes. Translated by Isabella Aparecida Nogueira Leite. Juiz de Fora: Revista Ipotesi, 2018. https://doi.org/10.34019/1982-0836.2018.v22.25649.
———. *Polysystem Studies*. Tel Aviv: Tel Aviv University Press, 1997.
Gandra, Alana. "País tem 10,7 milhões de pessoas com deficiência auditiva, diz estudo." Agência Brasil, October 10, 2019. Accessed February 4, 2020. http://agenciabrasil.ebc.com.br/geral/noticia/2019-10/brasil-tem-107-milhoes-de-deficientes-auditivos-diz-estudo.

Hessel, Carolina; Karnopp, Lodenir; Rosa, Fabiano. *Cinderela Surda.* Canoas: Editora da Ulbra, 2018.

Kinsey, Arthur A. *Atas: Congresso de Milão [de] 1880.* Rio de Janeiro: Ines, 2011.

Lacombe, Milly et al. *Over the Rainbow: um livro de contos de fadxs.* São Paulo: Planeta, 2016.

Lefevere, André (ed.). *Translation/History/Culture: A Sourcebook.* Shanghai: Shanghai Foreign Language Education Press, 2004.

López, Alberto. *Charles Michel de l'Epée, o pai da educação pública para surdos.* São Paulo: El país, 2018. Accessed February 4, 2020. https://brasil.elpais.com/brasil/2018/11/24/cultura/1543042279_562860.html.

MEC. *Decreto n. 5.626—Regulamenta a Lei no 10.436, de 24 de abril de 2002, que dispõe sobre a Língua Brasileira de Sinais—Libras, e o art. 18 da Lei no 10.098, de 19 de dezembro de 2000.* Brasília, 2005. Accessed February 3, 2020. https://presrepublica.jusbrasil.com.br/legislacao/96150/decreto-5626-05.

Quadros, Ronice Muller de; Karnopp, Lodenir Becker. *Língua de sinais brasileira: estudos lingüísticos.* Porto Alegre: Artmed, 2004.

Sutton, Valerie. *Manual 1—Noções básicas sobre sigwriting.* La Jolla: Center for Sutton Movement Writing, 2009. Accessed February 4, 2020. http://www.signwriting.org/archive/docs12/sw1177_SignWriting_Basics_Instruction_Manual_Sutton_PORTUGUESE.pdf.

Unesco. *The Salamanca Statement and Framework for Action on Special Needs Education: Adopted by the World Conference on Special Needs Education; Access and Quality.* Salamanca: Unesco, 1994. https://unesdoc.unesco.org/ark:/48223/pf0000098427.

III

Post-human and
Post-truth Cinderellas

Chapter Ten

Dragons, Magical Objects, and Social Criticism

Reimaging the Cinderella Trope in Tui T. Sutherland's
The Lost Heir

Rachel L. Carazo

According to Jack Zipes, "Cinderella is probably the most popular fairy tale in the world,"[1] and the "Cinderella" trope in which a neglected,[2] albeit a beautiful, kind, and gifted female receives help in order to escape from her difficult stepfamily, marry a prince, and join the royal family has had several recent iterations in film and literature, making it a "cultural script" that crosses multiple social boundaries.[3] Even though this reconfiguring, especially those examples that parody or overturn the goals of the trope, offer important social commentaries, the protagonists are generally *human*. Yet what happens when Cinderella becomes represented by a dragon named Tsunami in *The Lost Heir*, the second novel in Tui T. Sutherland's *Wings of Fire* series? Not only does this nonhuman assemblage of dragons include a RainWing, a NightWing, a SandWing, and a MudWing in addition to Tsunami, who is a SeaWing like her newly discovered royal family, but the overturned "Cinderella" trope also allows the *objects* of the tradition to become powerful players in re-creating and commenting upon it. In the end, Tsunami does not stay to become Queen. Neither does she get her "happily ever after" with her "prince," Riptide. Nevertheless, Tsunami's stepfamily of dragonets becomes ascendant, marking a turn in modern culture in which stepfamilies are more common and in which materialism and consumerism have power, just like the written works that Queen Coral writes, the harness that she keeps around her daughter Anemone, and the statue of Coral's deceased daughter, Orca, have their own powers. As a result, this chapter argues that the *nonhu-*

man nature of the Cinderella figure in *The Lost Heir* is what allows for the novel to fully critique the "Cinderella" story and comment upon the need to unite women, positively view the modern stepfamily, consider the effects of materialism and consumerism—especially as aspects of vibrant matter[4]— and account for the growing importance of multiculturalism in modern culture, especially since "[i]n this process lies the enduring vitality of the fairy tale; a vitality that will persist so long as old tales stir the creative impulse."[5]

CINDERELLA AND HER *HUMAN* ITERATIONS

While many scholars, such as Marina Warner[6] and Andrew Teverson,[7] remind readers that the "Cinderella" trope existed in folktales that are often as old as oral tradition, the modern versions of "Cinderella" that resonate with most people are Perrault's version, the Brothers Grimm's version, or a combination thereof. Yet in these popular iterations of the trope, which Disney's 1950 and 2015 films have helped to imprint in people's minds, Cinderella is traditionally *human*. Nevertheless, in order for "Cinderella" to "seem timeless" for every generation, there should be specific differences, maturations, and adaptations of the narrative to represent the idea that, in truth, the story has "no history, but [. . .] too many histories" which makes it "plural and many voiced."[8] As a result, cultural and societal concerns often change in its (re)telling. Sometimes the body and character of Cinderella herself adapts; sometimes the setting changes; sometimes she does not marry. These realities indicate that "[t]he Cinderella tale [is not] [. . .] based on a preexisting essence or model of an unproblematic expression of 'culture,' but rather focuses on the transfers, appropriations, manipulations, and recreations that give it an ever-changing existence, significance, and relevance in its manifold 'de-territorializations.'"[9]

Since the "Cinderella" story is inherently meant to change and adapt, it is unsurprising that contemporary environmental and animal studies issues have begun to affect its presentation. The nonhuman animals in fairy tales have begun to gain more notice as agents, but scholars have still taken time to overcome the bias that "[s]tories like Cinderella now belonged to the *people* [emphasis added], with the result that they were able to retell Cinderella stories in ways that made sense to their tellers and to the stories' hearers."[10] Even though nonhuman agents partake in the story, especially in animated versions in which they can speak or become beloved characters in their own right, it becomes a significant oversight that scholars do not consider the story to *belong* to them as well. However, in versions when Cinderella and the main characters are represented by nonhuman animals, this oversight begins to be reconciled. In fact, when the "Cinderella" story follows the experiences of *dragons*, which are fantastical nonhuman animals, the impact

becomes amplified since the "Cinderella" trope demonstrates how it is possible to not only offer agency to a nonhuman animal, but also to give autonomy to one that does not even exist in real life.

DRAGONS: POWERFUL SYMBOLS IN A FAIRY-TALE UNIVERSE

The dragon has become a powerful figure in pop cultural and literary studies.
Even though its medieval associations "as an allegory for all the evils in the
world"[11] and as a troublesome creature that needs to be defeated have pro-
liferated throughout history, modern representations, such as those in *Drag-
onheart, How to Train Your Dragon,* and *Eragon,* have avoided these
"stereotypes [that, like fairy tales] take the form of clichés and stock characters"[12] by portraying dragons in more positive ways: as guides, friends, companions, or allies. Thus, to create a heroic, albeit anthropomorphized nonhuman group[13] of young dragons in *Wings of Fire* follows this growing cultural
trend. Moreover, it situates dragons into the animal studies movement since,
like nonhuman animals in the visual and print arts, they have become "important symbols that humans use to make sense of the world and ourselves."[14] Such a re-creation of Cinderella as a nonhuman animal even functions this way in William Wegman's version of "Cinderella," which "uses
photographs of his Weimaraners to transform the timeless tale into 'a classic
for our time.'"[15] In addition, the nonhuman animals in previous, human-
centered versions have seemed to progress toward giving nonhuman agents
more consideration for their actions in the story. Ruth B. Bottigheimer
writes:

> In narrative terms each of the animal familiars amplifies Cinderella's personal-
> ity or extends her reach. Whether the result is intended or not, the process of
> externalizing agency away from Cinderella by introducing animals to solve her
> problems also effectively strips the heroine of individualizing characteristics.
> To put this another way, each new animal familiar in contemporary rewritings
> contributes to universalizing the Cinderella figure by denaturing personal indi-
> viduality.[16]

Even though Bottigheimer focuses on the loss of Cinderella's individuality as
a human, there are obvious gains being made by nonhuman agents in the
fairy tale, which hints at the ability for nonhuman animals to completely
partake in the plot itself.

As a result, even though Sutherland's *Wings of Fire* dragons are anthropomorphized, they are also used in literature just like real-life nonhuman
animals would be used. Thus, even though this chapter focuses on how
Tsunami and her companions fit into a human-centered "Cinderella" story
line, they could also effectively add to any study that aims to consider them

fully as nonhuman animals, albeit imaginary ones. Consequently, dragons
are no longer mere literary characters. Neither are they simple-minded beasts
that destroy and kill. Instead, they are highly relevant and modern *tools* that
writers and scholars can use when evaluating significant cultural, social, and
political issues in the real world.

SUMMARY OF *THE LOST HEIR*

Sutherland's second novel in the *Wings of Fire* series continues to follow the
five dragonets of destiny, Tsunami, Clay (MudWing), Glory (RainWing),
Sunny (SandWing), and Starflight (NightWing), after they have escaped
from Burn and Queen Scarlet in the SkyWing Kingdom, where several of the
dragons, including Tsunami, were forced to fight and kill in an arena. In fact,
Tsunami kills a dragon named Gill, which becomes important later in the
second novel, but, during this part of the story, the dragonets are intent on
looking for the SeaWing Kingdom so that they can hopefully get a better idea
of how to fulfill their destinies. Using the information that they gained from
their studies, they are searching for Tsunami's family, specifically since they
believe that Tsunami is the lost (and only) heir to the kingdom. As a result,
like Cinderella who starts humbly and ends up as a royal, Tsunami begins the
novel representing the "Cinderella" trope, "a universal metaphor to promote
an unjustly neglected subject, activity, region, or social cause."[17] Thus, the
aim of the story appears to be that the dragonets will resituate Tsunami in a
royal setting while they seek to follow the prophecy that has been set for
them to be the designators of the next SandWing queen, who will end the
war.

OVERCOMING DIVISIVE WOMEN:
EVIL (STEP)MOTHERS AND ENVIOUS SISTERS

Scholarly criticism about "Cinderella" has already uncovered many ways in
which the patriarchal and male-dominated influences in the narrative have
affected the female characters; in addition, modern reinterpretations of the
story have addressed these problematic aspects by giving females more agency and even the ability to refuse men. Yet the manner in which women are
often divisive and domineering with one another is also a "Cinderella" trope
that cannot be overlooked, an idea that Jack Zipes supports when he writes:
"what most of the tales, oral and literary, have in common is the conflict
between a young girl and her stepmother and siblings about her legacy."[18]
Stepmothers and stepsisters are primary antagonists to "Cinderella" figures,
and like Cinderella, Tsunami also experiences feeling divided from her own
family.

Tsunami's dreams about being the lost heir who has come to claim her rightful place in line for the throne of the SeaWing Kingdom are quickly blunted in two significant ways: the succession is antagonistic toward females, requiring one of the challengers to die in the battle for supremacy, and there is the presence of Tsunami's sisters and rivals for the throne—Anemone, who has already hatched, and several unhatched, albeit threatened eggs in the Royal Hatchery.

First, the manner in which dragons can succeed to the SeaWing throne is a system that overturns the male predominance over power. Females rule, and by focusing on a female-centered system, it "reveal[s] how power operates through the narrative, and, in revealing it, to expose and contest that construction of power."[19] In fact, male knowledge of the succession is quickly invalidated. Tsunami approaches the SeaWing Kingdom thinking, "according to Starflight, none of the queen's other female dragonets had survived to adulthood. Tsunami was the only living heir to the SeaWing kingdom. One day, she would be queen of the SeaWings."[20] Starflight, a male NightWing, is a scholar whose effort, in this case, faces scrutiny. He tries to serve as the authority on how the succession works based on books and culturally approved knowledge, which, in history, has been controlled by men. However, because he is incorrect about there being other heirs, his authority is immediately compromised, leaving Tsunami and her female-centered experiences at the core of this part of the narrative. As a result, criticisms against the patriarchy inherent in other versions of "Cinderella" have been eliminated in this case so that the nature of women who are in power can be surveyed instead. Yet because the presumed nature of fairy-tale women remains the same, this power structure becomes ripe for jealousy.

A Queen of the SeaWing Kingdom can only be deposed if she is challenged and killed by her daughter, a reality, along with Queen Coral's personality, that leads Tsunami to feel that "[s]he preferred the image in her head that she'd dreamed about her whole life—the loving queen from *The Missing Princess*"[21] instead of a self-destructive family. For Tsunami, who thinks that she has just achieved her dream of returning to her birth family, the idea of killing her mother—especially after she has unknowingly killed her father in the previous novel—and creating a division in her family is unthinkable or at least not urgent since she considers, "that day could be as far off as she wanted it to be. Not something she had to think about now."[22] Moreover, the fact that another sister, Orca, already challenged and lost to Queen Coral demonstrates to Tsunami the divisive and antagonistic nature of how SeaWings relate to one another. In fact, Orca's accidental loss when she was "impal[ed] on that narwhal horn she [Coral] has on the end of her tail" demonstrates how violent the battle for the throne can be.[23] Furthermore, the reality that Orca planned revenge in case she lost (and she did) by enchanting the statue of herself in the Royal Hatchery so that it will kill any hatchlings with royal blood serves as a way to control the succession from the grave and exhibits the true animosity she felt toward members of her own family.

Tsunami feels envious when she first realizes that Anemone is her sister. The narrator reveals how her thoughts associate *"Anemone"* with *"An enemy"*:[24]

> It took Tsunami a few moments to realize what Riptide had actually said. Her skin prickled, hearing *an enemy, an enemy*, until it sank in that he'd been saying a name.
> *Anemone*. Tsunami's sister. Another heir to the throne.
> So much for being special. So much for her guaranteed future kingdom.[25]

After living for years with a stepfamily, Tsunami thinks that she will be happy to meet her blood family. Yet as soon as she realizes that she has a sibling, she becomes envious. However, these feelings are more than just about power in the line of succession; they are also about perceptions of love and materialism. As Tsunami continues to evaluate Anemone, she frets that Anemone wears "tiny strands of pearls [. . .] woven around her neck and tail as if to match her mother's" and thinks, *"That could have been me, [. . .] I could have been the one with matching pearls and a matching throne and a mother who loved me, if the Talons hadn't stolen me from my home."*[26] Immediately, Tsunami makes these assessments even though she does not know her sister or the personal struggles that Anemone endures because she is an heir. This situation therefore serves as an example of Ann and Barry Ulanov's classic case of fairy-tale envy when the envier objectifies the envied and seemingly closes off all future productive communication or a chance for reconciliation with the envied.[27]

Nevertheless, because the use of a nonhuman dragon allows for a new perspective in the "Cinderella" tale, Tsunami's sense of envy follows Ann and Barry Ulanov's concept of seeing the good and bad of both sides of envy since,[28] by the end of the novel, the experience makes Tsunami more multidimensional than the Brothers Grimm's or Perrault's Cinderella ever were. The double-sidedness inherent in the situation begins to grow during Tsunami's first interaction with Anemone. According to the narrator, Anemone "was really tiny, no taller than a scavenger, and she didn't look very strong," which first makes Tsunami believe that *"I don't have to worry about her* [. . .] *She'd be easy to defeat, and obviously I'd make a better queen."*[29] From these considerations, it becomes evident that in addition to her envy, Tsunami is worried first and foremost about the succession and how *she* can control it.

This situation is not much different in earlier iterations of "Cinderella." Surely, the men in many of the version can control the royal succession through their own choices, but the women in Cinderella's family or household *do* determine how the succession will proceed as well. In versions where the stepmother denies Cinderella access to the ball, she makes this decision in order to try to remove Cinderella from being considered in the line of succession. Plus, when the royals arrive in the Brothers Grimm version to have the women try on the slipper, the stepsisters mutilate themselves in an attempt to fit their feet inside the slipper. Thus, there are ways in which women divide themselves over a succession to some form of power.

Nevertheless, because dragons are not humans—even though they are depicted in anthropocentric ways due to the human-made nature of Sutherland's novel—their ultimate determinations about the viability of dividing women and denying the good traits of the stepfamily become significant. One of the ways in which Ann and Barry Ulanov recommend for enviers (Tsunami) to reconcile themselves with the envied (her mother, Anemone, her lost place in the SeaWing Kingdom) is to actually interact with the envied by "cross[ing] over to each other's opposing emotions"[30] and to avoid objectifying them and "blank[ing] out persons in favor of qualities."[31] It is tempting for Tsunami to see Anemone as a threat, especially since Anemone's harness keeps her so close to Queen Coral. However, Tsunami knows that her behavior at their first encounter is wrong, which is why she "felt a stab of guilt for thinking about something like that on her first meeting with her real family."[32] As a result, Tsunami "held out one of her front talons to Anemone, and after a small pause, Anemone pressed her own talon against it."[33] Tsunami's overcoming of envy becomes more situated and evident as the novel progresses.

After Tsunami and Anemone begin to communicate with each other and to share stories about each other's struggles, the situation begins to change. For example, when Tsunami and Anemone finally sneak under a waterfall (which reaches the limits of Anemone's leash) and have a private moment away from Queen Coral, who is asleep, they discover that each has different, biased, and envious perceptions of the other. Tsunami has idealized royal power, which Anemone finds boring and overbearing; Tsunami also realizes that Anemone has her own problems: Coral and her ministers want to use her magical abilities as a weapon despite her protestations and they want her to marry Whirlpool, an unattractive dragon to both siblings. Thus, instead of feeling threatened by each other, they begin to unite and see each other as real dragons with both good and bad experiences, allowing them to fit with Queen Coral's simple exclamation that "And now I have two daughters!"[34]

Moreover, by the end of the novel, Tsunami is able to feel protective of the remaining unhatched sibling who faces danger in the hatchery. When she first arrived in the kingdom, she could have had a fourth sibling, but the magical statue leaves "[t]he little blue dragonet inside [. . .] strangled to death. Her neck was twisted in a horrible way, and her head flopped sadly," a moment that leads Tsunami to fully commit herself to her family because she is "in shock. It—*she*—was so tiny."[35] She then wonders, "Who would do this to a baby dragonet? How could anyone?"[36] Finally, in anger, she adds, "TO MY SISTER."[37] Tsunami's fury and protectiveness allow her to overcome her envy, and after Queen Coral kills the hatchery attendant, Tortoise, for allowing one of the eggs to be destroyed by this then-unknown threat, Tsunami risks her life and the wrath of her mother, who threatens, "[i]f anything happens to that egg [. . .] I'll lose two daughters that day," to save the hatchling.[38] And even once Tsunami realizes the danger of Orca's statue, the battle is not easy, for the statue "plowed into Tsunami and knocked her backward. Its weight bore down on her, crushing her against the floor."[39] Yet in the end, Tsunami manages to expose the magical enemy and have it destroyed. She also feels protective of her new sister and has the honor of naming her Auklet, a moment which overturns the evil stepmother (mother) and stepsister (sister) trope since Tsunami realizes that Coral loved her daughters "even though one of them would one day grow up to take her place" and that Coral's caring, which was "perhaps a little too much" was nevertheless "better than not caring at all."[40]

Through this process, the cycle of envy in a "Cinderella"-based episode ends. The women are in fact reconciled with one another, and the notion that women must be divisive in order for Cinderella to mature and feel self-actualized is overturned. Such a change relates to calls for more inclusiveness between women in modern society and fits with Zipes's complaint against the "Cinderella" trope since "the message of this underdog in all its iterations has become somewhat hackneyed, and it may be time to reconsider a total remake in keeping with the changing role of women in society or to abandon her story altogether."[41] While Tsunami does not like the system of succession, which remains in place despite her reconciliation with her royal relatives, she accepts it and the position that she now has within this system no matter if she becomes Queen or not. This situation therefore creates a unique situation in which a Cinderella-character can both oppose and accept a system at the same time, allowing readers "to reinterpret the fairy tale: to transform our attitudes to the narrative, and, in so doing, to encourage us to reconsider what the tale is capable of doing."[42] In many versions of the story, Cinderella must either accept or deny the slipper. Yet in this case, when Cinderella is a dragon who remains royal even if she is not in power or married, the fairy tale can be expanded to more complex social situations, leaving the slipper always within reach.

RIPTIDE: THE NEGLECTED PRINCE, THE HERO-IN-WAITING

The predominance of the prince in the "Cinderella" tradition, whose primary roles are to be handsome, rich, and powerful, becomes completely overturned in *The Lost Heir* even though these classic elements are still present in different forms. While Riptide, the socially "neglected" son of Webs,[43] who originally stole Tsunami (in her egg) from the Royal Hatchery, serves as Tsunami's romantic interest, the notion of having a royally accepted suitor is also embodied by Whirlpool, a "dark green dragon with pale green eyes" and an "oily and slow" voice[44] who serves Queen Coral and who is considered as a suitor first for Anemone and then for Tsunami until Whirlpool's evil character becomes known. As a result, like Cinderella and her stepsisters, the role of suitor for Princess Tsunami is split between different characters. Thus, using dragons in place of humans allows for a revisioning of gender roles in the "Cinderella" tradition that does more than just "feminize" these male dragons.

The first difference occurs because, instead of Riptide being the privileged prince, Tsunami is a princess dealing with the royalty that is already *hers* by blood. Just like the physical wealth of her family is obvious, with castles, and jewels, Tsunami even has physical markings that prove her bloodlines. When Shark, the queen's brother, seeks confirmation of Tsunami's heritage, Riptide points out her "glow patterns," for

> Under her wings, when she lit them up, the luminescent stripes formed spirals around the outer edges. Starbursts shaped like webbed dragon footprints branched away from the lines in the middle [. . .] [while] [m]ost of them [the other Sea Wings] had smaller starbursts and no spirals. Only Shark's [royal] patterns matched her own.[45]

The one important quality that Tsunami is missing, though, is the ability to speak Aquatic, and it is her relationship with Riptide that begins this process. Riptide chases her because he interprets her accidental use of Aquatic, "Hey, sparkling teeth. I totally love three of your claws but not the others, and I wish your nose was a herring so I could eat it, and also your wings sound like sharks snoring"[46] to mean that Tsunami likes him romantically. Yet even after Riptide assesses that she is a friend, mostly because she "look[s] sad," he still asks, "So where did you come from, and what's wrong with you?"[47] What is *wrong* is that she does not speak Aquatic, a clear sign that she is not ready to assimilate with SeaWing, much less *royal* SeaWing culture. Nevertheless, because Tsunami's nonverbal cues and frustrated expression about being "raised by [an] idiot" SeaWing named Webs convinces Riptide that she is sincere, he agrees to bring all the dragonets to the Summer Palace.[48] This scene is therefore significant because it exemplifies how "Cinderella" figures manage to move in society through their ability to *communicate* with the prince. Now that the male is of lower status, his goodness earned through difficult experiences, social exile, and the ability to speak a dragon language that uses his glowing scales brings him into the role of a dual-Cinderella with Tsunami.

Moreover, the biological nature of using dragon stripes and scales to communicate is a physical difference from humans that allows for the pro- blematizing of critiques against appearances in "Cinderella stories."[49] In- stead of the Cinderella character being seen as superficial due to her physical presentation, a dragon *must* learn how to use his or her body for a communi- cative advantage, for, as Tsunami realizes, dragons under water "couldn't just pop up to the surface every time they needed to chat."[50] So while Cinde- rella *may* present herself like a royal at the ball to show her good qualities as a marriage partner, Tsunami *must* learn Aquatic to prove herself as a SeaW- ing, for "*how can [she] be queen of the SeaWings if [she] doesn't even speak their language?*"[51] This situation would be akin to Cinderella having to prove herself to be human. Consequently, by reversing the genders and then by allowing for multiple neglected "Cinderella" figures, these dragons allow for an innovative way to see body, communication, and biology as proof of being a species itself rather than being part of a hierarchy.

Whirlpool's status as a suitor is therefore needed to show the other side of the problem. As a minister for Queen Coral, using communication to try to gain status is his primary aim throughout the novel. Nevertheless, because he is a villain who tries to kill Tsunami, who imprisons the dragonets, and who sides with Blister, his membership as a SeaWing, in spite of his ability to speak Aquatic and his "appearance" as an upstanding dragon, also provides another component to the argument. Whirlpool might be the "neglected" suitor—by Coral, Anemone, *and* Tsunami—but he lacks the goodness of character that is also necessary to be considered a dragon (i.e., human) in the same sense as Tsunami and Riptide. Thus, unlike in most human-oriented versions of "Cinderella," which indicate that blood (biological inheritance) is not necessarily important—for Cinderella does not need a special bloodline to marry a prince—in the world of dragons, blood is still important in deter- mining goodness. Tsunami is good because she is royal and because she strives to be a "SeaWing dragon"; Riptide is good because he is related to Webs and because he has been driven into goodness by neglect. Whirlpool, though, is evil because he has not suffered neglect and because he has no known relatives who are good.

The fact that Riptide struggles and suffers as an outcast also develops this goodness in much the same way as Tsunami has suffered in hiding with the other dragonets. Unlike the Brothers Grimm's and Perrault's Cinderella, Tsu- nami is socially awkward with her prince. When Tsunami first encounters him, she accidentally insinuates that she likes him romantically and causes him to chase her. After she realizes her mistake, she finds herself being protected by him and feeling piqued when Queen Coral does not support him due to his kinship with Webs, the SeaWing who stole Tsunami (as an egg) from the hatchery. When Queen Coral comments, "He can't be trusted. Webs is his father. Their bloodline is tainted with betrayal," Tsunami thinks, "But she'd liked Riptide [. . .] *Poor Riptide* [. . .] It wasn't his fault his father had turned traitor, but he suffered for it anyway."[52] Thus, just like Riptide defends Tsunami even when he does not have to, Tsunami defends Riptide and becomes more defensive of him as she learns more about his character.

Even though many of her feelings are involuntary, for when Anemone mentions marriage "[a]n image of Riptide flashed in her [Tsunami's] head" even though she considers it "ridiculous, because she hardly knew him either" and because she "do[es]n't have time to get married" but has "to stop the war and save the world,"[53] it is evident that she has become fond of him in a way that resembles Cinderella's early meetings with the prince before the fitting of the slipper. The notion that hers is a real romance also appears since Tsunami admits to having crushes on Starflight and Clay. However, now she finds that Riptide is "a SeaWing who looked at her as if he didn't see a future queen, or a father killer, or anything but a dragon whom he liked very much."[54] She also places more value on her growing feelings for him than being heir to the throne, which seems to be tied to Cinderella's own traditional goodness. At one point, "[s]omething tingled in the air between them, like the sky outside, waiting for the storm" and Tsunami thinks, *"This is* MOST *improper for the future SeaWing queen [. . .] But maybe I'd rather have this than a throne anyway."*[55]

Furthermore, these commonalities do not end at the conclusion of the novel. While both become romantically interested in each other and learn to protect each other, they are ultimately forced to separate. Riptide tells her: "I really am sorry. I hope next time . . . well, I hope there is a next time. When things are better for everyone."[56] Riptide must help protect the Summer Palace and Tsunami must continue forward with her fellow dragonets, ultimately toward the RainWing Kingdom. However, the quip that Tsunami offers when she leaves him harkens back to her former awkward state when "she flashed one of the patterns he'd taught her. *All right.* Then she added *squid-brain*, and Riptide smiled before turning to fly away into the heart of the battle."[57]

This ending serves as a direct counterexample to traditional "Cinderella" versions since "[a]n ordinary girl's marrying up the social scale is fundamental to the modern Cinderella plot."[58] Instead, Riptide is the ordinary prince who does not move up the social ladder in this episode. In addition, having a male Cinderella in Riptide also serves as a counterpoint to many human male Cinderellas. According to Ruth B. Bottigheimer, "[d]ifferent kinds of plots accommodate a boy Cinderella protagonist in today's world. For contemporary boys, the Cinderella tale means coming from behind and winning."[59] Yet because Riptide is forced to flee and leave behind his love interest, he is not "coming from behind and winning" here.[60] Surely, he has captured Tsunami's affection (as well as the hearts of readers), but he does not end this "Cinderella" episode with a victory in any definite way besides being good to the heroine. Thus, male dragons allow for another reimagining of the "Cinderella" trope in this manner.

Moreover, the dragons do not marry at the end of the novel, which, while uncommon since Daniel Aranda "found only one version that poses Cinderella explicitly as a character who is not marriageable,"[61] does allow for the dragons to critique the marriage plot of the "Cinderella" story line. However, even if the non-marriage of Tsunami and Riptide makes one wonder if "a romantic attraction [can] survive if it transgresses social conventions,"[62] they nevertheless part as *equals* in a relationship that remains open at this point. This fits with the classic ending of the "Cinderella" tale in a different way since a parting in this sense does not symbolize divorce or hopelessness, but a sense of giving destiny a chance, or as Tsunami says, "she wanted the chance to decide,"[63] which is similar to the married endings of other versions of the story in which the "happily ever after" assumption does not offer any specific details about the rest of their lives. In effect, then, dragon princes in the "Cinderella" tradition allow for any neglected family members related to the main heroine (hero) to benefit from her goodness, thus overturning the idea that Cinderella stands alone in the tradition. And in modern society, where concepts of equality, expansive online networks, which often serve as surrogate "blood' and family, and the importance of ethics have become global phenomena, it becomes evident how expanding the idea of how the "Cinderella" trope can be shared among many Cinderellas and connected families fits with current social trends.

DRAGONS, ROYALTY, AND OBJECTS

Materialism and consumerism are aspects built into the premise of "Cinderella," and they constitute what Kathryn A. Hoffman calls "object studies" or "thing studies"[64] and what Jane Bennett calls "vibrant matter,"[65] especially since contemporary cultural symbols of "Cinderella" include "products from dolls and toys to DVDs, video games, e-books, apps, dresses, magic wands, tiaras, trinkets, and cosmetic cases."[66] When Cinderella is in rags, dirty, and poor, she reflects the social desire for readers to have what is considered to be opposite of this state. When it is time for her to go to the ball to meet the prince, her transformation involves material goods and the superficial necessities needed to highlight how the consumption of objects matter. For Marina Warner, this assessment means that "in a more settled and prosperous world, the longing in fairy tales for a safer, more comfortable life looked like rank consumerism and cynical upward mobility, cost what may," which many traditional versions of the "Cinderella" trope are beginning to reassess.[67] For example, Maía Fernández-Lamarque, in her study of Spanish-language versions of "Cinderella," discusses how in one version, Noé Martínez's *Cinderella siempre quiso un Wonderbra* (2009) (*Cinderella Always Wanted a Wonderbra*), the character Paulina "constantly comments that a (Visa) credit card is what every woman [i.e., Cinderella] needs."[68] Nevertheless, using nonhuman animals adds another layer to critiquing consumerism as a fairy-tale end goal, especially since many real-life nonhuman animals are often involved in the testing of consumer products.[69] Thus, for Tsunami, her dragonets, and Riptide (the prince), their draconic characteristics allow for them to stand outside of traditional human perspectives and critique aspects of materialism within the novel.

As dragonets growing up in a cave in secrecy, the material possessions that they had were limited to dire necessities and educational materials. As a result, the materialism and consumerism of other dragon kingdoms stands starkly against this meager background. Moreover, for Tsunami, who is the daughter of a queen, the idea of growing materially as well as in a familial and authoritative way appears to be her main goal upon learning this truth. As a result, when she reaches the Summer Palace and encounters its material riches she is awed.

> Four pillars of blue-tinted white stone spiraled out of the water, winding toward one another until they formed a towering pavilion in the middle of the lake. The pavilion had twelve circular levels, each one smaller than the one below. There were few walls, most of them very low, and the whole structure was latticed with curving shapes and holes and little wading pools.[70]

Not only does the rich complexity of the palace impress her, but its naturalness and balance with the surrounding environment also astounds her, making her think, "It didn't look like it had been built; it looked as if it had grown that way, although Tsunami was pretty sure that was impossible."[71] Such an observation seems to link royalty and its physical manifestations of wealth as natural and out-of-reach for everyday dragons in a way similar to the apparent separateness of the prince's royal family in traditional "Cinderella" versions. Thus, this material display becomes as "natural" to the powerful as the pools and waterfalls in which it is situated in the SeaWing Kingdom.

Due to these perceptions, which fit with Tsunami's fairy-tale dreams of being the lost heir, she is ready to take her place as a titled possessor of it and "want[s] to make a good impression on the dragons of her kingdom."[72] In fact, the connection that the palace has to her physical appearance—her stripes—connects material aspects to her in a vibrant way.[73] According to the narrator, "[a] spiraling starburst of webbed talon-print shapes was carved into the floor and filled with glittering water, lined all along the bottom with tiny pearls. Tsunami realized the pattern was the same as the one on her wings."[74]

Even the thrones are bejeweled. The queen's throne is "studded with eme-
ralds and sapphires and shot through with gold lines in the shape of waves,"
while the "smaller throne [is] carved to match, with the same patterns made
of tinier gemstones,"[75] which further connects perceptions of physiognomy,
power, and materialism.

Even though, according to the narrator, "[a]ll dragons loved treasure,"[76]
which is a characteristic carried over from many folktale interpretations of
the creatures,[77] the pearls that Queen Coral wears also represent the consumerist tendencies of these particular royals. Later, Coral even invites Tsunami to join in this consumption as "[s]he leaned forward and draped the pearls
around Tsunami's neck."[78] Tsunami is quite appreciative of the gesture and
finds them to be "heavy and smooth, sliding coolly across [. . .] [her]
scales."[79] In fact, she considers them her "*first treasure*" since "[i]t was a
strange thrill, having something of her very own" and since it "was more than
a shiny, beautiful thing. It belonged to Tsunami and nobody else. And it
made her look even more like her mother."[80] Thus, Tsunami likes the pearls
because their richness is something that she feels that she can own, especially
after she has owned nothing, and because they link her to her mother, which
fits with ideas of social inclusion (and competition) which are often associated with consumption.[81]

Nevertheless, this "Cinderella" dragon story is incomplete without elements of social critique. It does not take long for Tsunami to feel the real
burden that owning things and being a part of this royal system causes.
Because Tsunami appears to value the first set of pearls so much, Queen
Coral

> smiled at this and produced another long strand of pearls, these a shimmering
> pale purple and oddly shaped instead of round.
>   With expert talons, Queen Coral wound them around Tsunami's chest and
> wings. They were beautiful, but it was strange to have something weighing her
> down. Tsunami felt almost as if she was wearing a harness of treasure. She
> wasn't about to complain, though. The Talons of Peace had never given the
> dragonets beautiful things.[82]

In this moment, the true significance of these pearls as pieces of vibrant
matter[83] and objects of cultural critique appear. Rather than Cinderella being
improved and uplifted by gaining a palace, jewels, and a royal title, she feels
more and more weighted down. The mention of the word "harness" is especially important in this context since the harness is a definite image of re-
straint and constraint in the royal household. As a result, even though Tsunami is not yet ready to abandon the palace and return to her attempt to fulfill
the prophecy, which is supported by a peace organization, she *does* notice
that these objects are not as ideal as they seem.

Another group of objects that have an important function in the novel and that are worth noting is Queen Coral's writings/scrolls. The story of her lost heir and missing daughter is what allowed the dragonets to learn about the SeaWing Kingdom. Thus, the scrolls themselves are pieces of vibrant matter that led them toward their experiences with the SeaWings. [84] Moreover, the fact that Queen Coral's stories are popular and relate her directly to consumption through royally made commodities is critical to this "Cinderella" situation. Just like Coral's stories "have never been more popular," with the "latest [. . .] [being] bought by every single SeaWing in the tribe," [85] the story of the prince looking for the woman whose foot fits in the slipper travels widely and is consumed by every woman hoping to marry him. As a result, when Coral tells Tsunami, who is not interested in reading these stories, that "my writing is about *everything*," it becomes evident that for these dragon royals, the consumption of their own tales and their physical manifestations has become "[m]ore important than how to fight the war" [86] and ensure that the proper queen rules over the Sand Kingdom. Consequently, these objects and how they convey meaning control the trajectory of life for *all* dragons.

This image becomes compounded by the harness, which Coral forces Anemone to wear and for which Tsunami is fitted, so that she can keep them close and safe from the unknown enemy who is trying to kill her living (Tsunami) and unborn daughters. Tsunami sees that the harness is made of "a stretchy, gummy, clear material that seemed to cling to Anemone's scales" and that keeps her "trapped" and "tether[ed]" to Coral. [87] The harness therefore best symbolizes the glass slipper, which, in this case, has a negative "performative identity," [88] for many writers and scholars see it as a constraining object that links Cinderella to her fate [89] and indicates how upward mobility could itself be considered a "harness" constraining her to a certain consumerist and material lifestyle, "a veritable emblem of late capitalist commodity fetishism." [90] The ability of the harness to change size and "suddenly [shrink] until" fitting Tsunami, [91] which stems from Anemone's magic, also relates to scholarly interpretations of the glass slipper that find that "crystal and glass have a potentially malleable form." [92]

The magic that is "part of the fabric of everyday [fairy-tale] reality" [93] and that animates certain objects in the novel also literally relates to Jane Bennett's vibrant matter [94] since objects passively *and* actively assert a force on characters in the novel. Certain dragons also have magical abilities, which can be used for good or evil purposes. Even though Anemone is an "animus" who is trying to stall being used by her mother and the council to create weapons, such as "enchant[ing] the Sky Kingdom's palace to cave in on all the SkyWings," and "curs[ing] a spear so it will search for Burn's heart and not stop until it kills her," she does not want to be used in this manner, a reality that makes not only the products of her power into objects, but that also makes her into one. [95] The fact that the power to enchant objects debilitates the self is also evident when Anemone tells Tsunami: "[e]very time an animus dragon uses her power, she loses a bit of herself."[96]

The true danger of objects thus appears in the struggle between Tsunami and the statue of Orca in the hatchery, which has been enchanted to kill any dragonets with royal blood. Like other objects made into truly vibrant matter[97] by animus dragons, such as "chess pieces [. . .] [that] play themselves" and "jewels [that] poison anyone who trie[s] to steal them,"[98] Orca's statue is an object of consumption that Queen Coral especially valued but that turns against its possessors. Similarly, Collette and Ravel's "prophetic insight" that "Walt Disney would exploit" consumers with toys and other merchandise that seemed to be "living, conscious beings, independent of the [. . .] [consumer's] make-believe" also critiques how people depend on objects that can, in some form or fashion, injure those who create, purchase, and possess them.[99] Due to this reality, in which this dragon Cinderella realizes how materialism and consumption in society control and destroy what they aim to protect, Tsunami wonders "[d]id she even *want* to be queen here?"[100] and eventually decides against staying in her "inherited" kingdom. In the end, she realizes that even though the Royal Hatchery is *"where I should have hatched"*[101] she also understands "how her life should have been if she'd hatched here and been raised by her own mother. None of them would have happened. She'd have been dead within the first week, her neck snapped like the sad little dragonet in the eggshell."[102]

In the end, consumption, materialism, and the presence of vibrant objects[103] as signs of progress become heavily critiqued because the dragons, while anthropomorphic, are still separated enough from the contemporary motions of capitalistic human society to fully critique them. Tsunami and her "royal" companions, whose status as the dragonets of destiny nevertheless make them important even if they are not seen that way in the SeaWing Kingdom, are able to choose goodness over materialism and consumption, which is something that is normally impossible when "neglected"[104] Cinderella characters marry their "princes" and become royals in an object-reliant social system.

CONCLUSION: THE RISE OF MULTICULTURALISM AND THE FUTURE OF NONHUMAN CINDERELLAS

Since Tsunami's "Cinderella" story line differs from traditional iterations of the fairy tale, it is unsurprising that, instead of staying with the royals, whose culture is fixed in its aggressive and materialistic ways, Tsunami chooses the dragonets over her bloodlines. At the end of the novel, she tells her mother: "I don't belong here [. . .] I'm not doing what I was hatched to do. I don't speak the underwater language. I don't understand the Council. [. . .] my destiny is somewhere else. I have to go stop the war. With my friends."[105] Tsunami therefore chooses a mixed-species group of a NightWing, a Rain-Wing, a MudWing, and a SandWing instead of her blood relatives (i.e., traditional fairy-tale rendering). Such a choice comes at a time when contemporary society often measures family through means other than blood: stepfamilies, especially "stepmother families,"[106] pets,[107] global friends, and even parasocial relationships with celebrities[108] are also familial considerations that expand beyond previously set borders and create a multicultural understanding of the world and its narrative traditions.

Most emphatically, Tsunami's choice destroys the idea of the stepfamily being the divisive element in the "Cinderella" story line. At the beginning of the novel, Tsunami even thinks that being a member of the same tribe is critical when she thinks: "Perhaps the problem with her friends was that they were from different tribes, all stubborn and muddled up instead of sensible like SeaWings. Maybe her own kind would understand her better. They'd *appreciate* her instead of yelling at her."[109] Nevertheless, the reality is that her blood relatives do not necessarily treat her better; neither do the SeaWings. As a result, she realizes that love and family can be found anywhere. In this case, she finds this sense of belonging with her fellow dragonets of destiny, with whom she has had some difficulties—and even ignored them for a time during her early visit to the Summer Palace while Coral held them in a cave. Yet, by the end of the novel, after all the dragonets are imprisoned and helped to escape by Anemone, the significance of choosing sisters over being divisive as well as relying on the multicultural family and the *lowly neglected* prince who remains in-waiting appears. Tsunami confirms this notion when she equates the dragonets with home, thinking, "She was surprised at how warm and happy she felt to be back with her friends again" and "[t]his was how she'd expected to feel among the SeaWings—like she was coming home."[110] She considers her obligation to the dragonets to be stronger as well, thinking, "Too late now. She had this other family, not at all normal, and they needed her more than anyone."[111] Moreover, Tsunami ends the novel with a mature consideration, a characteristic "Cinderella"-type metamorphosis[112] that aligns, in this case, with her emotions and that combines what she has learned from *both* families,

> *I will*, Tsunami thought, *but not because I think I'm the greatest and everyone should listen to me. I'll keep trying to lead you because it's the only way I know to keep you all safe. And maybe sometimes I'll have to listen, the way Mother listens to her Council, and sometimes I won't be able to do exactly what I want.*
>
> But even when she was mad at her friends, she knew she could trust them. And she had to be the kind of dragon they could trust as well."[113]

Consequently, these aspects demonstrate how much a contemporary Cinderella figure can learn from the experience of being Cinderella, just like scholars can learn from studying multiple iterations of the fairy-tale trope. Thus, using dragons in a version of "Cinderella" can not only provide new ways of viewing the narrative, but also of relating the trope to modern society.

Therefore, it is evident from the way in which Tsunami's "Cinderella" story reveals important insights about contemporary society, especially concerning divisive women, lowly princes, materialism and consumerism, the rise of multicultural—and even nonhuman families—and the role of nonhuman animals in the fairy-tale tradition that the use of any nonhuman in a fairy tale will become and continue to be an important way of encouraging social critique. This idea fits with Andrew Teverson's idea that fairy tale

> is a genre that enables writers to hold a mirror up to their society, reflecting the anxieties and preoccupations of the era, but it also furnishes writers with a means of responding to their society indirectly, using the fabulous and otherworldly qualities of the genre as a mask for social satire, and, more affirmatively, as a means of speculating about how things might be different.[114]

Having a dragon Cinderella is different, but it nevertheless emphasizes very common issues of contemporary society and its growing interest in dragons as cultural characters. Nevertheless, despite these scholarly benefits, the reality that "Cinderella," "a global cultural icon that keeps pace effortlessly with new social media and communication networks,"[115] is still a great story cannot be overlooked. No matter if her character is the good and beautiful young woman of Perrault and Brothers Grimm, or the powerful and psychologically maturing dragon of *The Lost Heir*, "Cinderella" still endures and partakes in significant contemporary narratives that "push the reader to recognize, question, and potentially reject culturally constructed expectations and desires,"[116] which indeed keep her as one of the most famous literary and cinematic figures in human (and nonhuman) history.

NOTES

1. Jack Zipes, "The Triumph of the Underdog: Cinderella's Legacy," in *Cinderella across Cultures: New Reflections and Disciplinary Perspectives*, ed. Martine Hennard Dutheil de la Rochère, Gillian Lathey, and Monika Woźniak (Detroit: Wayne State University Press, 2016), Location 7513.

2. Martine Hennard Dutheil de la Rochère, Gillian Lathey, and Monika Woźniak, "Introduction: Cinderella across Cultures," in *Cinderella across Cultures: New Reflections and Disciplinary Perspectives*, ed. Martine Hennard Dutheil de la Rochère, Gillian Lathey, and Monika Woźniak (Detroit: Wayne State University Press, 2016), Location 194.

3. de la Rochère, Lathey, and Woźniak, "Introduction," Location 489.

4. Jane Bennett, *Vibrant Matter: A Political Ecology of Things* (Durham, NC: Duke University Press, 2010), vii.

5. Andrew Teverson, *Fairy Tale (The New Critical Idiom)* (London: Routledge, 2013), 142.

6. Marina Warner, *Once Upon a Time: A Short History of Fairy Tale* (Oxford: Oxford University Press, 2014), xviii.

7. Teverson, *Fairy Tale*, 3.

8. Teverson, *Fairy Tale*, 5.

9. de la Rochère, Lathey, and Woźniak, "Introduction," Location 469.

10. Ruth B. Bottigheimer, "Cinderella: The People's Princess," in *Cinderella across Cultures: New Reflections and Disciplinary Perspectives*, ed. Martine Hennard Dutheil de la Rochère, Gillian Lathey, and Monika Woźniak (Detroit: Wayne State University Press, 2016), Location 1008.

11. Martin Arnold, *The Dragon: Fear and Power* (London: Reaktion Books, 2018), Location 2024.

12. Jan Van Collie, "The Illustrator as Fairy Godmother: The Illustrated Cinderella in the Low Countries," in *Cinderella across Cultures: New Reflections and Disciplinary Perspectives*, ed. Martine Hennard Dutheil de la Rochère, Gillian Lathey, and Monika Woźniak (Detroit: Wayne State University Press, 2016), Location 5999.

13. Teverson, *Fairy Tale*, 22.

14. Margo DeMello, *Animals and Society: An Introduction to Human-Animal Studies* (New York: Columbia University Press, 2012), Location 5860.

15. Sandra L. Beckett, "Revisualizing Cinderella for All Ages," in *Cinderella across Cultures: New Reflections and Disciplinary Perspectives*, ed. Martine Hennard Dutheil de la Rochère, Gillian Lathey, and Monika Woźniak (Detroit: Wayne State University Press, 2016), Location 5760.

16. Bottigheimer, "Cinderella," Location 1058–1071.

17. de la Rochère, Lathey, and Woźniak, "Introduction," Location 194.

18. Zipes, "Triumph," Location 7504.

19. Teverson, *Fairy Tale*, 136.

20. Tui T. Sutherland, *Wings of Fire: The Lost Heir* (New York: Scholastic Press, 2012), 6.

21. Sutherland, *Wings*, 185.

22. Sutherland, *Wings*, 6.

23. Sutherland, *Wings*, 183.

24. Sutherland, *Wings*, 76.

25. Sutherland, *Wings*, 76.

26. Sutherland, *Wings*, 77.

27. Ann Ulanov and Barry Ulanov, *Cinderella and Her Sisters—The Envied and the Envying* (Einsiedeln [Switzerland]: Daimon Verlag, 2012), Location 1194.

28. Ulanov and Ulanov, *Cinderella*, Location 1194.

29. Sutherland, *Wings*, 78.

30. Ulanov and Ulanov, Cinderella, Location 1194.

31. Ulanov and Ulanov, Cinderella, Location 235.

32. Sutherland, *Wings*, 78.

33. Sutherland, *Wings*, 78.

34. Sutherland, *Wings*, 86.

35. Sutherland, *Wings*, 146.

36. Sutherland, *Wings*, 146.

37. Sutherland, *Wings*, 146.

38. Sutherland, *Wings*, 155.

39. Sutherland, *Wings*, 236.

40. Sutherland, *Wings*, 246.

41. Zipes, "Triumph," Location 8112.

42. Teverson, *Fairy Tale*, 136.

43. de la Rochère, Lathey, and Woźniak, "Introduction," Location 194.

44. Sutherland, *Wings*, 90.

45. Sutherland, *Wings*, 52.

46. Sutherland, *Wings*, 35.

47. Sutherland, *Wings*, 37.
48. Sutherland, *Wings*, 37.
49. Maía Fernández-Lamarque, *Cinderella in Spain: Variations of the Story as Socio-Ethical Texts* (Jefferson, NC: McFarland & Company, Inc., Publishers, 2019), Location 743.
50. Sutherland, *Wings*, 36.
51. Sutherland, *Wings*, 36.
52. Sutherland, *Wings*, 85.
53. Sutherland, *Wings*, 104.
54. Sutherland, *Wings*, 128.
55. Sutherland, *Wings*, 130.
56. Sutherland, *Wings*, 284.
57. Sutherland, *Wings*, 284.
58. Bottigheimer, "Cinderella," Location 1084.
59. Bottigheimer, "Cinderella," Location 727.
60. Bottigheimer, "Cinderella," Location 727.
61. Daniel Aranda, "Moral Adjustments to Perrault's Cinderella in French Children's Literature (1850–1900)," in *Cinderella across Cultures: New Reflections and Disciplinary Perspectives*, ed. Martine Hennard Dutheil de la Rochère, Gillian Lathey, and Monika Woźniak (Detroit: Wayne State University Press, 2016), Location 2901.
62. Mark Macleod, "Home by Midnight: The Male Cinderella in LGBTI Fiction for Young Adults," in *Cinderella across Cultures: New Reflections and Disciplinary Perspectives*, ed. Martine Hennard Dutheil de la Rochère, Gillian Lathey, and Monika Woźniak (Detroit: Wayne State University Press, 2016), Location 4479.
63. Sutherland, *Wings*, 284.
64. Kathryn A. Hoffman, "Perrault's 'Cendrillon' among the Glass Tales: Crystal Fantasies and Glassworks in Seventeenth-Century France and Italy," in *Cinderella across Cultures: New Reflections and Disciplinary Perspectives*, ed. Martine Hennard Dutheil de la Rochère, Gillian Lathey, and Monika Woźniak (Detroit: Wayne State University Press, 2016), Location 1263.
65. Bennett, *Vibrant*, vii.
66. de la Rochère, Lathey, and Woźniak, "Introduction," Location 381.
67. Warner, *Once*, 132.
68. Fernández-Lamarque, *Cinderella*, Location 1612.
69. DeMello, *Animals*, Location 633.
70. Sutherland, *Wings*, 65–66.
71. Sutherland, *Wings*, 66.
72. Sutherland, *Wings*, 66.
73. Bennett, *Vibrant*, vii.
74. Sutherland, *Wings*, 70.
75. Sutherland, *Wings*, 71.
76. Sutherland, *Wings*, 84.
77. Arnold, *Dragon*, Location 1358.
78. Sutherland, *Wings*, 84.
79. Sutherland, *Wings*, 84.
80. Sutherland, *Wings*, 84.
81. Lauren A. Siegel and Dan Wang. "Keeping Up with the Joneses: Emergence of Travel as a Form of Social Comparison among Millennials." *Journal of Travel & Tourism Marketing* 36, no. 2 (2019): 159. https://doi.org/10.1080/10548408.2018.1499579.
82. Sutherland, *Wings*, 107.
83. Bennett, *Vibrant*, vii.
84. Bennett, *Vibrant*, vii.
85. Sutherland, *Wings*, 113.
86. Sutherland, *Wings*, 114.
87. Sutherland, *Wings*, 101.
88. Rebecca-Anne C. Do Rozario, "Comic Book Princesses for Grown-Ups: Cinderella Meets the Pages of the Superhero," *COLLOQUY text theory critique* 24 (2012): 199, accessed September 4, 2019, www.arts.monash.edu.au/ecps/colloquy/journal /issue024/do_rozario.pdf.

89. Rona May-Ron, "Rejecting the Glass Slipper: The Subversion of Cinderella in Margaret Atwood's *The Edible Woman*," in *Cinderella across Cultures: New Reflections and Disciplinary Perspectives*, ed. Martine Hennard Dutheil de la Rochère, Gillian Lathey, and Monika Woźniak (Detroit: Wayne State University Press, 2016), Location 3222.

90. de la Rochère, Lathey, and Woźniak, "Introduction," Location 367.

91. Sutherland, *Wings*, 158.

92. Hoffman, " Perrault's," Location 1451.

93. Warner, *Once*, 19.

94. Bennett, *Vibrant*, vii.

95. Sutherland, *Wings*, 208.

96. Sutherland, *Wings*, 209.

97. Bennett, *Vibrant*, vii.

98. Sutherland, *Wings*, 73.

99. Warner, *Once*, 169.

100. Sutherland, *Wings*, 227.

101. Sutherland, *Wings*, 144.

102. Sutherland, *Wings*, 221.

103. Bennett, *Vibrant*, vii.

104. de la Rochère, Lathey, and Woźniak, "Introduction," Location 194.

105. Sutherland, *Wings*, 249.

106. Jason B. Whiting, Donna R. Smith, Tammy Barnett, and Erika L. Grafsky, "Overcoming the Cinderella Myth: A Mixed Methods Study of Successful Stepmothers," *Journal of Divorce & Remarriage* 47, no. 1/2 (2007): 107, accessed February 1, 2020, doi:10.1300/J087v47n01_06.

107. DeMello, *Animals*, Location 3515.

108. Markus Wohlfeil, Anthony Patterson, Stephen J. Gould, "The Allure of Celebrities: Unpacking their Polysemic Consumer Appeal," *European Journal of Marketing* 53, no. 10 (2019): 2025, accessed December 13, 2019, doi: 10.1108/EJM-01-2017-0052.

109. Sutherland, *Wings*, 24–25.

110. Sutherland, *Wings*, 180.

111. Sutherland, *Wings*, 281.

112. Ashley Riggs, "Multiple Metamorphoses, or 'The New Skins' for an Old Tale: Emma Donoghue's Queer Cinderella in Translation," in *Cinderella across Cultures: New Reflections and Disciplinary Perspectives*, ed. Martine Hennard Dutheil de la Rochère, Gillian Lathey, and Monika Woźniak (Detroit: Wayne State University Press, 2016), Location 4018.

113. Sutherland, *Wings*, 291.

114. Teverson, *Fairy Tale*, 47–48.

115. de la Rochère, Lathey, and Woźniak, "Introduction," Location 186–200.

116. Riggs, "Multiple," Location 4323.

BIBLIOGRAPHY

Aranda, Daniel. "Moral Adjustments to Perrault's Cinderella in French Children's Literature (1850–1900)." In *Cinderella across Cultures: New Reflections and Disciplinary Perspectives*, edited by Martine Hennard Dutheil de la Rochère, Gillian Lathey, and Monika Woźniak, Location 2828–3182. Detroit: Wayne State University Press, 2016. Kindle.

Arnold, Martin. *The Dragon: Fear and Power*. London: Reaktion Books, 2018. Kindle.

Beckett, Sandra L. "Revisualizing Cinderella for All Ages." In *Cinderella across Cultures: New Reflections and Disciplinary Perspectives*, edited by Martine Hennard Dutheil de la Rochère, Gillian Lathey, and Monika Woźniak, Location 5604–5938. Detroit: Wayne State University Press, 2016. Kindle.

Bennett, Jane. *Vibrant Matter: A Political Ecology of Things*. Durham, NC: Duke University Press, 2010.

Bottigheimer, Ruth B. "Cinderella: The People's Princess." In *Cinderella across Cultures: New Reflections and Disciplinary Perspectives*, edited by Martine Hennard Dutheil de la

Rochère, Gillian Lathey, and Monika Woźniak, Location 705–1241. Detroit: Wayne State University Press, 2016. Kindle.

de la Rochère, Martine Hennard Dutheil, Gillian Lathey, and Monika Woźniak. "Introduction: Cinderella across Cultures." In *Cinderella across Cultures: New Reflections and Disciplinary Perspectives*, edited by Martine Hennard Dutheil de la Rochère, Gillian Lathey, and Monika Woźniak, Location 176–700. Detroit: Wayne State University Press, 2016. Kindle.

DeMello, Margo. *Animals and Society: An Introduction to Human-Animal Studies*. New York: Columbia University Press, 2012. Kindle.

Do Rozario, Rebecca-Anne C. "Comic Book Princesses for Grown-Ups: Cinderella Meets the Pages of the Superhero." *COLLOQUY text theory critique* 24 (2012): 191–206. Accessed September 4, 2019. www.arts.monash.edu.au/ecps/colloquy/journal/issue024/do_rozario.pdf.

Fernández-Lamarque, Maía. *Cinderella in Spain: Variations of the Story as Socio-Ethical Texts*. Jefferson, NC: McFarland & Company, Inc., Publishers, 2019.

Hoffman, Kathryn A. "Perrault's 'Cendrillon' among the Glass Tales: Crystal Fantasies and Glassworks in Seventeenth-Century France and Italy." In *Cinderella across Cultures: New Reflections and Disciplinary Perspectives*, edited by Martine Hennard Dutheil de la Rochère, Gillian Lathey, and Monika Woźniak, Location 1255–1895. Detroit: Wayne State University Press, 2016. Kindle.

Macleod, Mark. "Home by Midnight: The Male Cinderella in LGBTI Fiction for Young Adults." In *Cinderella across Cultures: New Reflections and Disciplinary Perspectives*, edited by Martine Hennard Dutheil de la Rochère, Gillian Lathey, and Monika Woźniak, Location 4382–4760. Detroit: Wayne State University Press, 2016. Kindle.

May-Ron, Rona. "Rejecting the Glass Slipper: The Subversion of Cinderella in Margaret Atwood's *The Edible Woman*." In *Cinderella across Cultures: New Reflections and Disciplinary Perspectives*, edited by Martine Hennard Dutheil de la Rochère, Gillian Lathey, and Monika Woźniak, Location 3199–3593. Detroit: Wayne State University Press, 2016. Kindle.

Riggs, Ashley. "Multiple Metamorphoses, or 'The New Skins' for an Old Tale: Emma Donoghue's Queer Cinderella in Translation." In *Cinderella across Cultures: New Reflections and Disciplinary Perspectives*, edited by Martine Hennard Dutheil de la Rochère, Gillian Lathey, and Monika Woźniak, Location 4018–4369. Detroit: Wayne State University Press, 2016. Kindle.

Siegel, Lauren A. and Dan Wang. "Keeping Up with the Joneses: Emergence of Travel as a Form of Social Comparison among Millennials." *Journal of Travel & Tourism Marketing* 36, no. 2 (2019): 159–175. https://doi.org/10.1080/10548408.2018.1499579.

Sutherland, Tui T. *Wings of Fire: The Lost Heir*. New York: Scholastic Press, 2012.

Teverson, Andrew. *Fairy Tale (The New Critical Idiom)*. London: Routledge, 2013. Kindle.

Ulanov, Ann and Barry Ulanov. *Cinderella and Her Sisters—The Envied and the Envying*. Einsiedeln (Switzerland): Daimon Verlag, 2012. Kindle.

Van Collie, Jan. "The Illustrator as Fairy Godmother: The Illustrated Cinderella in the Low Countries." In *Cinderella across Cultures: New Reflections and Disciplinary Perspectives*, edited by Martine Hennard Dutheil de la Rochère, Gillian Lathey, and Monika Woźniak, Location 5952–6348. Detroit: Wayne State University Press, 2016. Kindle.

Warner, Marina. *Once Upon a Time: A Short History of Fairy Tale*. Oxford: Oxford University Press, 2014. Kindle.

Whiting, Jason B., Donna R. Smith, Tammy Barnett, and Erika L. Grafsky. "Overcoming the Cinderella Myth: A Mixed Methods Study of Successful Stepmothers." *Journal of Divorce & Remarriage* 47, no. 1/2 (2007): 95–107. Accessed February 1, 2020. doi:10.1300/J087v47n01_06.

Wohlfeil, Markus, Anthony Patterson, and Stephen J. Gould. "The Allure of Celebrities: Unpacking their Polysemic Consumer Appeal." *European Journal of Marketing* 53, no. 10 (2019): 2025–2053. Accessed December 13, 2019. doi: 10.1108/EJM-01-2017-0052.

Zipes, Jack. "The Triumph of the Underdog: Cinderella's Legacy." In *Cinderella across Cultures: New Reflections and Disciplinary Perspectives*, edited by Martine Hennard Dutheil de la Rochère, Gillian Lathey, and Monika Woźniak, Location 7504–8349. Detroit: Wayne State University Press, 2016. Kindle.

Chapter Eleven

Cyborg-erella

Marissa Meyer's Cinder as a New Type of Other

Alexandra Lykissas

As Archer Taylor says, "no other tale has so many early, independent, and widely scattered versions,"[1] so it is no wonder that there are so many twentieth and twenty-first century versions of "Cinderella" in all different genres. There is something about this story of the hardworking maid who simply wants to go to a ball, that speaks to our cultural need to repeatedly revisit this story that dates back to Ancient Egypt.

In this chapter,[2] I will examine one of the most unique adaptations of the "Cinderella" story, which is found in *The Lunar Chronicles* by Marissa Meyer. Through my analysis of parts of the initial four-book series and the representation of the main character Cinder as a cyborg, I will argue that this version of "Cinderella" shows a new form of Othering, and acts as a warning against all types of Othering, particularly in a post-humanist world. Through using both intersectional feminist theories of Othering and post-humanist theories, I will conclude that Cinder's representation provides critical commentary about how society treats those who do not fit the norms of society through the vein of fairy tales. First, a brief background of the variants of "Cinderella" is necessary in order to understand how Meyer used those foundational texts to reimagine a new, yet not so new, version of the story that speaks to issues in our contemporary moment. Then, I will establish my theoretical frameworks of intersectionality and the post-human which I will use to analyze *The Lunar Chronicles*.

"Cinderella" is one of the most adapted fairy tales because it speaks to our innate desire to be accepted for who we are and to be able to overcome difficult beginnings. Its origins, however, stem from a variety of cultures and times, with the oldest variant, often cited as the story of Rhodopis, from

Egypt recorded by Strabo in the first century BCE. Another text that is often cited as one of the original literary variants is the Chinese tale of "Yeh-hsien" from the ninth century CE.[3] However, contemporary readers are more familiar with the versions written by Marie De France from the twelfth century and Charles Perrault from the late seventeenth century. Perrault's *Mother Goose Tales* version first introduced the fairy godmother, pumpkin carriage, and glass slippers.

The Perrault version, from seventeenth-century France, is the one most closely associated with the Disney animated film adaptation from 1950 that has since permeated global popular culture. The other "Cinderella" variants, particularly "Aschenputtel" from the Brothers Grimm, are often much darker than the Perrault version, including "Donkeyskin" where the father wishes to marry and bed his own daughter. As Maria Tatar summarizes in *The Classic Fairy Tales*, "the plots of the 'Cinderella' stories are driven by the anxious jealousy of biological mothers and stepmothers who subject the heroine to one ordeal of domestic drudgery after another."[4] Despite the disturbing father-daughter desire of the "Donkeyskin" version of this tale type "again and again, mothers are the real villains, extracting promises that end by victimizing both father and daughter. Everywhere we look, the tendency to defame women and to magnify maternal evil emerges. Even when a tale turns on a father's incestuous desires, the mother becomes more than complicit: she has stirred the trouble in the first place by setting the conditions for her husband's remarriage."[5] The pursuit of selfish, individualistic desires as well as the demand for authoritarian rule over the domestic space establishes this concept of maternal evil. This is more clearly seen in the Brothers Grimm version of the story. In this "Cinderella," the stepmother treats Cinderella like a maid in her own house, positioning her as "The Other" within her own household. By forcing her to perform menial tasks like picking out all the lentils thrown into the fireplace and not allowing her to engage in the norms of society, like going to the ball, the stepmother has made Cinderella an outsider despite the fact that she was not born into this position. She is treated poorly by both her stepmother, who wields ultimate power in the domestic confines of the home, and her stepsisters, who treat her as a slave to their every whim. This example of "maternal evil" as evidenced by the authoritarian rule of the stepmother is furthered by the stepmother's desire for upward mobility through wanting her daughters to marry the prince. After the ball, when the prince is seeking the woman who got away, Cinderella's stepmother tries to make the prince choose one of her daughters. She does this by cutting off their toes and heels to force their feet to fit into the slipper. This is an example of the price of beauty and riches: how women have to suffer in order to be considered beautiful and what women will do to be the most beautiful in order to land the heart of a prince. The prince only realizes he's been manipulated by Cinderella's stepmother and stepsisters after he sees the blood gushing from their feet. By subjecting her daughters to bodily harm for the sake of fitting into a shoe, the stepmother illustrates that she will do anything so that she can be the mother of the future Queen. This deception leads to her daughters having their eyes plucked out by doves (or blackbirds depending on the version) at the wedding of Cinderella and her prince—leaving them with a permanent reminder of their treachery. At the end of the story, reader is left with the lesson to all women that the only way they can marry a prince is to be honest about who they are, even if they are an outsider in their society, because if they are deceptive, they will be punished.

"Cinderella" has become a text that represents both maternal evil and being able to overcome the worst in human nature, as evidenced in the character of the stepmother. As Tatar explains, "'Cinderella' has been reinvented by so many different cultures that it is hardly surprising to find that she is sometimes cruel and vindictive, at other times compassionate and kind."[6] However, much of these evil intentions are omitted from more recent versions of the story, lessening some of the more critical commentary seen in earlier variants.

The story of Cinder in *The Lunar Chronicles*, however, provides critical commentary on a society consumed by technology, while also providing an investigation into a new variation of intersectional feminism. This links to other contemporary feminist fairy tales by addressing the importance of intersectional representations within contemporary popular culture in order to reflect the diversity of American society. The concepts of intersectionality have been around in the discussions related to feminism for more than two hundred years, but the term was originally defined by Kimberlé W. Crenshaw in 1989 when she argued how the experiences of Black women were not a separate idea of "Black" and of "women," but were interconnected and interrelated.[7] Patricia Hill Collins expanded on these ideas to include other areas of women's experiences including religion, socioeconomic class, and sexuality, saying that all of these elements affect women's lives in different ways.[8] It is necessary to provide these intersectional representations in fairy-tale adaptations because as Jack Zipes says, "from *Cinderella* (1950) and *Sleeping Beauty* (1959) up through *The Princess and the Frog* (2009) and *Tangled* (2010), the Disney fairy-tale films have followed conventional principles of technical and aesthetic organization to celebrate stereotypical gender and power relations and to foster a world view of harmony consecrated by the wedding of elite celebrity figures."[9] Many popular fairy tales project a white, Eurocentric version of the stories, which do not reflect a twenty-first-century global society, while also perpetuating an unconscious bias toward these hegemonic heteronormative representations, which have been greatly influenced by Disney's animated film versions; however, *The Lunar Chronicles* offers an example of intersectional representations of femininity, particularly related to identity and class.

In *The Lunar Chronicles*, the main character Cinder is a cyborg—a new type of "Other" in science fiction. The concept of the Other is often set in opposition to culturally accepted norms, as postcolonial critic Gayatri Spivak explains in "Can the Subaltern Speak?" In this foundational postcolonial text, she explains how "the intellectual is complicit in the persistent constitution of Other as the Self's shadow."[10] Those that are labeled as "the Other" do not fit socially accepted norms and instead reflect the opposite of what we define as socially accepted. However, it is the dialectical relationship between the Other and Self that makes Spivak's definition appropriate for my study, because in identifying "the Other" we are identifying that which we fear within ourselves.

The acceptance of self is critical in this text because it represents not only an acceptance of self, but an acceptance of self as one who is labeled as the Other. In science fiction, this is even more difficult because as a cyborg, Cinder does not belong in her society. Since cyborgs are a new representation of the Other, and by Cinder accepting all of who she is, she is also accepting herself as the Other position in her society. This is significant because as feminist scholar Donna Haraway claims, "the main trouble with cyborgs, of course, is that they are the illegitimate offspring of militarism and patriarchal capitalism, not to mention state socialism. But illegitimate offspring are often exceedingly unfaithful to their origins. Their fathers, after all, are inessential."[11] Haraway continues by arguing that "a cyborg world might be about lived social and bodily realities in which people are not afraid of their joint kinship with animals and machines, not afraid of permanently partial identities and contradictory standpoints."[12] Her argument, while seemingly unaccepting of the realities of cyborgs, actually positions the cyborg as the Other who is neither wholly human nor wholly machine, but something else entirely that exists in an in-between space.

While the cyborg has often been positioned as this in-between, as neither human nor machine, many post-human feminist scholars argue that the cyborg is, in fact, a feminist figure because of this dual positionality. Genevieve Lloyd discusses how "woman" is often equated with irrationality, and as such, she is not logical, therefore, she cannot be fully human.[13] Furthermore, technology has often been equated with masculinity and has been designated as a male realm, even in anonymous places like online video games (see Gamergate controversy for more about this), but this technological gendered difference is a social construct, as Judy Wajcman examines in *Feminism Confronts Technology*.[14] Additionally, while the assumption is often that women are "bad at technology," as Kim Toffoletti argues, "they are often symbolically aligned with technology,"[15] particularly in science fiction popular culture as an avenue through which to investigate male anxiety about technology, production, and the feminine space. As Toffoletti argues "[The post-human condition] is the bodily transformation and augmentations that come about through our engagements with technology that complicate the idea of a 'human essence.' The posthuman emerges by interrogating what it means to be human in a digital age."[16] In science fiction films, we often see women made into robots, thus removing their humanity, and in this representations, as Toffoletti suggests, "it is through the gendered assumptions inherent in a definition of humanity and subjectivity that woman is Othered, paradoxically as both nature and technology, thus exploitable and subject to masculine mastery."[17] From this understanding of women existing as neither belonging in society or in a technological society, I argue that making Cinder a female cyborg is that much more important for a current popular culture audience because her subjectivity investigates a new kind of Othering (that of the cyborg), she also represents how one can manage the dualities of their nature.

Judith Butler argues in *Gender Trouble* (1990) about the formation of identity as being gendered. Butler examines how the formation of identity and gender are socially constructed to fit particular social norms:

> In other words, the "coherence" and "continuity" of "the person" are not logical or analytic features of personhood, but, rather, socially instituted and maintained norms of intelligibility. Inasmuch as "identity" is assured through the stabilizing concepts of sex, gender, and sexuality, the very notion of "the person" is called into question by the cultural emergence of those "incoherent" or "discontinuous" gendered beings who appear to be persons but who fail to conform to the gendered norms of cultural intelligibility by which persons are defined.[18]

This concept of identity is furthered in the contemporary science fiction novel where the concept of the post-human (or those that mix human features with machines, aliens, etc.) because it forces the reader to question how we treat everyone, even those who might be what we consider to be less-than-human. In *The Lunar Chronicles*, Cinder, as a cyborg, is an outsider who does not fit in with the fully-machine androids, nor does she fit in with humans. This outsider position is significant because it provides the reader with an example of someone who is able to accept their outsider status to use it to their benefit, instead of allowing it to be a hindrance.

To provide a little bit more context about the story, in this series, the main character Cinder is a mechanic-cyborg, and like the foundational "Cinderella" story, she is also a servant to her stepmother and stepsisters. As Cinder tells the reader early on in the narrative, "Legally, Cinder belonged to Adri [her aunt] as much as the household android and so too did her money, her few possessions, even the new foot she'd just attached. Adri loved to remind her of that."[19] She has no agency since, as a cyborg, she is the property of her adoptive mother. Additionally, her positionality as a cyborg in a science fiction narrative, allows her to represent a different type of intersectional feminism where she is seen as The Other not because of her race or social status (though this is part of her intersectionality), but more so because of nebulous status as human. Her intersectionality is further complicated by the discovery at the end of the first novel that not only is she a cyborg and only 64 percent human as the reader is told throughout the novel, but Cinder also discovers that she is Lunar, a different race of human that colonized the moon, and she is also the long-lost Lunar princess Selene, the rightful heir to the throne of Luna (the moon colony): "Throughout the four novels in the series, the reader meets Cinder's new fairy tale friends, as they conspire to overthrow Levana, the current Queen of Luna, who nearly killed Cinder during a fire when she was a small child. The other characters include Wolf/ the wolf from Little Red Riding Hood, Scarlet/Little Red Riding Hood, Winter/Snow White, Cress/Rapunzel, and Thorne/Prince from Rapunzel."[20] Levana and most Lunar people are gifted with the power to manipulate other people's bioelectricity, which allows them to force their victims to do whatever they want and see only what they want them to see. For example, Levana changes her appearance using her Lunar power, in order to cover up her scarred face so she appears to be the most beautiful woman in the galaxy. This ability to create a false narrative of oneself positions this story squarely within the post-human theoretical space because this becomes another way to investigate the concept of reality.

For Cinder, she exists in a universe where she has always been positioned as lower than everyone around her. In this universe, cyborgs and androids are greatly discriminated against because of their status as not fully human. This positionality outside of humanity allows others to take advantage of them through only allowing them to be servants or to have service jobs. We first learn about this discrimination because of the draft for cyborgs to be "volunteered" to be tested for an antidote to the Letumosis plague:

> Subjects had been carted in . . . to act as guinea pigs for the antidote testing. It was made out to be some sort of honor, giving your life for the good of humanity but it was really just a reminder that cyborgs were not like everyone else . . . They were lucky to have lived this long, many thought. It's only right they should be the first to give up their lives in search for a cure.[21]

Because they are part machine, cyborgs are labeled as being inhuman because it is assumed that they have no humanity. Cinder's stepmother, Adri, asks Cinder, "do your kind even know what love is? Can you feel anything at all, or is it just . . . programmed?"[22] These questions further reflect the complicated dual nature of the cyborg as being viewed as not fully human, therefore they must not have the full range of human emotions. This then begs the question about whether the only distinction between being considered human and being inhuman is showing one's emotions.

The reader learns this discrimination has been reinforced by laws that make cyborgs and androids the property of their masters with no rights. As we learn in the third novel of the series, *Cress*:

> [Cyborgs] weren't citizens. Or, they were, but it was more complicated than that, had been since the Cyborg Protection Act had been instated by [Prince Kai's] grandfather decades ago. The act came after a series of devastating cyborg crimes had caused widespread hatred and led to catastrophic riots in every major city in the Commonwealth. The protests may have been prompted by the violent spree, but they were a result of generations of growing disdain. For years people had been complaining about the rising population of cyborgs, many of whom received their surgeries at the hands of taxpayers.
>
> Cyborgs were too smart, people had complained. They were cheating the average man out of his wages.
>
> Cyborgs were too skilled. They were taking jobs away from hardworking, average citizens.
>
> Cyborgs were too strong. They shouldn't be allowed to compete in sporting events with regular people. It gave them an unfair advantage.
>
> And then one small group of cyborgs had gone on a spree of violence and theft and destruction, demonstrating just how dangerous they could be.
>
> If doctors and scientists were going to continue to perform these operations, people argued, there needed to be restrictions placed on their kind. They needed to be controlled.[23]

This discrimination, enforced by law, reflects how cyborgs are equated to other types of Othered groups throughout history and the justification for dehumanizing them reflects nationalistic tendencies that occur during times of heightened anxiety. In contemporary American society, for example, we have seen the same arguments used when discussing immigrants from Latin America throughout the last thirty years, particularly the arguments about taking jobs away from citizens. This has continued during today's current debate about refugee children and those seeking asylum. The argument against the strength of cyborgs and how they shouldn't be allowed to compete in sports is akin to the argument against Black athletes in the last half of the twentieth century, and more recently against female athletes who have higher testosterone levels (cf. Caster Semenza case in track and field) and transgender athletes. We also saw similar arguments during the Brexit debates in the United Kingdom regarding non-British groups living in the UK.

In addition to new types of intersectional feminine representations, the cyborg as a subjective being represents the duality of "lived" or "human" experience—in this story in particular, we see the duality of Cinder's life on multiple levels. She is both machine and human, Lunar and Earthen, mechanic and Queen, and interestingly Cinderella and Snow White. This story combines so many elements that it helps us to understand a multitude of experiences, thus a new type of intersectionality. One of the major components of the post-human is that duality and the concerns about balancing one's humanity in a technological world.

Throughout all four novels, Cinder gradually accepts both her Lunar abilities and her cyborg nature. By claiming agency over her life, she is able to reclaim her throne as Princess Selene by announcing her claim to the throne and revealing who Levana truly is under her veil. This acceptance allows her to work with the others in order to create a united front against Levana, which is the only way they'll be able to reinstate Cinder on the Lunar throne. The characters first collaborate when they first secretly make their way onto the Lunar colony, despite being fugitives. They must work together to get past the Lunar guards when they are hiding in the hold of Thorne's ship. Thorne creates a diversion so everyone else can escape the thaumaturge (Levana's high-ranking government official) who was searching the ship.[24] Then, Cinder uses her Lunar abilities to take over control of Wolf, which is her first active act of accepting her supernatural ability to control others as the Lunar princess. She then tells him to attack the guards who were covering the landing bay, while Iko also attacks the other guards. These diversions allow everyone else to get off the ship without being seen. Then, Cinder tells Cress as everyone distracts the Lunar guards in order to get Cress into the electronics area in order to pen the palace doors, "we'll cover you,"[25] emphasis on the *we*. They all collaborate to protect each other: "Thorne creates a diversion, Wolf and Iko act as warriors to protect everyone else, Cress uses her electronic know-how to open the doors, while Cinder tries to lead them and keep them together, in order to eventually reveal the true Levana to the Lunar people."[26] This emphasizes how once they are all able to accept their true natures, particularly Cinder, then they can work together to defeat Levana.

The group collaboration between Cinder and her friends, and the Lunar people showcases how disparate groups can work together if they have a common goal. This message is needed in our world that continues to be segregated by class, race, religion, and gender. Cinder's initial video message that is projected to the entire Lunar colony proves that the group can disrupt Levana's propaganda and surveillance, which allows the Lunar people to see that they are more similar than Levana has told them. This event also affects Levana's access of control. After this, Cinder's group and those who had been ostracized in Levana's society are able to come together, under threat of death in order to start their revolution.

After a few people are killed as a way to get information about where Cinder is hiding, Cinder decides to reveal herself and tells Wolf, "It's the people's revolution now, not mine."[27] Much like previous revolutions throughout history, it becomes about the people, not an individual ruler— Cinder is just the impetus for the revolt that was waiting to happen on Luna. Prior to coming out of hiding, however, Cinder questions whether she did the right thing starting the rebellion and bringing all of the Lunar people into her revolt, but Scarlet reminds her, "No one is dying for *you*. If anyone dies today it will be because they finally have something to believe in. Don't you even think about taking that away from them now."[28] What she began had quickly become a revolution for the Lunar people to retake Luna for themselves.

When the siege on the capital city, Artemisia, begins, Cinder reminds both groups: "Remember, our safety lies in numbers. [Levana] keeps the sectors divided for a reason. She knows that she's powerless if we all stand together, and that's exactly what we're going to do."[29] She emphasizes that success lies in their ability to overwhelm Levana and her guards because their numbers will be greater than Levana's guards; it is in numbers that they have power over Levana even if she can mentally manipulate others. This reaches a climax when the group moves collectively toward the central city of Artemisia, with people from the outer sectors of Luna, joining them as they move closer to the city. Despite everyone working together, the people are disenfranchised until Cinder airs the second video of Levana's true face that is scarred and tortured as a result of the fire she set many years before trying to kill Cinder. Cinder is the only one who can see through Levana's illusion because of her positionality as the Other, the cyborg. This revelation reinvigorates all of those trying to overthrow Levana's tyrannical rule.

Cinder's cyborg mechanisms, which were installed to save her life after that fire when she was child, tell her when people are lying, which is why she was able to see through Levana's façade. Additionally, a microchip was implanted on her spine which allows her to resist the Lunar glamour. Both of which reinforce the importance of her duality as both cyborg and human. In *Cinder*, when she sees Levana for the first time, her visual sensor tells her that it's all *"Lies . . . When she looked up again, the illusion of goodness had faded . . . She was brainwashing them."*[30] In this moment, Cinder learns the truth about the Lunar glamour, the supernatural ability to change people's thoughts. The reader learns, "this was the effect of the Lunar glamour, the spell to enchant, to deceive, to turn one's heart toward you and against your enemies. And amid all these people who despised the Lunar queen, Cinder seemed to be the only one who had resisted her."[31] In this moment of realization, it becomes clear that while Cinder's society may position her as the Other, both because of her cyborg nature and her genetics as Lunar (which we learned about right before this moment), it is that cyborg nature that allows her to eventually overthrow Levana and reclaim her throne. In the final novel, after they all sneak onto Luna, Cinder is captured by Levana and put on trial. It is at this trial that Cinder is able to record a video of Levana's true self up close:

there was Levana, but not Levana. She was recognizable only by the red wedding gown.

Beneath the glamour, her face was disfigured from ridges and scars, sealing shut her left eye. The destroyed skin continued down her jaw and neck, disappearing beneath the collar of her dress. Her hair was thinner and a lighter shade of brown, and great chunks were missing where the scars had reached around to the back of her head. More scars could be seen on her left arm where her silk sleeve didn't hide them.

Burns.

They were scars created from burns.

. . . A wretched scream sent a shock of cold water over Cinder's body . . .

It was working. The queen was losing control. She was being forced to see the truth beneath her own glamour, and she could do nothing to stop it. [32]

When Cinder plays this video later, this seemingly breaks Levana because the truth had been revealed. Her entire existence was an illusion. As the cliché phrase says, "the truth will set you free" and for the Lunars, the revelation of Levana's true self releases them from her illusion. This allows the Lunar people to take over Levana's castle and for Cinder to eventually overthrow Levana. The revelation of Levana's true self is juxtaposed with Cinder's own revelation of her truth in *Cinder*; however, instead of it breaking her, Cinder's truth sets her free.

Even though this young adult text ends with a nice happily-ever-after, reinforcing many of the fairy-tale and young adult genre expectations, the Lunar people are still ruled by a monarch. Their rebellion was not one to instate a democracy, even though Cinder says she plans to eventually dissolve the monarchy to create a democracy. They have replaced one authoritarian ruler with someone who seems to be a more benevolent ruler, but Cinder is still the singular person who rules over all of Luna. Whether Cinder will end up as an authoritarian is yet to be seen, but *Winter* does leave the reader feeling like everything will work out—an antidote for the Leutomosis plague is being dispersed throughout Earth, Levana is no longer in charge, and all the fairy-tale characters have ended up together. The world feels right again and all because Cinder was able to resolve her duality of self—using both her cyborg and Lunar abilities to overthrow Levana while still maintaining her humanity by working together with others.

In the story's resolution:

we learn that the collaboration between the characters will not stop just because Cinder has reclaimed her throne, illuminating for the reader that collaboration to affect social, political, and/or cultural change does not end with the overthrowing of an authoritarian. The story ends when all the characters help Cinder/Selene gain her agency in order to become queen and rebuild Luna, in addition to helping to distribute the Leutomosis vaccine to Earth and to help rebuild the Earthen cities the Lunar warriors destroyed. It is uncertain whether

Cinder becomes queen as a way to show what Ann Sexton examines in her poem "Snow White," that female fairy tale characters who end up in power will become like the evil queen: jealous of those who are younger and more beautiful, authoritarian as a ruler, and desirous of being the most beautiful; or if she will become a new type of woman in power, a benevolent sovereign who does not reflect anxieties about female rulers, but subverts those fears in order to break the binary of monstrous female authority versus innocent youth.[33]

In *The Lunar Chronicles*, the examination of how society positions people as the Other becomes of primary importance to the story's resolution, but it is through the acceptance of her positionality as the Other that Cinder is able to reclaim her throne while proving to everyone that cyborgs are more human/ humane than many humans.

NOTES

1. Archer Taylor, "The Study of the Cinderella Cycle," in Alan Dundes, ed., *Cinderella: A Folklore Casebook* (New York: Garland Publishing, 1982), 117.

2. Sections of this chapter have been previously published as part of the article "Popular Culture's Enduring Influence on Childhood: Fairy Tale Collaboration in the Young Adult Series *The Lunar Chronicles*," in *Global Studies of Childhood*, Sept. 2018, and in the doctoral dissertation *When Fairy Tales Collide: Collaborative Fairy Tales as Postmodern Feminist Discourse in 21st Century Novels, Graphic Novels, and Visual Culture*, from Indiana University of Pennsylvania.

3. Maria Tatar, "'Cinderella' Introduction," in *The Classic Fairy Tales: A Norton Critical Edition*, 1st ed. (New York: Norton Publishing, 1999), 101.

4. Ibid., 102.

5. Ibid., 105.

6. Ibid., 102.

7. Kimberlé Crenshaw, "Demarginalizing the Intersection of Race and Sex: A Black Feminist Critique of Antidiscrimination Doctrine, Feminist Theory and Antiracist Politics," *University of Chicago Legal Forum* 1989, no. 1, article 8 (1989). Accessed April 7, 2018, http://chicagounbound.uchicago.edu/uclf/vol1989/iss1/8.

8. Patricia Hill Collins, *Black Feminist Thought: Knowledge, Consciousness, and the Politics of Empowerment* (New York: Hyman, 1990).

9. Jack Zipes, *Grimm Legacies: The Magic Spell of the Grimms' Folk and Fairy Tales* (Princeton: Princeton University Press, 2015), 102.

10. Gayatri Spivak, "Can the Subaltern Speak?" In *Colonial Discourse and Post-Colonial Theory: A Reader*, ed. Patrick Williams and Laura Chrisman (New York: Columbia University Press, 1993), 75.

11. Donna Haraway, "A Cyborg Manifesto: Science, Technology and Socialist-Feminism in the Late Twentieth Century," in *The Cybercultures Reader*, ed. David Bell and Barbara M. Kennedy (New York: Routledge, 2000), 293.

12. Ibid., 295.

13. Genevieve Lloyd, *The Man of Reason: "Male" and "Female" in Western Philosophy*, 2nd ed. (London: Routledge, 1984), ix.

14. Judy Wajcman, *Feminism Confronts Technology* (Cambridge, UK: Polity Press, 1991), 137.

15. Kim Tuffoletti, *Cyborg and Barbie Dolls: Feminism, Popular Culture and the Posthuman Body* (London: IB Tauris, 2007), 23.

16. Ibid., 13.

17. Ibid., 23.

18. Judith Butler, *Gender Trouble: Feminism and the Subversion of Identity* (New York: Routledge Classics, 1990), 17.

19. Marissa Meyer, *Cinder* (New York: Feiwel and Friends, 2012), 24.

20. Alexandra Lykissas, "Popular Culture's Enduring Influence on Childhood: Fairy Tale Collaboration in the Young Adult Series *The Lunar Chronicles*," *Global Studies of Childhood*, Sept. 2018, 308.

21. Ibid., 28–29.

22. Ibid., 63.

23. Marissa Meyer, *Cress* (New York: Feiwel and Friends, 2014), 306.

24. Marissa Meyer, *Winter* (New York: Feiwel and Friends, 2015), 170.

25. Ibid., 176.

26. Lykissas, "Popular Culture."

27. Ibid., 355.

28. Ibid., 351.

29. Ibid., 651.

30. Meyer, *Cinder*, 205.

31. Ibid., 206.

32. Meyer, *Winter*, 692–693.

33. Lykissas, "Popular Culture," 313–314.

BIBLIOGRAPHY

Butler, Judith. *Gender Trouble: Feminism and the Subversion of Identity*. New York: Routledge Classics, 1990.

Collins, Patricia Hill. *Black Feminist Thought: Knowledge, Consciousness, and the Politics of Empowerment*. New York: Hyman, 1990.

Crenshaw, Kimberlé. "Demarginalizing the Intersection of Race and Sex: A Black Feminist Critique of Antidiscrimination Doctrine, Feminist Theory and Antiracist Politics." *University of Chicago Legal Forum*, 1989, no. 1, article 8 (1989). Accessed April 7, 2018, http://chicagounbound.uchicago.edu/uclf/vol1989/iss1/8.

Haraway, Donna. "A Cyborg Manifesto: Science, Technology and Socialist-Feminism in the Late Twentieth Century." in *The Cybercultures Reader*, edited by David Bell and Barbara M. Kennedy, 291–324. New York: Routledge, 2000.

Lloyd, Genevieve. *The Man of Reason: "Male" and "Female" in Western Philosophy*, 2nd ed. London: Routledge, 1984.

Lykissas, Alexandra. "Popular Culture's Enduring Influence on Childhood: Fairy Tale Collaboration in the Young Adult Series *The Lunar Chronicles*," *Global Studies of Childhood*, Sept. 2018, 304-315. doi: 10.1177/2043610618798932.

Meyer, Marissa. *Cinder*. New York: Feiwel and Friends, 2012.

———. *Cress*. New York: Feiwel and Friends, 2014.

———. *Winter*. New York: Feiwel and Friends, 2015.

Spivak, Gayatri, "Can the Subaltern Speak?" In *Colonial Discourse and Post-Colonial Theory: A Reader,* edited by Patrick Williams and Laura Chrisman, New York: Columbia University Press, 1993, pp. 66–111.

Tatar, Maria. "'Cinderella' Introduction." *The Classic Fairy Tales: A Norton Critical Edition*, 1st ed. 1999.

Taylor, Archer. "The Study of the Cinderella Cycle," in Alan Dundes, ed., *Cinderella: A Folklore Casebook*, New York: Garland Publishing, 1982, p. 117.

Tuffoletti, Kim. *Cyborg and Barbie Dolls: Feminism, Popular Culture and the Posthuman Body*. London: IB Tauris, 2007.

Wajcman, Judy. *Feminism Confronts Technology*. Cambridge, UK: Polity Press, 1991.

Zipes, Jack. *Grimm Legacies: The Magic Spell of the Grimms' Folk and Fairy Tales*. Princeton: Princeton University Press, 2015.

Chapter Twelve

Once Upon a Time in Nazi-Occupied France

Inglourious Basterds, *Cinderellas, and Post-truth Politics*

Ryan Habermeyer

A decade since its release, Quentin Tarantino's *Inglourious Basterds* (2009) remains a strange postmodern mash-up of genres: war film, spaghetti western, dark comedy, and as indicative of my title, a fairy tale.[1] Surprisingly, little scholarly attention has been directed at Tarantino's intertextual use of the fairy tale beyond superficial acknowledgment of the framing device in the opening sequence—"Once upon a time in Nazi-occupied France . . ."[2]— as a means to explain the film's blatant historical liberties. Film reviewers at the time of its release pounced on the allusion, using it to critique the film in turns as a misleading fantasy;[3] "flagrantly fantastical";[4] and "a nutbrain fable . . . lodged in an uneasy nowheresville between counterfactual pop wish fulfillment and trashy exploitation."[5] It is an understatement to say the film has aged better than the litany of knee-jerk reviews.

The derisive use of "fable" at first glance suggests the film is simplistically coded as a fairy tale as a kind of tongue-in-cheek artificial guise to construct an escapist allohistory. This is Michael Richardson's approach when he writes that fairy-tale framing is "an attempt to mark the film as mere fantasy, set in a time and place distant from the present, thus immunizing it from criticisms about its lack of authenticity or realism."[6] Beyond its oversimplified conclusions, the problem with this interpretation is its colloquial usage of fairy tale as synonymous with falsity, distortion, misrepresentation, or even outright lie, as if Tarantino's fairy-tale framing naïvely announces, *Don't mind the troubling politics of this film—it's* just *a fairy tale*. It is difficult to imagine that an auteur like Tarantino, who pored over the script for *Basterds* for more than a decade and calls it his masterpiece (at least before he announced *Once Upon a Time in Hollywood* his masterpiece), feels the need to conceal his politics behind a fairy-tale screen rather than use the fairy tale to enhance the political underpinnings of the film.[7] Certainly, *Inglourious Basterds* is not fabulist cinema in the vein of Guillermo del Toro's *Pan's Labyrinth*, or Jan Svankmajer's *Little Otik*, but a closer examination suggests the aesthetic is deliberate and purposeful, not merely a careless sleight of hand to abuse history and whisk the spectator away into an ironic cinematic fantasy.

This article examines the folkloric spaces of Tarantino's *Inglourious Basterds*, mapping the intersections where fairy tale meets historiographic meta-cinema. I argue that fairy tales—in particular, scattered, Cinderella themes and motifs—constitute an integral element of *Basterds*, not merely a casual aesthetic trope haphazardly evoked but appropriative gestures entangled in the multivalent politics of the film, which are all the more resonant in what is being called the post-truth era.

Tarantino's use—and abuse—of folklore is not without precedent, especially in the context of Nazi propaganda. As Helge Gerndt has argued, "*Volkskunde* during the National Socialist period was a booming business."[8] Nazi nationalism, according to Louis Snyder, looked back on and stressed a number of traits in the folktale collections of Jacob and Wilhelm Grimm as exemplary of the German spirit, including patriarchal authoritarianism, mystical militarism, and violence toward the outsider.[9] Elizabeth Dalton goes so far as to say, "Nazi ideologues enshrined the Grimm's *Kinder- und Hausmärchen* as virtually a sacred text, a special expression of the spirit of the *Volk*."[10] Additionally, academic research in German folklore undertaken during the Nazi era underscored motifs of racial purity, Nordic cultural supremacy, and the glorification of the peasantry.[11] Despite party official Alfred Eyd announcing in 1935 that "the German folktale shall become a most valuable means for us in the racial and political education of the young," Nazi ideological misconstruction of folklore seldom rewrote the tales to emphasize Aryan features, rather, as fairy-tale scholar Jack Zipes observes, "educators, party functionaries, and literary critics [made enormous efforts to] revamp the interpretation of the tales in accordance with Nazi ideology."[12]

One of the more prolific mediums for disseminating folkloric propaganda during the 1930s was the cinema. The ideological dimensions of Nazi cinema, what Mary Elizabeth O'Brien has called the enchantment of reality, have been widely documented,[13] but until recently very little scholarship specifically investigated Nazi fairy-tale cinema. Ron Schlesinger's monograph, *Rotkäppchen im Dritten Reich: die deutsche Märchenfilmproduktion zwischen 1933 und 1945* (2010), is one of only two detailed studies I am aware of that brings to light the phenomenon of Nazi fairy-tale cinema.[14] As Schlesinger documents, between 1933 and 1945 the Reich Film Chamber (*Reichsfilmkammer*) produced no less than nineteen films based on fairy tales, including versions of *Puss in Boots* (*Gestiefelten Kater*: 1935), *Sleeping Beauty* (*Dornröschen*: 1936), *Snow White and the Seven Dwarfs* (*Schneewittchen und die sieben Zwerge*: 1939), and *Hansel and Gretel* (*Hansel und Gretel*: 1940). These fairy-tale films of the Third Reich—entertaining, ideologically subtle, and projecting moral wholesomeness while couched in faux innocence—were screened in large metropolitan areas and occupied territories alike, and reflected ideological nuances: a justification for invading Poland can be seen in *Snow White*, while *Little Red Riding Hood* (dressed in her swastika-imprinted cloak) is saved from the belly of the wolf by an SS soldier. Tickets were affordable for the average German household and films played in theaters for lengthy periods of time to ensure the widest possible spectatorship.[15]

To suggest that the fairy tale is merely a frivolous framing device in *Inglourious Basterds* is a disingenuous assertion that not only ignores the aforementioned historical context but neglects the folkloric spaces represented in the film. Christoph Waltz in the role of Nazi lieutenant Hans Landa, a charismatic sociopath, embraces his larger-than-life identity as the "Jew Hunter" in his interrogation efforts to locate Jewish "enemies of the State." Later, Landa performs as a diabolical Prince Charming by sleuthing Bridget von Hammersmark's Cinderella slipper as a sign of her treason. The SS soldier Frederick Zoeller performs as the heroic folk soldier elevated to wartime celebrity thanks to the Goebbels propaganda production, *Nation's Pride*, a pseudo-documentary film-within-a-film ironically directed at Tarantino's request by Jewish-American Eli Roth, who also happens to play the part of Donny Donowitz in the ensemble cast of the vigilante Basterds. Donowitz, who goes by the persona "The Bear Jew" and murders Nazis by bludgeoning them with a Louisville Slugger, has such an otherworldly presence that, in the film, Hitler wonders if he is a Golem, an anthropomorphic monster from Jewish folklore. Not to be outdone, the captain of the Basterds, Aldo Raine, is known as Aldo the Apache who claims, as an ancestor, the legendary mountaineer Jim Bridger who has been the subject of much American folklore. Indeed, much of the mystique of the Basterds relies not on their military prowess—they are often clumsy if not buffoonish—but the folkloric identities they assume to terrorize the Nazi psyche. When Raine recruits the Basterds he makes it a point to say, "The German will be sickened by us . . . will talk about us,"[16] as if acknowledging the virtues of weaponizing folklore on the battlefield.

Thus Michael Richardson's critique that the Basterds "remain relatively faceless: we learn nothing of the backstories of the soldiers . . . with many lacking names entirely" is an accurate observation but misses the mark.[17]

Folk and fairy-tale characters, evidenced by Max Lüthi's canonical study *The European Folktale: Form and Nature*, are purposefully flat, one-dimensional, nameless figures who serve as vehicles for the plot and exist as ideological expressions.[18] By intentionally eschewing psychological realism Tarantino ironically reimagines history as a series of performed folklores. The Basterds triumph largely because they create a living, oral folklore of themselves on the battlefield and beyond, whereas the Nazis (with the exception of Landa) are doomed as stereotypical caricatures. If we adopt Jack Zipes's approach that fairy tales are largely narratives projecting utopian futures, then the image of the Basterds carving swastikas on the foreheads of Nazis is a symbolic imprinting of a failed folklore. William Brown rightly observes that "*Inglourious Basterds* makes explicit reference to how the German Reich understood the powerful affective nature of cinema," to which I would add his use of folklore and fairy-tale motifs are deliberate choices responding to how the Nazis appropriated folkloristics.[19]

This conscious attention to folklore does not seem strange in the context of Tarantino's oeuvre. Tim Roth rehearsing his "Commode Story" joke as Mr. Orange in *Reservoir Dogs* is a kind of urban drug lore; and in *Pulp Fiction* characters wax eloquent on foot massages and Christopher Walken delivers an infamous monologue on the precarious placement of watches in Vietnamese prison camps. Certainly this does not mean that every time a joke or anecdote appears in a film it is an homage to folk narrative; but, with Tarantino these long, digressive pieces of dialogue, these stories-within-stories, these oratories, are allotted a privileged position in the diegetic space of the film and constitute part of his aesthetic signature.

The two fairy tales Tarantino directly alludes to and reappropriates throughout *Inglourious Basterds* are "Little Red Riding Hood" and "Cinderella." The heroine of the film, Shosanna Dreyfus, is subtly coded as a reimagined Red Riding Hood. Having escaped the Jew Hunter Landa, we next see Shosanna—whose name in Hebrew means *rose*—running a movie theater in occupied Paris under the alias Emmanuelle Mimieux.[20] During her first encounter with the love-stricken Frederick Zoeller she wears a red petticoat, an otherwise insignificant detail until she appears in a stunning red dress to the premiere of *Nation's Pride* in the final chapter where she enacts her revenge against the Nazis. The two most well-known variants of the Red Riding Hood tale-type come from Charles Perrault and the Brothers Grimm.[21] In the former, Red Riding Hood is abruptly devoured by the wolf and Perrault's morals read as misogynistic cautionary tales that any sexual indiscretion or violation is the fault of young women. The Brothers Grimm variant introduces the motif of the huntsman who rescues Red Riding Hood and the grandmother, emphasizing heroic masculine intervention in the lives of naïve women.

Unlike the passive folktale heroine beset by a supernatural adversary, Tarantino's Red Riding Hood becomes an active agent in her own salvation. In a deleted portion of the script Shosanna justifies her revenge with a very folkloric rationalization: "In a wolf fight, you either eat the wolf or the wolf eats you. If we're going to obliterate the Nazis, we have to use their tactics."[22] The reference to the Nazis as wolves echoes movie starlet spy Bridget von Hammersmark's comment in the La Louisiane tavern, "If any of these wolves gets out of line, I'll kick their ass!"[23] while simultaneously reflecting the historical reality of the ambivalent popularity of "Little Red Riding Hood" during the National Socialist period.[24] Hitler's self-imposed nickname in private circles was "Wolf" (an Old High German form of Adolf), and he used numerous variations of "wolf" as names for military headquarters throughout the portions of Europe he conquered: Wolfsschanze (East Prussia), Wolfsschlucht (France), and Werwolf (Ukraine). As a revisionist Red Riding Hood, Shosanna inverts the classic motifs as well as Nazi propaganda by becoming the hunter and luring the Nazi wolves into her theatrical den to enact a retributive justice.

Cinderella allusions in *Basterds*—the shoe left behind in the La Louisiane tavern, the prince in search of the foot to fit the slipper—are immediately recognizable even for those only vaguely familiar with the tale, but beyond functioning as plot devices it seems like an odd intertextual choice given that Cinderella is traditionally concerned with persecuted heroines seeking to restore lost social status through an advantageous marriage. The film teases that von Hammersmark's Cinderella will assist Red Riding Hood Shosanna to triumph over the wolfish Nazis in a kind of feminist fairy-tale utopian conclusion, but such a fantasy is violently dispatched when the Nazi prince Landa kills von Hammersmark in a gruesome strangulation scene and Shosanna kills and then is killed by Zoeller. So why Cinderella?

Despite its presence of a strong female heroine in Shosanna, *Basterds* is predominantly a masculine, not feminine, fantasy and Landa is Tarantino's masculinist Cinderella. As previously mentioned, fairy tales depict flat, one-dimensional characters lacking psychological complexity. This is true of all the characters in *Basterds* with the exception of Hans Landa. Landa is the only fairy-tale character in the film who attempts to transcend his characterization and in the final chapter seeks to create a new folklore of himself, shedding the Jew Hunter epithet and becoming the anti-Nazi double agent. We might read Landa as a trickster, that strange figure in myth and folklore who transgresses social boundaries, indulges in taboos, and is neither wholly virtuous nor malevolent but an ambivalent creature both foolish and erudite. We can only wonder if Tarantino chose the name Hans for its generic quality connoting a kind of German everyman, or if it is a subtle allusion to the persistent use of the name Hans in German folktales. There is "Clever Hans," in which a fool botches his engagement; and "Hans in Luck," an inverted rags-to-riches tale in which a man rids himself of his fortune. Perhaps the most interesting intertextual parallel is "Hans My Hedgehog," a fantastical and at times nonsensical tale of a human-hedgehog hybrid, who, through a series of adventures undergoes psychological and physical metamorphoses, shedding his animal skin and inheriting a wealthy kingdom.[25] Although classified in the Aarne-Thompson-Uther index as "In Enchanted Skin" tale-type, "Hans My Hedgehog" can be viewed as a masculinist Cinderella, which is precisely what Landa wishes to be. The Brothers Grimm tale "Allerleirauh" (translated as either "Thousandfurs" or "All Fur") is a Cinderella variant, like Perrault's "Donkey-Skin," in which a persecuted heroine must disguise herself in animal skins to escape an incestuous father. Both "Hans-My-Hedgehog" and "Cinderella" are tales of trickery and deceit; both tales utilize similar motifs of how clothing/skins can simultaneously disguise one's identity and reveal one's inner or true nature. The anxieties revolving around (mis)recognition wrought by false clothing/skins are dramatized in the concluding moments of *Basterds* when Raine questions Landa about removing his Nazi uniform and assimilating into American society. Carving the swastika on Landa's forehead can be construed then as a final Cinderella gesture. Hans My Hedgehog punishes the wicked princess by having her remove her beautiful clothes before bloodying her with his quills and sending her back to the kingdom in shame. The Brothers Grimm variant of "Cinderella" ends with the stepsisters cutting off their heels trying to fit into the slippers, after which pigeons peck out their eyes, blinding them for their attempted deceit. It is as if Raine marks Landa as a false Cinderella who attempted to use deceit couched in quasi-virtuous intent to transform his social and cultural status, scarring rather than restoring his humanity.

The fairy tale has long been pressed into the service of politics and by consciously evoking "Cinderella" and other forms of folklore, Tarantino positions his film within post-truth discourse. At the time of *Basterds'* release in 2009, post-truth was a fringe concept that has since gained traction in both academic and public discourses.[26] Following the Brexit referendum and Donald Trump's surprise victory in the 2016 American election, the Oxford English Dictionary elected *post-truth* as its Word of the Year while a companion institution, Gesellschat für deutsche Sprache, selected *postfaktisch* (post-factual) as the German word for 2016. It remains a disputed term, lacking a consensus definition while exhibiting multivalent inflections across the diverse fields of politics, philosophy, journalism, history, sociology, psychology and literature. The *OED* defines post-truth as "circumstances in which objective facts are less influential in shaping public opinion than appeals to emotion and personal belief." But "truth" has always been a contested sphere and to argue *post-truth* is a unique era where affect is privileged over rationality resulting in the diminishing value of veracity and honesty in public discourse feels limiting and oversimplified if not historically naïve.

Fake news, conspiracy theories, (internet) rumors, echo chambers and hoaxes are not novel phenomena; rather, the political weaponization of (mis)information—not seen in America since the nineteenth century—coupled with fringe ideologies carving out a prominent presence in mainstream cultural discourse have made distinguishing between fact and fiction a Herculean task. Beyond the decline in shared assumptions of fact and—as former president Barack Obama has stated—social groups "operating in completely different information universes,"[27] a post-truth culture, I argue, is one characterized by the waning of collective truth-seeking. It is the deliberate manufacturing and trafficking of misinformation; it is undermining objective facts to engineer a privatized social reality that conforms to idealized perceptions or utopian aspirations both nostalgic (right-wing) and progressive (left-wing). I see at the core of post-truth culture a fundamental paradox: even as our epistemic practices have expanded as a result of information technologies and virtual platforms, our hermeneutics have narrowed. That is, as a species we know more than we ever have; and yet our perceptions of "truth" are both polemically disparate and constricted so as to reinforce blind allegiance to pre-packaged ideological precepts.

The fairy tale—orally transmitted for millennia and subject to all manner of appropriation, revision, contamination, speculation and embellishment—is a perfect companion for reflecting and interrogating the concept of post-truth. Hans Landa's ominous exchange with the dairy farmer LaPadite in the opening chapter, "I love rumors! Facts can be so misleading, but rumors, true or false, are often revealing,"[28] reflects the close connection between folklore and post-truth. Herbert Lutz, a German-born physicist conscripted into the Hitler Youth programs of the 1930s, where propaganda and post-truth flourished, stated to *Stürmer* magazine, "The truth didn't mean anything: distortion was enormous. It was almost like reading dirty fairy tales."[29] Numerous critics have seized on Tarantino's deliberate misrepresentation of historical events, leading to interpretations of the film as duplicating Nazi fascism and accusations of Holocaust denial.[30] But such allohistorical revisionism can be construed as yet another folkloric impulse. Folk- and fairy tales lack stable origins: there are neither "official" nor "original" versions of tales like "Little Red Riding Hood" or "Cinderella," no prioritized urtext, but rather multiple variants reflective of their respective historical and cultural periods. Even Jacob and Wilhelm Grimm, who saw folklore as a reflection of the history and the collective consciousness of a nation, not only misrepresented their folktales as narratives collected from the illiterate German peasantry, but blurred the distinction between veracity and fabulation by adapting, rewriting, and editorializing the tales for decades to reflect their shifting aesthetic and ideological purposes.[31] It is tempting to think of Tarantino as a twenty-first-century Grimm brother whose film presents a "bastardized" variant of officially-sanctioned history. Much in the way folktales transformed as they passed from the hands of one storyteller to another, World War II history becomes just another folkloric artifact, what we might call in the post-truth era an "alternative fact."

However, transforming history into a fairy-tale doppelgänger of "alternative facts," while problematic, seems designed less to distance us from historical memory than to pull us closer to it. To grossly misrepresent history—especially the celebrated mythos of virtuous Allies and evil Nazis—is not to suggest that history as we know it does not exist but forces the spectator into an uncomfortable intellectual meditation on and confrontation with the notion of "historicity" and "fact." "What will the history books read?" Landa muses near the film's finale, poetically concluding, "In the pages of history, every once and while, fate reaches out and extends its hand."[32] This seems like a meta-cinematic commentary on Tarantino himself reaching into the pages of history and, far from imposing a nostalgic order on historical memory slipping beyond our grasp, disjointing and alienating us further from a pre-packaged World War II nostalgia.

Similar to how "Hans My Hedgehog" is a tale of disenchantment in which the hedgehog-human hybrid must shed the false animal skin to reveal his true self, so is Tarantino's post-truth film concerned with disenchanting perceived historical certainties. Each chapter in *Basterds* is framed around a series of interrogation scenes: Hans Landa's initial interrogation of the French dairy farmer LaPadite; Aldo Raine's interrogation of captured Nazi soldiers (narratologically mirrored against Hitler's interrogation of the surviving soldier); Hans Landa's interrogation of Shosanna/ Emmanuelle in the French café; the game playing in the La Louisiane tavern which doubles as an interrogation sequence; and finally Hans Landa's interrogation of Aldo Raine in the final chapter. The film's investment in interrogation as a narrative device underscores its thematic interest in interrogating historiography, including the most sacrosanct narrative in modern American history: the nationalist mythos of American exceptionalism. As Charles Taylor has astutely observed, "The attacks on *Inglourious Basterds* are a lesson not just in class-based prejudices about who should be able to use history as the raw material of drama, but in the willed naiveté that still exists about the virtuousness of the Second World War."[33] Tarantino exposes this naiveté by transforming the so-called "Greatest Generation" into a vigilante band of misfits seeking allied victory by coupling sensationalistic violence with folkloric mystique. The Basterds are supposedly an American alternative to the Nazis, yet in a very post-truth gesture appear to lack any significant difference, moral or otherwise. They not only frequently disguise themselves as Nazis but the opening two chapters are virtually mirror images of one other with Landa the Jew Hunter's interrogation of LaPadite followed by the massacre of Jews echoed with Aldo Raine's interrogation of Nazis and Donowitz the Bear Jew's brutal execution of the Nazi captain. Thus the fairy-tale-ness of

Inglourious Basterds acts as an epistemological rupture, a deliberate mistruth contaminating our assumptions of the historical past. As Cristina Bacchilega has eloquently written, fairy tales are "ideologically variable desire machines,"[34] so reimagining history as a post-truth folklore allows Tarantino to use World War II as ground zero for contesting American identity, particularly its implicit self-representation as a Cinderella.

A more subtle collapsing of the American/Nazi binary comes in the film's closing moments when Lieutenant Raine, anxious of Landa's attempted metamorphosis from Nazi Jew Hunter into heroic American double agent, carves a swastika on his forehead. "When you get to your little place on Nantucket Island, I imagine you'll take off that handsome-looking SS uniform, ain't ya?"[35] Raine says, once again conjuring the ambivalent Cinderella motif of clothing that both disguises and reveals identity. "Now that I can't abide," Raine continues, "I mean, if I had my way, you'd wear that goddamn uniform for the rest of your pecker-sucking life. . . . But at some point, you're going to have to take it off. So, I'm going to give you something you can't take off."[36] As the gruesome disfiguration proceeds, the low-angle camera shot looks up at Raine, effectively shifting the point of view so that the spectator becomes the Nazi Landa. When Raine, staring into the camera, smiles and says, "I think this just might be my masterpiece,"[37] it echoes an earlier moment where Josef Goebbels's documentary *Nation's Pride* is hailed as the propaganda minister's masterpiece. The final sequence, which occurs in a secluded forest as so many fairy tales do, clearly establishes Landa as the grotesque Cinderella of the film while simultaneously staging American anxiety toward a very real historical reality, namely, how a thousand little Führers—to borrow a phrase from Robert Jackson, the Supreme Court Justice and Nazi prosecutor at Nuremberg—white-washed their histories after the end of the war and successfully assimilated into postwar American society. Hans Landa seems to be Tarantino's nod to high-profile former Nazis like Wernher von Braun, Otto von Bolschwing, Otto Ambros and Hubertus Strughold who—through the Bibbidi-Bobbidi-Boo of moral ambivalence—emigrated as part of the secretive government program Operation Paperclip,[38] many of them transforming into American citizens.[39]

If this final scene is the narrative climax of Landa's failed Cinderella transformation, then it is also a final thematic interrogation of America's narrative of itself as a Cinderella nation. "Cinderella" is the perfect fairy-tale intertext for a post-truth allohistorical film because it evokes a tale that is quintessentially associated with the triumph of the underdog—the rags-to-riches, Algeresque trope that underpins the essence of America's cultural ethos. But the "Cinderella" tale, especially the Brothers Grimm variant which enacts a retributive punishment on the wicked stepsisters, also thematically questions the porous boundaries between deceit and truthfulness. As in many fairy tales, the eponymously persecuted heroine disguises herself and temporarily deceives the prince hoping to reveal her true self. However sympathetic we are to her predicament, however justifiable her motivations, her behavior is nonetheless ethically questionable. Comparably, the stepsisters in the Brothers Grimm variant cut off their heels and toes in an effort to fit their feet into the slipper and deceive the prince. Viewing Landa as the failed Cinderella suggests viewing Raine, his binary counterpart, as the wicked stepsister who does not hesitate to disobey military orders, deceive, and perpetuate folkloric rumor and mistruth in order to secure American victory. By ending abruptly on such an anti-happily ever after and morally ambivalent conclusion, Tarantino's final swastika carving scene seems to be asking the American spectator: Is "Cinderella" the story we want to tell about ourselves?

Although released in 2009, Tarantino spent a decade writing the script, the *Inglourious Basterds*, placing its composition firmly within the social instability of 9/11 and subsequent War on Terror and Iraq Invasion. It would be disingenuous to view the film as an allegory of those wars, nor do I think Tarantino is crafting a 1:1 analog between Nazi atrocities and American imperialism. However, as Italo Calvino once suggested, in times of social upheaval artists turn to fables and Tarantino's subversive "Cinderella" story, questioning the moral foundations of America's geopolitical power and global cultural hegemony, can be read in the context of its cultural production, namely, the destabilizing crisis in the Middle East wrought by American military quagmires and an interventionist foreign policy which, retrospectively, appears built on post-truth alternative facts.

Tarantino's fairy-tale historiography seems less disjointing when we consider the remarkable linguistic and semantic malleability of said tales in the first decades of the twenty-first century. As Ann-Marie Cook has argued, the fairy tale offered a fascinating framework for public discussions of the War on Terror and Iraq War.[40] Thus, former UN chief weapons inspector Scott Ritter described the American government's claims about Iraqi sovereignty to be "as fictitious as any fairytale ever penned by the Brothers Grimm";[41] South-African-British judge Johan Steyn of the House of Lords, following the London bus bombings of 2005, accused those who argued the Iraq War made the world a safer place as perpetuating a fairy tale;[42] and during the Democratic presidential primary, Bill Clinton referred to then-candidate Barack Obama's Iraq War opposition as "the biggest fairy-tale I've ever seen."[43] Perhaps the most striking thread weaving fairy tales and politics came from conservative presidential adviser Karl Rove. Rove, a chief architect of the invasion of Iraq under George W. Bush, admitted the very post-truth political tactic of transforming imagination into reality in 2004 when he told reporter Ronald Suskind he and other neoconservatives no longer needed to conform to the "reality-based community": "We're an empire now, and when we act we create our own reality. And while you're studying that reality—judiciously, as you will—we'll act again, creating other new realities, which you can study too, and that's how things will sort out. We're history's actors . . . and you, all of you, will be left to just study what we do."[44] Ira Chernus concisely summarized Rove's fairy-tale political strategy as "When policy dooms you, start telling stories—stories so fabulous, so gripping, so spellbinding that the king (or in this case, the American citizen who theoretically rules our country) forgets all about a lethal policy."[45]

Or, to phrase it differently, Rove suggests in a post-truth world "truth" is a variable fairy-tale thing changing upon every retelling. In Tarantino's case, we uneasily watch history's actors (the Basterds) savagely create ambivalent new realities (the revenge fantasy against Hitler). *Basterds*, I think, implicitly pushes back against the post-truth rhetoric contextualizing the War on Terror and Iraq invasion by cautioning against converting battlefield performativity with its misrepresentations, falsifications and folklores into everyday reality. This seems hinted at in the scene at the La Louisiane tavern where three of the Basterds—Lt. Archie Hicox, Sgt. Hugo Stiglitz and Corporal Wilhelm Wicki—pose as Nazis while trying to extract information from German spy Bridget von Hammersmark. It is a domestic scene, quite distinct from the rest of the film in tone, and staged as an elaborate card guessing game. Throughout the scene language conceals even as it reveals. Almost entirely in German, the scene is linguistically disorienting and makes the spectator skeptical of language and what may or may not be lost in translation. Even before Hicox blows his cover as an Allied spy with a casual gesture, his unusual German accent draws suspicions and proves his undoing. The consequences of language games are deadly: only Bridget von Hammersmark survives the bloody shootout. Viewed in the context of the deceitful rhetoric accompanying the War on Terror, the scene suggests that if words fails us and cannot be trusted then certainly history's actors—in Tarantino's case, duplicitous Americans—spinning tales cannot be trusted either. It feels reminiscent of the self-described moral in Kurt Vonnegut's novel, *Mother Night*, about the fictional Howard W. Campbell Jr. who spies for the Allies during the war but is on trial in Israel as a Nazi war criminal having inadvertently inspired white nationalists in America: "We are what we pretend to be, so we must be careful about what we pretend to be."[46]

Tarantino may very well have only superficial intentions with his fairy-tale allusions. Perhaps, as David Denby has criticized, the film fails to give us a single character with whom we can identify and abuses the realities of history. But by crafting deliberately flat, one-dimensional characters and rejecting a conclusion of stabilized hierarchy—the happily ever after motif—Tarantino's fairy-tale historiography is a purposeful rupture in our sense of fixed historicity that cuts off the spectator from an affective viewing experience. Estranged from our ability to create simplified emotional attachments to stereotypical World War II tropes and thus easily reinscribe nationalistic folklores, *Inglourious Basterds* provokes a troubling confrontation with the legacy of American postwar hegemony: thinking more and feeling less about the past at a time when foreign policy rhetoric is imbued with an enchanted semantics that signals, in very Scheherazade fashion, a War on Terror ever after.

NOTES

1. Tarantino is highly engaged with and cognizant of genre (and genre-deconstruction) in all of his films and *Basterds* is no exception. In an interview with *Cahiers du Cinéma* during the 2009 Cannes Film Festival he stated that the first two chapters are an homage to the Western, the third chapter a French New Wave, and the fourth and fifth chapters a classical war/mission film a la *The Dirty Dozen*. See Sharon Willis, "'Fire!' in a Crowded Theater: Liquidating History in *Inglourious Basterds*" in *Quentin Tarantino's* Inglourious Basterds: *A Manipulation of Metacinema*, ed. Robert Von Dassanowsky (New York: Continuum, 2012), 166–167.

2. "Chapter One: Inglourious Basterds," *Inglourious Basterds*, directed by Quentin Tarantino (Universal Pictures Home Entertainment, 2009), DVD.

3. This is a paraphrase of the final lines of Daniel Mendelsohn's review, "Tarantino Rewrites the Holocaust," in *Newsweek* (13 August 2009). The full quote is: "Facts can be so misleading," Hans Landa, the evil SS man, murmurs at one point in *Inglourious Basterds*. "Perhaps, but fantasies are even more misleading. To indulge them at the expense of the truth of history would be the most inglorious bastardization of all."

4. Ben Walters, "Debating *Inglourious Basterds*," *Film Quarterly* 63, no. 2 (Winter 2010): 20.

5. David Denby, "Americans in Paris," *The New Yorker,* 17 August 2009. https://www.newyorker.com/magazine/2009/08/24/americans-in-paris.

6. Michael D. Richardson, "Vengeful Violence, *Inglourious Basterds*, Allohistory, and the Inversion of Victims and Perpetrators," *Quentin Tarantino's* Inglourious Basterds: *A Manipulation of Metacinema* (New York: Continuum, 2012), 102.

7. There are no current studies to my knowledge of Tarantino's repeated intertextual references to the fairy tale in his films. Besides the obvious allusion in *Once Upon a Time in Hollywood* (2019), *Kill Bill: Vols. 1 & 2* (2003, 2004) both make several subtle allusions to assassin Beatrice Kiddo/The Bride as a "Sleeping Beauty" figure.

8. Helge Gerndt, "Folklore and Socialism: Questions for Further Investigation," *The Nazification of an Academic Discipline* (Bloomington: Indiana Press, 1994), 2.

9. Louis Snyder, *The Roots of German Nationalism* (Bloomington: Indiana University Press, 1978), 36.

10. Elizabeth Dalton, "Introduction," *Grimm's Fairy Tales* (New York: Barnes & Noble Classics, 2003), xxviii.

11. Hermann Bausinger, "Nazi Folk Ideology and Folk Research," *The Nazification of an Academic Discipline: Folklore in the Third Reich* (Bloomington: Indiana University Press, 1994), 11.

12. Jack Zipes, *Fairy Tales and the Art of Subversion: The Classical Genre for Children and the Process of Civilization* (New York: Wildman Press, 1983), 139–140.

13. See O'Brien's study, *Nazi Cinema as Enchantment: The Politics of Entertainment in the Third Reich* (Suffolk, UK: Camden House, 2004). Additional notable studies include: David Welch, *The Third Reich: Politics and Propaganda* (New York: Routledge, 1993); and *Propaganda and the German Cinema, 1933–1945* (New York: I.B. Tauris Publishers, 2001). See also Hilmar Hoffmann, *The Triumph of Propaganda: Film and National Socialism, 1933–1945.* Trans. John A. Broadwin and V. R. Berghahn (Providence, RI: Berghahn Books, 1996); and Susan Tegel, *Nazis and the Cinema* (London: Hambledon Continuum, 2007).

14. The other is by Cornelia Anett Endler. *Es war einmal . . . im Dritten Reich. Die Märchenfilmproduktion fur den nationalsozialistichen Unterricht* (Frankfurt am Main: Peter Lang Publishing, 2006).

15. Due to my limited capabilities with German, the information in this paragraph represents an abbreviated summary of main ideas and concepts Mr. Schlesinger graciously shared with me from his monograph during a series of email communications between August and October 2015.

16. "Chapter Two: Inglourious Basterds," *Inglourious Basterds*, Tarantino.

17. Richardson, "Vengeful Violence," 102.

18. Lüthi's monograph repeatedly examines the deceptive superficiality of folktales. For in-depth discussions of the aforementioned characteristics in the folktale, see chapters 1 ("One-Dimensionality"), 2 ("Depthlessness"), and 3 ("Abstract Style").

19. William Brown, "Counterfactuals "Counterfactuals, Quantum Physics, and Cruel Monsters in Quentin Tarantino's *Inglourious Basterds*," *Quentin Tarantino's* Inglourious Basterds: *A Manipulation of Metacinema* (New York: Continuum, 2012), 252.

20. It is impossible to say how deliberate Tarantino's choice of names is, but it bears mentioning the name Shosanna alludes to a woman in the biblical Apocrypha who is persecuted and falsely accused of adultery before being saved by the prophet Daniel. Emmanuelle is the feminized cognate of the Hebrew name Immanuel, meaning "God is with us" and one of the messianic epithets for Jesus Christ.

21. Perrault's variant, "Le Petit Chaperon rouge," was published in his collection, *Histoires ou contes du temps passé, avec des moralités: Contes de ma mère l'Oye* (1697). The Grimm variant, "Rotkäppchen," was included in the first edition of the folk and fairy-tale collection, *Kinder- und Hausmärchen* (1812).

22. Patrick McGee, *Bad History and the Logics of Blockbuster Cinema:* Titanic, Gangs of New York, Australia, Inglourious Basterds (New York: Palgrave MacMillan, 2012), 186. Ta-rantino echoes this sentiment in an interview with Jordanna Horn in the *Jewish Daily Forward* in which he justified his violent aesthetics and historical liberties by stating, "If you're dealing with people like Nazis . . . well, you either eat the wolf or the wolf eats you." Qtd. in Jordana Horn, "Glorious Bastard," *Forward* 21 August 2009. https://forward.com/culture/112638/glori-ous-bastard/.

23. "La Louisiane," *Inglourious Basterds*, Tarantino.

24. Maria Tatar points out the Nazis concocted an allegorical reading of the text with the Jewish wolf menacing and victimizing the German people (*The Hard Facts of Grimm's Fairy Tales* [Princeton: Princeton University Press, 2003], 41). Jack Zipes's influential study, *The Trials and Tribulations of Little Red Riding Hood* (London: Routledge, 1993) notes how Werner von Bülow penned a propagandistic essay using Red Riding Hood as a principle motif to promote German nationalism while Ulrich Link used the tale to ironically critique the blind conformity inherent to Nazism (53–54). A 1937 film by Fritz Genschow, *Rotkäppchen und der Wolf,* financed by Goebbels's Ministry of Propaganda, follows the titular heroine in a cloak adorned with swastikas who is saved by an SS soldier.

25. The Grimms first published the tale, "Hans mein Igel," in 1815 in Vol. 2 (no. 22) of their *Kinder- und Hausmärchen.* Beginning with the second edition, the tale was assigned number 108.

26. According to the *OED*, the term was coined by Steve Tesich in a 1992 essay in *The Nation.* At the time of *Basterds'* release in 2009, the only serious cultural engagement with the concept was Ralph Keyes's 2004 study, *The Post-truth Era,* which intertextually referenced *Pinocchio* and *Alice in Wonderland* while critiquing the entanglement of mass media and American politics. *OED* editors observed a 2,000 percent increase in the term's usage between 2015 and 2016. See Amy B. Wang, "'Post-truth' Named 2016 Word of the Year by Oxford Dictionaries" in *Washington Post,* 16 November 2016. https://www.washingtonpost.com/news/the-fix/wp/2016/11/16/post-truth-named-2016-word-of-the-year-by-oxford-dictionaries/.

27. Obama's comments came during an interview with David Letterman during the inaugural episode of the web television talk show, *My Next Guest Needs No Introduction.* The full quote is, "What the Russians exploited, but it was already here, is we are operating in completely different information universes. If you watch Fox News you are living on a different planet

than you are if you listen to NPR." See the episode, "It's a Whole New Ball Game Now" *Netflix*, 12 January 2018.

28. "If a Rat Were to Walk In," *Inglourious Basterds*, Tarantino.

29. Eric Johnson and Karl-Heinz Reuband, *What We Knew: Terror, Mass Murder, and Everyday Life in Nazi Germany: An Oral History* (New York: Basic Books, 2006), 148.

30. On his blog ("Recommended Reading: Daniel Mendelsohn on the New Tarantino," *Jonathan Rosenbaum*, 29 July 2019. https://www.jonathanrosenbaum.net/2019/07/recommended-reading-daniel-mendelsohn-on-the-new-tarantino/), film critic Jonathan Rosenbaum praised Daniel Mendelsohn's review in the *Newsweek* and panned *Inglourious Basterds* as "a film that seems morally akin to Holocaust denial." Michael Richardson's article, "Vengeful Violence: *Inglourious Basterds*, Allohistory, and the Inversion of Victims and Perpetrators," in *Quentin Tarantino's* Inglourious Basterds: *A Manipulation of Metacinema* (New York: Continuum, 2012), concludes, "Tarantino's film . . . seeks to appropriate fascist tactics, and in doing so ultimately replicates, not critiques, Nazi aesthetics" (95).

31. For a more comprehensive study of the Grimm Brothers' editorializing, see John M. Ellis, *One Fairy Story Too Many* (Chicago: University of Chicago Press, 1983).

32. "That's a Bingo," *Inglourious Basterds*, Tarantino.

33. Charles Taylor, "Violence as the Best Revenge Fantasies of Dead Nazis," *Dissent* 57, no. 1 (Winter 2010): 103.

34. Cristina Bacchilega, *Postmodern Fairy Tales Gender and Narrative Strategies* (Philadelphia: University of Pennsylvania Press, 1997), 7.

35. "Aldo's Masterpiece," *Inglourious Basterds*, Tarantino.

36. Ibid.

37. Ibid.

38. See Annie Jacobsen's definitive study: *Operation Paperclip: The Secret Intelligence Program That Brought Nazi Scientists to America* (New York: Little, Brown and Co., 2014).

39. As journalist Eric Lichtblau documents in his book, *The Nazis Next Door: How America Became a Safe Haven for Hitler's Men* (Boston: Mariner Books, 2014), it was not just high-profile Nazi scientists and military personnel who benefited from Operation Paperclip, but average soldiers and citizens, many with questionable histories concealing gruesome Nazi pasts, while others participated in the everyday banal bureaucracy of the Nazi war machine.

40. Ann-Marie Cook, "From the Enchanted Forest to the Desert: Reading *The Brothers Grimm* as Anti-War Critique," *The Monstrous Identity of Humanity: Proceedings of the Fifth Global Conference* (Oxford: Interdisciplinary Press, 2007), 174.

41. Scott Ritter, "Three Iraq Myths that Won't Quit," *AlternNet*, 26 June 2006. https://www.alternet.org/story/38011/three_iraq_myths_that_won%27t_quit.

42. Joshua Rozenberg, "Judge Attacks 'Fairy Tale' Over Iraq War," *The Telegraph*, 18 October 2005. https://www.telegraph.co.uk/news/uknews/1500956/Judge-attacks-fairy-tale-over-Iraq-war.html.

43. William Kristol, "The Democrats' Fairy Tale," *New York Times*, 14 January 2008. https://www.nytimes.com/2008/01/14/opinion/14kristol.html.

44. Ronald Suskind, "Faith, Certainty and the Presidency of George W. Bush," *New York Times Magazine*, 17 October 2004. https://www.nytimes.com/2004/10/17/magazine/faith-certainty-and-the-presidency-of-george-w-bush.html. The original article attributes this quote to a "high official" in the Bush administration, which was later acknowledged to be Rove.

45. Ira Chernus, "Karl Rove's Scheherazade Strategy," *Mother Jones*, 7 July 2006. https://www.motherjones.com/politics/2006/07/karl-roves-scheherazade-strategy/.

46. Kurt Vonnegut, *Mother Night* (New York: Dial Press, 2009), v.

BIBLIOGRAPHY

Bacchilega, Cristina. *Postmodern Fairy Tales: Gender and Narrative Strategies*. Philadelphia: University of Pennsylvania Press, 1997.

Bausinger, Hermann. "Nazi Folk Ideology and Folk Research." In *The Nazification of an Academic Discipline: Folklore in the Third Reich*, edited by James R. Dow and Hannjost-Lixfeld, 11–33. Translated by James R. Dow. Bloomington: Indiana University Press, 1994.

Brown, William. "Counterfactuals, Quantum Physics, and Cruel Monsters in QuentinTarantino's *Inglourious Basterds*." In *Quentin Tarantino's* Inglourious Basterds: *A Manipulation of Metacinema*, edited by Robert von Dassanowsky, 247–270. New York: Continuum, 2012.

Chernus, Ira. "Karl Rove's Scheherazade Strategy." *Mother Jones*, 7 July 2006. https://www.motherjones.com/politics/2006/07/karl-roves-scheherazade-strategy/.

Cook, Ann-Marie. "From the Enchanted Forest to the Desert: Reading *The Brothers Grimm* as Anti-War Critique." In *The Monstrous Identity of Humanity: Proceedings of the Fifth Global Conference*, edited by Marlin C. Bates IV, 171–182. Mansfield College, Oxford: Interdisciplinary Press, 2007.

Dalton, Elizabeth. "Introduction." In *Grimm's Fairy Tales*, xv–xxxiii. New York: Barnes & Noble Classics, 2003.

Denby, David. "Americans in Paris." *The New Yorker,* 17 August 2009. https://www.newyorker.com/magazine/2009/08/24/americans-in-paris.

Gerndt, Helge. "Folklore and Socialism: Questions for Further Investigation." *The Nazification of an Academic Discipline.* Bloomington: Indiana Press, 1994, 2–7.

Hoffmann, Hilmar. *The Triumph of Propaganda: Film and National Socialism, 1933–1945.* Translated by John A. Broadwin and V. R. Berghahn. Providence, RI: Berghahn Books, 1996.

Horn, Jordana. "Glorious Bastard." Forward. 21 August 2009. https://forward.com/culture/112638/glorious-bastard/.

Johnson, Eric A., and Karl-Heinz Reuband. *What We Knew: Terror, Mass Murder, and Everyday Life in Nazi Germany: An Oral History.* New York: Basic Books, 2006.

Kristol, William. "The Democrats' Fairy Tale." *New York Times*, 14 January 2008. https://www.nytimes.com/2008/01/14/opinion/14kristol.html.

Lichtblau, Eric. *The Nazis Next Door: How America Became a Safe Haven for Hitler's Men.* Boston: Mariner Books, 2014.

McGee, Patrick. *Bad History and the Logics of Blockbuster Cinema:* Titanic, Gangs of New York, Australia, Inglourious Basterds. New York: Palgrave MacMillan, 2012.

Mendelsohn, Daniel. "Tarantino Rewrites the Holocaust." *Newsweek*, 13 August 2009. https://www.newsweek.com/tarantino-rewrites-holocaust-79003.

Obama, Barack. "It's a Whole New Ball Game Now." Interview by David Letterman. *My Next Guest Needs No Introduction,* Season 1, Episode 1, 12 January 2018, Netflix.

Richardson, Michael D. "Vengeful Violence: *Inglourious Basterds*, Allohistory, and the Inversion of Victims and Perpetrators." In *Quentin Tarantino's* Inglourious Basterds: *A Manipulation of Metacinema*, edited by Robert von Dassanowsky, 93–112. New York: Continuum, 2012.

Ritter, Scott. "Three Iraq Myths that Won't Quit." *AlternNet*, 25 June 2006. https://www.alternet.org/story/38011/three_iraq_myths_that_won%27t_quit.

Rosenbaum, Jonathan. "Recommended Reading: Daniel Mendelsohn on the New Tarantino." *Jonathan Rosenbaum* 29 July 2019. https://www.jonathanrosenbaum.net/2019/07/recommended-reading-daniel-mendelsohn-on-the-new-tarantino/.

Rozenberg, Joshua. "Judge Attacks 'Fairy Tale' Over Iraq War." *The Telegraph.* 19 October 2005. https://www.telegraph.co.uk/news/uknews/1500956/Judge-attacks-fairy-tale-over-Iraq-war.html.

Snyder, Louis. The Roots of German Nationalism. Bloomington: Indiana University Press, 1978.

Suskind, Ronald. "Faith, Certainty and the Presidency of George W. Bush." *New York Times Magazine,* 17 October 2004. https://www.nytimes.com/2004/10/17/magazine/faith-certainty-and-the-presidency-of-george-w-bush.html.

Tarantino, Quentin, dir. *Inglourious Basterds*. 2009. Universal City, CA: Universal Pictures Home Entertainment, 2009. DVD.

Tatar, Maria. *The Hard Facts of Grimm's Fairy Tales.* Princeton: Princeton University Press, 2003.

Taylor, Charles. "Violence as the Best Revenge: Fantasies of Dead Nazis." *Dissent* 57, no. 1 (Winter 2010): 103–106.

Vonnegut, Kurt. *Mother Night.* New York: Dial Press, 2009.

Walters, Ben. "Debating *Inglourious Basterds.*" *Film Quarterly.* 63, no. 2 (Winter 2010): 19–22.

Wang, Amy. "'Post-truth' Named 2016 Word of the Year by Oxford Dictionaries," *The Washington Post*, 16 November 2016. https://www.washingtonpost.com/news/the-fix/wp/2016/11/16/post-truth-named-2016-word-of-the-year-by-oxford-dictionaries/.

Zipes, Jack. *Fairy Tales and the Art of Subversion: The Classical Genre for Children and the Process of Civilization.* New York: Wildman Press, 1983.

Zipes, Jack. *The Trials and Tribulations of Little Red Riding Hood.* London: Routledge, 1993.

Conclusion

A Postmodern Princess

*Rhetorical Strategies of Contemporary
"Cinderella" Adaptations*

Suzy Woltmann

The primary texts explored in this collection extend the legacy of the "Cinderella" fairy tale through the lens of *wokeness*. Contemporary revisionism also rewrites the traditional fairy tale in a postmodern way. The notion of literary ephemerality, or the inability to name or otherwise grasp potential narrative concepts, demonstrates the project of the postmodern adaptation: to question, destabilize, and show how there might be a variety of perspectives for any otherwise authoritative narrative. To conclude the collection, this epilogue identifies different rhetorical strategies employed in contemporary "Cinderella" variations. Strategies that allow for a transformative adaptation and empowered readership at the cross-section of the genre include perspective plurality, intertextual queering, and collaborative originality.

In many ways, the postmodern adaptation inherently strives toward wokeness. It draws from a source text or source texts to build upon past works and retells the events of a known narrative in a way that encourages readers to question what they think they know. Rather than simply pushing back against canonical fairy tales, however, postmodern adaptations assert "the unique subjectivity of every individual and a consequent insistence on a plurality of perspectives rather than any single truth."[1] The strategies that allow for a transformative adaptation (perspective plurality, intertextual queering, and collaborative originality) exist on a gradient and are by no means closed categories. However, while these categories are often fluid, this detailed grammar extends the work of Mikhail Bakhtin, Gerard Genette, Linda

Hutcheon, Cristina Bacchilega, Jack Zipes, and others to theorize the work being done in contemporary fairy-tale adaptations.

PERSPECTIVE PLURALITY

The first rhetorical strategy that engenders transformative adaptations is perspective plurality. Heteroglossia, or many voices within a single work, lends itself to perspective plurality, the idea that no matter the event or situation people will have different interpretations of it. Perspective plurality takes place when many characters have voice. Cinderella is traditionally represented as a passive, largely silent character, so rewriting her as someone with agency and voice encourages perspective plurality. The narration and formal structure of many adaptations question representation in source texts, which then encourages readers to be open to perspective plurality. This shows the malleability of narrative as well as the impossibility of getting to the "true story" unless all voices, particularly those historically silenced, are heard. Adaptations often encourage perspective plurality through the portrayal of many points of view in their texts, including diverse forms of representation. African-American feminist scholars claim that oppression takes place intersectionally, through racism, sexism, classism, and other forms of hierarchy and subjugation.[2] Hazel Carby shows how traditional feminist theory does not create space for black women's experiences, but that heteroglossic approaches to literature may allow for their voices to be heard.[3] Cheryl Wall argues that heteroglossia allows African-American women writers to revise, signify, and subvert literary tropes.[4] Henry Louis Gates, Jr. further shows how signification and parody are employed by African-American authors to "create a new narrative space for representing the recurring referent of . . . the so-called black experience."[5] This amplifies Zora Neale Hurston's statement that "originality is the modification of ideas."[6] By including heteroglossic voice that leads to perspective plurality, adaptations that challenge normative representations of race in the "Cinderella" fairy tale encourage interactive readership and resistant readings.

As Camille Alexander argues, simply adding a nonwhite character does not inherently make an adaptation woke.[7] However, portrayals of racial and ethnic diversity in fairy-tale revisionism allow for a proliferation of voices unheard in traditional versions. The portrayal of Cinderellas of color adds to the discursive web of "Cinderella" adaptations, as does the introduction of Cinderella's stepsister's narrative, Cinderfellas, nontraditional fairy godmothers, and so on.[8] Jennifer Donnelly's *Stepsister*, for example, adds the perspective not only of Isabelle, the "ugly" stepsister who cuts off her toe to marry the prince, but also her sister Tavi, childhood sweetheart Felix, and the co-conspirators Fate and Chance, who argue about how her life should turn out.[9] Perspective plurality suggests "that to re-write or to re-present the past in fiction and in history is, in both cases, to open it up to the present, to prevent it from being conclusive and teleological."[10] Simultaneously, many adaptations open up the present to the past, which implies that writing—and reading—are ongoing processes. These texts ironically indicate a difference that opens up the adaptation's source text to questioning while also showing that the newly written narrative can and should be questioned too.

INTERTEXTUAL QUEERING

Similarly, portrayals of nonnormative genders and sexualities encourages perspective plurality by queering the known tale. This practice disrupts the patriarchal impulse of authoritative canonical texts. Relying on scholarship from Cristina Bacchilega, Eve Sedgwick, Jennifer Orme, and Tison Pugh, I call this process queering because it offers a "queer invitation" to investigate the liminal space between adaptations and source texts.[11] Adaptations that can be read through the lens of wokeness offer a queer invitation because they imply that there is not a single narrative truth but instead a web of dialogic sources that each have something to offer. This implication destabilizes the notion of an authoritative canon and opens up both adaptations and sources to queer potentiality, or a disruptive force that pushes against normative readings and encourages alternative ways of understanding. "Cinderella" adaptations intertextually queer source texts through representations of nonnormative genders and sexualities and through methodological queering. Instances of representations of nonnormative genders and sexualities in "Cinderella" adaptations include Emma Donaghue's *Kissing the Witch: Old Tales in New Skins* (1997), which writes a queer Cinderella; Francesca Lia Block's *The Rose and the Beast* (2000), which subverts normative gender roles in "Cinderella" adaptations; Malinda Lo's *Ash* (2009), with a lesbian Cinderella; Marisa Meyer's *Cinder* (2013), which writes a cyborg Cinderella; S. T. Lynn's *Cinder Ella*, whose protagonist is Black and transgender; Andrew Lloyd Webber's *Cinderella* musical (2019), in which Prince Charming is romantically intrigued by a Duke; and most recently, Columbia Pictures's decision to sign Billy Porter to play the fairy godmother in an upcoming *Cinderella* film (2021).

Intertextual queering moves away from the binary view of gender and sexuality that is often enforced through the ideology of heteronormativity. Further, it encourages readers to rethink portrayals of gender and sexuality in traditional fairy-tale variations and extends the legacy of these texts while also allowing for a proliferation of desires. Surface queering and methodological queering often intersect. For example, I argue elsewhere that in *Ash*, Lo goes further in her project to queer the "Cinderella" story than simply writing a lesbian Cinderella. She also "intertextually and metatextually queers the 'Cinderella' story by including non-heteronormative relationships; depicting the queer time of fairy tales, dreams, and the carnivalesque; and demonstrating how certain gender and sexual identities are privileged."[12] By queering characters in the story as well as the genre itself, Lo draws attention to the process of narrative-making.

Methodological intertextual queering often takes place through metafictional parody, demythologizing, and framing devices. In many ways, adaptations are inherently metafictional because they remind readers that they are reading a fictional work, particularly one that responds to another fictional work. The term metafiction, originally popularized by William H. Gass, has been given its most extensive critical treatment by Patricia Waugh in *Metafiction: The Theory and Practice of Self-Conscious Fiction*. Waugh finds that metafiction implies that reality and history themselves are constructed—that the very structures we are interpellated into may be a figment of imagination.[13] Linda Hutcheon extends Waugh's work to define metafictional parody as "repetition with critical difference,"[14] leading the way to her later definition of adaptations as repetition with difference. The "critical" is what provides the stakes here: what it is that makes the difference between source text and adaptation critical enough to count as metafictional parody.

Metafictional writing is postmodern because it encourages its readership to think about the process of narrative-making. The term *"postmodernism, when used in fiction, should, by analogy, best be reserved to describe fiction that is at once metafictional and historical in its echoes of the texts and contexts of the past."*[15] Since adaptations act as palimpsests that draw attention to their source text(s) as well as the revised work, they work metafictionally to remind readers that they are, in fact, works of fiction. According to Werner Wolf, explicit metafiction directly comments on the construction of text as part of storytelling, while implicit metafiction uses other disruptive techniques to prompt readers to remember that they are reading a work of fiction.[16] Many contemporary fairy-tale adaptations use both techniques in a way that imply that not only are the adaptations fictional but so are authoritative source texts. Metafictional works often parody their source text(s) as well as the process of reading and writing itself. However, "to parody is not to destroy the past; in fact, to parody is both to enshrine the past and to question it. And this is the postmodern paradox."[17] By parodying the historical past of the time their source texts were created and the literary past of paying tribute to an authoritative text, metafiction extends the legacy of its predecessors while simultaneously inviting readers to question it. While comparable, metafictional demythologizing exposes the process of myth-making itself while working to unravel it. Adaptations that demythologize their source texts point out our inability to comprehend myth while ironically creating it anew.

Metafictional parody is often achieved in contemporary adaptations through the conceit of the narrator directly questioning their source text or its author. This strategy involves the narrator speaking directly to an audience—presumably readers—to tell them that the story they have heard is either incorrect or is not the full story. This reminds readers that the narrative they are reading is a fictional retelling of another fiction, therefore metafictionally encouraging questions of narrative authority. For example, in one of Cinderella's songs in *Into the Woods*, she angrily chants "nice good nice good" while tying up her stepsister's hair.[18] This intertextually and amusingly signifies Cinderella's normative depiction as nice and good while showing how she might resist that description.

Further, contemporary "Cinderella" stories demythologize source texts by showing that the writers of traditional fairy tales were perpetuating a historical fiction themselves. No matter its historical roots, mythology necessitates a historical foundation, since myth is "chosen" by history rather than a natural evolution.[19] In other words, myth's major purpose is to assimilate beliefs, and its permanence (or not) is due to its historical meaning. Although it appears objective or what Mikhail Bakhtin would call authoritative speech, myth's meanings are often political; but the quality of myth is that it always seeks to disguise its own historicity. By reworking the familiar in a different way, it encourages readers to conceptualize the known through a new lens. All adaptations defamiliarize readers from the known quantity of the original work. However, defamiliarization of myth holds a particular gravitas, since myth is already itself alienated from its meaning. This twist is taken further through Barthes's idea that in postmodernity, text is not authoritative but rather "a multi-dimensional space in which a variety of writings, none of them original, blend and clash."[20] This rests on his notion of the death of the author, which says that neither the author nor a literary work is autonomous. Because the fairy-tale adaptation turns in upon itself, readers are always aware of its metafictional implications and the space between texts.

Woke adaptations also intertextually queer their source texts through framing devices that draw attention to the process of narrative-making. In Bacchilega's discussion of framing in postmodern fairy-tale adaptations, she argues that these strategies include externalization, metaphor, narration, and actual reflection.[21] Refraction and the frame itself allows for the postmodern narrative's reflection.[22] Assuming "that a frame always selects, shapes, (dis)places, limits, and (de)centers the image in the mirror, postmodern retellings focus precisely on this frame to unmake the mimetic fiction."[23] In other words, these retellings give us a funhouse mirror version of their source texts and, in doing so, draw attention to the normative mirror image and its own frame. This is particularly explored in "Cinderella" adaptations through reliance on the makeover, when Cinderella changes from dirty, impoverished cleaner to beautiful princess-to-be. In *The Devil Wears Prada*, for example,

Andy's makeover scene provides a frame through which to view the rest of the film; it is later exposed as a reliance on artifice that turns her against the fashion industry.[24] This framing parodies Cinderella's makeover scene in traditional texts while also extending it to the twenty-first century. While similar to frame stories, framing devices intertextually queer a larger constellation of recursive, mirroring, and mimetic strategies than simply providing a story within a story. Any adaptation works to reframe their source text, but adaptations working toward wokeness do so in a way that destabilizes the mirror image as well as the notion of the frame itself.

Many contemporary "Cinderella" adaptations, such as *Confessions of an Ugly Stepsister* and *Sex and the City*, use the internally persuasive dialogue of first-person narration in a way that challenges authoritative fairy-tale texts. However, a few, such as *Ash*, use third-person framing, which omnisciently and ironically proposes that this narrative is the correct one. Third-person framing is "a form of ventriloquism that highly complicates the issue of narrative accountability."[25] While many fairy-tale adaptations work to undermine the possibility of authority in any given narrative through the rhetorical strategy of first-person subversion, texts that rely on third-person framing encourage readers to ironically question both texts. Using this framing, authors challenge what readers have heard about the "Cinderella" story and expose the process of literary mimesis. In doing so, contemporary adaptations provoke a metafictional look at the processes of writing and writerly reading.

COLLABORATIVE ORIGINALITY

"Cinderella" adaptations also rely on collaborative originality, or the ways that texts refer to a variety of signifiers. These include interdiscursive realms of shared knowledge: "literature, visual arts, history, biography, theory, philosophy, psychoanalysis, sociology, and the list could go on."[26] Collaborative originality is about the relationships between texts and the discourses and sociohistorical realms in which they operate; and collaborative originality, like metafiction, can be explicit or implicit. For example, *Confessions of an Ugly Stepsister* refers explicitly to the Perrault and Brothers Grimm variations as well as the notorious Disney film.[27] It also implicitly refers to literary fairy tales as a genre, historical events, psychoanalytic notions, and poetry; its epigraph is from Howard Nemerov's "Vermeer."[28] This interdiscursive referentiality reminds readers of the various structures that allow for the writing—and reading—of Maguire's adaptation.

References and allusions in adaptations interdiscursively show Cinderella's historiography. Since she meets real people, it implies that her story is also real. Turned inverse, this implication means that readers are reminded how narratives, too, are emplotted. Therefore, Cinderella's encounters with popular culture or historical events ironically verify her tale while simultaneously undermining it. Hilary Duff's portrayal of the heroine, Sam, in *A Cinderella Story* relies on an ironic twist to the typical "Cinderella" story line: instead of losing a shoe while fleeing from Chad Michael Murray's prince character, she loses her phone.[29] This kind of ironic signaling metafictionally exposes the process of adaptation itself. Contemporary adaptations refer intertextually to their source texts and also to other modes of discourse to empower readers to take a second look at known narratives. The postmodern condition is an uncertain one founded in unverifiable discourse, the dissolution of the metanarrative, or simple disbelief. By showing the seemingly endless amalgamation of factors that lend themselves to the construction of any text, interdiscursive references in "Cinderella" variations imply that all narratives are constructed and so are open to questioning, therefore engendering a woke readership.

CONCLUSION

Many contemporary "Cinderella" adaptations enact a transformative process on their source texts to destabilize narrative authority while also extending the legacy of any given source text. Authors that produce writerly texts often use the rhetorical strategies of perspective plurality, intertextual queering, and collaborative originality. These strategies encourage the reader to question how literary worlds are constructed and connected, thereby also encouraging postmodern critique. This collection theorizes a way to look at contemporary "Cinderella" adaptations by tracing the adaptive impulse through the lenses of forms of power and empowerment. The adaptations addressed herein disrupt canonical source texts and rewrite the "Cinderella" story in a way that drastically alters the way readers approach the fairy tale. Because of the inherent intertextuality of adaptations, they are not just responses to their source texts, but instead change how readers view and interpret source texts and the web of similar texts. That readers have read the actual pre-text does not really matter. Instead, the transformative adaptation responds in some way to our shared understanding of a text's cultural legacy. Viewing patterns at the cross-section of the genre gives a more comprehensive view of just how these strategies work—and therefore, how they work toward wokeness. In this way, the "Cinderella" story that has so enchanted the world has continued into the twenty-first century with new, fabulous takes on a postmodern princess.

NOTES

1. Jeremy Rosen, *Minor Characters Have Their Day: Genre and the Contemporary Literary Marketplace* (New York: Columbia University Press, 2016), 143.

2. Kimberle Crenshaw headed the Critical Race Theory (CRT) movement that introduced intersectional theory in 1989. Black women felt isolated from the feminist movement, which was led primarily by white women. Crenshaw argues that the experience of being a black woman cannot be broken down into just race or gender but must be understood in tandem.

3. Hazel Carby, "White Woman Listen! Black Feminism and the Boundaries of Sisterhood," *The Empire Strikes Back: Race and Racism in Seventies Britain* (London: Hutchinson, 1982), 17.

4. Cheryl Wall, *Worrying the Line: Black Women Writers, Lineage, and Literary Tradition* (Chapel Hill: The University of North Carolina Press, 2005).

5. Henry Louis Gates Jr., *The Signifying Monkey: A Theory of African American Literary Criticism* (Oxford: Oxford University Press, 2014), 121.

6. Zora Neale Hurston, "Imitation," *Negro* (New York: Negroes Universities Press, 1969), 42.

7. See chapter 7.

8. Gregory Maguire, *Confessions of an Ugly Stepsister* (New York: Harper Collins, 2009).

9. Jennifer Donnelly, *Stepsister* (New York: Scholastic Press, 2019).

10. Linda Hutcheon, *Narcissistic Narrative: The Metafictional Paradox* (London: Methuen, 1980), 209.

11. Jennifer Orme, "A Wolf's Queer Invitation: David Kaplan's *Little Red Riding Hood* and Queer Possibility," *Marvels & Tales* 29.1 (2015): 87.

12. Suzy Woltmann, "'Beneath It All Something as Yet Unnamed Was Coming into Focus': A Queer Reading of Malinda Lo's *Ash*," *Marvels & Tales* (Fall 2020).

13. Patricia Waugh, *Metafiction: The Theory and Practice of Self-Conscious Fiction* (London: Methuen, 1984), 7.

14. Hutcheon, *Narcissistic*, 12.

15. Ibid., 3.

16. In "Metareference across Media: The Concept, its Transmedial Potentials and Problems, Main Forms and Functions," in *Metareference across Media: Theory and Case Studies* (Amsterdam: Rodopi). He further designates direct/indirect metafiction, critical/non-critical metafiction, and generally media-centered/truth- or fiction-centered metafiction.

17. Hutcheon, *Narcissistic*, 6.

18. "Prologue," *Into the Woods,* directed by Stephen Sondheim (Walt Disney Studios, 2014).

19. Roland Barthes, *Mythologies* (New York: Noonday Press, 1972), 108.

20. Ibid., 146.

21. Cristina Bacchilega, *Fairy Tales Transformed* (Detroit: Wayne State University Press, 2013), 28.

22. Ibid.

23. Ibid., 35–36.

24. *The Devil Wears Prada*, directed by Wendy Finerman (20th Century Fox Home Entertainment, 2006).

25. Ibid., 34.

26. Linda Hutcheon. *Narcissistic,* 12.

27. Maguire, *Confessions.*

28. Ibid., 5.

29. *A Cinderella Story*, directed by Mark Rosman (Warner Bros. Pictures, 2004).

BIBLIOGRAPHY

Bacchilega, Cristina. *Fairy Tales Transformed*. Detroit: Wayne State University Press, 2013.

Bakhtin, Mikhail. *The Dialogic Imagination: Four Essays by M. M. Bakhtin*, ed. Michael Holquist. Austin: University of Texas Press, 1981.

Barthes, Roland. *Mythologies*. New York: Noonday Press, 1972.

Carby, Hazel. "White Woman Listen! Black Feminism and the Boundaries of Sisterhood." *The Empire Strikes Back: Race and Racism in Seventies Britain*. London: Hutchinson, 1982. 212–235.

A Cinderella Story, dir. Mark Rosman. Warner Bros. Pictures, 2004.

The Devil Wears Prada, dir. Wendy Finerman. 20th Century Fox Home Entertainment, 2006.

Donnelly, Jennifer. *Stepsister*. New York: Scholastic Press, 2019.

Gates, Henry Louis Jr. *The Signifying Monkey: A Theory of African American Literary Criticism*. Oxford: Oxford University Press, 2014.

Hurston, Zora Neale. "Imitation." *Negro*. New York: Negroes Universities Press, 1969.

Hutcheon, Linda. *Narcissistic Narrative: The Metafictional Paradox*. London: Methuen, 1980.

Into the Woods, dir. Stephen Sondheim. Walt Disney Studios, 2014.

Maguire, Gregory. *Confessions of an Ugly Stepsister*. New York: Harper Collins, 2009.

Orme, Jennifer. "A Wolf's Queer Invitation: David Kaplan's *Little Red Riding Hood* and Queer Possibility." *Marvels & Tales* 29.1 (2015): 87–109.

Rosen, Jeremy. *Minor Characters Have Their Day: Genre and the Contemporary Literary Marketplace*. New York: Columbia University Press, 2016.

Wall, Cheryl A. *Worrying the Line: Black Women Writers, Lineage, and Literary Tradition*. Chapel Hill: The University of North Carolina Press, 2005.

Waugh, Patricia. *Metafiction: The Theory and Practice of Self-conscious Fiction*. London: Methuen, 1984.

Wolf, Werner. "Metareference across Media: The Concept, Its Transmedial Potentials and Problems, Main Forms and Functions." *Metareference across Media: Theory and Case Studies*, ed. Werner Wolf, Katharina Bantleon, and Jeff Thoss. Amsterdam: Rodopi, 37–38.

Woltmann, Suzy. "'Beneath It All Something as Yet Unnamed Was Coming into Focus': A Queer Reading of Malinda Lo's *Ash*," *Marvels & Tales* (Fall 2020).

Index

About the Contributors

Dr. **Camille S. Alexander** is an assistant professor of English Literature at UAE University. She completed her PhD in English at the University of Kent and an MA in Literature from the University of Houston, Clear Lake. Dr. Alexander's research interests include Caribbean studies and literature; Black British literature; American film; and third-wave feminism. She is currently researching Indian culture in Indo-Trinidadian literature using the novels of Lakshmi Persaud and has recently been published in the edited collection *Voodoo, Hoodoo and Conjure in African-American Literature: Critical Essays* and *The Journal of Popular Culture*.

Rachel L. Carazo has a graduate degree in English from Northwestern State University and is earning a second graduate degree in Library Science at the University of Southern Mississippi. She has published several essays in edited collections and is currently editing a collection on the film *Gladiator* (2000). She has also written a novel, *The Vaindrian Queen*, and the second novel of the series, *The Edelstein*, will soon be complete.

Christine Case is a PhD student at the University of Pittsburgh specializing in fairy-tale adaptation, queer theory, and cultural studies. She received her MA from the University of Chicago and her BA from Williams College, and she has recently presented at conferences on Mary Martin's *Peter Pan* and Broadway's *Frozen*.

Brittany Eldridge obtained her MSc in Comparative Literature from the University of Edinburgh in 2017. She is a current PhD candidate at the University College London. Her interests lie in studying the mother figure in fairy tales and their adaptations, both literary and film.

Dr. **Ryan Habermeyer** is assistant professor at Salisbury University. He is the author of the prizing-winning collection of fabulist short stories, *The Science of Lost Futures* (2018). He is currently at work on a novel as well as revising his dissertation into a scholarly monograph tentatively titled *Fairy-Tale Phantoms: On the Cultural Hauntings of Ever After*, which examines the intersections of spectral aesthetics and social politics in fairy-tale narratives embedded in twentieth and twenty-first century transnational literature and film.

Loraine Haywood has completed a master of theology at the University of Newcastle, Australia. Her interests include the Religious and Theological themes and motifs of chaos, apocalypse, sacrifice, salvation, and Saviour narratives used as popular icons in film. She applies theories of psychoanalysis in her research using the works of Sigmund Freud, Jacques Lacan, Jean Baudrillard, Todd McGowan, and Slavoj Žižek to support her theories. Her latest research involves *Game of Thrones*, as a pop culture phenomenon and a religious icon.

Svea Hundertmark is a doctoral candidate at Christian Albrecht University at Kiel, Germany. She holds a master of arts and a master of education degree in English/American studies and German studies. The topic of her dissertation is the American fairy tale film of the twenty-first century. She works as a research associate for the chair of Teaching English as a Foreign Language at the English Department of Kiel University.

Christian Jiminez has published essays on gender, mass media, the superhero genre, Harold Pinter, James Cameron, and Steven Spielberg. Forthcoming essays will cover race in American television and conspiracy theory. He has taught at various colleges and is currently working on epic fantasy.

Dr. **Alexandra Lykissas** is a tenure-track professor of humanities at Seminole State College of Florida where she regularly teaches adaptations of fairy tales in all types of artistic forms. She recently published an article related to how *The Lunar Chronicles* shows the importance of fairy tales in popular culture and the rise of a new type of fairy tale called the collaborative fairy tale, in the September 2018 issues of *Global Studies in Childhood*. Dr. Lykissas completed her PhD at Indiana University of Pennsylvania in English literature and criticism in August 2018.

Dr. **Carolina Alves Magaldi** is a professor of literary studies and literary translation at the Federal University of Juiz de Fora. She teaches and supervises at the graduate program in literary studies at the same university and is head of the research group Prisma—Interculturality and Translation. She recently organized a volume of the *Ipotesi Journal* regarding literary rewritings and cultural perspectives, focusing on the contributions of the Polysystem Theory to comprehend such phenomena.

Dr. **Sarah E. Maier** is full professor of English and comparative literature director of interdisciplinary graduate studies and university teaching scholar at the University of New Brunswick. After several pieces for the Brontë bicentennials, including work for *The Lost Manuscripts* (2018), recent work with Brenda Ayres includes *Reinventing Marie Corelli for the Twenty-First Century* (2019), *Victorian Children and their Animals* (2019), *Neo-Gothic Narratives* (2020) and *Neo-Victorian Madness* (2020).

Lucas Alves Mendes is a Brazilian sign language teacher. He is a graduate of the Federal University of Juiz de Fora and a master's degree student at the same university. He worked for three years as the head of accessibility at SENAC/JF, a professional education institution in Brazil.

Dr. **Aoileann Ní Éigeartaigh** is a lecturer in literature and cultural studies at Dundalk Institute of Technology, Ireland. She is the coeditor *of Borders and Borderlands in Contemporary Society* (2006), *Rethinking Diasporas: Hidden Narratives and Imagined Borders* (2007) *and Exploring Transculturalism* (2010), and has published articles on literature, film, and cultural theory. She delivered the 2019 W. A. Emmerson Memorial Lecture to the Irish Association for American Studies on the topic of "Contested Narratives and Liminal Spaces in the Novels of Juan Rulfo and George Saunders."

Jessica Raven is a graduate student in interdisciplinary studies at UNB Saint John. She is currently putting her lifelong love affair with fairy tales to good use by writing her thesis on obsolete fidelity in transmedial fairy-tale adaptations like ABC's *Once Upon a Time* and Netflix's *The Witcher.*

Dr. **Suzy Woltmann** earned her Phd in literature from the University of California, San Diego, where she teaches literature and writing courses. She specializes in adaptations studies, gender and sexuality, and intertextuality. She is published on topics including gender and sexuality, adaptations, neo-slave narratives, and fairy tales. Her current book project theorizes transformative adaptations that encourage interactive readership.

www.ingramcontent.com/pod-product-compliance
Lightning Source LLC
Chambersburg PA
CBHW022306280326
41932CB00010B/1001